COLONEL GRENFELL'S WARS

George St. Leger Grenfell

COLONEL GRENFELL'S WARS

The Life of a Soldier of Fortune

Stephen Z. Starr

LOUISIANA STATE UNIVERSITY PRESS
BATON ROUGE

To I-J. E. S.
In gratitude and love

. . . in her hands life blossoms and bears fruit.
Beloved and loving, she grows old beside
Her husband, mother of children fair and honored;
Her name shines out among all womankind,
And on her ways a grace lies, like the Gods' . . .

SEMONIDES OF AMORGOS

ISBN 0-8071-0921-5
Library of Congress Catalog Card Number 71-142339
Copyright © 1971 by Louisiana State University Press
All rights reserved
Manufactured in the United States of America
Printed by Parthenon Press, Nashville, Tennessee
Designed by Albert R. Crochet

Preface

BOOKS are written for a great many reasons. This biography of George St. Leger Grenfell was written for only one reason—I enjoyed doing it.

Grenfell has a unique place in Confederate hagiology. A talented British cavalry officer whose bravery became a byword but whose congenital restlessness nullified his effectiveness, a "character" whose idiosyncrasies made him a man of mark in the most individualistic of all armies, his posthumous fame nevertheless rests not on what he did, but on what he chose to tell his friends about his life as a soldier of fortune before the Civil War, in Europe, Africa, Asia, and South America. His tales of glamorous derring-do on four continents made a great impression on a parochial generation of Americans. These tales, alas, were largely a fantasy, the product of his own romantic imagination, of his need to clothe himself in a glittering aura of color and high adventure. To puncture these harmless pretenses, even for the sake of historical accuracy, is not an adequate reason for a biography. Grenfell has earned a place in the Confederate Valhalla by his activities and fate after he had severed his official relations with the South. His fate, especially, raises questions about the conflicting rights of an individual to receive justice and those of a government which deems its existence threatened, which are not without contemporary relevance. It will be for the reader to judge whether these things are an adequate justification for an addition to the vastly overburdened shelves of Civil War biography.

The writing of George St. Leger Grenfell's life has brought me dividends beyond the pleasure I have derived from the task itself. It has given me the friendship of William H. Wright of Los Angeles, California, whose wise counsel and strict devotion to the nearly lost art of correct English usage have added immeasurably to whatever merit the book possesses. The title is his suggestion. Miss Anne Glyn-Jones of Haywards Heath, Sussex, England, began by searching through the Foreign Office and Colonial Office papers in the Public Record Office, London, for material bearing on Grenfell's life in Tangiers, but as her work progressed, her interest in Grenfell grew; she made the project her own, and I owe to her ingenuity, resourcefulness, and enthusiasm much of the material that will be found in chapter two, and she will recognize the result of her suggestions throughout the book. Anthony H. Packe, of Burnham, Bucks., England, Grenfell's great-grandson, has not only supplied the photograph which forms the frontispiece of this volume and granted me the unrestricted use of the Grenfell family papers in his possession, but has given me also his encouragement, hospitality, and friendship. Major General R. F. B. Naylor, c.b., c.b.e., d.s.o., of Dancer's Hill House, Barnet, Herts., England, has graciously allowed me to read and make use of the letters of his grandmother, George St. Leger Grenfell's eldest daughter. I owe a special debt to T. Harry Williams, Boyd Professor of History at Louisiana State University, Baton Rouge; I can only hope that this biography is not entirely undeserving of the championship of a master of the craft. My thanks are due also to Professor Joseph E. Holliday of the University of Cincinnati for his critique of the first version of the manuscript; to The Rt. Hon. the Lord Grenfell, t.d., for permission to consult the Grenfell family tree in his possession; and to my friend, David DuVivier, for searching the French archives for a trace of Grenfell's activities in Paris in the 1830s.

A project such as this bestows on the fortunate author the freedom of the City of Scholarship. All doors are opened to him.

It is a delightful corrective to the currently fashionable grim view of our culture to encounter nothing but cordiality and unstinted helpfulness from the many librarians, archivists, and scholars to whom one must turn for information and assistance. I hope I will be forgiven if, because of considerations of space, I do not list by name all those who have responded so generously to my inquiries or have given me access to, and permission to quote from, manuscript material in their custody. Thanks to them, scholarship is a constant pleasure.

Lastly—and lastly only because there must be a last—this book owes its existence to the wise advice of Dr. Starr Ford, my physician and dear friend.

STEPHEN Z. STARR

COLONEL GRENFELL'S WARS

Chapter I

APRIL 10, 1865. The morning newspapers of Cincinnati, on the Ohio River, used their largest, boldest type to proclaim the great news from Appomattox Court House. General Lee had surrendered the Army of Northern Virginia to U. S. Grant on the previous day. Lee and his army had been the palladium of the Confederacy. Their surrender meant the defeat of secession. Rebellion had been smashed and the Union restored. Above all, there was an end to the killing. Just three days short of the fourth anniversary of its start in Charleston harbor, the bloody Civil War was now virtually ended.

Cincinnati had gone wild with joy a week earlier, on April 3, when Secretary of War Edwin M. Stanton's telegram arrived, announcing the fall of Richmond. Within thirty minutes the glorious tidings that the Confederate capital was at last in Union hands had spread through the city. All business came to a halt, the entire population poured into the streets to celebrate, every house flew the Stars and Stripes, all the church bells rang, factory and steamboat whistles blew, and cannon on the Public Landing on the riverbank fired a salute.

The news of Appomattox was even more glorious, and planning was quickly begun to signalize the great event in a fitting manner. A Grand Celebration was to take place four days later, on Good Friday, to honor the triumphant conclusion of the war.

3

Punctually at 6 A.M. on the fourteenth all the bells in the city—church bells, fire alarm bells, steamboat bells and factory bells—were to ring out to accompany the firing of a one-hundred gun salute. At noon sharp and again at 6 P.M., the bells were to peal, to chime an obbligato to a second, and then a third, one-hundred gun salute. Every church in the city was to hold a service of thanksgiving in the morning, civic dignitaries were to deliver suitable patriotic orations throughout the day, and the festivities were to close at nightfall with a grand torchlight procession.[1]

The enthusiasm, the huzzahs, the "delight . . . in every countenance," were everywhere in evidence in Cincinnati on the tenth except in the courthouse, where three men, known collectively as the "Chicago Conspirators," were on trial before a military commission. The long trial, now in its thirteenth week, had begun on Monday, January 9, and at 2 P.M. on Monday, April 10, while the excitement in the city outside was at its height, the presentation of evidence having been concluded a few days earlier, Judge Robert S. Wilson of Chicago, the first of the defense attorneys to speak, rose to address the court on behalf of his client.

The senior of the three prisoners present in the courtroom was Judge Buckner S. Morris, a native of Augusta, Kentucky. He had long been a resident of Chicago and was a prominent figure in that city's political life. First a Whig, then a Know-Nothing, and finally a Democrat, Morris had been mayor of Chicago, judge of the Circuit Court of Illinois, and, in 1860, was the unsuccessful candidate for the governorship of Illinois on the Breckinridge-State Rights-Democratic ticket.[2] The second defendant, Charles Walsh, had served for five years in the United States army in the Florida War; he settled in Chicago when the war ended and became a prosperous draying contractor, achieving at the same time a degree of prominence in local politics. He had served as sergeant-at-arms of the Illinois legislature and in 1862 ran unsuccessfully for the post of sheriff of Cook County on the Democratic ticket. In

[1] Cincinnati *Daily Gazette*, April 10, 1865.
[2] Chicago *Tribune*, November 8, 1864.

4

the later years of the Civil War, he became notorious as a "virulent Irish Copperhead." [3]

The third member of the strangely assorted triumvirate of prisoners was George St. Leger Grenfell, a British subject who had come to America in the spring of 1862 to fight for the Confederacy. He served for a time as General John Hunt Morgan's adjutant general, then as inspector of cavalry, with the rank of lieutenant colonel, in General Braxton Bragg's Army of Tennessee, and then as assistant inspector general of General "Jeb" Stuart's Cavalry Corps of the Army of Northern Virginia.

When the trial had begun three months earlier, eight prisoners were before the court. One, Charles Travis Daniel, escaped; another, Benjamin M. Anderson, committed suicide in prison; the third, Vincent Marmaduke, was acquitted and discharged from custody midway through the trial; the fourth, R. T. Semmes, whose case was submitted to the court without argument on February 15, had been found guilty; the fifth, George E. Cantrill, was granted a separate trial because of ill health.

The prisoners were being tried under martial law before a military commission of nine army officers sitting as judges. The indictment consisted of two charges. The first accusation recited that they had conspired, "in violation of the laws of war, to release the rebel prisoners of war . . . at Camp Douglas, near Chicago . . . by suddenly attacking said camp, on or about the evening of the eighth of November . . . [1864] with a large number of armed men." And the second, that they had conspired, "in violation of the laws of war, to lay waste and destroy . . . the city of Chicago . . . by capturing the arsenal in said city, cutting the telegraph wires, burning the railroad depots, taking forcible possession of the banks and public buildings, and leaving the city to be sacked, pillaged and burned by the rebel prisoners of war confined at Camp Douglas." [4]

[3] *Ibid.*
[4] *Message from the President of the United States, in Answer to a Resolution of the House of Representatives of the 19th of December, Transmitting Papers Relative to the Case of George St. Leger Grenfel [sic]; House Executive Documents,*

It had taken six sittings of the court, from January 9 to January 19, to dispose of the preliminary formalities, and fifty-four sessions for the presentation of evidence, first by the prosecution and then by the defense. The parade of witnesses ended in the sitting of April 6, and after a three-day adjournment to give the defense attorneys time to prepare their closing addresses to the commission, the court met at 2 P.M. on the tenth to hear Judge Wilson sum up on behalf of the prisoner, Charles Walsh. He was followed on the next two days by T. W. Bartley and T. M. Ray, speaking for the defendant Morris; E. G. Asay with another speech for Walsh; and finally, on the thirteenth, by Robert Hervey speaking for Grenfell. After Hervey had spoken, the commission adjourned for four days to enable Lieutenant Colonel Henry Lawrence Burnett, the prosecutor (judge advocate), to review the voluminous evidence and prepare his reply to the speeches for the defense.

On the evening of April 14, while the commission was in recess, President Lincoln was assassinated. It was universally believed in the North that he was the victim of a conspiracy hatched and nurtured by the leaders of the Confederate government.[5] The Chicago Conspiracy, also hatched in Richmond, failed. The assassination plot succeeded. Inevitably, the northern mind would find a deadly parallel between the conspiracy that had resulted in the murder of the beloved President and the other conspiracy for which Grenfell, Morris, and Walsh were on trial. It is hardly possible, a century after the event, in an age when political assassinations have become commonplace, to conceive of the extent of the shock and horror which the killing of the President in the very hour of the victory of the Union, inspired throughout the North, and indeed, throughout the world. Nor did the judge advocate fail to capitalize on this feeling when he delivered his closing

---

39th Congress, 2nd Session, No. 50 (Serial 1290), 22; hereinafter cited as *House Executive Documents*.

[5] Benjamin P. Thomas and Harold M. Hyman, *Stanton: The Life and Times of Lincoln's Secretary of War* (New York, 1962), 422.

address to the court only four days later, while the body of President Lincoln lay in state in the East Room of the White House:

> Judge Morris and such as he, taught that Abraham Lincoln, the pure patriot, was a tyrant, a usurper, a despot, unfit to live, and the result is his death . . . they have been teaching and reiterating Abraham Lincoln's unconstitutional usurpations and oppressions, until today the nation stands, as it were, hushed in woe under the universal gloom occasioned by the death of its pure, beloved chief. You are the men that at the last great day will be responsible for this foul deed . . . ye are the men that will be held responsible by this people, whose wail ascends to heaven this day because their champion is dead.[6]

In very truth, the bloody ghost of the murdered President was with the members of the court when they retired later that afternoon to deliberate on their verdict.

After its recess, the commission met on the eighteenth to hear Colonel Burnett sum up for the prosecution. He began by reading a telegram from Secretary of War Stanton, ordering him to report at once in Washington "to aid in the examination respecting the murder of the President." [7] Then he launched into his oration. The climax of his powerful forensic effort was his attack on Grenfell. The judge advocate saved him to the last, for maximum effect, and tore into him without mercy:

> As to this man Grenfell, I confess I have no sympathy with him; no sympathy for the foreigner who lands in our country when this nation is engaged in the struggle for human rights and human liberty, and who takes part in the quarrel against us, and arrays himself on the side of those who are trying to establish tyranny and slavery. I have no sympathy for the man whose sword is unsheathed for hire and not for principle; for whom slavery and despotism have more charms than freedom and liberty. The motive of such a one does not rise even to the dignity of vengeance . . . his sword has gleamed in every sun, and has been employed on the side

[6] *House Executive Documents*, 587–88.
[7] *Ibid.*, 573.

7

of almost every nationality. . . . He was a fit instrument to be used in this enterprise. What to him would be the wail of women and little ones? What to him would be the pleadings of old men and unarmed citizens? [8]

The courtroom was then cleared and, with these bitter words ringing in their ears, the members of the court began their deliberations. It was late in the evening when it was announced that they had reached a decision. The prisoners, their attorneys, and the public having taken their places in the courtroom, the president, Colonel Charles D. Murray, Eighty-ninth Indiana Infantry, read the verdict of the court. The nine military justices acquitted Judge Morris; Charles Walsh was found guilty and sentenced to five years' imprisonment. Grenfell was also found guilty, and with "two thirds of the members concurring," was sentenced "to be hung by the neck until he is dead, at such time and place as the commanding general may direct." [9]

Who was "this man Grenfell," whom Burnett had denounced in such bitter terms?

In late June, 1862, a recruit, who introduced himself as Colonel George St. Leger Grenfell, late of the British army, rode into the camp of John Morgan's Second Kentucky Cavalry in Knoxville, Tennessee, to take up the post of regimental adjutant. The troopers of Morgan's regiment beheld a ramrod-straight six-footer, a man no longer young, but with a spare, wiry, angular figure, and an erect, soldierly bearing. The newcomer had a stern, weather-beaten, bronzed face framed in dark hair and side-whiskers, with a look in his eye that was sometimes fierce and hawklike, sometimes coldly aloof and supercilious. Many, if not most, of Morgan's boys had been brought up on Sir Walter Scott's romances, and Grenfell had been in camp for only a few hours before someone decided that he bore a remarkable resemblance to Sir Brian de Bois Guilbert, the grim Templar of *Ivanhoe*.

[8] *Ibid.*, 593–94.
[9] *Ibid.*, 573–74.

It was evident that the Englishman had the habit of command. His name suggested aristocratic origins, and it was understood that he had earned his high rank by virtue of many years of distinguished service in his country's army. As the weeks passed, and he began to feel at home in his new surroundings and his reticence began to thaw in response to the amiable, easy-going courtesy of the Kentuckians, Grenfell told a few chosen friends about his life before the Civil War. His stories were of dangerous, bloody doings in strange corners of the world, and as his tales were passed along from man to man, the aura of mystery and romance which surrounded Colonel Grenfell grew and flourished mightily.

Truly, Grenfell's tales were spectacular and almost unbelievable. He had a brother, he said, much older than himself, who served as an officer under the great Duke of Wellington in the Peninsular War against the French. This brother's body servant foraged a kid from a Spanish peasant for his master's mess; the outraged peasant complained, and as the beneficiary of the servant's misdeed, Grenfell was court-martialed. This so angered their father that he refused to permit the younger son, George St. Leger, to follow his older brother into the army. Not to be thwarted in his powerful inclination toward a military career, young Grenfell thereupon ran away from home, enlisted in a French cavalry regiment in Algeria, and fought in the earliest battles that led to the French conquest of that country. After serving out his term of enlistment, he established himself in Tangier. What is more, "Although not a convert to the faith of Mahomet, [he] was quite willing, with a broad cosmopolitan view of social matters, to conform to the prevalent customs of the community in which he dwelt, and accordingly became connected by marriage with a number of the first and most influential families of the place." [10] Or, in less Victorian terms, Grenfell had acquired the four wives permitted by the Prophet to the faithful—but not, so far as can be determined, to resident aliens of the Christian faith—and established

[10] These stories of Grenfell's career are based on Basil W. Duke, *Reminiscences of General Basil W. Duke, C.S.A.* (New York, 1911), 150; and Duke, *A History of Morgan's Cavalry* (Bloomington, 1960), 180.

a harem. Had this been Grenfell's only tale about his past, it alone would have justified the respectful and, in this particular, envious awe in which he was held by the unsophisticated country boys of Morgan's command.

Some years later, the French besieged Tangier, and Grenfell commanded a Moroccan battery that inflicted severe damage upon them. Escaping from the French, he fought for more than four years under the Emir Abd-el-Kader in his unsuccessful revolt against French rule in Algeria.[11] Continuing his career as a soldier of fortune,

> He fought the Riffe pirates off the coast of Morocco, and then served with Garibaldi in South America. Finally, tiring of this irregular and barbarous strife, and desirous of settling down to a more Christian and civilized kind of warfare, he returned home and . . . obtained a commission in the English service. He fought in India during the greater part of the Sepoy rebellion, and then in the Crimean War, attaining the rank of lieutenant-colonel.[12]

In 1863, when Grenfell served as inspector of cavalry under General Braxton Bragg, Lieutenant Colonel Arthur J. L. Fremantle, a young British Guards officer, visited Bragg's Army of Tennessee. He was eager to meet Grenfell, and one of the high points of the diary in which he set down vivid descriptions of everyone he met and all he saw in a three-month tour of the Confederacy, is his account of his encounter with his fellow countryman. Having spent three days in Grenfell's company, Fremantle decided that he was "one of the most extraordinary characters" he had ever met.[13] Grenfell told him he had served for three years in a French lancer regiment, rising in rank from private to sublieutenant. Later, while living in Tangier, he was a "sort of consular agent." Next, he said, he fought the French for four and a half years under Abd-el-Kader. Then he fitted out a yacht "and carried on a private war with the Riff pirates." This was followed by service as brigade

[11] Duke, *Reminiscences*, 150.
[12] *Ibid.*, 150.
[13] Arthur J. L. Fremantle, *The Fremantle Diary*, ed. Walter Lord (New York, 1960), 127.

10

major in the Turkish Contingent in the Crimean War. When the war ended, he saw service in the Indian Mutiny, and after that, was engaged "in war in Buenos Aires and the South American republics." [14]

In the late fall of 1863, having left the Army of Tennessee under mysterious circumstances, Grenfell was on the staff of the most renowned of Confederate cavalrymen, General Jeb Stuart. In November a portion of Stuart's cavalry corps was encamped on the farm of John Minor Botts near Culpeper, Virginia, and making free with what little the Federal army had left of his fences, feed, and livestock. Grenfell tried without much success to protect Botts's property. For two weeks he was a guest in Botts's house and spent the evenings in talk with his appreciative host. As was only natural, he spoke of his past. He told Botts he had been a colonel in the British army. His services in the Crimean War, he said, were rewarded by the British government with an appointment "in some public capacity" to South America, "where he had settled down on a large body of land, devoting himself to the pursuits of agriculture and raising sheep, in which vocation he was employed at the time of the breaking out of the rebellion." [15]

A month or so after his stay with Botts, another traveler from overseas met Grenfell and later wrote a few words about him. This was Fitzgerald Ross, who himself had had an unusual career before he came to America to view the Civil War from both sides of the line. An Englishman by birth, educated at the universities of Heidelberg and Gottingen, captain in a regiment of Hungarian hussars in the Austrian army, Ross, like Fremantle, saw the Civil War with the eyes of a professional soldier, but he was neither as perceptive nor as skillful with the pen as Fremantle.[16] Ross met Grenfell during the Christmas season of 1863, when the latter was about to give up his post of assistant inspector general of Stuart's

[14] *Ibid.,* 119.
[15] John Minor Botts to Joseph Holt, June 17, 1865, in *House Executive Documents,* 637.
[16] Fitzgerald Ross, *Cities and Camps of the Confederate States* (Urbana, 1958), xiv.

cavalry. In the following summer they met again and spent a month or more together on a fishing and hunting excursion in northern New York and Canada. Nevertheless, Ross's account of Grenfell is disappointingly meager; either Grenfell did not see fit to confide in him as he had confided in Fremantle, Botts, and Basil Duke of Morgan's regiment, or, what is more likely, Ross repeated in his sketchy references to his compatriot only a fraction of what Grenfell had told him about his past. Ross wrote that "few men can have seen and done more fighting" than Grenfell, who "at one time commanded the bodyguard of Abd-el-Kader. At another time he fitted out a privateer and cruised on his own account against the Riff pirates. He has served in Turkey, India, South America, and I know not how many other places." [17]

There are inconsistencies, contradictions, and anachronisms in these stories, and many differences in detail, but on the surface they add up to the life story of a more than ordinarily restless but otherwise quite typical soldier of fortune, who, by an accident of birth, happened to be British. He might equally well have been French, or Polish, or Hungarian, or German, for in the middle of the nineteenth century, adventurers and soldiers of fortune of every nationality, or none, were to be met with in every quarter of the globe. Perhaps it was the final flowering of the Romantic spirit, warring against the ever more constricting social rigidities of the Victorian, or more properly, the Bourgeois Era, that led these men beyond the edges of the known world and the too-firmly circumscribed boundaries of a settled society. Many of them would doubtless have agreed with Stendhal that: "The very perfection of civilization would be a combination of all the delicate pleasures of the nineteenth century with a more frequent presence of danger." Soldiers of fortune, empire builders, explorers, missionaries, pioneers—they devoted their lives to the quest for the unknown, the new, the marvelous, those things which lay just beyond the horizon or just beyond normal experience. In the

[17] *Ibid.*, 172.

eighteenth century, soldiers of fortune had been itinerant practitioners of the profession of soldiering; but in the nineteenth century, even soldiers of fortune were caught up in the spirit of the time, and, more often than not chose their employers on idealistic grounds, and "drew their swords" (as they would have phrased it) for a cause and not for pay.

Had Grenfell been what Colonel Burnett called him, one "whose sword is unsheathed for hire and not for principle," a mere mercenary, had he brought nothing more to the Confederacy than his sword, his military skills, and his tales of a gaudy past, he might merit casual mention as an exemplar of a dying profession which was about to be wiped out by the growth of an all-pervasive nationalism. He was, after all, only an obscure member of a glamorous fraternity whose British contingent alone included Sir Richard Burton, General "Chinese" Gordon, and many more of the same exotic stamp, if lesser notoriety.

But Grenfell was something more than a soldier of fortune or something less; perhaps he was something altogether different, not to be pigeonholed under any simple label. A long and rocky road led him from the security of an upper middle-class British boyhood to America, a road that ran through the Paris of the Restoration and the July Monarchy, to Gibraltar, Morocco, the Crimean War, and South America. The life of an adventurer and the rejection of roots are there, plainly enough, but the casually selfish repudiation of loyalties is missing. A mercenary who fights for the mere pleasure of fighting, for whom irresponsibility is freedom and the violence and danger of war are a necessary drug, is easy enough to understand. Nor is there anything mysterious about the mercenary's scorn for loyalties or allegiances of any kind, personal or national, the *ubi bene, ibi patria* spirit. But what is one to make of a soldier of fortune who is a devoted adherent of the cause for which he fights, and who retains his allegiance to it long past the point at which the most elementary prudence would have dictated its abandonment?

A legendary figure in his lifetime was Colonel George St. Leger Grenfell, C.S.A., and a creature of high romance after his death.[18] Who and what was the creature of flesh and blood behind the legend and the romance?

[18] For examples of Grenfell's fame in the literature of the Civil War, see Dee Alexander Brown, *The Bold Cavaliers: Morgan's 2nd Kentucky Cavalry Raiders* (Philadelphia, 1959); Cecil F. Holland, *Morgan and His Raiders* (New York, 1942); James D. Horan, *Confederate Agent: A Discovery in History* (New York, 1954); Ella Lonn, *Foreigners in the Confederacy* (Chapel Hill, 1940); Howard Swiggett, *The Rebel Raider: A Life of John Hunt Morgan* (Indianapolis, 1934). For an interesting example of the fantastic legends that clustered about Grenfell among his contemporaries, see Milford Overley, "Old St. Leger," *Confederate Veteran*, XIII (1905), 80–81.

Chapter II

THE COURSE of George St. Leger Grenfell's life was a continuing act of violence against the sanctities of Victorian life, and especially against its inmost essence, the family. And indeed, the large Grenfell family was an overpowering aggregation, even by the ample Victorian standard.

The Grenfells hailed from the small town of Marazion in Cornwall, the long and rugged peninsula in the southwestern corner of England. The founder of the family fortunes was Pascoe Grenfell, born in 1728. A man of enterprise and energy, he engaged in the mining and smelting of tin and copper, for which Cornwall had been famous even in antiquity. The nearly continuous dynastic wars in the latter half of the century provided a ready market for Pascoe Grenfell's metals. The youngest of his ten children, George Bevil Granville Grenfell, migrated to London, where in 1804 he married his first cousin once removed, Caroline Granville, granddaughter of his paternal uncle.[1]

When George Grenfell and Caroline Granville, George St. Leger's parents, were married, the Grenfells were already people of substance. One of George's older brothers, Pascoe, after learning the secrets of finance in the great Amsterdam banking house of Thomas and Adrian Hope, made a large fortune; in association

[1] Some members of the family used the more aristocratic spelling of "Granville" of the family name.

15

with his father and others, he expanded greatly the family mining and smelting operations and also engaged in banking.[2] He solidified the family's social position by taking as his second wife, Georgina St. Leger, daughter of the first Viscount Donerail. A member of Parliament for many years, he enjoyed a wide reputation as an authority on financial questions. In the light of his nephew's later association with the Confederacy, it is not without interest that Pascoe Grenfell was a zealous supporter of William Wilberforce in the latter's successful fight to abolish slavery in the British colonies.[3]

Even by the standards of the time, the Grenfells were an exceptionally prolific and hardy race. Seven to ten children were the family norm and an amazingly large proportion of them survived the perils of infancy and childhood. In the course of years, Grenfells achieved or married distinction. One of George St. Leger Grenfell's first cousins married the novelist Charles Kingsley, another the historian James Anthony Froude. John Pascoe Grenfell became an admiral and commanded the Brazilian navy. In a later generation, a Grenfell became *sirdar* of the Egyptian army, a British field marshal and a peer. The poet Julian Grenfell was killed in action in World War I, as was also his brother. Francis and Riversdale Grenfell, nephews of Field Marshal Lord Grenfell, and known to their contemporaries as "the brilliant Grenfell twins," also gave their lives in World War I, Francis after winning the most coveted of all decorations for bravery, the Victoria Cross.[4] The twins were two of a family of thirteen; of the nine brothers in the family, three besides the twins died in the service of their country;

[2] The elder Pascoe Grenfell came across Thomas Hope just after the latter had been relieved of all his cash and valuables by a highwayman; Hope expressed his gratitude for Grenfell's kindness in providing him with the funds he needed to continue his journey by taking the younger Pascoe as an apprentice in his bank in Amsterdam. The younger Pascoe was described as "well known throughout England as . . . a man of talent and of great liberality, commensurate with his almost unexampled success in commerce." Davies Gilbert, *The Parochial History of Cornwall* (London, 1838), II, 216.

[3] *Dictionary of National Biography* (London, 1917), VIII, 553.

[4] The twins had the further distinction of having their biography written by their friend, John Buchan, *Francis and Riversdale Grenfell* (London, 1920).

one, Robert, was killed in the charge of the Twenty-first Lancers at Omdurman in which Lieutenant Winston Churchill, temporarily attached to the regiment, also participated.

George St. Leger Grenfell was born in London on May 30, 1808. On September 19, he was christened in St. Paul's, Covent Garden, and received the names George Stleger [*sic*] Ommanney.[5] The second of his names was given him as a compliment to his godmother, the aristocratic wife of his uncle Pascoe. The family name appears in the baptismal register as "Greenfell," neither the first nor the last of many such misspellings.

To be born into such a family as the Grenfells gave one a start in life from a secure base of economic and social well-being, a world of certainties, whose foundation was an unquestioning belief in the worth of industry, integrity, and discipline, and whose inhabitants shared the confident expectation that these virtues would be amply rewarded both in this world and the next. But these families also produced the eternally restless, to whom all certainties were an abomination, who could fulfill themselves only by seeking a world beyond the physical and emotional horizons of the parish pump. George St. Leger Grenfell was one of these. With singleness of vision and fixity of purpose, he might have become a pioneer, a seeker, or a revolutionary; lacking both, he became a drifter, a vagabond, and a mere rebel.

The multiplicity of George Bevil Grenfell's commercial and financial interests suggests that his family enjoyed a comfortable degree of prosperity.[6] His son George's schooling probably began in Penzance, whither the family moved in 1815. Five years later, the boy was sent to "college" (as he later called it) in Holland, for the practical education not then available in the classically oriented British grammar schools. He wrote many years later that during the four years of his schooling in Holland, his parents allowed him only one visit to his home. The feeling of rejection that this en-

[5] Baptismal Register, St. Paul's, Covent Garden (Parish Office, London).
[6] George Bevil Grenfell was a freeman of the Worshipful Company of Founders and was elected a steward in 1811. He was a partner in the banking house of Boase, Grenfell, Boase, and Company, in the tin smelting firm of Grenfell and Boase, and in a second tin smelting firm, Geo. Grenfell & Sons.

forced separation from his family evidently aroused may well have had a share in turning an unruly adolescent into a reckless adult whose destructive impulses were beyond anyone's—and especially his own—ability to control.

Late in the century, there were still old people in Penzance who told tales of "Mr. George's" daredevil pranks. "Old Mrs. Borlase" recalled the occasion when he had held her out at arms' length over the ocean, atop a high cliff at Land's End, despite her screams and struggles; but he remained in her memory "as the most dangerously fascinating man she ever met," and she remembered also that his charm was such that no one could bear him malice or fail to forgive him for his many misdeeds.[7]

After finishing his education in Holland, Grenfell wrote in later life, he toured the Continent with a relative and then settled in Paris.[8] At no time did he run away from home to enlist in a French cavalry regiment in Algeria. He did, however, perform military service of a sort during his residence in Paris. With friends who were members of the French Royal Guard, he took part in the three days of street fighting in Paris in July, 1830, that brought about the downfall of the Bourbon monarchy, and thereafter was a member for five years of the French National Guard. Service in the guard had its hazards, but in respect of military glamor, this bourgeois militia was a far cry from a "French lancer regiment" serving in Africa.[9]

[7] Lucy Galton, one of Grenfell's granddaughters, to Marie Pearce-Serocold, Marazion, —, 1900. In the possession of A. H. Packe (one of Grenfell's great-grandsons), Tile House, Burnham, Bucks., England. Documents from this source will be cited hereafter as Packe Papers.

[8] Grenfell to John Drummond Hay, April 15, 1845; Foreign Office-Morocco, General Correspondence (Public Record Office, London), FO 99/36. Documents from this collection will be cited hereinafter as FO-Morocco. For reasons referred to later in the text, in all the letters and documents in this collection for the period 1844-48 Grenfell is addressed and referred to, and himself uses, the surname St. Leger. To avoid unnecessary confusion, his true surname of Grenfell has been substituted for St. Leger in all quotations from and references to these documents.

[9] "All the shopkeepers are enrolled." Thomas B. Macaulay, undated family letter from Paris; quoted in G. Otto Trevelyan, The Life and Letters of Lord Macaulay (New York, 1876), I, 157.

18

Grenfell did not actually settle in Paris until the late 1820s. He was sent there by his family after he had worked for some years in the London offices of his father's firms, and had demonstrated a degree of extravagance and financial irresponsibility that made it necessary to remove him from the temptations and undesirable associations of London. His father's decision to have him work as a partner in the Paris branch of one of his firms, and thus give him a fresh start in a new environment, proved to be a catastrophic mistake. Grenfell engaged in speculations, the exact nature of which can no longer be determined, for which he used or pledged the assets of the firm. The speculations failed and his father, who as a partner was fully liable for the firm's debts, was ruined. As a result, Grenfell senior deemed it necessary to formally disinherit his scapegrace son, and as an outgrowth, apparently, of the same transactions, Grenfell himself was later tried and convicted *in absentia* by a French court for the forgery of a commercial instrument and sentenced to six years' imprisonment at hard labor.[10]

[10] This greatly abbreviated version of Grenfell's life in Paris has been reconstructed from the following sources: his own untruthful account (Grenfell to John Drummond Hay, April 15, 1845, in FO-Morocco, FO 99/36); notices concerning the dissolution of his father's firms in the London *Gazette*, II (1836) 2476; *The Annual Register for 1837* (London, 1838), 171–85; F. G. Hilton Price, *A Handbook of London Bankers* (London, 1890-91), *passim*; George Elwick, *The Bankrupt Directory: being a complete register of all bankrupts . . . from December 1820 to April 1843* . . . (London, 1843); the will of George Grenfell, Sr., on file in the Principal Probate Registry, London; a manuscript note, signed "E. K. Naylor," captioned "Some Details of the life of Nellies [sic] grandfather, George Ommany [sic] Grenfell, by herself, May, 1928," in the possession of Major General R. F. B. Naylor (one of Grenfell's great-grandsons), Barnet, Herts., England (Documents from this source will be cited hereinafter as Naylor Papers); and an undated memorandum from the French Ministry of the Interior to the Ministry of Foreign Affairs, a copy of which was given in November, 1847, by the French chargé d'affaires in Tangier to the British consul, John Drummond Hay, and forwarded by him to the British Foreign Office on November 12, 1847 (in FO-Morocco, FO 99/35). It is this memorandum which states explicitly that Grenfell was tried and convicted *in absentia* for forgery and sentenced to six years' imprisonment at hard labor. It should be said in fairness to his memory that a diligent search has failed to turn up any evidence in support of this statement. The records of the Palais de Justice in Paris from 1830 on were destroyed during the Revolution of 1848. The official law journal of the period, the *Gazette du Palais*, makes no mention of any proceedings against Grenfell, nor does his name appear in any of the following collections of documents for the period 1826–40, deposited in the Archives de France, Paris: Series F-7, *Police Générale;* Series F-80, *Algérie;*

19

At some time in 1840 Grenfell left or fled from France and returned to London. His Parisian transgressions were forgiven by his loyal and long-suffering family. A place was even made for him in one of his father's firms. He was joined in London by his wife, Hortense Louise Wyatt, a girl of mixed English and French parentage, whom he had married in 1833, and their daughters, Caroline Hortense, born in 1834, and Marie Emilie Jeanne, born in 1838.[11] His return to respectability was marked by his admittance to the Founders Company in November, 1840.[12] But the return of the prodigal did not prove to be a durable success. Whatever promises of future good conduct Grenfell may have made to his family and to himself, it was not in his nature to settle down to a sober and respectable career in commerce. He managed to keep his congenital restlessness in check for a time—one senses the restraining influence of his "nice, quiet, steady" wife—but three years in the role of the industrious apprentice was as much as he could endure.[13] In the fall of 1843 he decided to try a new venture under a new name in new surroundings; in October of that year, he obtained a Dutch passport made out to "George St. Leger," the name he was to bear for the next twelve years.[14]

There is ample documentation of Grenfell's activities for the next several years. From 1844 to 1848 he managed to be the center

Series BB-17, BB-18 and BB-30, *Ministèrè de la Justice*. Nonetheless, the author has been unable to arrive at any convincing reason for refusing to accept the statement.

[11] Caroline Grenfell's birth certificate dated December 2, 1834 (*Extrait du Registre des Actes de Naissance de la 8e Mairie*), in Naylor Papers; Marie Grenfell's birthdate supplied by A. H. Packe.

[12] Founders Company, Minutes of the Court of Assistants, entry for November 10, 1840. Guildhall, London, MS6331, Vol. VIII.

[13] The description of Grenfell's wife is in Lucy Galton to Marie Pearce-Serocold, Marazion, —, 1900, in Packe Papers.

[14] A copy of the passport, good for six months (Grenfell was still using it four years later) is enclosed with a dispatch of August 28, 1847, from the governor of Gibraltar, Sir Robert Wilson, to the Colonial Office, London. Colonial Office—Gibraltar, General Correspondence (Public Record Office, London), CO 91/182, Encl. 2. Documents from this collection will be cited hereinafter as Gibraltar-General Correspondence. The French Ministry of the Interior memorandum referred to in note 10 above states that while living in Paris, Grenfell had called himself "Grenfell de St. Leger."

of international complications and a source of embarrassment to the British government. He was the subject of an endless correspondence between the British consulate in Tangier, the governor of Gibraltar and his subordinates, the Foreign Office and the Colonial Office in London, numerous officials of the Sultan of Morocco, and representatives of the French Foreign Office, all of whom had the placid routine of their official lives disturbed by the activities of the irrepressible "George St. Leger." [15]

On January 10, 1844, Grenfell presented his Dutch passport at the police office in Gibraltar.[16] The Rock, however, was merely a way station to his ultimate destination, which was Tangier, across the Straits. He claimed a year later that he settled in Tangier on an impulse; actually, he said, he had intended to look for cheap farmland in Italy or Greece, but having gone on a hunting trip to Tangier with some of the officers of the British garrison at Gibraltar, he fell in love "with the wildness of the country, the beauty of the climate [and] the cheapness of the land," and decided to settle there instead.[17] But there is good reason to think that something other than the "love of agricultural pursuits" he professed to have, led him to Tangier.[18] The French conquest of Algeria, begun in 1830, was resisted by Abd-el-Kader, emir of the province of Mascara, at the head of the Berber tribes of western Algeria. When serious fighting broke out in 1840, it became evident that the emir's ability to keep his forces in the field depended largely on the recruits and supplies that came to him from Morocco, and especially on the arms and munitions his agents purchased for him in England and delivered through Gibraltar and Morocco. There is no firm evidence to link Grenfell to this risky traffic in arms, but the French government was sure he was involved in it and it is nearly certain that their belief was well founded.

[15] He will be referred to as Grenfell both in the text and in quotations from documents.

[16] Gibraltar-General Correspondence, CO 91/182, Encl. 2.

[17] Grenfell to John Drummond Hay, April 15, 1845, in FO-Morocco, FO 99/36.

[18] Ibid.

In 1844 Tangier was a squalid Oriental town with a population of seven thousand, important because of its location on the Straits and because, as the residence of the foreign consuls, who also acted as their countries' diplomatic agents, it was the only window to the modern world of Sultan Mulai Abd-er-Rahman's decrepit "empire." After many generations of misgovernment, even the fertile countryside around Tangier, including the farm, three miles from the city, that Grenfell leased, had become a scrubwood wilderness crawling with snakes and lizards. To venture beyond the gates of Tangier unarmed was suicidal. Nevertheless, Grenfell set about the task of clearing his land, planting crops, and restoring the dilapidated buildings on the property. These activities were enlivened by violent quarrels with his lazy and thievish workmen. After he had invested most of his ready cash in the farm, a stroke of luck came his way; the British vice-consul, Henry John Murray, employed him to help with the clerical work of the consulate at a wage of ten shillings per day.[19]

Grenfell had hardly entered upon his duties at the consulate when the long-smoldering trouble between France and Morocco blazed up. Its basis was French resentment of the help Abd-el-Kader was getting from and through Morocco. The French presented the sultan with an ultimatum, and to make sure that it was treated with respect, sent a squadron of battleships to Tangier under the command of the Prince de Joinville, third son of King Louis-Philippe. Acting on the knowledge that the prince intended

[19] For the history of the French conquest of Algeria and for the career and personality of Abd-el-Kader, see G. B. Laurie, *The French Conquest of Algeria* (London, 1909); Paul J. L. Azan, *L'Emir Abd-el-Kader* (Paris, 1925); Francis R. Flournoy, *British Policy Towards Morocco in the Age of Palmerston, 1830–1865* (London, 1935); and J. Lucas-Dubreton, *The Restoration and the July Monarchy* (New York, 1929). For Tangier and Morocco in the 1840s, see L. A. E. Brooks, *A Memoir of Sir John Drummond Hay* (London, 1896); Xavier Durrieux, *The Present State of Morocco: A Chapter of Mussulman Civilization* (London, 1854) and Walter B. Harris, *France, Spain and the Rif* (London, 1927). Grenfell's troubles with his workmen are referred to in John Drummond Hay to Lord Palmerston, June 21, 1847 in FO-Morocco, FO 99/39; Hay states that Grenfell had spent £600 to rehabilitate the property. For Grenfell's employment at the consulate, see E. W. A. Drummond Hay to Lord Aberdeen, October 3, 1844, in FO-Morocco, FO 99/19 and January 16, 1845, in *ibid.*, FO 99/29.

22

to bombard Tangier, Murray sent Grenfell to Gibraltar for help to remove British nationals from the threatened city. The arrival of the French ships had raised to fever pitch the xenophobia and religious fanaticism of the Moors. Tangier was occupied by an undisciplined horde of irregular soldiery of the Moroccan army, and the wild Kabyle tribesmen of the interior, who had a sixth sense for loot, appeared in droves. Conditions in the city became so bad that even the Moorish lieutenant governor was afraid to venture into the streets.[20] Grenfell could have remained in Gibraltar but chose to return to Tangier, notwithstanding the actual danger to his life. It was known that he had lived for some years in France and his wife was thought to be French. This was enough to brand him as a "French spy." Then he added fuel to the flames; in a typically reckless gesture, he lowered the flag of the French consulate as a formal, and in the circumstances, redundant, token of the severance of French-Moroccan diplomatic relations.[21] As a result, it became necessary for the lieutenant governor to assign him a guard of six reliable soldiers to protect his life.

Even before the arrival of the French squadron, the British consul, E. W. A. Drummond Hay, had hurried off to the sultan's residence at Rabat to persuade him to give in to the French ultimatum. His mission was successful, but at dawn on August 6, a few hours before he reached Tangier with the news, the prince began the long-threatened bombardment of the city. The French ships rode at anchor only a half-mile from shore. Nevertheless, their fire was remarkably ineffective; a few Moorish guns were disabled, two gunners were killed, and a half-dozen wounded. But the return fire of the Moorish batteries, manned mostly by renegade Christians, was hardly better. The ships sustained a few nicks and scratches, and casualties, in what Parisian newspapers described as a "brilliant exploit," were twenty sailors slightly wounded. Throughout the action, the Moorish gunners were seen dashing out

[20] Henry J. Murray to Commodore Nicholas Lockyer, July 28, 1844, in FO-Morocco, FO 99/21. Lockyer commanded a British "squadron of observation" that was sent to Tangier to keep watch on the Prince de Joinville's activities.
[21] Admiral Owen to the Admiralty, July 30, 1844, in FO-Morocco, FO 99/21.

of their works to pick up unexploded French shells which they promptly fired back at the ships. The bombardment went on until midafternoon, when the ships drew off and the artillery duel ceased.[22]

Grenfell was undoubtedly in Tangier on August 6, but whether he actually "did a little business with the Moorish batteries," or commanded one of them, as he later claimed, cannot be established; at any rate, the latter seems quite unlikely.[23] It is a fact, however, that during these troubles, his house and crops were destroyed and his livestock and farming implements were stolen. He was then to learn that by the custom of the country, he could not look to the Moorish government for compensation for his losses, because they occurred in time of war, and the British authorities did not consider it expedient to exert any pressure on his behalf.[24]

Directly and indirectly, the bombardment and its aftermath increased greatly the workload of the British consulate, and for the next two years the new consul, John Drummond Hay, who succeeded to the post upon the death of his father, continued Grenfell's part-time employment. Indeed, for four months in the summer of 1846, he had the rank and title of acting vice-consul while Henry John Murray was on leave. Grenfell's clerical duties were varied from time to time with more congenial assignments. In the spring of 1846 he accompanied Hay on a ceremonial visit to the sultan's court, then at Marrakesh, and had the task of making the formal presentation of Queen Victoria's gifts to the sultan and his principal dignitaries.[25] A few months earlier, he had deputized for Hay as host on a hunting trip arranged for a party of French

---

[22] Prince de Joinville, *Vieux Souvenirs, 1818–1848* (Paris, 1894), 391 *passim;* Lockyer to Admiral Owen, August 6, 1844, Lockyer to the Admiralty, August 9, 10, and 11; numerous dispatches from Sir Robert Wilson to the Colonial Office and from E. W. A. Drummond Hay to the Foreign Office, all in FO-Morocco, FO 99/21. *Cf.* Durrieux, *Present State of Morocco,* 46.

[23] Duke, *Morgan's Cavalry,* 180; Duke, *Reminiscences,* 151.

[24] Memorandum in Grenfell's handwriting, undated and unsigned, captioned "Account of losses sustained by George St. Leger at Tangier," in Packe Papers. E. W. A. Drummond Hay to Lord Aberdeen, October 17, 1844, in FO-Morocco, FO 99/18.

[25] There is a fascinating description of the journey in Brooks, *John Drummond Hay,* 76–123.

visitors headed by the author of *The Count of Monte Cristo*, Alexandre Dumas. The novelist was astonished by Grenfell's bizarre costume; he was hatless in the hot African sun, and his legs were bare. "A kind of pair of drawers came below his knees, and a kind of gaiter covered his ankles." Dumas ventured to question him about his unconventional costume; Grenfell cited the tale of the philosopher Diogenes, who, having discarded all his possessions except a wooden drinking bowl, threw it away after seeing a child drinking water out of his cupped hands; he was a disciple of Diogenes, Grenfell said, and seeing Arabs going barelegged and Negroes bareheaded, he discarded his hat and stockings. His sartorial eccentricities apart, Dumas described Grenfell as "one of the most agreeable men [he had] ever met" and a splendid hunting companion who "knew the country to a marvel and in all its details." [26]

Grenfell's employment at the consulate ended in September, 1846. For the next six months, there is no mention of his name in the records of the consulate. When it reappears in March, 1847, it is in an ominous conjunction with smuggling and the Emir Abd-el-Kader.

Three years before, after being defeated in Algeria, Abd-el-Kader had taken refuge in eastern Morocco and from that secure neutral haven, continued his harassment of the French. After the bombardment of Tangier nine months later, the Moroccan government had to be far more circumspect in aiding him than it had been. Abd-el-Kader had always enjoyed the enthusiastic support of the Moroccan people in his war against the infidel French, and when the sultan's government, under French pressure, began to interfere with his activities and with the flow of supplies to him, he decided to make himself sultan of Morocco in place of Abd-er-Rahman, whose authority and prestige had been badly damaged by the bombardment of Tangier.

It was at this point in the emir's fortunes that the first recorded direct contact between him and Grenfell occurred. In March, 1847, Hay reported to the British Foreign Office that Grenfell

[26] Alexandre Dumas, *Impressions de Voyage-Le Veloce* (Paris, 1871), 62–66.

25

and two companions named Clark and Moore had just returned from a visit to Abd-el-Kader's camp; Hay wrote that the French consul had complained to him about the visit, but that he had convinced his French colleague that the British government had not "the slightest connection with the wild schemes of these adventurers." [27] Grenfell himself explained later that, in the course of the visit, Moore made a "contract for certain stores of which he had been informed the Emir was in much need"; he did not identify the "certain stores" but it is obvious that they were arms and ammunition. [28]

Abd-el-Kader had often tried over the years to establish contact with the British government, but his advances had always been rebuffed. Now he took advantage of Grenfell's visit to enlist his services as an intermediary. No doubt he was encouraged to do so by what Grenfell told him about his highly placed and politically powerful connections in England. In a lengthy report to Lord Palmerston, the British foreign secretary, Grenfell wrote that Abd-el-Kader had claimed, no doubt correctly, that he had the secret support of the principal Moroccan tribal chiefs and government officials, and could make himself sultan in a month's time, given British good will. If, the emir said, Britain kept her hands off as between the sultan and himself and kept the French from interfering, then he would reward her with important economic concessions in Morocco as soon as he was in control of the country. The charm for which Abd-el-Kader was famous had an undoubted effect on Grenfell, and it was evident also that he was greatly flattered to be asked by the "gallant and enlightened" emir to intercede on his behalf with the all-powerful British government. He described his host in the most attractive terms and spoke glowingly

[27] John Drummond Hay to "Mr." [sic] Addington, March 27, 1847, in FO-Morocco, FO 99/35.

[28] Grenfell to Lord Palmerston, May 1, 1847, in FO-Morocco, FO 99/35. As to the nature of the "certain stores," Sir Robert Wilson wrote to Earl Grey on August 4, 1847: "[Grenfell] moreover has . . . been represented to have been connected with Abd-el-Kader and supplied him with arms, ammunition, etc., and had been to his camp, which avowed facts and statements, whether true or false, have been the subject of frequent representations on the part of the French Consul resident in Gibraltar." Gibraltar-General Correspondence, CO 99/36.

of "the respect almost amounting to adoration" that was felt for him throughout Morocco.[29]

Grenfell's venture into diplomacy and his eloquent presentation of the emir's cause helped Abd-el-Kader not at all, but were to prove disastrous to himself.

On the day after he reported to Lord Palmerston on his interview with Abd-el-Kader, Grenfell had to address a very different kind of letter to the foreign secretary. He had to solicit Palmerston's help in the difficulties that had sprung up between the Moorish government and himself within a few days after he completed the delivery of Moore's "certain stores" to the emir. John Hay told him that a Moorish merchant named Doucaly had requested the consulate to prevent his return to Tangier or to forbid him to remain there if he did return, on the ground that he had been smuggling leeches out of the country in violation of the monopoly of that trade which Doucaly had been granted by the Moroccan government.[30] Hay had told Doucaly that he, as consul, did not have the authority to force Grenfell to leave the country, whereupon Doucaly departed with the threat that he would apply to the sultan himself for an order for Grenfell's expulsion from Morocco.[31]

All this Grenfell described to Lord Palmerston. He admitted that he had been engaged in the illicit export of leeches, but he neglected to mention that his associates in the venture were a woman "who called herself" the wife of a self-styled Count St. Marie, and the "Count" himself, who had fled to Tangier to escape prosecution as a swindler in his native Belgium.[32] Indeed, he wrote that his partner was the son-in-law of the Portuguese consul and pleaded in

[29] Grenfell to Lord Palmerston, May 1, 1847, in FO-Morocco, FO 99/35.

[30] In the nineteenth century, bleeding, or phlebotomy, was still a common method of therapy, and leeches, widely used for this purpose, were an important article of commerce, France alone importing 57.5 million of them in one year. The swamps of Morocco were a prolific breeding ground of leeches, whose commercial value was recognized by the Moroccan government by the grant of export monopolies to well-connected and suitably grateful merchants. These export monopolies, like all other Moroccan trade regulations, were habitually evaded with impunity.

[31] Grenfell to Lord Palmerston, May 2, 1847, in FO-Morocco, FO 99/39.

[32] Henry J. Murray to Grenfell, April 11, 1848, in FO-Morocco, FO 99/36.

27

extenuation of his conduct that various forms of smuggling were the normal occupation of the European residents of Tangier, and were even indulged in by most of the foreign consuls. He was certain, he said, that the move to have him banished from Morocco, "as being a Man known to be averse to French Interests and French Domination" there, had been instigated by the French. He closed with an earnest plea for the protection of the British government and stated that expulsion from Morocco would mean his financial ruin.

Grenfell's letter to the foreign secretary was followed six weeks later by Hay's official report on the case, consisting of a twenty-one-page account plus thirty pages of supporting documents. This was a leisurely age, when the problems of a single unimportant British subject were deemed of sufficient consequence to justify the expenditure of so much ink, paper, and time, and to require the personal attention of Her Majesty's Secretary of State for Foreign Affairs. Hay had to concede that there was "considerable foundation for the several accusations . . . brought against . . . Grenfell," but he too expressed the opinion, in proper diplomatic language, that "the Moors were urged on . . . by certain underhand counsels," namely the French, because of Grenfell's dealings with Abd-el-Kader.[33]

Hay's report was not written until the Grenfell Affair, as it may be called, had entered the official stage by the receipt at the consulate on May 18 of a communication from the provincial governor, Sidi Bou Selham, in which Hay was requested to order Grenfell to leave the country; should he refuse to leave, the governor said, the government could not be responsible for his safety. Sidi Bou Selham justified his request on three grounds, not one having any ostensible connection with Grenfell's dealings with the emir. First, there were the many complaints against Grenfell by his workmen, whom he thrashed with great regularity; second, the complaints of merchants whose trade he injured with his smuggling activities; and third, that he had committed an unpardonable insult

[33] John Drummond Hay to Lord Palmerston, June 21, 1847, in FO-Morocco, FO 99/39.

28

against the Mohammedan religion. Grenfell, said the governor in closing, "ought to be sent out of the country. He is not thankful to God. You must oblige him to go, otherwise he will bring about a very disagreeable affair to yourself." [34]

The insult to religion the governor referred to was not exaggerated and showed Grenfell at his hot-tempered worst. It appears that as he was walking along the street with his gun on his shoulder and his hunting dogs at his heels, a boy expressed the national hatred of foreign Unbelievers by throwing a stone at him. The boy then ran, with Grenfell in hot pursuit, and took refuge in a mosque; Grenfell, with his gun and his dogs, ran into the building right behind him. In his anger, he forgot what he and all other Europeans in Tangier knew very well, namely that the Moroccans were so fanatically jealous of the sanctity of their places of worship that a Jew or a Christian who entered a mosque, even inadvertently, was customarily given the choice of instant conversion to Islam or death. By taking his gun and his dogs into the building, Grenfell aggravated an already serious offense.

Under existing treaties between Great Britain and Morocco, Grenfell could not legally be expelled from the country, and the consulate had no power to force him to leave if he chose to stay. Nevertheless, Hay persuaded him to leave Tangier voluntarily and to remain in Gibraltar until the reply of the Foreign Office to his own report arrived.[35] Grenfell departed after he was given written permission by Sidi Bou Selham to return to Tangier to wind up his affairs after the excitement over the mosque incident had died down.[36]

Within a few days after Grenfell left Tangier, the nearby villagers had thoroughly plundered his farm and to make sure that he

[34] Sidi Bou Selham to Hay, May 17, 1847, in *ibid*. In some of the documents, the governor's name is written "Sidi Bouselham," or "Sidi Booselham Ben Aly."

[35] John Drummond Hay to Grenfell, May 21, 1847, in FO-Morocco, FO 99/39; Grenfell to Hay, June 4, 1847, in *ibid*.

[36] Hay's letter to Sidi Bou Selham requesting the grant to Grenfell of a permit to return to Tangier, and the permit itself, are not in the records, but a letter from Hay to Grenfell dated June 18, 1847 (FO-Morocco, FO 99/39) speaks of the receipt of the permit by the consulate "this day," and recites the conditions under which Grenfell was authorized to return to Tangier for fourteen days.

had nothing to which to return, the Moroccan government took steps to have his lease canceled on a trumped-up technicality.

Grenfell's affairs were in this state on July 31, when Lord Palmerston's instructions were sent from London to Murray, once again in charge of the consulate in Hay's absence. His Lordship's orders were very much to the point and were couched in the breezy and arrogant language for which he was deservedly famous. Murray was directed to tell the Moorish authorities that: "All the complaints but one made against . . . [Grenfell were] trivial and futile; and could [not] afford the slightest ground for his expulsion." [37] The exception, Grenfell's entry into the mosque, was dismissed in cavalier fashion: ". . . thus to intrude into a Moorish Sanctuary was an unjustifiable outrage upon the religious feelings of the Mohammedan population, for which no doubt some atonement was due. But for that proceeding the Moorish Authorities, if not urged on by foreign influence would have been satisfied by some moderate present of money for the use of the Mosque." It will be noted that Palmerston too recognized that the French were at the bottom of Grenfell's difficulties. The foreign secretary went on to instruct Murray to communicate these observations to Sidi Bou Selham, and to say to that gentleman in the foreign secretary's own words,

> that if . . . [Grenfell] should remain in Morocco, the Moorish Government will be held answerable for his safety . . . and . . . you are specifically instructed to warn the Moorish Govt. that the British Govt. will not permit any injury, violence or other wrong which may be done towards any British subject in Morocco to pass with impunity; that Great Britain has the power to punish wrongs to Her Majesty's subjects by whomever committed; and that it will be well for the Govt. of Morocco not to give to Great Britain any just cause of complaint.

The Moorish government was to be told, the dispatch concluded, that if Grenfell chose to leave the country in deference to its

[37] This and the two quotations which follow are from Foreign Office to Henry J. Murray, July 31, 1847, in FO-Morocco, FO 99/34.

wishes, the British government would "require" that he be compensated in full for the losses that the forced abandonment of his property would entail.

That is how the lion roared when he still had teeth and claws and the willingness to use them. But before this dispatch arrived in Tangier, Grenfell had fatally compromised his own situation. He had left Tangier in early June and made no move for six weeks to use his permit to return. Then, on August 1, he received word in Gibraltar that the permit had been revoked because of his failure to avail himself of it within a reasonable time, and also because he had been heard to utter "serious menaces" against certain Moorish merchants.[38] If, as is likely, the revocation was intended to provoke him to some sort of retaliation, it succeeded admirably. Within two days after learning that he would not be allowed to reenter Morocco, he hired a boat, and with a single sailor as a companion, crossed the Straits to Tangier. When the lieutenant governor learned of his arrival, he stationed armed men along the mole and the beach with orders to shoot if Grenfell tried to land and, as an added precaution, sent a launch manned by a dozen of his soldiers to anchor close to Grenfell's boat and keep an eye on him. The soldiers whiled away the time by shouting insults in Arabic and Spanish at Grenfell, varied with promises to board his vessel and cut his throat during the night. Prudent for once, he did not allow the obscenities and threats to provoke him to retaliation, although the strain on his hair-trigger temper must have been well-nigh unbearable.

After two days in the harbor and the exchange with the consulate of a long succession of notes, which, on his side became more and more abusive, Grenfell had to recognize at last that he could accomplish nothing by remaining in the port and thus set sail for Gibraltar. Murray thereupon sent Lord Palmerston a lengthy report of these momentous proceedings, supported by copies of all the relevant letters and documents.[39] To make certain that no department of the British government remained in igno-

[38] Sidi Bou Selham to Murray, August 3, 1847, in FO-Morocco, FO 99/39.
[39] Murray to Lord Palmerston, August 10, 1847, in *ibid.*

31

rance of the affair, Sir Robert Wilson, the governor of Gibraltar, made haste to inform the colonial secretary also.[40]

By going to Tangier without waiting for the foreign secretary to make his wishes known, and with knowledge that his permit to return had been rescinded, Grenfell put himself hopelessly in the wrong. He had taken the law into his own hands and thereby relieved his government of the burden of taking his part in what was at best a rather messy affair. Also, with an incomprehensible obtuseness, while he was soliciting Palmerston's good offices to retrieve his position in Morocco, and knowing full well that the French, the prime cause of his misfortunes, were watching his every step, he chose this very time to apply for a visa to visit Abd-el-Kader again, with a Russian nobleman, Prince Demidoff, and one Joseph Benjunes, whom Governor Wilson described as "a Jew of discreditable reputation," as his companions. His application for a visa was refused, and Wilson sent a voluminous report of this latest imbroglio to the Colonial Office, whence it was promptly forwarded to the Foreign Office, whose officials read it even while they had to respond to his protestations of innocence and ill usage and his pleas for assistance.[41] As a result, he was now told in rather curt language that the Foreign Office declined to have anything more to do with him and his problems.[42]

The exchange of letters between Grenfell and the Foreign Office ended in the spring of 1848. Earlier, in December, 1847, a concerted attack by the sultan's forces on one side and the French on the other, destroyed Abd-el-Kader's armies; the emir was forced to surrender, and his fight for Algerian independence came to an end. Grenfell was barred from returning to Morocco, and there was no longer any money to be made out of gunrunning for the emir. For the next several years, Grenfell's wife, a talented teacher and a capable manager, was the financial mainstay of the family. She founded an excellent school for girls in Gibraltar. She held

[40] Robert Wilson to Earl Grey, August 4, 1847, in FO-Morocco, FO 99/36.
[41] Grenfell to H. Morgan, August 25, 1847; Wilson to Earl Grey, August 25, 1847, in Gibraltar-General Correspondence, CO 91/182.
[42] Foreign Office to Grenfell, December 13, 1847, in FO-Morocco, FO 99/35.

the family together and with occasional help from her erratic and impractical husband, provided a comfortable and happy home for her daughters.[43]

Grenfell, meanwhile, in partnership with a succession of individuals whose quality can be surmised from the terms in which they were referred to in the family correspondence: the "nasty, grasping" Genoese, Mateos, the aforementioned Joseph Benjunes, "Berzel the Jew," and others of the same type, engaged in "trade" —a euphemism for smuggling—on the Barbary Coast. Grenfell's contribution to these partnerships, which usually ended in quarrels and recriminations, was his knowledge of Morocco and the reckless courage needed to navigate the pirate-infested waters along the Moroccan coast, while his partners supplied the capital, stayed safely in Gibraltar, and took the lion's share of the profits. On one of these voyages Grenfell was attacked "by about 100" pirates.[44] He and his crew barely escaped with their lives, and apparently this was only one of several such incidents. These encounters were the basis of the tales he told of having fitted out a yacht or a privateer to carry on "a private war with the Riff pirates."

At some time during these years of Grenfell's feckless existence, possibly in 1855, the cumulative effect of his vagaries, his irresponsibility and his frequent "scrapes" proved too much for his wife. After twenty-two years of marriage, she left her husband. A formal divorce would have been out of the question, but the separation proved to be permanent. Mrs. Grenfell moved to Paris and there established a girls' school which acquired an excellent reputation and was much favored by American and British families living in the French capital.[45]

[43] A third daughter, Blanche Isabel, had been born to the Grenfells in 1841. Family tree supplied by A. H. Packe.

[44] Grenfell to the London *Times*, November 7, 1848; published in the issue of November 20, 1848.

[45] Hortense Grenfell's activities can be pieced together to some degree from a long series of letters written to her by her eldest daughter, Caroline (who had been married to her cousin, Robert Granville, a lieutenant in the Twenty-sixth Regiment of Foot, on August 30, 1851) from August, 1851 to July, 1855, in Naylor Papers.

A letter written by Grenfell's eldest daughter to her mother reveals that in May or June, 1854, he gave up his seafaring life and obtained a position "in the ordnance" at Gibraltar.[46] The Crimean War had broken out, and with Gibraltar serving as the principal staging point for supplies going to the British forces in the Crimea, its ordnance depot became a scene of intense activity. But with a war in progress, a dull desk job could not hold Grenfell for long, notwithstanding his forty-seven years. The Allies—the British, French and Turks—had agreed that in addition to sending their regular troops to the Crimea, they would also raise a special force of about twenty-five thousand men, to be organized as a self-contained "legion" with infantry, artillery, and cavalry components, to be known as the "Anglo-Turkish Contingent." The Turks were to furnish the enlisted men and a portion of the noncommissioned officers; the British, in addition to bearing the expenses, were to supply the officers, who were to be transfers from the Indian army and volunteers commissioned from civilian life, who could show "previous gallant service, knowledge of languages, general experience and skill in military training and acquaintance with the habits of Mahommedan soldiery."[47] Grenfell met some of these qualifications; the proper strings were no doubt pulled on his behalf, and on April 24, 1855, the London *Gazette* announced that "Henry St. Leger, Esq." was commissioned captain in the Contingent as of March 27. A week later, a correction changed the name of the newly commissioned captain to George St. Leger Grenfell.[48]

It will be observed that Grenfell now resumed his true patronymic. He had written his brother-in-law, "Perhaps it would be as well if you left word . . . that my name is George St. Leger

[46] Caroline Granville to Mrs. Grenfell, June 22, 1854, in *ibid.*

[47] F. Peel to an unnamed correspondent, March 29, 1855, in War Office-Crimea, Miscellaneous Letters (Public Record Office, London), WO 6/79. The history of the Anglo-Turkish Contingent will be found in Sir Adolphus Slade, *Turkey and the Crimean War: A Narrative of Historical Events* (London, 1867), 379–85, and in a series of letters from an unnamed correspondent in the *Illustrated London News*, XXVI (June 23, 1855), 630, 632; and XXVII (July 2, September 1, 15, 29, November 3, and December 8, 1855), 67, 251, 314, 370, 515, 659.

[48] London *Gazette*, April 24, 1855, p. 1575; May 1, 1855, p. 1669.

Grenfell . . . to prevent any mistake in case of my flattening a bullet." [49]

When his commission was gazetted, Grenfell was already on his way to Turkey with a group of Contingent officers from England.[50] When they arrived in Constantinople on May 12, they found that as a result of bad luck, mismanagement, and inertia, there were as yet no troops for them to command. They were quartered in the luxurious palace of the Russian embassy and employed their overabundant leisure in sightseeing expeditions and in cursing the Turks and all things Turkish. Eventually, and with much reluctance, the Turks assembled twelve thousand troops, about half the planned number; a camp was formed outside Constantinople, and the British officers could at length begin to learn Turkish and to become acquainted with the men they were to command.

While the Contingent was being assembled, another interesting body of troops, the "Osmanli Irregular Cavalry" (also known from the name of its British commander as "Beatson's Horse"), was in process of formation. The enlisted men of this unit were Turkish irregular cavalry, the redoubtable *bashi-bazouks*, whose atrocities and unruliness were a byword even in the Turkish army.[51] As a result of high-level army politics, General Beatson was ordered to turn over his 2,600 troopers to the Contingent to form the nucleus of its cavalry component, and it was to that unit that Grenfell was assigned. He proved to be conspicuously successful in controlling his company of ruffians, and his all-around competence as an officer was rewarded by appointment to the post of brigade major of the cavalry division, which gave him the responsibility of plan-

[49] Grenfell to A. H. L. Wyatt. The first page of the letter, which no doubt showed the date, is missing; the second page, from which the quotation in the text is taken, is attached to Colonel Wyatt to the Secretary for War, April 25, 1855, in War Office, Memorandum Papers, Commander in Chief (Public Record Office, London), WO 31/1080.

[50] Grenfell sailed from England on April 21, 1855, aboard the government-chartered steamer *Zebra*. British Ministry of Transport, General Register and Record Office of Shipping and Seamen, Llandaff, Cardiff.

[51] W. H. Russell, *The War: From the Landing at Gallipoli to the Death of Lord Raglan* (London, 1855), 125.

ning the training program of the division and of issuing all operational orders to it. However, the appointment did not carry with it an advance in rank; he retained his captaincy to the end of his service with the Contingent.[52]

At the end of August, 1855, Major General Robert J. H. Vivian, commander of the Contingent, reported his troops ready for active service. It then developed that no one wanted them. The War Office sent nine orders in succession from London, each contradicting its predecessor, as to where, how, and when they might be employed. In the midst of these indecisions, the fortress of Sebastopol fell to the Allies. The outcome of the war was now virtually settled, and, as a practical matter, the Contingent had lost its reason for being before it had fired a shot in battle. Sporadic fighting, however, went on for some time longer. In the autumn, the Allies decided to occupy the city of Kerch, in order to sever the best supply line to the Russian troops still in the Crimea. The task was assigned to the infantry and artillery of the Contingent. After taking possession of the city, General Vivian found himself under constant harassment by large bodies of Cossacks of the Russian army. To deal with them, Vivian sent orders to his cavalry to join him as speedily as possible.

On November 17, the transports carrying the Contingent's cavalry, its horses, and baggage arrived at Kerch. Everyone was eager to land, and the officers especially were delighted at the near prospect of a chance to earn distinction after six months of preparation. But it was fated that the cavalry was to reap no laurels and, indeed, was not even to have a chance to fight. It was discovered that, in keeping with the incredibly bad logistics of the entire war, the transports drew too much water to enter the shallow harbor, and no one had thought to provide for lighters to ferry the cavalry ashore. After twenty-four hours of a fruitless search for some way to effect a landing and amid much fuming and cursing on the part of the disappointed officers, the armada hoisted anchor and returned

[52] *The Annual Army List* for 1855 and for 1856 shows Grenfell as holding "Local and Temporary Rank of Captain."

ignominiously to Constantinople without the cavalry ever having set foot on shore or seen a Russian.

During the winter of 1855, the war slowly faded out of existence and came to a formal close with the signing of the Peace of Paris in February, 1856. During this time, and for some months longer, the Contingent remained in being, the infantry and artillery at Kerch and the cavalry at Constantinople. Not until May, 1856, did the War Department order that all the Contingent officers, except those who had to proceed to England on duty, were to receive their discharges at Constantinople. There was, however, a considerable delay in the execution of these orders. Grenfell was not appointed brigade major until the following month and his service with the Contingent did not terminate until late in August or early September.

Chapter III

WITH THE DEACTIVATION of the Turkish Contingent, Grenfell, nearing fifty, was cast adrift once more, without occupation, income, or ties whose claims he was willing to honor. Through no fault of its own, the Contingent had had a lackluster career and its officers had no martial accomplishments to boast about. Grenfell did not, in any proper sense of the word, "fight" in the Crimean War, but for something over a year, he had been an officer in a regularly organized army, he had learned much about the handling of an unruly band of irregular cavalry, and his appointment as brigade major attests to his efficiency and competence as an officer.

The six years from the late summer of 1856 to the spring of 1862 are a shadowy period of Grenfell's life. None of his statements to his American friends about his life in these years, of fighting in the Sepoy Mutiny in India, of a "civil appointment" and farming in South America, is inherently impossible or even improbable, but apart from a few indirect indications, there is no firm evidence to support any of them.

No doubt Grenfell had become friendly with some of the Indian army officers serving with him in the Contingent and, with nothing to keep him in Europe, he might well have gone with them to India when the Contingent was disbanded, to enjoy at modest cost his favorite sport of hunting. If he went to India in the fall of 1856, he may well have been there still in May of the following year, when the Sepoy Mutiny broke out; in that case he would unquestionably have volunteered for service. However, a search of the surviving records has failed to turn up his name as one of those who fought the mutineers; but the hectic months before the mutiny was suppressed were not a time for the careful compiling of records and rosters and the formal issuance of commissions.[1] The evidence being wholly negative and the fact not impossible, he should, perhaps, be given the benefit of the doubt on this point.

Grenfell's stories of being in South America stand on a different footing. A family tradition has it that while he was crossing the Atlantic with "a heterogeneous collection of men emigrating to South America," there was a mutiny on board and, singlehanded, he put down the mutiny by shooting the ringleaders. In another version, the mutineers are identified as "a party of bashi-bazouks, formerly commanded by Grenfell, that were emigrating to South America under his leadership." In either version, this is a fascinating addition to the Grenfell canon, and one wishes that a substantiation of it were possible; unfortunately, there is no mention of a mutiny on board a ship bound for South America in the exhaustive shipping news section of the London *Times* in the years 1856 to 1860, and Grenfell himself did not speak of the incident in the tales he told in America about his pre-Civil War adventures.

The absence of any mention of his name in the records of the British consulate general in Buenos Aires may be taken as proof that Grenfell had no "civil appointment" to take him to South America.[2] On the other hand, a number of incidental comments in letters he wrote in later life, in circumstances where there was no reason to boast of imaginary adventures, establish the fact that he did reside in Argentina for some time prior to 1862. He was then one of the eight thousand British subjects who, as their consul general in Buenos Aires reported in 1859, were engaged in sheep

[1] Communication from India Office Library, Commonwealth Relations Office, London.
[2] Foreign Office-Argentina, General Correspondence (Public Record Office, London), FO 6/237.

and cattle raising and agriculture in that country.[3] His well-to-do relatives, impressed perhaps by his good record in the Contingent as an augury of a permanent reformation, may well have supplied the capital for still another fresh start in a new country. If, as is nearly certain, Grenfell did reside in South America in these years, it would have been in character for him to dabble in the civil commotions and military coups and countercoups which were already the normal means of political activity in the "South American republics," but there is a total absence of corroboration of Grenfell's claims on this point.

In April, 1862, Grenfell appeared in Charleston, South Carolina, aboard the blockade-runner *Nelly*.[4] That much is fact. However, there is nothing tangible to show why and when he left Argentina; no indication, unless his congenital restlessness is an adequate indication, of the reasons which led him to risk his life in a foreign war; and no evidence whatever of his motives in choosing the Confederacy, rather than the North, to fight for. One can only assume that however good his intentions may have been at the start of his venture in Argentina, it was probably not long before farming palled on him. He was not cut out to lead for very long the life of a peaceful husbandman. Indeed, no one was less suited by temperament to remain long in one place or pursue a humdrum occupation for any length of time. The subsequent course of Grenfell's life makes it evident that advancing years had not cooled his blood, nor had they made him willing to settle down to slippers and a chair by the fireside. Restlessness, the craving for change, for excitement were in his blood. The poet Julian Grenfell who also traced his lineage back to Pascoe Grenfell and Cornwall, wrote of himself as one "who every year has an increasing desire to live in a blanket under a bush, and will soon get bored with the bush

[3] *Ibid.*, FO 6/216.
[4] *The Vidette*, August 17 (actually August 27), 1862; copy in the John Hunt Morgan Papers, Southern Historical Collection, University of North Carolina Library, Chapel Hill; hereinafter cited as Morgan Papers. *The Vidette* was a camp newspaper issued irregularly by members of the Second Kentucky Cavalry. The "August 17" issue contained an article on "Col. George St. Leger Grenfell," reprinted from the Knoxville, Tennessee, *Register*.

and the blanket." [5] One may contrast this with a letter our Grenfell wrote in 1864:

> I know nothing of my future movements, but leave them all to fate. . . . But it does not much matter; we have all got to live a certain time, and when the end comes, what difference will it make whether . . . I died in a four-poster bedstead with a nurse and phials on the bed table or whether I died in a ditch? [6]

Julian Grenfell's cousin, Auberon Thomas Herbert, was described by a close friend as "a gipsy to the core of his being, a creature of the wayside camp, wood smoke, and the smell of earth." [7] And what was said of Julian Grenfell and Auberon Herbert might have been said with equal justice of their relative in an earlier generation, George St. Leger Grenfell: "Some very ancient forebear was reborn in [them]."

Grenfell did not go directly from South America to Charleston. He went first to Europe. He was in England for a time, and visited his daughter Marie, recently married to Charles Pearce-Serocold and living near Oxford in Buckinghamshire.[8] He also visited his childhood home in Penzance and made a lasting impression on the inhabitants; it was said of him several years later that he was "covered with scars, [the] master of 13 languages, many of which he spoke so well as to make his nationality doubtful, and possessed . . . a fund of good spirits and anecdote which rendered his society very agreeable." [9] Before leaving England, he had his photograph taken; dressed for the occasion in the conservative black broadcloth uniform of the day of the middle and upper classes, he ap-

---

[5] John Buchan, *Pilgrim's Way* (Cambridge, 1940), 60-61.

[6] Grenfell to Marie Pearce-Serocold, October 11, 1864, reproduced in Mabel Clare Weaks (ed.), "Colonel George St. Leger Grenfell," *Filson Club History Quarterly*, XXXIV, No. 1 (1960), 8.

[7] Buchan, *Pilgrim's Way*, 61.

[8] Grenfell family tradition communicated to the author by A. H. Packe.

[9] "Col. George Grenfell, of Penzance," *Cornish Monthly Illustrated Journal* (May, 1868), n. p. The writer of this article, published anonymously, gave it as his opinion that Grenfell's career "surpasses anything that could be born of the most romantic conceptions of the novelist, exuberant or eccentric as his fancy might be." As to Grenfell's knowledge of languages, he was fluent in English, French, and Arabic and probably had a good knowledge of Dutch, Spanish, and Turkish; seven languages of the thirteen with which this article credits him are thus unaccounted for.

pears in the photograph, at least in dress, the very image of Victorian respectability.[10] The photograph shows him as he was when he appeared in America a few weeks later: a wiry figure, glossy dark hair without a trace of gray, a rather scraggly moustache and beard, his head firmly cocked to the left in a jaunty, devil-may-care pose, and a supercilious look in his eye. Grenfell was nearly fifty-four when the photograph was taken, and by the standards of the day, was on the threshold of old age, but he appears to be a man in the prime of life and vigor.

From England, Grenfell crossed over to France, and on March 1, called on John Slidell, the emissary of the Confederate government to the Emperor Napoleon III.[11] Slidell gave him the letters of introduction which, in the fashion of nineteenth century travelers, Grenfell felt it necessary to have. He was probably introduced to Slidell by Adolphe Thibaudeau, a man of influence in Parisian financial circles and husband of his wife's sister Blanche.

One of Slidell's letters of introduction was addressed to General Robert E. Lee. After landing in Charleston, Grenfell went on to Richmond, where he arrived toward the end of April, and presented his letter to the general. A short time before, Lee had been appointed to a post corresponding to that of a present-day Chief of Staff of the Army, being charged "with the conduct of military operations in the armies of the Confederacy." [12] He was thus in a position to provide Grenfell with a suitable assignment. There is no record of the conversation between the two men, but its outcome makes it evident that the breadth and caliber of the military experience Grenfell claimed to possess and the modesty of his demands made an excellent impression. He had with him letters of recommendation from high-ranking British officers, and doubtless stressed his service in the Crimean War. It would appear, however,

[10] The date of this photograph, and the photograph itself, have been given to the author by A. H. Packe.
[11] Grenfell to P. G. T. Beauregard, May 20, 1862; in RG 109, War Department Collection of Confederate Records; General and Staff Officers; File of G. St. Leger Grenfell (National Archives, Washington, D.C.); hereinafter cited as Grenfell Papers-National Archives.
[12] Douglas Southall Freeman, *R. E. Lee: A Biography* (New York, 1941), II, 5.

that he also began in this interview the practice, which was to become a habit, of exaggerating his military accomplishments; he claimed to have held the rank of colonel, and represented himself as "late of the British Army." [13] These embellishments of the truth were probably quite unnecessary. The mere fact that a British gentleman had crossed the sea to offer his sword to the Confederacy was recommendation enough. It was already evident in the spring of 1862 that the South had an ample supply of officers who combined the utmost bravery with a profound ignorance of military administration. Had Grenfell given General Lee a wholly factual account of his military experience, it would have been sufficient to assure him a cordial welcome. He had been trained in just those areas of military lore in which the Confederate armies were most deficient: tactics, training, discipline, and administration. He was a valuable acquisition, and he heightened the good impression he had already made by making it clear that unlike the general run of gentlemen volunteers from abroad, he wanted neither high rank nor a showy staff appointment.

General Lee decided that the western armies of the Confederacy were most in need of Grenfell's talents and skills, and sent him West with, according to Grenfell, an appointment as aide-de-camp to General P. G. T. Beauregard, but actually with nothing more than a letter of recommendation, albeit highly complimentary in tone, addressed to the general:

> Col. G. St. Leger Grenfell late of the British Army generously offers his Services in defense of our Invaded Country. Wishing to make his Service as agreeable to him as possible, I have recommended to him to attach himself to your Army. His information is so extended & his experience so varied, that there is hardly any position in which he could not be useful. He however asks no particular position, but prefers leaving that to the qualifications he may exhibit & the Service he may render desiring at present the opportunity of duty in the field. From the testimonials in his favour from high British officers and other letters I have seen, I can with Confidence recommend him to your kind attention.[14]

[13] R. E. Lee to P. G. T. Beauregard, April 26, 1862, in Grenfell Papers-National Archives.

[14] *Ibid.*

Even if it were not for the precise terms of Lee's letter, Grenfell's claim that Lee had appointed him aide-de-camp to General Beauregard would be incredible. With his meticulous sense of military courtesy and protocol, the general would not have presumed to appoint someone to the personal staff of another general officer, especially one so notoriously touchy about the prerogatives of his rank as "The Great Creole."

In his postwar story about Grenfell, General Basil Duke wrote that he had been assigned to duty with John Hunt Morgan by General Lee, to give him "the kind of service to which he had been most accustomed." [15] General Duke's memory was at fault on this point. Grenfell's own version, that on his way to Beauregard's headquarters he met Morgan and decided to join him, is borne out by the surviving documents.[16] Beauregard's headquarters were at Corinth, Mississippi, at this time. In the seven weeks of April and May, 1862, while his army was established there, Beauregard lost as many men from typhoid fever and dysentery as he had lost in the bloody battle of Shiloh.[17] Grenfell left Richmond for Corinth at the end of April or the beginning of May, but he had hardly begun his journey when he suffered a severe attack of dysentery. He had to interrupt his journey in Montgomery and had to remain there for three weeks before he was well enough to travel. The epidemics of typhoid and dysentery at Corinth were by that time common knowledge throughout the South. Still weak from his own illness, Grenfell decided not to risk an immediate trip to Corinth and went instead to Mobile to recuperate. It was there that he met Morgan during the last week in May. The two men took an immediate liking to each other and Grenfell there and then put away General Lee's letter of recommendation and joined Morgan's "Corps of Rangers" as a "private Soldier." [18]

[15] Duke, *Reminiscences*, 150.
[16] *House Executive Documents*, 598.
[17] T. Harry Williams, *P. G. T. Beauregard: Napoleon in Gray* (Baton Rouge, 1954), 152.
[18] Grenfell to Beauregard, May 30, 1862, in Grenfell Papers-National Archives. Grenfell went on to explain: "After having proved by some active Service my devotion to the Southern cause I may claim your recognissance [*sic.*] hereafter with more justice and satisfaction to myself than I could now do, as an utter Stranger." The letter is signed "G. St. Leger Grenfell, Lieut. Col."

Colonel John Hunt Morgan, in whose command Grenfell was about to begin his service in the Confederacy, was born in Alabama in 1825 and grew to manhood in Lexington, Kentucky. At nineteen he enlisted in the First Kentucky Cavalry for service in the Mexican War and saw action in the battle of Buena Vista, in which Colonel Jefferson Davis and Captain Braxton Bragg so greatly distinguished themselves. Returning to Lexington after the war, he became a successful manufacturer and businessman and kept alive his interest in military matters by organizing the Lexington Rifles, a gaudily uniformed militia company of which he was elected captain. When the Civil War broke out, Kentucky declared its determination to remain neutral, which, however, did not prevent its citizens, many strongly pro-Union and many just as strongly pro-South, from an open and energetic display of their sympathies. Morgan paraded his secessionist leanings by flying a large Confederate flag over his factory. When Confederate forces crossed the state boundary into Kentucky in September, 1861, and the Federals retaliated by occupying a number of strategic points and the larger cities in the state, the official neutrality of Kentucky became a dead letter. The state was in the Union to stay, and with Federal troops in possession of Lexington, Morgan and his Rifles decided it was time to leave the city. They departed in great secrecy on the night of September 20 and joined the Confederate forces assembling in Bowling Green, Kentucky.[19]

One of the many stanzas of a half-serious "poem" printed in a Cincinnati newspaper in 1863, describes thus Morgan's departure for the wars:

> But Fame of John's expanding mind
> Possession full had gotten,
> And so he left his woolen mills,
> To go and save King Cotton.[20]

During the first winter of the war, Morgan and the Rifles engaged in scouting and raiding excursions on a minor scale. These operations had very little military value but they served as an ex-

[19] Holland, *Morgan and His Raiders*, 21–41.
[20] Cincinnati *Commercial*, August 14, 1863.

cellent course of training, and, in the midst of the general inactivity, brought Morgan's name to the notice of the Confederate high command. They also established the pattern for his subsequent conduct as a commander of cavalry.

The worst of Morgan's qualities as a military commander was the excessive indulgence with which he handled his men. His kindness toward his troopers went well beyond what he might have been expected to show friends and neighbors from Lexington, which many of them were. His naturally kindly disposition should have been hardened by the responsibilities of command, but was not. As a result, he had the affection of his men, and as the successes of "Morgan's command" made their name and his a household word in the Confederacy and beyond, he gained their admiration as well.[21] The affable camaraderie between Morgan and his men, however pleasant it may have been for all concerned, had another, far less desirable, aspect. A military organization cannot be run with the casual egalitarianism of a gentlemen's club. It must have discipline. Morgan was far too lenient and easygoing to try to raise the state of discipline of his command even to the modest Confederate norm. The very last letter Grenfell wrote him closed with the admonition Morgan must have heard from him many times before: "Keep up discipline, whatever you do! Put in a good firm A. A. G. who will take the odium of a little necessary severity off your shoulders and bear it himself, and support him." [22]

It is doubtful if on balance, Morgan gained as much for the Confederacy with his military successes as he lost because he failed to make a real effort to control the depredations committed by his undisciplined troopers in Kentucky and Tennessee. Operating normally at a distance from their base, Morgan's men lived off the country. Food for themselves, feed for their mounts, supplies of all kinds, in fact, whatever they needed, they took from the civilian population, and frequently took what they did not need, simply

[21] India W. P. Logan (ed.) *Kelion Franklin Pedicord of Quirk's Scouts, Morgan's Kentucky Cavalry, C.S.A.* (New York, 1908), 35.
[22] Grenfell to John H. Morgan, March 30, 1864, in Morgan Papers. "A. A. G." is the abbreviation for assistant adjutant general.

46

because it was there for the taking. And they took from friend and foe alike. It was said, especially in the later years of the war, that a single visit by Morgan's command was usually enough to turn devout Confederate sympathizers into strong Unionists. Morgan's name became a synonym for horse stealing, marauding and, at the end, for undisguised banditry. Morgan closed his eyes to such things. Whether from weakness, or indifference, or amiability, he did not make the necessary effort to check the predatory habits of his men, even after it was obvious that they injured the military effectiveness of the command; and he seemed equally indifferent to his troopers' straggling on the march, their lengthy absences from the ranks, and their habit of obeying orders, except in battle, only when it suited them to do so.

Even more destructive in the long run than the laxity of command was the fact that Morgan's inability to discipline his men was coupled with an equal inability to discipline himself. An incurable romantic, unstable, moody, erratic, unpredictable, and, it must be said, neither very shrewd nor very intelligent, Morgan operated as if he had been a solitary knight-errant on the lookout for crossroads adventures. If he ever thought of the Civil War as something more than a gaudy tournament, he gave no indication of it. He lacked the singleminded ruthlessness of Nathan Bedford Forrest, just as he lacked Forrest's hardheaded appreciation of the uses of irregular cavalry. He had not a particle of the killer instinct and his judgment was the victim of the glamor of his activities. He took a childish delight in his own successes, describing them in letters to his friends as "brilliant affair[s]."[23] He was as much dazzled as were his many admirers back in the Bluegrass by the superficial glitter of his exploits, and as little capable as his friends were of an objective appraisal of their true military value. One of his own men, better qualified than most to judge, called him in retrospect a hero of romance, not of fact.[24]

[23] Morgan to Irby Morgan, August 24, 1862. Quoted in Julia Morgan, *How It Was: Four Years Among the Rebels* (Nashville, 1892), 172.
[24] John B. Castleman to Thomas Henry Hines, February 7, 1867, in Thomas Henry Hines Papers, University of Kentucky Library, Lexington; hereinafter cited as Hines Papers.

Beauregard retreated to Corinth after the battle of Shiloh. He spent the succeeding weeks preparing the best reception he could muster for the heavily reinforced Union armies moving toward him, under the uninspired leadership of Major General Henry W. Halleck, with the speed of a glacier. The energetic and imaginative Beauregard was not content to have his men dig trenches and throw up earthworks pending the arrival of the Union army. During the retreat from Shiloh, he had been impressed by Morgan's resourcefulness and now decided to put to use his talent for independent action. He instructed Morgan to increase the size of his command from a "squadron" of three companies to a full regiment, gave him fifteen thousand dollars for expenses, and ordered him to make life as unpleasant as possible for General Halleck by operating on his line of communications. Adding a few detachments of horse to his command, Morgan set off on April 26 to beat up the country in Halleck's rear and intercept his supply trains.

Despite the smallness of the force with which Morgan started out, the raid began auspiciously and all went well until he reached Lebanon, Tennessee, 170 miles from his starting point. There the lack of discipline produced disaster. On May 4, when the raiders reached Lebanon, night was falling. They had had a hard day's ride, it was raining, and the night promised to be cold and dismal. Most of the 325 troopers took up quarters with the hospitable townsfolk. Sentries were posted and pickets were stationed on the roads leading into town. The good people of Lebanon, feeling sorry for the sentries and pickets out in the night, plied them with whiskey to counteract the deleterious effect of the chill rain. Excessively well warmed on the inside, the guards decided their services were not needed, inasmuch as the Federal cavalry would not venture out on so unpleasant a night, and they drifted off to the nearest houses and barns for a well-earned night's sleep. The roads leading into Lebanon were left unpicketed and unwatched. Just before dawn, a force of 600 Federal troopers, made up of parts of the First Kentucky (Union) Cavalry and the Seventh Pennsylvania Cavalry, and led by the redoubtable Colonel Frank Wolford, known as "Old Meat Axe," galloped into town. The surprise was complete. Morgan and his men came tumbling out of the houses and, considering the adverse circumstances, put up a remarkably good fight, but they were greatly outnumbered and the surprise made any organized resistance impossible. Nearly half the Confederates were taken prisoner; Morgan himself and the rest of his men fled. After a wild ride of twenty-one miles, known thereafter as the "Lebanon Races," a mere 20 of the 325 crossed Stone's River to safety. The rest were killed, captured, or scattered to the four winds.[25]

Returning to Chattanooga after this humiliating experience, Morgan set about reorganizing his command. The original three companies were reconstituted with recruits from Kentucky and men who had escaped from Lebanon. Two companies of Texas cavalry were given permission to join him. Three hundred members of the First Kentucky (Confederate) Infantry, having completed their original term of enlistment, decided to do their fighting as cavalry thereafter and reenlisted under Morgan. A cavalry company from Mississippi joined, and another from Alabama, and later a Partisan Ranger unit from Georgia. Morgan now had a full regiment, which was officially designated as the Second Kentucky Cavalry. The regiment moved to Knoxville, and under the inspiration of the scholarly and thoughtful Lieutenant Colonel Basil Duke, Morgan's brother-in-law and second in command, began to drill in the battle tactics for which Morgan was to receive credit, although they were actually devised by Basil Duke.[26]

[25] Sergeant E. Tarrant, *The Wild Riders of the First Kentucky Cavalry* (Louisville, 1894), 82–91; Duke, *Morgan's Cavalry*, 159–62.

[26] Controversy about the authorship of Morgan's contribution to the development of the new cavalry tactics was rife as early as 1866, when General Duke wrote: "I shall certainly claim, for I firmly believe, that Genl Morgan was the author of that system of operations which . . . made our cavalry so effective. . . . No matter in what sense 'revolutionized cavalry tactics' is used, it was he who did it." Duke to T. H. Hines, April 3, 1866, in Hines Papers. Notwithstanding Duke's loyal and modest disclaimer, we are convinced that it was he himself, and not Morgan, who was the author of these innovations. There was a great deal of truth in the remark of the historian of the Seventh Pennsylvania Cavalry, who wrote: "The general opinion of Union officers, who had the honor of meeting [Morgan's] command in battle, was that [George D.] Prentice, of Louisville, told the truth when he said: 'Someone might hit Duke on the head and knock Mor-

Based on the system developed in the "Old Army" for use by small bodies of cavalry operating against Indians, and adapted by Duke to the needs of regiments and brigades, the new tactics produced a new kind of fighting force, vastly different from traditional cavalry. It was manifestly impossible to give men and horses the two years of rigorous training considered indispensable to form a cavalry force on the European model, one able to execute the elaborate evolutions the manuals prescribed for large bodies of cavalry. Moreover, the nature of the terrain in the hills of Kentucky and Tennessee, heavily wooded for the most part, with scattered small clearings lined with high fences, and narrow, winding paths for roads, made the normal (in the traditional sense) shock tactics of cavalry virtually impossible. Duke's substitute was an intelligent adaptation of the mobility of cavalry to the talents and weaknesses of his human material, the limitations imposed by the terrain, and the lack of time for adequate training. Unhampered by the orthodoxies of a formal military education and with typical American pragmatism, he discarded those elements of textbook dogma which were unsuited to the conditions in which he had to operate and transformed what was left into the essentially new concept of a force of mounted riflemen. He laid it down that in battle, a small portion of the command was to remain mounted and held in reserve "to act on the flanks, cover a retreat or press a victory," but the bulk of the force was to fight dismounted, deployed in a single line curved forward at its two ends, and moving to the attack at the double-quick or at a run. The men were to be armed with infantry rifles, the medium Enfield by choice, rather than the cavalry carbine.[27] No reliance was to be placed on the saber.

A body of cavalry employing Duke's tactics, unlike cavalry operating along traditional lines, did not need to rely on infantry support; it *was* infantry. It retained the mobility of cavalry, but primarily only as the means of rapid movement between engage-

gan's brains out.'" William B. Sipes, *The Seventh Pennsylvania Volunteer Cavalry* (Pottsville, Pa., n.d.), 20.

[27] Duke, *Morgan's Cavalry,* 173-76.

ments, for raids deep into enemy territory, and for independent operations on the enemy's line of communications.

Morgan's regiment was encamped in Knoxville in late June, assimilating Colonel Duke's novel ideas, when Grenfell arrived with a note of introduction from Morgan. Grenfell explained that he had come to take up the duties of adjutant, having been appointed to that post by Morgan when they met in Mobile. Duke later wrote that when Morgan met Grenfell, he "fell in love with him on first sight," and impressed with the Englishman's personality and qualifications, appointed him without further ado to his staff.[28] There were no bothersome formalities of enlistment in the Confederate army. Grenfell simply "joined." As for rank, the British colonelcy he claimed was sufficient; he was "Colonel Grenfell" and a Confederate commission would have added nothing to what he already had.

Lieutenant Colonel Basil Wilson Duke, whom Grenfell now met, had been born near Georgetown, Kentucky, and lacked only two days of being exactly thirty years his junior. Duke was a great-nephew of Chief Justice John Marshall. He had attended colleges in Danville and Georgetown, Kentucky, and after studying law at Transylvania College in Lexington, moved to St. Louis to practice his profession. In the summer of 1861, he returned to Lexington to marry Henrietta Hunt Morgan, John Morgan's only sister. He enlisted in his brother-in-law's Lexington Rifles and was elected first lieutenant. He served under Morgan until the latter's death in September, 1864, and succeeded him in command of what had then become the Morgan Brigade. With the remnants of this once famous unit he escorted President Davis on his flight from Richmond in April, 1865. Quietly brave, intelligent, possessed of an uncompromising sense of duty and loyalty, honorable to the bone and possessing a most attractive personality, Basil Duke was the embodiment of the finest qualities of the best type of Confederate officer.[29]

[28] Duke, *Reminiscences*, 151.
[29] James W. Henning, "Basil Wilson Duke, 1838–1916," *Filson Club History Quarterly*, XIV (1940), 59–64.

Chapter IV

THE NEWLY APPOINTED ADJUTANT of the Second Kentucky Cavalry entered a strange world on joining his regiment at Knoxville. The physical setting was the camp of a regiment of cavalry, with its rows of tents and horselines, superficially similar to the cavalry camp of the Turkish Contingent at Constantinople. But in all the essentials, it is quite evident that the differences between the Confederate cavalrymen and the troopers of the contingent were astronomical. There was much that Colonel Grenfell could contribute to the military education of the Second Kentucky, but to become an effective teacher, he had to learn much himself and unlearn just as much. He had to accustom himself first of all to the casual atmosphere of a service in which every trooper was, and expected to be, treated with a relaxed camaraderie by those of his boyhood friends and fellow gentlemen whom he helped to elect as officers; a service in which prewar social standing counted for more than the adventitious badges of military rank, and bravery in battle more than either.[1] A mere lieutenant or captain, raised to office by the suffrages of the enlisted men of his company, was not likely to be held in awe by his constituents. And the exalted titles of major or even colonel

---

[1] A typical situation in Morgan's regiment is shown by the comment of one of his men: "I enlisted . . . in Captain G. M. Coleman's company, composed mostly of my boyhood schoolmates." Henry L. Stone, *"Morgan's Men": A Narrative of Personal Experience* (Louisville, 1919), 6.

meant little in an organization in which the lowly private who was in charge of the mule train was always addressed as "Colonel" Leathers, by virtue of his prewar service in the Kentucky legislature. Titles were a greatly depreciated currency in an era in which so many were "tinseled with the usual harmless military . . . titles of that old day of cheap shams and windy pretense," as Mark Twain put it in one of his acrid comments on the prewar South.

Actual authority in a regiment like Morgan's flowed not from mere rank, but from force of character, ability, and above all, bravery. As Grenfell noted after a brief acquaintance with his new associates, "every atom of authority had to be purchased by a drop of . . . blood." [2] Moreover, an officer was expected to confine the exercise of his right to give orders mainly to the battlefield. If he tried to assert it in camp, he was at once stamped as a martinet and his life was made a burden and a tribulation accordingly. If his men chose to wander away from camp of an evening, to straggle on the march, to do a little visiting or foraging whenever the spirit moved them, or to take a lengthy and unauthorized leave when there was no fighting going on, it was not for an officer to interfere. Nor did the men consider it proper to have the hardships of drill and guard-mount inflicted upon them when they were recuperating from the fatigues of their latest expedition and building up their strength for the next; the necessary chores of caring for the horses, mending clothing, refurbishing gear, writing letters, and reading the mail and the newspapers left little enough time for the more pleasant camp pastimes of visiting, horse racing, card playing, cockfighting, and gander pulling.

If Grenfell needed a reminder that the Second Kentucky Cavalry was not an organization of regulars, all he had to do was to look about him. In common with the majority of Confederate cavalry units, especially in the West, the regiment was plagued by shortages. Uniforms were practically nonexistent; most wore what they had on when they left home to enlist, or what was left of it, and when that wore out, replaced it by getting more clothing from home and completed the ensemble with parts of Federal uniforms

[2] Fremantle, *Diary*, 127.

53

taken from prisoners. More serious was the shortage and the lack of uniformity of weapons. Before captures from the Union army, the Confederacy's never-failing source of supply, remedied the situation, Morgan's men made do with a miscellany of shotguns, sporting rifles, and relics of the Mexican War. When they started on their first and most successful raid into Kentucky—the first operation in which Grenfell participated—200 of the total of 826 men had no firearms at all and carried clubs in lieu of more effective weapons.[3] The supply of blankets, accoutrements, and camp gear was totally inadequate. But, to compensate for these shortages, the men wore the largest, noisiest spurs they could find and broadbrimmed hats pinned up on one side with a crescent or a star, in the style affected by Morgan himself.[4] And many of them carried huge bowie knives, formidable in appearance but of no military utility whatever.

The one article essential to a cavalryman that Morgan's troopers did have was horses, and in the first two years of the war, with the riches of Kentucky to draw upon, they usually had good ones. At the beginning, every man brought his own horse from home, or bought one with money borrowed from friends and in some cases from Morgan himself. Later, the procurement of mounts was handled in the more informal fashion described by Union Major General Jacob D. Cox:

> John Morgan's foot is on thy shore
> Kentucky! O Kentucky!
> His hand is on thy stable door
> Kentucky! O Kentucky!
> You'll see your good gray mare no more,
> He'll ride her till her back is sore
> And leave her at some stranger's door,
> Kentucky! O Kentucky! [5]

It may be taken as certain that the young men of the Second Kentucky, fresh from the towns, villages, and farms of Kentucky, Alabama, Georgia, Texas, and Mississippi, were equally as curious

[3] Duke, *Morgan's Cavalry,* 181–82.
[4] Stone, *"Morgan's Men,"* 5.
[5] Holland, *Morgan and His Raiders,* 121.

about the new adjutant from overseas as he was about them. He provided the purveyors of camp gossip, that most prolific source of misinformation, with a field day. His physical appearance was sufficiently arresting to start the regimental rumor mill running at full speed. His stature, his bearing, "as strong as a bull and alert as a tiger," his youthful energy, the blue coat of his Turkish Contingent uniform, his commanding manner, were a major topic of discussion around the campfires.[6] But curiosity turned to suspicion and reserve as soon as he began to exercise the duties of his office, which he lost little time in doing.

The proper designation of Grenfell's post was assistant adjutant general. Officially, his function was to relieve the regimental commander of a multitude of administrative and housekeeping duties, to prepare returns and reports, to draft orders for the signature of his chief, and to issue routine orders himself in his name. In effect, he was the colonel's administrative assistant. In actual practice, the duties of the position varied greatly with the predilections, abilities, and zeal—or lack thereof—of the individual adjutant and of his chief. There is little direct evidence to show the full range of the duties Grenfell actually performed as assistant adjutant general and later as adjutant general, his promotion to the higher post having occurred shortly after the return of the regiment from its July, 1862, raid into Kentucky.[7] That he perfomed some or all of the

[6] The quotation in the text and the reference to Grenfell's bearing and youthful appearance are from the reminiscences of Thomas L. Russell, a member of Morgan's regiment, printed in the Pittsburgh, *Dispatch*, February 25, 1894, under the title "Told by Thos. L. Russell." Fremantle and Duke were also impressed by Grenfell's apparent youth; Fremantle, *Diary*, 120; Duke, *Reminiscences*, 154.

[7] Duke, *Morgan's Cavalry*, 203. Duke is explicit on the subject of Grenfell's promotion, and his statement is borne out by Morgan's reference to Grenfell as "acting adjutant general" in his report on the fight at Hartsville, Tennessee, on August 21, 1862. U.S. War Department, *The War of the Rebellion: A Compilation of the Official Records of the Union and Confederate Armies* (Washington, 1880–1901), Series I, Vol. XVI, Part I, 881; hereinafter cited as "OR". All references are to Series I unless noted otherwise. On the other hand, a dispatch written by Grenfell himself on November 27, 1862, is subscribed by him as assistant adjutant general. *OR*, Vol. XX, Part II, 427–28. But only two days later, he signed another dispatch as acting adjutant general. *Ibid.*, 110–11. In the absence of any official record of his promotion, it is impossible to determine if General Duke's recollection was in error or if Grenfell was careless about the use of his proper title.

nominal duties of the post is indicated by his few surviving orders, and by General Duke's recollection that he persistently disregarded the regulations laid down by the Confederate War Department for the form of reports and followed instead the style "he had learned in the English service," presumably as brigade major of the Turkish Contingent cavalry.[8]

Actually, however, and from the start, Grenfell was a great deal more than a mere administrative staff officer. He was able to offer Morgan and Duke, both of them virtual novices, sound advice on training and the technique of cavalry operations. Equally important, he believed in the need for discipline and was willing to incur the unpopularity that resulted from any effort to inculcate it. But in his efforts to establish camp and march discipline, he failed to recognize, or chose to ignore, the fact that Morgan's troopers were neither Turkish regulars with an ingrained habit of obedience to authority, nor *bashi-bazouks* who could be broken to obedience with the bastinado. Consequently, he drew upon himself the hostility of the men, who, as one of them later wrote, "did not take kindly to the rigid discipline which he sought to enforce . . . that might have passed with ordinary enlisted men, but which would not go down with young gentlemen who, outside matters military, regarded themselves as the peers of his master the Prince of Wales." [9] What the consequences of such hostility could be was demonstrated not long after Grenfell left the command, when one of his successors in the post of adjutant was killed by a Captain Murphy, whom he had placed under arrest for robbing a citizen.[10]

Grenfell had the support of the more knowledgeable officers, and of Basil Duke in particular, but the frontier tradition of rugged individualism was too much for him. He did his best to stop unauthorized absences from camp and straggling on the march, but he was fighting a losing battle. Not that he met active resistance.

[8] Duke, *Morgan's Cavalry*, 181.
[9] Russell, "Told by Thos. L. Russell."
[10] Basil W. Duke, "A Romance of Morgan's Rough Riders," in George W. Cable (ed.), *Famous Adventures and Prison Escapes of the Civil War* (New York, 1939).

On the contrary; his reckless bravery and his eccentricities soon made him a "favorite with the troopers of the Blue Grass country," an officer respected and admired as a fighter and a "character," and the men were willing to humor him up to a point; but they simply could not see the sense of all the drilling, obedience, and military formality that the strange British colonel made so much fuss about.[11] He tried, but he was not able to accomplish much. Morgan's regiment started its military career with the tendency "for every man to be his own captain and manoeuver his own forces," and so it remained despite Grenfell.[12]

In the area of tactics, Grenfell was more successful. He offered advice and suggestions which Morgan was glad to follow. One historian implies that Grenfell taught Morgan the proper technique of a cavalry advance through hostile country, with a carefully picked twenty-five-man detachment of scouts preceding the column at a distance of four hundred yards and a chain of vedettes connecting the advance detachment with the main body and picketing all intersecting roads until they were cleared by the entire column.[13] Elementary as such precautions were, especially in the hilly, heavily wooded country in which Morgan normally operated, it was just such rudiments that Morgan and his officers, amateurs to a man, had to learn. Moreover, Grenfell was apparently responsible for the establishment of a permanent corps of guides and scouts, to replace the unsystematic practice of assigning men to these exacting duties at random, whenever the occasion called for it.[14] It has been claimed that Grenfell taught the regiment all that the men ever learned of such basic cavalry skills as firing from the saddle, training green horses to stand under fire, and the like.[15] The general impression of contemporaries was that Grenfell and Duke were Morgan's "chief advisers," the former being particu-

[11] Russell, "Told by Thos. L. Russell."
[12] J. W. Dyer, *Reminiscences: or Four Years in the Confederate Army* (Evansville, 1898), 165.
[13] Swiggett, *Rebel Raider*, 59–63; cf. Duke, *Morgan's Cavalry*, 187–89.
[14] Morgan, *How It Was*, 190; cf. Duke, *Morgan's Cavalry*, 187–88.
[15] Brown, *The Bold Cavaliers*, 70.

larly well fitted for the role by his "experience and skill." [16] By common repute also, in the North as well as in the South, Grenfell was far more than an uncommonly colorful staff officer. The translator of the Prince de Joinville's book on the Army of the Potomac recorded that Grenfell (who, he wrote, had "resigned his Queen's commission and left a lucrative post in India . . . to put his sword at the service of the South") was Morgan's "second in command." [17]

There is no evidence, direct or indirect, to connect Grenfell with the evolution of the tactical ideas we have credited to Basil Duke. These concepts were the direct antithesis of the cavalry doctrine, exemplified by the bloody absurdity of the charge made by the Light Brigade at Balaklava, that was in vogue in the British Army and, by extension, in the Contingent cavalry when Grenfell was associated with it. But there were points of striking similarity between Duke's and Abd-el-Kader's tactics, just as there were many traits which, as soldiers, Morgan's Kentuckians and Abd-el-Kader's tribesmen had in common. It may be assumed, even in the absence of evidence, that Grenfell's stories of what he had seen and heard of the emir's methods played some part in the elaboration of Duke's ideas. The two men were on the best of terms, and it would have been strange if Duke had not sought Grenfell's counsel on subjects which the Englishman was so well qualified to discuss.

By all accounts, Grenfell was a useful, "efficient officer, energetic and constant in his attention to duty." [18] He brought to the Second Kentucky a fund of knowledge which was of great value to that body of willing but inexperienced warriors. But he failed to teach them the value of discipline. Here his precepts ran counter to their mental and emotional heritage.[19] No one had to teach these boys

[16] Sally R. Ford, *Raids and Romance of Morgan and His Men* (Mobile, 1864), 123.
[17] Prince de Joinville, *The Army of the Potomac, Its Organization, Its Commander, and Its Campaigns,* tr. Wm. H. Hulbert (New York, 1862), 111, note G.
[18] Duke, *Reminiscences,* 154.
[19] Thomas F. Berry, *Four Years With Morgan and Forrest* (Oklahoma City, 1914), 16: ". . . this command of rough riders . . . were all high-born freemen and gentlemen. . . . Such men do not require the rigid discipline of regulars to

(which most of them were) courage and endurance, and they were more than sufficiently pugnacious to need no encouragement to fight. On the other hand, they had no interest in performing parade ground evolutions with the precision of British regulars or in executing elaborate tactical maneuvers on the battlefield. Without question, Grenfell contributed greatly to Morgan's military education, as Morgan was prompt to admit. For example, he ended his official report on his July, 1862, raid with the statement: "I feel indebted . . . particularly to Col. St. Leger Grenfell for the assistance which his experience afforded me." [20] But it is going too far, as one of Morgan's biographers has done, to credit him with Morgan's greatest successes or to equate his value to Morgan with that of Baron von Steuben to Washington. [21]

The military history of the Confederacy has a curiously tide-like quality. The first half of 1862, when Grenfell joined the Second Kentucky, was a period of ebb-tide, and the fortunes of the South were at a low point. The fine fervor with which it started the war had subsided and many of the illusions of the first weeks were gone. No one, certainly no soldier, thought any longer that one Confederate could lick any five of "Lincoln's hirelings." The first battle of Bull Run, which had provided considerable justification for that delusion, had been fought in July, 1861, but since that victory, the Confederate armies had sustained one setback after another. Only a few days before Grenfell's arrival at Charleston, it had become certain that General George B. McClellan was about to move his huge army against Richmond. To meet this threat, General Joseph E. Johnston had found it necessary to abandon the position at Manassas, practically within sight of Washington, that he had held ever since the Bull Run battle. Western Virginia had already been lost to the Confederacy. In the West, Brigadier General Ulysses S. Grant had captured Forts Henry

---

make them soldiers." Berry, an arrant plagiarist and a compulsive liar, might have been at a loss to define "high-born freemen and gentlemen," but his comment is an accurate reflection of the average Confederate cavalryman's attitude toward discipline.

[20] *OR*, Vol. XVI, Part I, 770.

[21] Swiggett, *Rebel Raider*, 59.

and Donelson and opened the Tennessee and Cumberland rivers to a Union advance deep into Confederate territory; other Federal forces took Fort Columbus and Island No. 10, and General Beauregard had suffered a costly check at the hands of Generals Grant and Buell at Shiloh, on the Tennessee River. At the end of May, Beauregard had to give up Corinth, whither he had retreated after Shiloh. The border states of Missouri, Kentucky, and Maryland were more or less firmly in the hands of the Union. The blockade of the Confederate ports by the Union navy was becoming increasingly more effective. New Orleans had been captured by Commodore Farragut. Foreign recognition of the Confederacy, so eagerly hoped for, had not come to pass and was receding into an ever more distant and doubtful future. In the face of defeat and discouragement, southern morale had sunk to a very low point.

One Southerner who had not given way to discouragement, notwithstanding his own humiliating defeat at Lebanon, was Colonel Morgan, and he now proposed to carry the war to the enemy.

Grenfell had only a short time in which to get adjusted to his new environment. For some time prior to his arrival, Morgan had been contemplating a raid into Kentucky. The bulk of the Federal troops in the West were concentrated in Halleck's army in Corinth. The area north from there to the Ohio River was loosely held for the Union by a scattering of isolated battalions and regiments of regular troops and home guard units. Well supplied with information from his home state, Morgan concluded that by moving swiftly and boldly, he could disrupt the flow of supplies to Halleck's army via the Louisville & Nashville Railroad and carry alarm and despondency as far north as the Ohio River. On July 4, only two weeks after Grenfell's arrival, the Second Kentucky left its camp in Knoxville and, 826 strong, inadequately armed and poorly equipped, started North on what was to be Morgan's most glamorous raid.

In his report on this operation, Morgan boasted that in twenty-four days, his men rode more than a thousand miles, "captured seventeen towns, destroyed all Government supplies and arms in them, dispersed about 1,500 Home Guards and paroled nearly 1,-200 regular troops." [22] He might have added also that the raid accomplished nothing of lasting value. It proved only that given the great distances and poor communications of a sparsely settled area, lack of serious opposition, a friendly population, and a little luck, a small, fast-moving cavalry force under resourceful leadership could make a quick incursion into enemy territory, cause a moderate amount of damage and a great deal of confusion, and escape unscathed. But such raids do not win wars.

Nevertheless, this was an exhilarating time for the entire command, and especially so for Grenfell, with his taste for novel experiences. He remarked to Basil Duke that the raid "reminded him of the expeditions made by Abd-el-Kader into the territory held by the French." [23] He was seeing one of the most fertile and beautiful stretches of country in America; he was seeing it in congenial company and at its attractive best, the hills and rolling plains a vivid, intense green under the bright July sun. The pro-Confederacy people of the towns and villages of Central Tennessee and Kentucky through which he rode were enthusiastically hospitable and their Unionist brethren kept discreetly out of sight or joined in the fun. Food for the men and feed for their animals were abundant and were eagerly pressed upon the regiment at every halt. At each halt also, everyone was eager to gaze upon the fascinating and mysterious British adjutant who rode with Colonel Morgan. And finally, enemy resistance was negligible; there was just enough of it to add spice to the expedition.

Three days out of Knoxville, Morgan reached Sparta, Tennessee, at the edge of the Cumberland Mountains. He was joined there by a native who was to guide the column northwest across the mountains toward Kentucky. The guide was the notorious bushwhacker Champ (or Champe) Ferguson, who shares with William Quantrill the distinction of being the least likely to have a chapter of the United Daughters of the Confederacy named for

[22] OR, Vol. XVI, Part I, 770.
[23] Duke, Reminiscences, 154.

61

him. With the Civil War only a little more than a year old, Ferguson already possessed a considerable reputation as a guerilla. The war had provided him with a golden opportunity to put to use his uncommonly well-developed criminal tendencies. At his trial for murder in Nashville after the war, he was charged with the cold-blooded murder of fifty-three men and boys, probably fewer than half the number of killings Ferguson actually committed. His heroic efforts on behalf of southern independence usually took the form of gunning down unarmed and preferably wounded and helpless prisoners, while he himself was protected by his gang of armed cutthroats. He was hanged in October, 1865, wearing the new black suit and neat white shirt that were presented to him by the sympathetic ladies of Nashville, who had previously cheered his days in prison by sending him "special articles of food" to fortify him for the strains of his trial.[24]

In July, 1862, Ferguson's patriotic career had barely begun; he had only thirteen known killings to his credit but he was to double the number by the end of the year. Grenfell may well have recognized him as the spiritual kin of the Barbary Coast pirates.

The first encounter with the enemy on the march North occurred at Tompkinsville, Kentucky, a short distance above the Tennessee-Kentucky border, and resulted in the defeat of a 350-man detachment of the Ninth Pennsylvania Cavalry. In the short time Grenfell had spent with the Second Kentucky, he had seen and heard enough to have the "feel" of his environment and to recognize that, as a newcomer, a foreigner, and a staff officer, he was on trial, tolerated but not accepted. He realized that his effectiveness would depend on his willingness to set an example of reckless bravery on any and all occasions, and he therefore took the very first opportunity to show that his credentials in that respect were of the highest order. The Pennsylvanians were drawn up on the top of a ridge, their flanks and rear covered by dense woods. To get at them, the Second Kentucky, led by Duke, had to make

---

[24] For an excessively and undeservedly sympathetic biography of the squalid psychopath, see Thurman Sensing, *Champ Ferguson, Confederate Guerilla* (Nashville, 1942).

a frontal assault across a belt of open fields; they attacked on foot, on the run. When they were still sixty yards from the enemy, Grenfell spurred his horse forward between the two lines, and "risking the fire of both, leaped a low fence behind which the enemy were lying and began lashing at them right and left with his saber." [25] Beset in front by Duke's men, and with the berserker figure of Grenfell in their midst, the Yankees broke and fled, leaving twenty-two killed, thirty or forty wounded, and thirty prisoners in the hands of the Confederates.[26] Morgan had his first resounding success, and Grenfell had made his mark in spectacular fashion and established his footing in the regiment. Everyone had seen with his own eyes that his "gallantry in battle was superb." [27]

One of the odd characters in the Second Kentucky was a meek-looking native of Canada named George Ellsworth. By virtue of his civilian profession of telegrapher, he was known in the regiment as "Lightning" Ellsworth. Thinking that his telegrapher's key might come in handy, he had brought it along on the raid. On the day following the fight at Tompkinsville, the raiders halted while Ellsworth, Morgan, Grenfell, and a small escort made a detour to scout the line of the Louisville & Nashville Railroad a few miles north of Glasgow, Kentucky. At a crossing bearing the euphonious name of Horse Cave, Ellsworth tapped the telegraph line, which followed the railroad right of way between Louisville and Nashville, and "read" the messages exchanged by the Federal military posts along the line, while his companions sat for several hours on the muddy railroad embankment in the midst of a severe thunderstorm and a driving rain.[28]

[25] Duke, *Reminiscences*, 158.

[26] The figures in the text are taken from Morgan's report; *OR*, Vol. XVI, Part I, 766–67. There is the usual wide divergence in the number of casualties claimed by one side and admitted by the other; Major T. J. Jordan, in command of the Ninth Pennsylvania detachment, reported only four of his men killed, seven wounded and nineteen taken prisoner. *Ibid.*, 754–55. In general, it is nearly impossible to reconcile Morgan's and Jordan's reports and Duke's account of this fight. *OR*, Vol. XVI, Part I, 754–56; Duke, *Morgan's Cavalry*, 184.

[27] Duke, *Reminiscences*, 154.

[28] Duke says that this exploit occurred at a place called Bear Wallow. From the standpoint of euphony, there is little to choose between Horse Cave and Bear Wallow. Duke, *Morgan's Cavalry*, 185.

On July 11, Morgan crossed the Green and Rolling Fork rivers, and arrived in the evening at Lebanon, Kentucky. The town was the site of a small Federal supply depot, which was duly captured with its guard of two hundred infantry, who put up only a token resistance. The local correspondent of the Louisville *Journal* sent his paper an account of Morgan's proceedings in the town, colored by his pro-Union bias, which was powerfully reinforced the following morning, when some of the troopers "chased the writer . . . a great distance, but failed to catch him." [29] He noted that Morgan did "not appear to care much for discipline, permitting his men to go as they please. The men had no general uniform, and were armed to suit their own taste. . . . Many of them had shot-guns; a few only had sabers, or bayonets." Morgan announced on the morning of the twelfth that the commissary stores in the captured depot would be divided among the poor; but said the *Journal* correspondent, "Only prominent rebels were so fortunate as to get any of the spoils." Morgan also failed to live up to his declaration that the property of the people of Lebanon would be respected: ". . . his men failed to do it, and he failed to make them do it when his attention was called to their misdemeanors. The soldiers stole horses by the wholesale. . . . Indeed, whenever they wanted anything, they . . . took it. They took the express wagon, and pressed Uncle Ben Spaulding's buggy into service." The correspondent gave it as his opinion that Morgan's troopers were mostly "of that class to which we apply the term 'sporting gentlemen,'" and he singled out for special mention "a big, degenerated [*sic*] Enlishman, named Colonel George St. Leger Grenville [*sic*]" whom Morgan ordered to burn down the depot and set fire to the Lebanon courthouse.

With their supply of effective firearms increased and the quality of their mounts improved by the spoils of Lebanon, the raiders moved northward through Perryville to Harrodsburg. The people of the latter town, noted for their Confederate sentiments,

[29] The Louisville *Journal* report, from which this and the subsequent quotations are taken, is reproduced in full in F. Senour, *Morgan and His Captors* (Cincinnati, 1865), 59.

were attending services in their churches on Sunday morning, July 13, when word came that Morgan and his men were approaching. At once the services and sermons were deserted and the populace rushed into the streets to welcome the visitors. Mrs. Maria T. Daviess was one of those who watched the cavalcade ride into town; she was swept up in the most memorable day in the history of the town. She wrote that the fearsome cavalrymen were actually only boys of all ages and sizes, riding an ill-assorted lot of horses and wearing clothing that was uniform only in being grimy and gray with dust.[30] Another eyewitness, typical of the "female secessionists" with whom Morgan was "a universal favorite," described thus the arrival of the raiders in her diary: "At last they came! Oh! the grand and glorious sight it seemed to us! Eleven hundred Southern horsemen, rushing on at full speed amid the waving of caps and the glancing of steel. . . . The men and boys rushed up the road to meet them giving shout for shout. The ladies waved handkerchiefs and threw flowers, and wept and almost shouted, too, as among the troops they saw brothers and sons and husbands."[31]

To make certain that everyone in Harrodsburg had the opportunity to see his men, Morgan led them on a circuit of the town and back to the Graham Springs grounds where he ordered a halt. The men dismounted under the elms, and when the handshaking and kissing were over and the horses had been tethered, the greatest picnic in Harrodsburg history got under way. The "fat of the land was furnished in rich abundance . . . and the larders of the loyal yielded up their stores as freely as the most rabid secesh" for, after all, many of Morgan's men were kinfolk and all of them were guests. While there were more visitors than the good people of Harrodsburg were accustomed to entertaining at one time, the exacting standards of Kentucky hospitality had to be

[30] Maria T. Daviess, *History of Mercer and Boyle Counties* (Harrodsburg, Ky., 1924), 101-102.
[31] G. Glenn Clift (ed.), *The Private War of Lizzie Hardin* (Frankfort, Ky., 1963), 85. The comment that Morgan was "a universal favorite . . . with the female secessionists" is from Senour, *Morgan and His Captors*, 47.

met, and met they were.[32] The only jarring note in the universal geniality of the occasion was struck by some of the less well mounted of the honored guests, who abused the privileges of hospitality by "exchanging" their inferior and worn-out animals for better horses owned by those of their hosts who were suspected of harboring Union sympathies. Loyal to her political convictions at the expense of her ethical standards, the aforementioned diarist noted that: "men were never kept in better order than Morgan's on that raid. After they left Harrodsburg even their enemies could say nothing of them except that they had taken horses and the letters from the postoffice." [33]

On Monday, after the raiders had taken an early morning departure, the town was a-buzz with the events of the memorable Sunday. Not the least spectacular of the tales making the rounds concerned that gallant, fascinating, and distinguished Englishman, named "Grenfell Ledger," the living image of Brian de Bois Guilbert, whose reserve had melted in the friendly atmosphere of Harrodsburg to such effect that he was seen giving a *gage d'amour* to a certain beauty of the town.

Lexington lies less than thirty miles northeast of Harrodsburg, and Frankfort slightly farther, to the northwest. Both cities were held by the Federals, and both could be readily reinforced through Louisville and Cincinnati. Except for the fight at Tompkinsville and some hard riding, until July 13 the raid had been no more demanding than a pleasant summer excursion, but after leaving Harrodsburg, Morgan had to mind his step. By continuing northward, he would place his small command into a position of some peril because the Federals could converge upon him from three points of the compass. Morgan, however, decided to gamble on the weakness of the Federal position. Brigadier General J. T. Boyle, the Federal commander in the area, could not mount much of a threat against the raiders; most of his troops had been hurriedly assembled. They consisted of poorly armed and undisciplined Home Guards with but limited mobility and moderate fighting capabilities, stiffened

[32] Daviess, *Mercer and Boyle Counties,* 102.
[33] Clift, *Lizzie Hardin,* 93.

by improvised battalions of convalescents from the military hospitals in Louisville. Officers on their way to or from the Union armies in Tennessee and Mississippi were virtually kidnapped to lead these *ad hoc* units.[34] Moreover, Morgan counted on being able to confuse Boyle about his own movements while at the same time getting accurate information about the location, strength, and movements of the Federals, from the many Confederate sympathizers in the area and from scouting detachments he sent out in all directions. Therefore, he continued his march to Georgetown, twelve miles beyond Lexington. After resting his men there for two days, he decided that he was not strong enough to attack either Lexington or Louisville with any hope of success and that the time had come to retreat. But he also decided on a stratagem; instead of going back the way he had come, he went north to Cynthiana with the object of confusing and upsetting the Federals by creating the impression that he was headed for Cincinnati; actually, he intended to cross the Licking River at Cynthiana and then head back to Tennessee by way of Somerset, Kentucky.

It has long been fashionable to treat General "Jerry" Boyle as a character out of low comedy. Much is made of the somewhat overwrought pleas for help he telegraphed to Generals Halleck and Don Carlos Buell, to the secretary of war, and even to the mayor of Cincinnati. The telegram President Lincoln sent to Halleck after reading Boyle's dispatches to the War Department—"They are having a stampede in Kentucky. Please look to it."—is held to be proof positive of Boyle's incompetence.[35] He is blamed for exaggerating the size of Morgan's command, and on the strength of the entertaining tales of "Lightning" Ellsworth's exploits, it is taken for granted that Boyle was befooled and befuddled by the telegrapher's fake dispatches. In truth, Boyle was excitable, but on this occasion he had good reason to be. Before Morgan demonstrated by this very operation the feasibility of cavalry raids deep into enemy-held territory, it occurred to no one that Central Ken-

[34] J. T. Boyle to Edwin M. Stanton, July 14, 1862 in *OR*, Vol. XVI, Part I, 739–40.
[35] *Ibid.*, 738.

67

tucky, shielded by large Federal armies many miles to the south, needed protection from the enemy. Hence, Boyle had virtually no troops at his disposal and had to improvise the defense of territory vitally important to the Union with an assemblage of Home Guards and convalescents. Morgan was careful to pick his way north through predominantly friendly territory, where he could count on help in misleading the Federals about his strength and destination.

Nevertheless, Boyle's estimate of Morgan's numbers was amazingly accurate. He was not only shrewd enough to realize that Confederate sympathizers were exaggerating Morgan's strength, but he also arranged to get accurate information by having the raiders shadowed.[36] One of his men actually "enlisted" in the Second Kentucky and kept him fully informed of its numbers and whereabouts. Moreover, Boyle made a faultless appreciation of his primary duties. He knew that he had to protect the Louisville & Nashville Railroad, the artery of supplies to the Union armies to the south, and to hold the key cities of Louisville, Lexington and Frankfort, and all this he managed to do. Finally, Morgan's efforts to mislead Boyle with Ellsworth's false telegrams were not so successful as he and others were pleased to suppose, for on July 15, Boyle reported to Secretary of War Stanton that Morgan's "operator had his instrument and attempted to deceive us . . . but was detected." [37]

Cynthiana, where the Second Kentucky arrived in mid-afternoon on July 18, is a small town of pleasant aspect located on the east bank of the Licking River. Because the town lay on the direct road between Lexington and Cincinnati, Boyle had ordered it occupied several days earlier to block Morgan's path to the Ohio River. General Duke thought that the town was held by "three or four hundred men of Metcalfe's regiment of cavalry, and about the same number of Home-guards"; his estimate is a tribute to the fighting qualities of the Cynthiana garrison, whose actual numbers were far

[36] Boyle to Stanton, July 13, 1862, and to Don Carlos Buell, July 15, 1862, in *ibid.*, 738, 741.
[37] Boyle to Buell, July 15, 1862, and to Stanton, July 15, 1862, in *ibid.*, 741.

smaller.[38] In command was the tough and resolute Lieutenant Colonel John J. Landram of the Eighteenth Kentucky Infantry. He had under him 75 raw recruits of the Seventh Kentucky Cavalry, 15 men of his own regiment, 205 Kentucky Home Guards, and 40 Ohio Home Guards from Cincinnati. His "artillery" consisted of a single 12-pounder howitzer, manned by a squad of Cincinnati firemen, led by their "Captain," William H. Glass. The total came to "about 340 men, the majority of them poorly armed and nearly all totally undisciplined." [39]

As Morgan neared Cynthiana from the south, along the west bank of the Licking, he encountered Landram's pickets and drove them before him, but to get at the Federals in the town, he had to cross the river. Landram's men occupied the houses lining the east bank, and their muskets commanded the approaches of the covered bridge that carried the Georgetown Pike over the river to the center of town. Having sent off strong detachments with orders to cross to the east bank at fords located some distance above and below the town and then to deliver a converging attack on the Federals from both flanks and the rear, Morgan had four companies dismount for a frontal assault across the bridge and over a waist-deep ford a short distance below it. This, the main attack, was making little headway against the rapid fire of the 12-pounder and the small-arms fire from the riverside houses, when the two flanking columns came charging into the Federal position. Simultaneously, Grenfell, wearing a scarlet forage cap, led Company C in a thundering mounted charge directly across the bridge. Attacked from three sides, nearly surrounded and heavily outnumbered, Landram's men held their ground; the firemen-turned-gunners particularly distinguished themselves. Although the fight could have only one outcome, the issue was still in the balance when Grenfell, still wearing his conspicuous forage cap and with a long saber

[38] Duke, *Morgan's Cavalry*, 199.
[39] Colonel Landram's report in *OR*, Vol. XVI, Part I, 756–59. Duke wrote his *History of Morgan's Cavalry* immediately after the end of the war, long before the publication of the *Official Records*. He had no means of verifying his estimate of Landram's numbers. More recent historians, who have faithfully copied General Duke's figures, do not have the same excuse.

in his fist, led two mounted charges against the Federals who had rallied at the railroad station and broke up the toughest core of resistance. For this, Duke singled him out for special commendation in his official report; he said: "I cannot too highly compliment Col. St. Leger Grenfell, who acted with my regiment, for the execution of an order which did perhaps more than anything else to gain the battle. His example gave new courage to everyone who witnessed it." [40] Grenfell came out of the fight with "eleven bullets through his horse, person and clothes, but was only slightly hurt." [41] One of the bullet holes was through his cap (General Duke wrote that the cap fitted "so tight upon his head that I previously thought a ball could not go through it without blowing his brains out") which thereafter became his own personal panache, to be worn whenever there was bloody work to be done.[42]

The fight at Cynthiana lasted less than two hours and gave rise to the usual conflicting claims of casualties. Landram reported the loss of seventeen killed and thirty-four wounded, and most of his men were taken prisoner; Morgan admitted to a loss of eight killed and twenty-nine wounded.[43] The total of twenty-five killed and sixty-three wounded was remarkably large for such a short engagement, but the fighting was at close quarters and in grim earnest. From a strategic standpoint, it was a pointless "battle"; a mere demonstration against the town would have served Morgan equally well, but by the standards of warfare, twenty-five lives was a small price to be paid for a slight error in strategic judgment.

As soon as the wounded had been attended to and the prisoners paroled, Morgan's men fell in for the long march back to Tennessee. The return, by way of Paris, Winchester, Richmond, and Somerset, was uneventful, for General Boyle had no cavalry and his infantry had no chance of catching the fast-moving raiders.

The only noteworthy incident of the retreat involved "Light-

[40] *OR,* Vol. XVI, Part I, 783.
[41] Duke, *Morgan's Cavalry,* 201.
[42] *Ibid.,* 201-202.
[43] For Landram's report of his casualties, see *OR,* Vol. XVI, Part I, 756-59; for Morgan's, *ibid.,* 782–83. Landram reported Morgan had at least 21 killed, whereas Morgan reported that Landram lost 194 killed and wounded.

ning" Ellsworth and Colonel Grenfell. The little village of Crab Orchard, Kentucky, lies halfway between Richmond and Somerset. The raiders arrived there shortly after dawn on July 21, after a thirty-six-hour march. Just outside the village, the column was fired on by a bushwhacker. Morgan's scouts tried to capture the man, but he escaped. Ellsworth, whose real or fictitious successes as a telegrapher had fired his martial ambitions, decided to show that he could succeed where the scouts had failed. While the command was halted at Crab Orchard for breakfast and a brief rest, he learned that the bushwhacker was the notorious and formidable "Captain" King. This information opened up the prospect of greater glory and increased Ellsworth's ardor. He organized an expedition consisting of himself and a gullible trooper to "get" King, whose house was not far from the village. Unfortunately, as it turned out, Ellsworth decided his own horse was not good enough for so perilous a venture, so he helped himself to Grenfell's charger, without the owner's permission or knowledge. On the horse was a saddle which Grenfell valued highly and tied behind the saddle was Grenfell's buff overcoat, in the pockets of which was all that remained of the gold he had brought to America with him. Ellsworth and his companion found King's house readily enough. The bushwhacker was enjoying a well-earned breakfast when the two Confederates arrived and summoned him to surrender. His reply was a volley from a shotgun and a revolver, which wounded Ellsworth's fellow guerilla hunter. Thereupon the brave telegrapher fled, with King in close pursuit. Ellsworth himself managed to escape, but in the excitement, Grenfell's charger broke away, complete with saddle, buff overcoat, and gold and was never seen again. Duke, who tells the story, adds that "St. Leger was like an excited volcano, and sought Ellsworth to slay him instantly. Three days were required to pacify him, during which time the great 'operator' had to be carefully kept out of his sight."[44]

[44] Duke, *Morgan's Cavalry*, 212–13.

Chapter V

ON JULY 28 the raiders reached sanctuary in Confederate territory and the regiment went into camp at Sparta, Tennessee. Morgan himself went on to Knoxville to report to General Edmund Kirby Smith on the results of the raid. In the absence of the easygoing colonel, Duke and Grenfell put the regiment through a course of drill and discipline the like of which it had never experienced before and was never to experience again. Guards were posted to keep the restless troopers from wandering away from camp "to go on a lark." As the need for more guards became evident, their numbers were increased until nearly half the regiment was on watch to keep the other half in camp. The men had expected a spell of rest and relaxation after the fatigues of the Kentucky expedition. What they got instead was an abundance of guard duty, drill on horseback and dismounted, dress parades and inspections. There were to be no more "Lebanon Races" if Duke and Grenfell could prevent it. Much emphasis was placed on the care and grooming of horses, accoutrements were refurbished, and firearms repaired and cleaned. It cannot be said that the men were enthusiastic over this program, which passed into the regimental folklore as "The Spartan Life," nor did it last long enough to produce a permanent effect. Only a month later, Grenfell had to forbid the issuance of passes to men whose arms were not in perfect order. And he reminded the officers that "the safety of the brigade may often depend upon the state of its arms, and too much attention cannot be paid . . . to this most important duty." [1]

Morgan, meanwhile, was conferring with General Smith. By describing the weakness of the Federal forces in Kentucky and voicing his conviction that the state was ready to rise and join the South if it were invaded by a Confederate army, he persuaded Smith of the feasibility of an invasion and of the great benefits to the Confederacy that would unfailingly result. Convinced by Morgan's sanguine advocacy, Smith undertook to win over Bragg, who had succeeded Beauregard in command of the main Confederate armies in the West. Smith's recommendation proved successful. The normally cautious Bragg took fire and even went Morgan one better; he envisaged the annexation of Kentucky as a mere prelude to even greater things, to the capture of Cincinnati and an invasion of Ohio. Having agreed on their objectives, the two generals decided on a two-pronged march into Kentucky. Smith was to move north from Knoxville to dislodge the Federal garrison at Cumberland Gap and was then to proceed northwest to Lexington. Bragg, meanwhile, starting from Chattanooga, was to bypass General Buell's forces at Nashville and beat him in a race to Louisville. Their two armies would then combine and, reinforced by the thousands of Kentuckians who were confidently expected to join them, march for the Ohio River.

Morgan was to make the initial move in this ambitious project. Smith ordered him to return at once to Sparta, gather up his command, and march to Gallatin, Tennessee, where he was to break up the Louisville & Nashville Railroad, cutting off Buell's army from its supply base at Louisville and forcing him to retreat.

Morgan left Sparta on this raid on the morning of August 10. From that day until January 5, 1863—five months—he and his men were almost constantly in the saddle, and it was his activities during this period that created his fame as a leader of partisan cavalry. These were Morgan's great days and the climax of his brief career. Until nearly the end of the five months, Grenfell was at his side. The glimpses of him are few and faint; he remained in the back-

[1] Order dated August 22, 1862; quoted in Morgan, *How It Was*, 193.

ground, as a good staff officer should. Nevertheless, the contrast between Morgan's course of unbroken success while Grenfell was with him, and the failures, defeats and disasters, the fumbling, erratic operations, the ever-widening dissociation from military realities that followed after they parted company is too striking to be a mere coincidence, and has been responsible for the belief that Morgan owed his greatest successes to Grenfell.[2]

Was it only an accident that Morgan's most memorable accomplishments occurred while Grenfell was with him, and were succeeded by a downward spiral of futility after the Englishman's departure? The surviving records are too sparse to support a valid judgment on this question. General Duke, the only one aside from the two principals who could have spoken with full knowledge of the facts, may well have been too loyal to his famous brother-in-law, and perhaps too much aware of the value of his memory as a shining symbol of the Lost Cause, to have any desire to disturb the Morgan legend. He may have been unwilling to admit even to himself that Grenfell's, to say nothing of his own, contribution to Morgan's successes was a subject for discussion. Notwithstanding the absence of firm evidence, it is tempting to think that in a life that was a succession of failures, this brief episode was attended with success. Had Grenfell been able to gain victories in his own name, it would have gone a long way to balance his accounts with life; failing that, he would at least have had the satisfaction of knowing that he had been instrumental in achieving successes for which another received credit. His pleasure in this knowledge would have been enhanced by his personal regard for Morgan and his devotion to the cause of the South.

Morgan reached Gallatin before dawn on August 12. The Federal garrison consisted of about 375 Wisconsin infantry commanded by the bearer of a distinguished name, Colonel William P. Boone. About two-thirds of Boone's small force was absent, guarding bridges and other vulnerable points along the railroad. Morgan's advance detachment made its way into Gallatin in the predawn

[2] Swiggett, *Rebel Raider*, 63.

darkness, undetected by Boone's pickets and sentries.[3] Boone himself was captured in the town. Duke and Grenfell then proceeded under a flag of truce to the Federal camp at the edge of town and demanded the surrender of the garrison. They told the senior officer present that he was surrounded by twenty-five hundred Confederates—a great exaggeration, but a permissible *ruse de guerre*—with the result that he agreed to surrender.[4]

With the garrison safely disposed of, Grenfell was treated to a novel and ingenious railroad-smashing performance. The most vulnerable point on the Louisville & Nashville, and the objective of the expedition, was an eight-hundred-foot-long tunnel a short distance below Gallatin. The tunnel had been driven through a ridge of slate seamed with veins of coal, and to prevent cave-ins, its walls and ceiling were supported by a massive structure of timbers. A short time after the surrender of the garrison, a train of nineteen cars loaded with hay for Buell's cavalry came chugging into Gallatin from the north and was captured. Obstacles were then placed far enough in the tunnel so that, when the engine came up against them, the entire train would be well inside the tunnel. The cargo of hay was set afire, and the blazing train was run into the tunnel at full speed, where it smashed against the obstructions and was derailed. The timbers caught fire and in turn ignited the veins of coal, and as the wooden supports burned away, the roof and walls of the tunnel collapsed. With the coal seams continuing to burn, several weeks passed before the repair crews could venture inside the tunnel, and several weeks after that were needed to clear away the debris, erect a new timber lining, and restore the blocked line to operation.[5]

[3] *OR*, Vol. XVI, Part I, 846.
[4] *Ibid.*, 856. Four weeks later, in a nearly identical situation (but on a far larger scale) at Munfordville, Kentucky, Union Brigadier General John T. Wilder requested and was granted General Bragg's permission to *count* the Confederate troops opposed to him. Having satisfied himself by a personal inspection that he was in fact so greatly outnumbered that resistance would be hopeless, Wilder surrendered. Kenneth P. Williams, *Lincoln Finds A General* (New York, 1956), IV, 63–64.
[5] The destruction of the tunnel and the capture of Gallatin are described in Duke, *Morgan's Cavalry*, 211–14. See also Holland, *Morgan and His Raiders*, 137–38, and Brown, *The Bold Cavaliers*, 104–107.

During the night of August 20 one of Morgan's scouts came to Gallatin with the information that a large force of Federal cavalry had left Hartsville, fifteen miles to the east, and was headed in his direction. A few days before, Buell had ordered his most competent cavalryman, Brigadier General Richard W. Johnson, to make up a force consisting of the most efficient companies of four cavalry regiments and drive Morgan away from his position at Gallatin astride the Federal supply line.[6] If Johnson had any misgivings about going after Morgan with an *ad hoc* unit, made up of troops who had never before worked together, he gave no sign of it; indeed, it was reported that he went about boasting that he would "catch Morgan and bring him back in a bandbox." [7]

Early on the morning of the twenty-first, Morgan led about eight hundred of his men out of Gallatin toward the advancing Federals, whose numbers were nearly equal to his, intending nothing more than a demonstration to frighten them off. Duke, however, persuaded him to give battle.[8] Duke's decision to stand and fight and his handling of the Second Kentucky in the ensuing battle justify a high opinion of his military capabilities. With the Union cavalry approaching, Duke had his men dismount and deploy in a long skirmish line behind a low fence on the western edge of a large meadow, three hundred yards across from east to west. The ends of his line were anchored in a cornfield and a patch of woods respectively, in both of which he posted mounted detachments as flankers. Johnson somehow decided that the Confederates were trying to escape and ordered a mounted charge against their line. His men formed up, drew sabers, and with bugles shrilling and flags and guidons flying, rode at Duke's line in the time-honored sequence of Trot-Gallop-Charge. The Confederates held their fire until the Yankees were only thirty yards away. Then they fired an aimed volley that dropped nearly two-thirds of the attackers or their mounts. The survivors retreated to their side of the meadow. With an obtuseness worthy of Lord Raglan at Balaklava,

[6] *OR*, Vol. XVI, Part I, 871.
[7] Duke, *Morgan's Cavalry*, 223.
[8] *Ibid.*, 218.

Johnson ordered a second mounted charge. This attack was repulsed also, with considerable loss to the Federals. Now the Union survivors retreated about a half-mile and with a spirit deserving of better leadership, halted to await a Confederate attack. Duke led his men forward in a dismounted charge which dislodged Johnson's troopers, who retreated some distance to the rear and reformed their line. Again the Confederates attacked on foot, and this time the Federals broke and fled, led by the Fifth Kentucky "in a style of confusion more complete than the flight of a drove of stampeded buffaloes." [9] The Union loss was stated to be sixty-four killed, many wounded, and about two hundred taken prisoner, General Johnson among them.[10] The Confederate loss was trifling. This fight confirmed Duke in his belief in the superiority of dismounted action over mounted charges and of the infantry rifle over the combination of carbine and saber.[11]

Following this engagement, Morgan moved his command to Hartsville. A by-product of his sojourn there was Volume One, Number One of *The Vidette*, a sprightly, one-page "newspaper" written, edited, set in type, printed, and published by Gordon E. Niles, a practicing newspaperman who had come from New York to serve with Morgan. The second number of the paper, published as an Extra and erroneously dated August 17, contained the reprint of a laudatory article in the Knoxville *Register* about Grenfell, describing him as "a distinguished officer of the British army . . . commissioned thirty-three years ago . . . and in active service almost ever since," who had come all the way from India to take part in the southern struggle for independence.[12] Someone, either the author or his informant, had drawn heavily on his imagination

[9] *OR*, Vol. XVI, Part I, 875.
[10] Duke, *Morgan's Cavalry*, 223. Morgan himself gave the tally of Federal losses as "some 180" killed and wounded and 200 taken prisoners. *OR*, Vol. XVI, Part I, 881. Inevitably, the Federal and Confederate reports of the engagement are so different that they could well be describing two entirely different encounters.
[11] Duke, *Morgan's Cavalry*, 223.
[12] A copy of the "August 17" issue of *The Vidette* is in the Morgan Papers. See note 4, chap. three above.

about Grenfell's past, but there was nothing fictitious about the comments on his deeds during the raid into Kentucky:

> We have heard the highest encomiums bestowed upon his behavior during the trip, by those who were with him, and it is due to Col. Grenfell to say that he commanded the respect and admiration of the entire command by his undaunted bravery, being always where bullets whistled thickest, and when, in the bloody streets of Cynthiana, his noble horse fell pierced by eleven bullets, his own clothing riddled, and himself wounded, he placed himself at the head of a small party detached from their command, and calling upon them to follow, he dealt such destruction among the enemy as to cause them to tremble at the sight of him.[13]

It may be taken for granted that Grenfell's penchant for being in the thick of the fight had been in evidence at Gallatin also, for in his report of the engagement Morgan wrote that "Col. St. Leger Grenfell . . . ably supported me." [14]

For the next three eventful months Grenfell as an individual is almost wholly lost to sight. When Morgan fought and routed Johnson, the Confederate invasion of Kentucky had already begun. General Kirby Smith had driven the Federals away from Cumberland Gap and was marching into the center of the state. Morgan, still at Hartsville, was ordered to join him at Lexington. He started north on the morning of August 29 and reached the city on September 4 after an uneventful march.

Lexington was the home of Morgan and of many of his men, and their entry into the city was a triumphal homecoming parade: "Almost the whole population had turned out to welcome them, lining the streets and cheering wildly as Morgan, dressed in the full uniform of a Confederate colonel, his cheeks flushed with pride and his eyes sparkling, led his proud riders down Main Street." [15] And indeed, Morgan had reason to be proud of his command; the Second Kentucky now numbered nearly 900 and

---

[13] *Ibid.* Niles was killed in action a few days after publishing the second number of *The Vidette.*
[14] *OR,* Vol. XVI, Part I, 881.
[15] Holland, *Morgan and His Raiders,* 146.

counting the separate squadron of Captain R. M. Gano's 200 Texans, he commanded 1,100 well-armed, well-equipped and well-mounted cavalrymen, with the aura of success about them.[16] And as they rode into Lexington,

> The bells throughout the city pealed joyously—men, women and young boys and girls, with smiles, tears, shouts and cheers rushed into the streets, waving white handkerchiefs and small Southern flags, and making the very air resonant with the strains of wildest joy. Wives pressed husbands to their bosoms, parents clasped sons in affectionate embrace. General gladness reigned throughout the vast multitude, and for hours the most intense interest every where prevailed.[17]

It is a pity that there is no record of what Grenfell, riding behind his colonel and possibly adding to the spirit of the occasion by wearing his famous scarlet forage cap, thought of the spectacular entry into Lexington, and whether it reminded him of the day, many years before, when he rode into Marrakesh in the suite of John Drummond Hay to visit the sultan of Morocco.

The entry into Lexington was a glorious event for Morgan and a stirring day for his admiring fellow townsmen, but within twenty-four hours, the glory and admiration had become sadly tarnished. The next day Grenfell found it necessary to issue stringent orders to put a stop to the illegal seizure of horses; to put teeth into the order, he announced that no leaves would be granted until Morgan was satisfied that the practice had ceased.

The plaudits of his home-town friends were the only satisfaction Morgan was to gain from Bragg's badly mismanaged invasion. The euphoria brought on by Smith's victory at Richmond, Kentucky, on August 29 and the large number of recruits who joined Morgan, increasing his total strength to eighteen hundred, induced visions of a permanent occupation of the state, the capture of Cincinnati, and even a raid to Chicago as practical and attainable objectives. But Bragg's hesitations and Buell's rapid recapture of the initiative aborted these ambitious projects. Bragg was forced to

[16] Duke, *Morgan's Cavalry*, 234.
[17] Ford, *Raids and Romance*, 291.

retreat, fighting the battle of Perryville on his way back to Tennessee.

During the later stages of the invasion, Morgan was sent eastward to intercept the retreat of his namesake, Brigadier General George W. Morgan, from Cumberland Gap to the Ohio River and to delay him until he could be attacked by Brigadier General Humphrey Marshall's infantry.[18] This assignment was followed by another even less glamorous. When Bragg began his retreat, Morgan was ordered to act as rear guard for the army. Both assignments required the performance of traditional cavalry functions, but they were not in keeping with Morgan's notions of fighting a war. He had acquired a taste for independent operations and however he may have rationalized it, he wanted his independence to continue. He could not discipline himself to accept a role, regardless of its military necessity and importance, that required him to follow orders and act in the anonymity of a subordinate position. That, in his view, was mere military drudgery. His successes and the adulation they had brought him had persuaded him that he could do more for the Confederacy on his own than as an adjunct of a plodding army. He had come to believe that cavalry raids of the hit-and-run variety could win the war.

The sequel was typical of the unfortunate lack of discipline, even in the higher ranks, that was a curse of the Confederate armies. Smith was cajoled into issuing an order which allowed Morgan to leave his post as rear guard and to return to Tennessee by a route of his own choosing. The route he had in mind was a return sweep to Lexington, thence southwest across Buell's line of communications between Louisville and Bowling Green, and on to Tennessee by way of southwestern Kentucky. Morgan had hardly started when he was overtaken by fresh orders from Smith; General Bragg desired him to head eastward into the mountains to guard the salt works, vitally important to the Confederacy, at Saltville, Virginia. Smith's courier handed these orders to one of Morgan's staff officers—it is to be hoped that the culprit was not

---

[18] Duke, *Morgan's Cavalry*, 256–60.

Grenfell—who "pocketed it and dismissed the courier. The officer reasoned that the salt works were in no danger . . . [and] that it was more important to operate upon the railroads, in front of Nashville, than to look after salt works." [19] Morgan eventually learned of the new orders, but he could see no reason to comply with them and calmly went ahead with his own plans.[20] The unnamed staff officer, who should have been cashiered for his inexcusable breach of discipline, suffered no ill consequences whatever. Morgan went off on his foray, and arrived back in Gallatin on November 4.[21] His eccentric two-week march accomplished nothing; the destruction of a few dozen of Buell's supply wagons, the capture of a few hundred Yankees who were promptly paroled, and the tearing up of a few hundred yards of railroad track had no effect whatever on Buell's operations.

Just before the start of this bootless excursion, Morgan decided to try in a more legitimate way to free himself of Bragg's control. It occurred to him—or it was suggested to him—to make use of the diplomatic skills which Grenfell as an ex-consular official was thought to possess, as well as his prestige as an experienced military figure from overseas, to present his case for independence to General Bragg and to the War Department in Richmond. Bragg was an obstinate individual, the most uncompromising opponent of irregular operations—of military irregularities of any description —of any of the Confederate army commanders. It required a high degree of optimism to expect him to consider sympathetically the unorthodox ideas Grenfell was to present to him. Nor was Grenfell's errand well timed. The Kentucky campaign, although manifestly a failure, was still in full swing, and it had given Bragg a costly lesson in the unreliability of Morgan's judgment. Bragg had hauled twenty thousand muskets North to arm the Kentuckians who, as Morgan had reported in July, were only waiting for the arrival of a Confederate army to "spring to arms." A mere two thousand Kentuckians had sprung to arms at Bragg's call; eighteen

[19] *Ibid.*, 294.
[20] Holland, *Morgan and His Raiders*, 155.
[21] Duke, *Morgan's Cavalry*, 282–93.

thousand of the twenty thousand muskets were even then being hauled back to Tennessee and would have been guarded by Morgan had he been in his proper place as part of the rear guard, instead of gadding about, no one knew where, among the Kentucky hills.[22]

Despite these unfavorable auguries, Grenfell accomplished his mission. Having had firsthand experience of Morgan's methods, and probably swayed by an exaggerated estimate of his talents, he was able to convince Bragg that his commander's greatest usefulness lay in the field of partisan operations. The arguments he used to win over the not easily persuadable Bragg are not known, but they did the trick. Grenfell wrote to Morgan that Bragg had expressed his consent in the most flattering terms and quoted him as saying that as far as he (Bragg) was concerned, Morgan already had an independent command.[23] If there was a hint of sarcasm in the remark, Grenfell failed to realize it. In the same letter, he gave Morgan the pleasing intelligence that Bragg was about to recommend him for promotion to brigadier general; he indulged in an uncharacteristic bit of flattery by adding, "may the Fates be propitious to you and may it soon be Major General."[24]

The winning over of Bragg was not the full extent of Grenfell's success as a diplomatist. In Richmond, he obtained a grant of $250,000 for the purchase of supplies for Morgan's greatly enlarged force, and permission for Morgan's quartermaster to buy and charge to the War Department whatever rations and supplies he needed that he could not get from Bragg's stores. He also obtained from the War Department a battery of six guns for Morgan. Grenfell's debut in the field of high-level military negotiations, a particularly thorny branch of the diplomatic art, was thus a brilliant success.

While Grenfell was in Richmond, Bragg's retreating army halted

[22] Don C. Seitz, *Braxton Bragg, General of the Confederacy* (Columbia, S. C., 1924), 206–207.

[23] Grenfell to John H. Morgan, Knoxville, November 9, 1862, in Morgan Papers.

[24] *Ibid.*

at Murfreesboro, Tennessee, to see what Buell would do next. Morgan set up his camp at Baird's Mill, on the road from Murfreesboro to Lebanon, Tennessee. Throughout November, notwithstanding Bragg's promise of independence, Morgan had to act under the orders of General Joseph Wheeler, Bragg's newly appointed chief of cavalry. After graduation from West Point, Wheeler had two years of service in the Regiment of Mounted Rifles in the "Old Army," and thus had a grounding in the dismounted tactics favored by his two unconventional subordinates, Morgan and Bedford Forrest. But he also accepted the traditional view that the proper role of cavalry was to operate in close conjunction with, and in support of, the infantry. Hence his orders required Morgan to perform the prosaic and distasteful scouting and patroling duties of conventional cavalry on the right wing of Bragg's army.[25]

Two dispatches Grenfell wrote during this period are preserved in the *Official Records.* One was a routine order concerning the delivery of paroled prisoners to the Union lines near Nashville.[26] The other was a courtly message addressed to General Wheeler, to convey Morgan's assurance that he "appreciates the very kind tone of your dispatches, and is happy to have earned your good opinion, and I am ordered to assure you that nothing shall be wanting on his part to insure the duration of those feelings of cordiality and esteem betwixt officers of the same arm which tend so much to the efficiency of the service." [27] Poor Wheeler, having the unenviable task of dealing with two such formidable subordinates as Morgan and Forrest, must have been gratified by the cordial tone, no less than the content, of this dispatch. The memory of it may well have been with him still when, forty years later, he had one of Grenfell's granddaughters as a guest in his home in Alabama.

[25] John P. Dyer, *"Fightin' Joe" Wheeler* (Baton Rouge, 1941), 15, 68–69.
[26] *OR*, Vol. XX, Part II, 110–11. The dispatch is dated Murfreesboro, November 29, 1862.
[27] Grenfell to Joseph Wheeler, "Cross Roads, near Murfreesborough [*sic*]," November 27, 1862, in *ibid.*, 427–28.

December 6, 1862, was a bitterly cold day. A deep blanket of snow and ice covered the ground in Central Tennessee. Morgan left his camp early that day to attack the large but isolated Federal garrison at Hartsville—an area with which he and his men were thoroughly familiar—posted there to protect the left flank of the main Federal position at Nashville. Morgan had under his command his own cavalry, now grown to a brigade of four regiments, plus two regiments of infantry which were assigned to him for the operation. Grenfell was given an opportunity to observe an American frontier invention; to cover as rapidly as possible the thirty-odd miles between Baird's Mill and Hartsville, Morgan ordered a "ride and tie" march. The cavalry and infantry started together, the cavalry on horseback and the infantry on foot. The cavalry rode on for three or four miles, dismounted, tied their horses to the trees, and went forward on foot. When the foot soldiers reached the horses, they mounted, and rode on until they were two or three miles ahead of the plodding troopers; they then dismounted and proceeded on foot, leaving the horses for the cavalry to ride, and so in turn.

Neither the infantry nor the cavalry took kindly to the "ride and tie" system, but it accomplished Morgan's purpose. The distance to Hartsville was covered in twenty-four hours, including the time needed for the slow operation of ferrying the infantry across the swollen, ice-cluttered Cumberland River in two small boats; the cavalry, led by Duke and Grenfell, swam across. Counting on the effect of surprise, Morgan attacked as soon as the leading half of his command reached Hartsville, and within an hour, with no more than about 1,250 of his men at hand, he captured nearly all of the 2,400-man Federal garrison. Fortunately for him, in command at Hartsville was a grossly incompetent officer, Colonel Absalom B. Moore of the 104th Illinois Infantry. Morgan was able to effect a surprise because Moore had failed to post pickets and outposts, and after the presence of the Confederates had already been discovered, Moore allowed them to form for the attack without firing a shot. Morgan's attack stampeded about a fourth of the garrison, whereupon Moore surrendered without further ado.[28]

This affair, so shameful for the Union, generated a great deal of noise and eventually came to the attention of President Lincoln, who demanded an investigation. It was shown that the blame rested squarely on Moore's shoulders, and General-in-Chief Halleck recommended that he be dismissed from the service in disgrace, for gross neglect of duty. Doubtless for political reasons, Halleck's recommendation was not acted upon, and Colonel Moore was permitted to remain as an ornament of the Union army.[29] What he lacked in soldierly qualities he more than made up for in vindictiveness, as Grenfell was to learn a few years later.

Colonel Moore had something besides his own disgraceful misconduct to store away with his memories of Hartsville. Before being led off to captivity, he witnessed a striking demonstration of Confederate logistics. It was intensely cold, and many of the Rebels lacked overcoats. The Federal prisoners having been collected, Moore's own regiment was ordered to fall in and was then given the command: "One Hundred Fourth Illinois, Attention! Come out of them overcoats!"[30] Having acquired overcoats in this simple but effective manner, the Rebels then exchanged their worn and ragged boots and shoes for Federal footwear of better quality in the same eminently practical fashion.[31]

One week after this eventful day, on Sunday, December 14, Grenfell participated in a very different enterprise. On that day, Brigadier General Morgan, promoted to that rank by President Jefferson Davis himself as a reward for his victory at Hartsville, married Martha Ready at her home in Murfreesboro.

The romance of Martha Ready and John Hunt Morgan is one of the most colorful entries in the catalogue of Confederate folk-

[28] Duke, *Morgan's Cavalry*, 309–14; *cf. OR*, Vol. XX, Part I, 43–62 (Union reports) and 62–72 (Confederate reports).
[29] General Halleck's endorsement on General Rosecrans' report of December 10, 1862. Halleck's recommendation was approved by Secretary of War Stanton, but Moore remained in the service until he resigned because of disability on September 9, 1863. *OR*, Vol. XX, Part I, 45.
[30] Brown, *The Bold Cavaliers*, 140.
[31] Duke, *Morgan's Cavalry*, 315.

lore, and their wedding has found a place in the annals of the Civil War similar to that of the ball at Brussels on the eve of Waterloo in the history of the Napoleonic Wars. And with good reason. The bridegroom wore for the occasion the full dress uniform of a Confederate general of cavalry. His ushers were General Bragg and his corps commanders, Generals John C. Breckinridge, William J. Hardee, and Benjamin F. Cheatham. The marriage service was read by Leonidas Polk, who wore the vestments of his high clerical office of bishop of the Episcopal Church of Louisiana over his uniform of a lieutenant general in the Confederate States army. The ceremony took place in the evening, and was followed by

> a great supper. . . . Supplies were still plentiful, and the supper included turkeys, hams, chickens, ducks, and "all the delicacies and good dishes of a Southern kitchen," while Colonel Ready's cellars still had a sufficient stock of wine to provide for the drinking of many toasts. Two regimental bands were on hand, and after supper there was dancing until the hour grew late. On the street outside, hundreds of soldiers assembled and celebrated the wedding with bonfires and cheers for Morgan and his bride.[32]

Grenfell had been strongly opposed to Morgan's marriage. He was apparently quite open in declaring his disapproval of it on principle, in that matrimony would inevitably make Morgan cautious and unenterprising, and thus destroy his usefulness as a partisan leader.[33] This was an anachronistic conception of the obligations of a soldier's life, and Morgan was certainly not the man to revive in his own person the monastic code of the military orders of the Middle Ages. Grenfell told Colonel Fremantle a few months later that he had actually tried to "avert" the marriage.[34] It is quite possible that in his outspoken fashion he had done precisely that and, if so, the resulting coolness and possible bitterness between the two men may have led to Grenfell's abrupt decision a few days after the wedding to seek more congenial employment elsewhere.

[32] Holland, *Morgan and His Raiders*, 177.
[33] Fremantle, *Diary*, 120.
[34] *Ibid.*

Whatever objections to the marriage Grenfell may have voiced beforehand, his disapproval did not interfere with his enjoyment of the festivities, to which, as a distinguished visitor and a member of the bridegroom's staff, he was invited as a matter of course. The romantic connotations and military trappings of a wartime wedding, of a ceremony performed by a bishop who was at the same time a general and corps commander, thawed even Grenfell's habitual reserve, and perhaps the process was aided by the bounteous supper and the contents of Colonel Ready's cellar. Grenfell not only unbent, but after the festivities were over and he, Basil Duke, and a group of other officers were on their way to their quarters, he regaled the company with "Moorish songs, with a French accent, to English airs, and was as mild and agreeable as if someone was going to be killed." [35] To question the veracity of a Kentucky gentleman is akin to *lèse majesté*; nevertheless, the unlikely conjunction in Basil Duke's account of Moorish lyrics, a French accent, and English tunes, suggests that his hearing may have been confused by the same vintages that caused his friend Grenfell to burst into song.

Within a week after the wedding, Grenfell and Morgan parted company. There are several explanations by contemporaries of this abrupt end of what had every appearance of a friendly and even warm relationship. None of these explanations is wholly convincing, and Grenfell himself, far from clarifying the situation, has muddied the waters by giving differing accounts of the separation.

By mid-December, Morgan's command had become unwieldy. It now consisted of seven regiments, the colonel of each of which reported directly to him. Either under pressure from Wheeler or on his own volition, Morgan decided to organize the seven regiments into two brigades. Duke was the obvious choice to command the first brigade. Command of the second was offered to its senior colonel, Adam R. Johnson of the Tenth Kentucky, but he declined the promotion, whereupon Morgan appointed Colonel W. C. P. Breckinridge to the post. Breckinridge, a Lexington

[35] Duke, *Morgan's Cavalry*, 322.

lawyer, newspaper editor, and member of a prominent Kentucky family, had joined Morgan with a newly raised battalion the day before the battle of Cynthiana; within a space of 24 hours, he enlisted as a private, was promoted to captain, and took part in his first battle. He had subsequently risen to the command of the Ninth Kentucky Cavalry. General Duke states that Grenfell had taken a violent dislike to Breckinridge and considered him unfit for brigade command; he carried his opposition to the appointment to such intemperate lengths that he received from Morgan a sternly worded request to desist.[36] There was a general impression in the command that Grenfell opposed the choice of Breckinridge because he felt that he himself should have been offered the post. Duke denied that this was the case. He and Grenfell talked over the Breckinridge appointment, and Duke was left with the impression that Grenfell's objections to it were disinterested.[37]

Whether or not this was so, Grenfell had every right to think that he was at least as well qualified as Breckinridge for brigade command. Had he been a Kentuckian, or at least a Southerner, the post may well have been his. No one in the command had a greater right to it, on the basis of age, seniority, military competence, devotion to the cause, and bravery. As one of the troopers of Breckinridge's own regiment wrote after the war, ". . . he always sought the post of danger. . . . He would permit none to lead him in a charge; in a retreat he was always nearest the enemy. Age had not cooled his blood, and at sixty his reckless daring won the admiration of our young Kentucky cavalrymen, the boldest of whom could not surpass him in dash and deeds of daring." [38] Morgan may have considered that it was more politic to appoint a Kentuckian rather than a foreigner to command Kentucky troops, or that he could not promote a volunteer aide over the heads of regularly commissioned colonels, or that Grenfell's rigidity on the subject of discipline militated against his success as a commander

[36] *Ibid.*, 325–26.
[37] *Ibid.*
[38] W. L. Chew, "Col. St. Leger Grenfell, C.S.A.," *Confederate Veteran*, XXXVI (1928), 446.

of partisan cavalry. Even Duke, who admired Grenfell, thought that his ideas of discipline were too severe to be effective in a command of highly individualistic volunteer cavalrymen. Grenfell, Duke wrote, "would have been invaluable as commander of a brigade of cavalry, composed of men who (unlike our volunteers) appreciated the 'military necessity' of occasionally having an officer to knock them in the head. If permitted to form, discipline, and drill, such a brigade . . . after his own fashion, he would have made gaps in many lines of battle, or have gotten his 'blackguards well peppered' in trying."[39] Finally, in preferring Breckinridge, Morgan may have been motivated merely by an entirely human resentment of the position Grenfell had seen fit to take in the matter of his marriage.

Whether or not Grenfell's objections to the Breckinridge appointment were disinterested, there is no doubt that he aired his views more vociferously than Morgan was willing to tolerate from a subordinate. Grenfell had evidently developed so possessive an attitude toward Morgan and his command that he came to feel not only that he had the right to offer suggestions on any subject having to do with the administration of the command, but also that Morgan was bound to follow them. If there was already an estrangement between the two men because of Grenfell's opposition to Morgan's marriage, it would have made the latter less patient with Grenfell's views on the Breckinridge appointment than he might have been otherwise. In fact he "requested him to desist from agitating" the matter.[40] His pride hurt by the snub, Grenfell decided to leave. So goes one story.

Grenfell himself said a year later that he "found [Morgan's command] a band of horse thieves and plunderers of public and private property, carrying on a system of warfare . . . which was revolting to his nature," and implied that it was disgust with the thieving propensities of Morgan's men that had caused him to leave.[41] The accusation was only too well founded, but Morgan's

---

[39] Duke, *Morgan's Cavalry*, 181.
[40] *Ibid.*, 326; see also Logan, *Kelion Franklin Pedicord*, 61.
[41] *House Executive Documents*, 637.

troopers did not become horse thieves and plunderers overnight; Grenfell saw as much unauthorized taking of horses and supplies in his first month with Morgan as he did in the last; and if the men's conduct was reprehensible when he found it intolerable in December, it was no less so when he tolerated it in July. Surely a man with the experience of irregular warfare on four continents that Grenfell laid claim to would not have been squeamish about a little looting. Quite possibly he did not approve of it, but it would be absurd to suppose that this alone would have caused him to leave Morgan.

Once Grenfell made up his mind to leave, for whatever reason, there was no legal way in which Morgan could compel him to stay, even if he had wanted to do so. Because Grenfell was not a regularly enlisted member of the Confederate army, he could come and go as he pleased. And so, on December 20, 1862, as Morgan's men were leaving camp on their famous "Christmas Raid," Grenfell gathered up his horses and baggage and departed for Bragg's headquarters at Murfreesboro in quest of a new post. But before leaving Baird's Mill, he was guilty of deplorably loose talk, as reprehensible in its way as the indiscipline in Morgan's command that he found so objectionable. On December 21, General George H. Thomas quoted a deserter from one of Morgan's regiments as stating he had heard Grenfell say that Morgan was about to lead his men into Kentucky to cut the Louisville & Nashville Railroad.[42]

[42] *OR*, Vol. XX, Part II, 214.

Chapter VI

MORGAN'S DEPARTED ADJUTANT GENERAL left behind him the memory of eccentricities which lost nothing in the telling in the years after the war. One man remembered that he made it a habit to bathe in every stream the column had to cross; the fact that a practice so eminently sensible in the summer heat of Kentucky and Tennessee was remembered suggests that Grenfell's hygienic habits were viewed with astonishment but were not widely imitated. Basil Duke mentions in a tone of obvious disapproval that Grenfell settled a misunderstanding with his landlord by thrashing him soundly; fighting with one's fists was not looked upon with favor among gentlemen in Kentucky, but after his dealings with his Moroccan workmen, it came quite naturally to Grenfell.[1]

The troopers, to whom Grenfell was "Old St. Leger," admired his "splendid courage," his courtly manners, and his lofty bearing, but not many liked him. They were repelled by his frequently "savage temper" and his "strict discipline." [2] But they were awed and fascinated by the stories of his past that filtered down to them from Duke and the other officers, with embellishments galore added along the way. He was credited with having exterminated, not

[1] For remarks on Grenfell's bathing, see Berry, *Four Years With Morgan*, 75 (Berry's only statement about Grenfell that is not a plagiarism from Basil Duke). For his fighting, see Duke, *Morgan's Cavalry*, 181; Duke, *Reminiscences*, 158–59.

[2] Milford Overley, "Old St. Leger," *Confederate Veteran*, CVXIII (1905), 80-81.

merely fought, the Moorish pirates; he had served, it was said, as a private in the Turkish army; he was wounded while fighting in the Opium War in China; as a captain of cavalry, he rode in the immortal Charge of the Light Brigade; while serving as an aide to Marshal Bazaine in the war in Italy in 1859, he was gravely wounded in the battle of Magenta; and "in the jungles of South Africa he made war upon the lions and tigers." [3] And then there was the most impressive story of all, that of his harem in Morocco. The mere names of the places where he had performed his exploits—the Barbary Coast, China, the Crimea, Italy, India, South Africa, South America—were strange and exotic, and as for the deeds and adventures, they outdid the marvels of romantic fiction.

Another kind of tale was related about Grenfell by one George W. Hull, formerly a private in the Second Kentucky. An unnamed young man had told him, Hull said, that he had been ordered by Brigadier General Adam Buford to "press" horses for a company of cavalry then being formed. Among the horses collected by this nameless individual and his helpers were several belonging to Grenfell. When Grenfell learned his horses had been taken, he enlisted the help of some civilians and caught the thieves. Not satisfied with recovering the horses, Grenfell fired several times at the men who had taken them, killing "a couple"; then he pulled out his knife and settled accounts with the ringleader by stabbing him in the back.[4] The story appears to have a foundation of fact. The young man whose name Hull did not mention was probably John T. Shanks, the Texas ne'er-do-well whose perjured testimony was to prove gravely damaging to Grenfell. Grenfell's own version of the story is that three days before the battle of Murfreesboro, at the end of December, 1862, Shanks and four helpers stole five of his horses; he pursued and caught the thieves and recovered his animals; Shanks himself got away, but Grenfell "punished the rest of the gang." [5]

[3] *Ibid.*
[4] *House Executive Documents,* 123.
[5] Grenfell, to "British Ambassador, Washington," Jan. 23, 1865, in Foreign Office—U.S., General Correspondence (Public Record Office, London), FO 5/1155; hereinafter cited as "U.S.-General Correspondence."

It will be noted that Grenfell did himself uncommonly well in the way of mounts. He owned five, when most Confederate officers were glad to make do with one or two. Also, advancing years had clearly not smoothed the rough edges of his temper, and to have his horses stolen by fellow soldiers would have incited to violence a much more peaceable individual than he was. It is not unlikely that he used his guns while pursuing the thieves, but there is nothing in his past or in his character to indicate that he was capable of shooting down or stabbing them after they had surrendered.

If Grenfell was capable of violence, he was also capable of kindness. Henry Lane Stone, another of Morgan's troopers, recalled that one day in the fall of 1862, as the command marched along a miserably bad mountain road in East Tennessee, he was doing his best to keep up on foot, leading his horse, whose back had become so sore that it could not be ridden. Grenfell came riding by with a led horse and, when he learned the cause of Stone's plight, gave him his spare horse and told him to keep the animal until his own got well.[6] The time was to come when Stone was able to return with interest the older man's kindness.

Of those Grenfell met while serving with Morgan there was one, Thomas Henry Hines, with whom his life was to be closely intermeshed in the years to come. Barely twenty in 1861, Hines organized a fifteen-man troop of cavalry in Lexington the day after news arrived of the firing on Fort Sumter and was elected its captain. A slightly built, slender, handsome lad, something of a classical scholar, he gave up a post on the faculty of a small college near Louisville to go soldiering.[7] Two weeks after its organization, his troop joined General Albert Sidney Johnston's army, and for the next several months it was used as an independent unit on scouting, bridge-burning and raiding expeditions. As a reward for a number

[6] Stone, *Morgan's Men*, 26.
[7] Hines's friend, John Castleman, described him as about five feet nine inches tall, weighing about 140 pounds, with penetrating eyes set deep under heavy brows. His photographs fully bear out the adjective "handsome." Hines, says Castleman, was "modest, courteous and imperturbable, with a voice as soft as that of a refined woman." John B. Castleman, *Active Service* (Louisville, 1917), 189.

of small successes, Hines was commissioned a lieutenant in the Confederate army. In January, 1862, he and his men were detailed to serve with Morgan, but after the Confederate evacuation of Nashville, the Hines troop decided to disband, on the curious ground that they had come together to serve in Kentucky and had no desire to fight in Tennessee. Hines was a civilian for the next few months. In May, 1862, he reenlisted with Morgan as a private, but at about the time Grenfell arrived on the scene, he was promoted in one jump to captain and was given command of a company in the Ninth Kentucky Cavalry.

In the months following the disbanding of his original command, Hines became expert in slipping in and out of Union-held territory in Kentucky. There was much crossing of the lines throughout the war, especially in the loosely held West. There was no language barrier to act as a deterrent and security arrangements were rudimentary; nevertheless, Hines played a dangerous game, for most of his journeys across the lines took him into territory where he was well known and in constant danger of betrayal. These expeditions probably began as clandestine visits to his sweetheart, but Hines had a taste for undercover operations and eventually made these visits the occasion for meetings with pro-Confederate and disaffected Kentuckians. The contacts he established at this time later helped to pave the way for Morgan's raids into the state.

There is a special kind of occupational hazard connected with such operations. Those who engage in them, perhaps because of the dangers they incur, are prone to form an excessively high estimate of the value of their cloak-and-dagger activities, and what is even more dangerous, they generally form an exaggerated opinion of what can be accomplished by such means. Notwithstanding his protestations to the contrary, Hines was not immune to these delusions. But during these months, he also developed a capacity for leadership and independent action remarkable in so young a man. From 1862 on he dealt on a plane of complete equality with men twice and three times his age, all of whom accepted his leadership and became his willing subordinates. Grenfell was one of these beginning in the spring of 1864 and became the chief victim of Hines's optimism or inexperience.

John Castleman, who was to be Hines's right-hand man in the conspiratorial activities which led to Grenfell's final catastrophe, was an officer in the Ninth Kentucky while Grenfell was with Morgan. He has given a revealing glimpse of what must have been an uncommonly attractive personality in the opening words of his autobiography: "I was born in the season of the wild rose and the elder blossom . . . at Castleton, my father's homestead in Fayette County, Kentucky." [8] The son of a prosperous family whose home lay a short distance outside Lexington, Castleman was twenty when the war began. Like all the Bluegrass gentry, at home on a horse and with a gun almost as soon as he could walk, Castleman secretly raised a troop of forty boys, of whom he was one of the oldest, and led them out of Lexington on a May night in 1862 to join Morgan in Knoxville. Two years later, he left Morgan and made his way to Toronto to join his friend Hines; there he shall be met again.

Grenfell had made a great reputation in his six months with Morgan and could feel assured of a warm welcome at General Bragg's headquarters at Murfreesboro, where he went to request a new assignment. Probably the best organizer and disciplinarian in the Confederate army, Bragg was predisposed in Grenfell's favor and forthwith gave him a temporary appointment as an aide on his personal staff, pending his assignment to a more suitable permanent post. [9]

Shortly after the bloody battle of Murfreesboro, in which Grenfell performed the duties of an aide in a manner which earned Bragg's praise, he was appointed inspector of cavalry on the staff of Major General Joseph Wheeler, Bragg's chief of cavalry. [10]

[8] *Ibid.*, 15.
[9] Grenfell's file in the National Archives contains no record of his appointment as aide on Bragg's staff, but he is referred to as such in Bragg's report on the battle of Murfreesboro. *OR*, Vol. XX, Part I, 671.
[10] *Ibid.*, 671, 760, 783. There is no record in Grenfell's file in the National Archives of the date of his appointment to Wheeler's staff. It would appear that Bragg, contrary to his usual practice, failed to observe the proper formalities in

Bragg must have been satisfied that Grenfell had the technical knowledge and experience for the post. And he must have known that Grenfell had demonstrated while he was with Morgan that, unlike many of the field-grade officers of Confederate cavalry, he recognized the crying need for system and regularity in the organization, training, and discipline in that excessively individualistic branch of the service. At the same time, however, it could be expected that whatever predisposition Grenfell may have brought with him from the "British service" in favor of rigidity and precision in training and tactics would have been tempered by his exposure to Confederate cavalry. His attitude would also have been affected by the realization that Bragg's troopers were not British regulars—that they were in fact a distinctive breed, requiring a gentle hand and the utmost elasticity and patience.

Joseph Wheeler, a graduate of West Point in 1859 and twenty-six years old in 1862, had been in command of Bragg's cavalry since mid-November. He had three regularly organized brigades, those of Forrest, Morgan, and John A. Wharton, plus two regiments of mounted infantry. Bands of irregular cavalry, calling themselves partisan rangers and bearing a great variety of blood-curdling names, were coming in to join existing regiments or to become parts of new ones. Wheeler had a hard core of relatively seasoned units with considerable campaigning experience to which newcomers could be added singly or in groups, but none with anything more than a faint tinge of formal training or discipline. To perfect his organization and to have the new men taught the rudiments of cavalry service, were major tasks. No less important or difficult was the problem of effecting some degree of uniformity in tactics among the heterogeneous units making up the command.[11] These essential tasks had to be performed in the intervals of active campaigning against the Federals. The Union

---

this instance, for in April, 1863, when Wheeler applied to the adjutant general for a commission for Grenfell, who had then been his inspector-general for several months, the secretary of war was advised by the adjutant general's office that the "appointment of Inspector Generals is not considered legal."

[11] Dyer, *"Fightin' Joe" Wheeler*, 75–77.

and Confederate armies lay in close proximity; to prevent a Federal advance, Wheeler had to maintain constant pressure on their line of communications. Hence some portion of his force was always absent on active service and his men were having almost daily scraps with the Yankees.

Grenfell's appointment as inspector of cavalry was not regularized until May, 1863. On April 2 Wheeler sent a dispatch through channels to Adjutant General Samuel Cooper in Richmond, recommending that Grenfell, whom he described as "a gallant, efficient and valuable officer and thorough soldier," who had "proven himself very useful" in the months he had already served as inspector general, be given formal appointment to that post, with the rank of lieutenant colonel.[12] Bragg added a most flattering endorsement, stating that he "consider[ed] Col[.] Grenfell a most meritorious and efficient officer. His services in the organization, etc. of . . . [the] cavalry are of great importance. On the battle field he is the soul of gallantry." General Joseph E. Johnston, an officer whose good opinion was not won lightly, also concurred with Wheeler's recommendation and wrote, "Col[.] Grenfell has been serving in this army with great zeal, courage and efficiency, without rank or pay, for more than a year. No one has better earned high rank than he." The dispatch bearing these favorable endorsements was submitted to the secretary of war on April 20 and, after some discussion as to whether Grenfell should be commissioned major or lieutenant colonel, the higher rank was agreed to and his appointment as inspector of cavalry was formally approved. His commission was issued on May 28, 1863, with seniority from May 2.[13] On August 10 Grenfell complied with the formality of accepting the commission; meanwhile, on May 17 Bragg issued formal orders assigning him to the post of inspector of cavalry.[14]

Grenfell found that Wheeler's conception of cavalry tactics was

[12] Wheeler's dispatch, bearing Bragg's and Johnston's endorsements, is in Grenfell Papers-National Archives.
[13] *Ibid.*
[14] Special Orders No. 141, in *OR*, Vol. XXIII, Part II, 854.

quite similar to Basil Duke's. In the months following the battle of Murfreesboro, Wheeler used his leisure time to write a manual of cavalry tactics.[15] Based on the methods he had learned as an officer in the prewar Regiment of Mounted Rifles, with the modifications suggested by the campaigns of the summer and fall of 1862, his tactical system was essentially that of mounted infantry. His purpose in writing the manual was not to advocate any new cavalry doctrine or to urge a return to the old, but to fill the "vital need for some system of cavalry tactics which would insure uniformity among the heterogeneous elements of mounted divisions calling themselves cavalry"; in other words, to make uniform and prescribe officially what had already become established, with many variations, as the habitual battle tactics of western cavalry.[16]

As already mentioned, Wheeler's West Point training made him more partial to orderly operations than were Morgan and Forrest, but he too was a devotee of the cavalry raid. His successes in that line were at times as great as those of his better-publicized subordinates and were usually of more immediate benefit to the main army.

All in all, Grenfell found Wheeler's tactical and strategic ideas quite similar to what he was already accustomed to. And the human material in Wheeler's command was the same as what he had known with Morgan, but perhaps even more uncouth, militarily speaking. Since he was in daily communication with Wheeler and living at his headquarters while the latter was writing his manual, he must have had some hand in its composition. One may assume, at least, that the ideas he expressed, his stories of Abd-el-Kader's exploits, and his accounts of what he himself had learned with the Turkish Contingent and under Morgan, are reflected to some degree in Wheeler's manual.

As inspector of cavalry, Grenfell was expected to assist Wheeler in organizing and training his men and in establishing some degree of discipline. He was required to perform inspections and to report

[15] Joseph Wheeler, *A Revised System of Cavalry Tactics for the Use of the Cavalry and Mounted Infantry, C.S.A.* (Mobile, 1863).
[16] Dyer, *"Fightin' Joe" Wheeler,* 101.

to Wheeler and Bragg on the condition and state of efficiency of the units he inspected. If he inspected any of Morgan's regiments, which would have been a somewhat embarrassing task, no record of it has survived. All of his reports have disappeared, but it is safe to assume that two of them, covering the regiments of Colonels Roddey and Patterson, are reflected, probably verbatim, in a general order issued by Bragg on April 2, 1863. It states that Grenfell had found the officers and men of the two regiments

> zealous in the performance of their respective duties . . . the discipline excellent, and the conduct of the men toward the citizens of the neighborhood . . . most praiseworthy. The arms were in good condition and the clothing of the men neat. . . . In the entire two regiments . . . only four horses were condemned as unserviceable. . . . The outposts of both regiments were visited . . . the pickets [were] well placed and the vedettes watchful.[17]

Manifestly, an inspection conducted by Grenfell was a thorough affair. The reference to the conduct of the men toward the civilian population is of special interest. This was a subject not usually investigated or commented upon; if it had been, the repute of Confederate cavalry in general and of Wheeler's men in particular might have been far better.

Colonel Fremantle's testimony bears out the fact that Grenfell did not take his duties lightly; he was, Fremantle writes, "the terror of all absentees, stragglers and deserters, and of all commanding officers who [were] unable to produce for his inspection the number of horses they have been drawing forage for." [18] It can be taken for granted that the thoroughness of his inspections did not endear him to regimental and brigade commanders, however much they may have admired his gallantry. On the whole, he was successful in the discharge of his rather invidious duties and earned the regard of Bragg and his corps commanders as a "most excellent and useful" officer.[19] The commanding general, usually so forbidding and contentious in his relations with his subordinates, went to ex-

---

[17] *OR*, Vol. XXIII, Part II, 737.
[18] Fremantle, *Diary*, 120.
[19] *Ibid.*

traordinary lengths to express his approval of Grenfell's services; he instructed his aide to send Grenfell a copy of the commendatory endorsement he had added to Wheeler's request that he be appointed inspector of cavalry.[20] And Wheeler himself was quite extravagant in his praise of his new subordinate; he wrote to the adjutant general that Grenfell's "conduct on the field during his career in this country does credit to the service in which he was educated." [21] Wheeler retained to the end of his life the admiration for Grenfell he expressed in his dispatches to General Cooper in 1863. He wrote Grenfell's daughter, Marie, in 1900 that her father had been a "thorough soldier and a very brave man. He would have been very valuable in command of troops and I had a great ambition to see him in that position. He was restless, however, and always seeking adventure." A year later, he wrote, "Your father was one of the bravest and best officers in the Confederate Army. A man of chivalry and generosity. If he had a fault it was his great fondness for adventure." [22]

Grenfell undoubtedly accompanied portions of Wheeler's cavalry on some of their frequent raids. Bragg's retreat after the battle of Murfreesboro had given the Federals possession of that city. The main body of Bragg's army was at Tullahoma, Tennessee, thirty-five miles to the south, and Bragg himself established his headquarters at nearby Shelbyville. Wheeler maintained a seventy-mile picket line in front of the Confederate army, and with the regiments not engaged in that duty, repeatedly raided Federal supply depots, wagon trains, and railroads. He even added a touch of novelty to these conventional operations by using cavalry to attack and burn a number of river transports hauling supplies for the Union army up the Cumberland. With none of Forrest's or Morgan's flair for the spectacular, Wheeler nevertheless harassed the Federal supply lines so effectively that he brought Major General William S. Rosecrans, the Federal commander, to the verge of

[20] Braxton Bragg to Grenfell, April 5, 1863, in Grenfell Papers-National Archives.

[21] Joseph Wheeler to Samuel Cooper, June 12, 1863, in *ibid*.

[22] Wheeler to Marie Pearce-Serocold, July 3, 1900, and Nov. 4, 1901, in Packe Papers.

abandoning Nashville.[23] He also caused Rosecrans to make life a burden for his superiors with innumerable requests for more cavalry to cope with the Confederate horse, and for more horses to replace the thousands of animals lost by his cavalry in one futile chase after another after Wheeler's elusive troopers.

Near the end of March, 1863, Grenfell was responsible for the rumor, which his associates were only too eager to believe, that France had at last recognized the Confederacy.[24] The rumor was false, but it is a fact that in his cat-and-mouse game with the South, Napoleon III came closer to recognition in the spring of 1863 than at any other time.

On May 30 Lieutenant Colonel Arthur J. L. Fremantle, a young man of twenty-eight on leave of absence from the Coldstream Guards for a visit to the Confederacy, turned up at Bragg's headquarters. Fremantle had landed at Matamoras, filled with "great admiration for the gallantry and determination of the Southerners" and a strong antipathy for "the foolish bullying conduct of the Northerners." [25] One of the first of Bragg's officers he asked to meet was Grenfell. He had already heard a great deal about his compatriot and looked forward to meeting him in the flesh. Grenfell's fame had by this time spread throughout the Confederacy, partly on the strength of his actual accomplishments and partly because he stood as a symbol of British sympathy for the South. Fremantle had been hearing tales of his glamorous exploits from many sources, and one can sense in his account of the few days they spent together that the reality did not disappoint his expectations.[26]

Grenfell, on his part, found in the young guardsman a sympathetic audience; he spoke to him freely about his own past and was equally free with his comments on the Confederate army and his experiences as a Confederate officer. He expressed a high re-

[23] Dyer, *"Fightin' Joe" Wheeler*, 100.
[24] J. A. Wharton to Leonidas Polk, March 25, 1863, in *OR*, Vol. XXIII, Part II, 725-26.
[25] Fremantle, *Diary*, 3.
[26] The account of Fremantle's stay in Shelbyville and of his conversations with Grenfell is based on *ibid*., 119–20, 126–29 and 130–31.

gard for Generals Bragg, Leonidas Polk, William J. Hardee, and Patrick Cleburne. Apart from these four—the omission of Wheeler, Morgan, and Forrest from the list is surely significant—he found no one to admire among the general officers of the Army of Tennessee and, indeed, he had a poor opinion of them as a group. Some were incompetent "political" generals, who owed their rank to their local prominence in civil life, or to the obligation of the Confederate government to "recognize" the states whence they hailed; others were military illiterates; still others were addicted to the bottle. But Grenfell conceded that they were good fighters to a man. He spoke also of the pernicious effect of politics on the military efficiency of the South, described the battle tactics of the Confederate cavalry, and told of his disappointment and sorrow over Morgan's marriage, declaring that his former commander, now that he had a wife, would never again be the man he had been.

But Grenfell also had some personal problems to talk about. On June 2, he escorted Fremantle on a visit to the cavalry outposts on the road toward Murfreesboro. The regiment on picket nearest the enemy happened to be the Fifty-first Alabama, through whose lines the Ohio Copperhead, Clement Vallandigham, had passed into involuntary exile only a few days earlier. The Alabama colonel considerably exceeded the requirements of southern hospitality by offering to send some of his men forward to have "a little fight" with the Federal outposts for the entertainment of his distinguished visitors. His offer was politely declined, whereupon the hospitable colonel had another thought: he turned out his regiment in a driving rain, to be inspected by his guests. As the two Englishmen rode back to Shelbyville after the inspection, Grenfell told Fremantle that he was in "desperate hot water" with the Tennessee authorities and was momentarily threatened with civil arrest on two charges. The first arose from his refusal to surrender to his master an escaped slave he had in his employ. The second and more serious charge was that he had been "illegally impressing and appropriating horses." The basis of the second charge, as reported by the army correspondent of the Mobile *Register*, was that some time before, Grenfell had met a soldier riding one horse and leading another; he accused the man of being a deserter and took his two horses, his equipment, and his money.[27] There is no adequate explanation of this unpleasant tale. If the incident was reported correctly—and Fremantle wrote that there were extenuating circumstances not mentioned in the article—then one is forced to choose between two conclusions equally discreditable to Grenfell: the first that the incident shows him at his highhanded worst; and the second that he used his rank to commit what is hardly distinguishable from highway robbery.

Whatever the truth of the "deserter" incident may have been, even Grenfell admitted that he had "acted imprudently" in the matter of the escaped slave. The Tennessee authorities, in any case, did not choose to allow Grenfell's military fame to prevent them from performing what they took to be their duty, and on the night of June 2, the sheriff arrested him.[28] He was caught while he was asleep, as he informed Fremantle in a rage in the morning. General Polk and his officers, with whom Fremantle was staying, were "much vexed at the occurrence," and Bragg gave a practical demonstration of his confidence in Grenfell by going bail for him to ensure his appearance in court in October.

Grenfell was not to appear in a Tennessee courtroom. Within a week after his arrest, he left the Army of Tennessee. There is no trustworthy explanation of his sudden departure from a post both honorable and congenial. John Morgan wrote his wife that Grenfell was dismissed by Bragg for some irregularity in his accounts, but he had the grace to add that "the service loses a fine soldier. He is certainly one of the most gallant men I ever saw." [29] There was nothing in Grenfell's duties as inspector of cavalry that re-

[27] The report of Grenfell's arrest in the Mobile *Register* was reprinted in an unnamed Charleston, South Carolina, newspaper, from which Fremantle clipped it. *Ibid.*, 131n.

[28] Documentation of Grenfell's difficulties with the Tennessee authorities is no longer obtainable. The Bedford County courthouse in Shelbyville, Tennessee, where these documents would have been stored, was destroyed by fire in a riot in 1935, and all court records for the years up to that date were burned. (Information supplied by Gene Parks, mayor of Shelbyville.)

[29] The letter is quoted in Holland, *Morgan and His Raiders*, 173, the Williamson Papers being given as the source. These papers are now in the Southern Historical

quired the handling of funds or the keeping of accounts. If he was indeed dismissed, it could only have been because Bragg held him blamable in one or both of the incidents which led to his arrest, but it seems highly unlikely that Bragg should have dismissed him within a week after going bail for him. In January of the following year, Grenfell received a cordial letter from Wheeler inviting him to rejoin his command.[30] Wheeler must have known the reason for Grenfell's abrupt departure from the Army of Tennessee, and it is highly improbable that he would have invited him to return if he had been dismissed in disgrace six months before. Nor would Wheeler have written to the adjutant general on June 12, 1862, at the very time when these events were taking place, in laudatory terms about Grenfell, if the latter had just left or was about to leave Tennessee for reasons discreditable to him.[31]

It may be assumed that Morgan repeated as fact a malicious camp rumor which, like most such rumors, was false. The most likely explanation of Grenfell's departure is that the indignity of being arrested like a common criminal, the loss of face, and the sense of being let down by his military superiors were too much for his pride. In telling Fremantle about his troubles, he had said that "the military were afraid or unable to give him proper protection." [32] He was always quick to take offense, and this blow to his dignity and self-esteem, plus a justified resentment of what he could have considered as grossly unfair treatment at the hands of people whose freedom he was fighting for, caused him to leave in anger and disgust. The absence of any hint in Fremantle's lengthy account of his conversations with Grenfell that the latter was in any way dissatisfied with his position under Wheeler supports the view that his leaving only a week later was an angry reaction to a personal humiliation. On the other hand, Wheeler

<hr />

Collection, University of North Carolina Library, Chapel Hill, and are known as the John Hunt Morgan Papers. The present writer has been unable to find in that collection the letter quoted by Holland.

[30] Grenfell to John H. Morgan, Jan. 29, 1864, in Morgan Papers.
[31] Joseph Wheeler to Samuel Cooper, June 12, 1863, in Grenfell Papers-National Archives.
[32] Fremantle, *Diary,* 127.

may have been correct in blaming Grenfell's action on his restlessness and craving for novelty and adventure.[33] He had spent six months with Bragg and Wheeler. The absence of stories about his exploits and activities during this period suggests that he had not made as conspicuous a place for himself under Wheeler as he had done under Morgan. Unquestionably, he failed to achieve the degree of identification with Wheeler personally and his widely scattered regiments as he had done with Morgan and his small, compact command. Then too, the relatively inactive period that followed the battle of Murfreesboro, lasting until late in June, may have seemed too dull after the adventures of the previous summer, and the duties of a staff officer too tame after the exciting life of a raider.

Grenfell had served the Confederacy for a year when he left Bragg. No record exists of his movements or whereabouts in the ensuing three months. There is nothing to suggest that in leaving Tennessee he had any purpose other than to go on fighting for a cause to which he seemed to be sincerely devoted. It may be conjectured, therefore, that he went from Shelbyville directly to Richmond to ask for a new assignment. He had a right to expect, on the strength of the reputation he had made in the West, that he would not be long out of employment. He was, in fact, well and favorably known in the highest quarters; when Colonel Fremantle interviewed Jefferson Davis on June 17, the President spoke to him of Grenfell and said that "he had heard much of his gallantry and good services." [34]

A minor mystery of Grenfell's life in America is the source of the money he lived on for two and a half years prior to November, 1864. He had served as a volunteer without pay while he was with Morgan. Upon being commissioned lieutenant colonel, he became eligible for the $185 monthly salary of that rank, paid in the already greatly depreciated Confederate currency. On September 8 he was paid for the period from May 2, the effective date of his

[33] Joseph Wheeler to Marie Pearce-Serocold, July 3, 1900, in Packe Papers.
[34] Fremantle, *Diary*, 168.

105

commission, to August 31, a total of $740.[35] So far as the records show, this was the only occasion when he drew his pay, although he continued to collect the forage allowances for his horses that he was entitled to. Even if he continued to accept his salary for the period from September 1, 1863 on, his real pay would have been quite meager in the face of the galloping inflation which by the latter part of 1863 had already become one of the major curses of the Confederacy. Besides, army pay was chronically in arrears, and even if Grenfell, who had none of the minor vices, was able to live inexpensively in the field, he had to have some money for food and lodging, clothing, travel, and incidental expenses. In one respect, at least, he pampered himself; when he left the Confederacy in the spring of 1864, he owned five horses, and by then, a good officer's mount was an expensive article indeed. If it is true that he lost all his gold when Ellsworth helped himself to his horse, then there is no way to account for the source of Grenfell's funds. He may have received remittances from his relatives in England, and the suspiciously large number of horses he owned at various times suggests that he may have traded in horses procured in ways that might not bear close scrutiny.[36]

The summer of 1863 brought with it the first signs foreshadowing the eventual defeat of the Confederacy. Until then, the successes of Lee and Jackson and the seeming inability of the North to develop competent military leadership gave some justification for the hope that the South might reenact the biblical triumph of David over Goliath. But Meade's victory at Gettysburg and Grant's capture of Vicksburg marked the beginning of the downward path which led to the end of southern independence. Shortly before these twin Federal victories, Bragg was maneuvered out of

[35] Voucher No. 614, Sept. 8, 1863, in Grenfell Papers—National Archives. It is to be noted that Grenfell was paid for a period of nearly three months subsequent to his departure from the Army of Tennessee. The fact that he was paid for these three months, during which he had no official duties, may perhaps be taken as an indication that he was or was considered to be on leave.

[36] A. H. Packe considers it possible that Grenfell received remittances from England; he has endeavored to trace the account books of Pascoe Grenfell and Sons, through whom such remittances would presumably have been transmitted, but was unable to locate them.

106

Tennessee in the opening moves of the long campaign which, with the temporary remission of Bragg's great but fruitless victory at Chickamauga, was to culminate in the fall of Atlanta, Sherman's March, and the final collapse of Confederate power in the West by Thomas' smashing defeat of Hood at Nashville. Grenfell's former chief, John Morgan, set off on July 2 on the most famous of his raids; undertaken in deliberate violation of orders, this militarily senseless venture into Indiana and Ohio ended in the capture of most of Morgan's command, the dispersal of the rest, and his own and his principal officers' imprisonment in the Ohio Penitentiary in Columbus.

Meanwhile, Grenfell's request for a new assignment had been granted. At the instance perhaps of General Lee, or of President Davis himself, he was given the post of assistant inspector general of the Cavalry Corps of the Army of Northern Virginia, commanded by Jeb Stuart. It may be said parenthetically that if Grenfell had been dismissed by General Bragg, a close friend of President Davis, it is quite unlikely that the President would have sanctioned this new and responsible assignment for him. The appointment was announced by Stuart on September 14 in a general order whose wording makes it evident that he acted in pursuance of instructions from General Lee's headquarters.[37]

Grenfell's period of service in the Army of Tennessee is illuminated to some degree by Fremantle's account of his meeting with him. Regrettably, there was no Colonel Fremantle to shed the same light on the three months he spent with Stuart. Captain Fitzgerald Ross met Grenfell briefly in December, 1863, but his modest reporting skill and too-brief acquaintance with Grenfell on this occasion produced a portrait less illuminating than those by Duke and Fremantle.

The scanty information that exists about Grenfell's tour of duty with Stuart suggests that the brief association of the two men was not a happy one. The flamboyant Stuart was under a cloud at this time. He had been criticized for allowing himself to be surprised by the hitherto despised Federal cavalry at Brandy Station in June;

---

[37] *OR*, Vol. XXIX, Part II, 721.

and the loss of the battle of Gettysburg was widely blamed on his erratic leadership of the Confederate cavalry during Lee's campaign in Pennsylvania. Stuart needed admiration more than most men, and to be criticized after years of adulation was a bitter blow to his self-esteem. And the appointment of an outsider to his staff may have appeared to him as an indication that he no longer had the full confidence of his superiors. It is evident that Grenfell was not made welcome by Stuart's devotedly loyal staff; this could not have happened if they had not merely reflected the attitude of their chief. Grenfell never overcame the handicap of having been foisted on Stuart, nor, apparently, was he given the opportunity to do so. It is significant that when Stuart's cavalry made its camp on John Minor Botts's farm in November, Grenfell spent a fortnight as a guest in Botts's house and was not where one would expect to find him, encamped with his chief and his fellow staff officers.

An even more significant indication of the hostility toward Grenfell is the story that he ran away at the fight with the Union cavalry under Generals John Buford and Judson Kilpatrick at Jack's Shop (Liberty Mills). The story is told in a sneering tone by Stuart's assistant adjutant general, Major Henry B. McClellan: "Grenfell became demoralized on this day. The fighting was closer and hotter than he liked. He was at my side when our regiments were trying to force Kilpatrick from the road. Seeing one of them recoil from the charge, Grenfell concluded that the day was lost. He took to the bushes, swam the river, returned to Orange Court House, and reported that Stuart, his staff, and his whole command were surrounded and captured." [38]

McClellan's malice is evident in his statement that Stuart employed Grenfell "somewhat as an inspector"; it slipped his memory that he himself had written the order announcing Grenfell's appointment as assistant inspector general of the cavalry corps, which was not the same thing.[39] Moreover, he ends his story with the statement that Grenfell was so ashamed of his cowardice "that he did not again show his face in our camp." This is a manifest un-

[38] H. B. McClellan, *I Rode With Jeb Stuart* (Bloomington, 1958), 376n.
[39] *Ibid.*, 375n.

truth which demolishes the whole miserable yarn. For the fight at Jack's Shop occurred on September 22, eight days, and not "several weeks," as McClellan has it, after Grenfell's appointment to Stuart's staff; two months later, during the Mine Run campaign, he was still at his post. Fitzgerald Ross met him on Christmas Day, a month later, and his account makes it clear that Grenfell was not only still on Stuart's staff, but that he was living at Stuart's headquarters at Orange Court House, where his tent and stables were "a model to be studied and worthy of such an old campaigner." [40]

If Stuart resented Grenfell's appointment to his staff and showed it by a frosty reserve or an open hostility, Grenfell on his part was far from happy in his new position. Perhaps he was becoming disenchanted with the fight for southern independence. It had been an appealing cause when active campaigning was afoot, and he could march and fight in congenial, appreciative company, with men like Duke, Morgan and Wheeler who looked up to him and toward whom he could have a feeling of friendship and personal loyalty. But to "fight for the Confederacy" in a time of inaction, in the midst of a Virginia winter, in the barren wilderness that northern Virginia had become, in the company of men who resented his presence among them and who meant nothing to him, was a far different thing; and he spoke to Ross with obvious nostalgia "of the stirring and fighting time when he was with Morgan in the West." [41] Perhaps he had become accustomed to the free and easy ways of the western cavalry and found it difficult to adjust to the more careful observance of military formalities in Stuart's command. When he joined Morgan, he had been no more of a newcomer than the majority of his associates. Later, when he served with Wheeler, he was part of an organization still in its formative stages. Now, for the first time, he had to adjust himself to an organization already in being, cemented by loyalties and traditions born of two years of living together and fighting side by side, led by a tightly knit group of officers who, so far from being impressed by his status as a foreigner of distinction or by

[40] Ross, *Cities and Camps*, 172.
[41] *Ibid.*, 172.

the glamor of his exploits with the western armies, made little effort to make him welcome or even to disguise their feeling that he was an interloper.

Perhaps Grenfell's unhappiness has an even simpler explanation, namely, the calendar. He was now nearly fifty-seven, and as he was to confess a short time later, he no longer had the resilience of youth. The hardships of service in the Confederate armies had broken the fighting spirit of many thousands of patriotic native Southerners, men who were Grenfell's juniors by three decades or more. He had led a harder life than most, and if he now grew weary of a cause that was not his own, it would be hard to blame him. His disillusionment shows clearly enough in his comments on the wanton destruction of private property by Stuart's men, and he spoke to Botts "with detestation of the practice of the Confederate army, in regard to the destruction of private property, as being contrary to the usages of civilized warfare and derogatory to the character of the government and officers that tolerated the custom." [42]

Apparently, however, there were more concrete reasons for Grenfell's discontent. Shortly after the turn of the year, he wrote Morgan that he had received "a most Complimentary" letter from General Lee "which lays open all Stuart's intrigues to get rid of me." [43] He does not say what these "intrigues" were, and there is no evidence, apart from his own statement, of anything Stuart may have done to have him removed from his staff. Nor is there any trace in Lee's records of any letter to Grenfell referring to his difficulties with Stuart. There is no reason to question Grenfell's statement, but whether he was right or wrong is less important than is his belief that such an intrigue existed.

Grenfell is also the sole source of information for Stuart's reason for wanting to be rid of him. In another letter to Morgan, he remarked that his "want of a musical ear, and a decided antipathy to the twang of the Banjo" were the grounds of his failure to find

[42] John Minor Botts to Joseph Holt, June 17, 1865, in *Executive Documents,* 637.
[43] Grenfell to John H. Morgan, February 15, 1864, in Morgan Papers.

110

favor with Stuart.[44] Cynical as it sounds, the remark may be quite factual. Jeb Stuart has a high place in the Confederate Pantheon; he is, in fact, a member of the Lee-Jackson-Stuart Trinity. But in his lifetime, he was not everyone's cup of tea. Those who were attracted by his high spirits and flamboyance were intensely devoted to him, but many were repelled by what they thought to be his naive exhibitionism. General Lafayette McLaws, for one, called his addiction to banjo music and his liking for publicity "the act of a buffoon to attract attention." [45] Stuart had a real fondness for a tune, and in winter camp his liking for gaiety, balls, charades, and music had full play. In the late months of 1863 the sound of banjo and fiddle and of male voices singing in chorus filled the air at the headquarters of the cavalry corps.[46] Grenfell had shown in his time with Morgan that he could unbend in congenial company, in a friendly, cordial atmosphere. But he found no sympathetic spirits like Basil Duke on Stuart's staff; on the contrary, he was met with the niggling hostility exemplified by McClellan's story about his "cowardice." Grenfell was not one to bear slights with patience and, doubtless, he reacted with a haughty reserve. He became the reproachful skeleton at the feast, and that would have been enough to cause Stuart to develop an active dislike for him.

There is no documentary evidence, other than Grenfell's own statements, of Stuart's hostility towards him or of any specific cause that might have given rise to it.[47] On the other hand, it can

[44] Grenfell to Morgan (a second letter), also dated February 15, 1864, in Morgan Papers.

[45] P. G. Hamlin, *"Old Bald Head": The Portrait of a Soldier* (Strasburg, Va., 1940), 133.

[46] Ross, *Cities and Camps*, 166-67.

[47] In June, 1864, Grenfell told Secretary of War Stanton that Stuart became very angry with him because he had reported accurately that the cavalry corps was only eight thousand strong, whereas Stuart falsely claimed to have, and was drawing rations for, nineteen thousand. *House Executive Documents*, p. 599. Grenfell implied that this led to his departure from Stuart's command. If Grenfell did submit such a report, it has not survived, nor is there any reflection of it in the correspondence of General Lee or the Confederate War Department. The story can hardly be true, because if Grenfell did report Stuart's strength as eight thousand, he merely confirmed Stuart's own reports, in which the effective strength of the Cavalry Corps is shown as about eight thousand throughout the

be said with certainty that Grenfell was not one of Stuart's admirers. Being the man he was, outspoken and tactless, he probably made no secret of his poor opinion of his chief. A separation was therefore inevitable. Grenfell left the corps some time between Christmas, 1863, and January 29, 1864. The exact circumstances are unknown, apart from two statements of Grenfell's. In one, he said that he was "relieved from duty with what remain[ed] of [Stuart's] Cavalry Corps"; in the other, he said bluntly that Stuart got rid of him.[48] In any case, the separation was clearly neither friendly nor pleasant, and no doubt both parties were relieved when they parted company.

months of September, October, November, and December, 1863. *OR,* Vol. XXXIX, Part II, 764, 811, 866. The "Aggregate Present *and Absent*" are shown as about eighteen thousand in all of these reports.

[48] Grenfell to John H. Morgan, two letters dated February 15, 1864, in Morgan Papers.

Chapter VII

O N JANUARY 7, 1864, the drabness of the third wartime winter at the Confederate capital was relieved briefly by the arrival in Richmond of John Hunt Morgan and his wife. In one of the most glamorous (or strangest) exploits of the war, he and Thomas Henry Hines escaped from the Ohio Penitentiary on the night of November 27. A large reward was offered for Morgan's recapture, and Federal troops scouted the roads he had to use on his way South, but by traveling at night and hiding by day, and with the indispensable help of Confederate sympathizers along the way, he reached friendly territory in safety. His dramatic escape made him the hero of the hour, and he went to Richmond to face the rigors of the enthusiastic popular and civic receptions which were to be tendered him.

Morgan had a second and more serious purpose in visiting the Confederate capital. He was eager to redeem his military reputation, and he needed the help of the War Department to reconstitute his command. Help, however, proved to be more difficult to get than he had probably anticipated. The Confederate authorities were willing to participate in the festivities honoring the popular hero, but to provide and equip a new command for a man whose irresponsibility had destroyed a fine force of 2,400 men was something else again. The War Department, struggling with the ever more difficult task of keeping up the numerical strength of the Confederate armies, was not eager to raise another force for Morgan to fritter away. Besides, General Bragg was now in Richmond as chief military advisor of President Davis, and he would have been more than human had he not used his considerable influence to block the plans of his intractable former subordinate; in fact, he threatened to have Morgan court-martialed for leading his force across the Ohio River the summer before, in disobedience of orders.[1] Thus, Morgan was thrown on his own resources and had to try to raise a new command through his own efforts, with only a minimum of official help. On January 13 he published a proclamation calling on his former soldiers to assemble in Decatur, Georgia. General Adam Johnson, one of his former brigade commanders, sent agents through the South to solicit donations to purchase equipment for the force Morgan hoped to raise. These, however, were ineffectual gestures, for even in that day of free-and-easy military administration, official backing and help were needed to organize and equip a respectable command.

It was at this time, and in these circumstances, that Grenfell became associated with Morgan once again. He was in Richmond when Morgan arrived and was at the side of his former commander on January 8, when the latter was tendered a civic reception by the mayor.[2] Grenfell wrote one of his daughters a short time later that he intended to return to Europe after leaving Stuart and had already advertised his horses for sale and booked passage on a blockade runner to Nassau; then, however, Morgan "put his claw" on him, and the memory of old associations and regard for his former chief impelled him to agree to stay on and become Morgan's adjutant general once more.[3]

Which of the two men made the first move toward a reconciliation is not on record. The lapse of a year since they had parted in anger probably made a formal reconciliation unnecessary. They simply resumed their old cordial relations. Grenfell was nostalgic

[1] Holland, *Morgan and His Raiders*, 298.
[2] Unidentified newspaper clipping, in Hines Papers.
[3] Grenfell to Marie Pearce-Serocold, March 18, 1864, in Weaks (ed.), "Colonel . . . Grenfell," 9.

114

for the brave days of 1862 and seemed to have the protective affection of an older brother for Morgan, whom he described as "the best gentleman and only Cavalry Officer except Forrest (who can't write his name) in the Service." [4] Morgan's high opinion of Grenfell has already been quoted. Now, facing a difficult situation in his relations with the War Department, he remembered Grenfell's successful diplomacy of 1862. He himself could not remain in Richmond; he had to go to Decatur to meet and organize the men he had invited to report to him there. Hence, he asked Grenfell to act *pro tempore* as his assistant adjutant general and stay in Richmond as his personal representative to rally political support, placate General Bragg, and cajole the War Department into a more helpful attitude.

Grenfell's transfer to Morgan was not effected without difficulty. On being formally relieved of duty with Stuart, he was ordered to report to General Joseph Johnston, who had replaced Bragg in command of the Army of Tennessee, as his inspector general of cavalry.[5] Johnston's report on the state of his cavalry makes it clear that Grenfell could have performed a useful function in the post, but he had no desire to serve again under Wheeler.[6] He applied to the adjutant general for a change of orders to authorize him to serve under Morgan, and when the request was refused, resigned his lieutenant colonel's commission.[7] The resignation was accepted, leaving him free to join Morgan as a volunteer.

Grenfell accepted a formidable assignment, and he tackled it with enthusiasm. Clearly, he was pleased to be needed and to be once again in a position of responsibility. On the other hand, his readiness to throw in his lot with Morgan shows that the years had not improved his sense of the practical. He was badly at fault in his judgment of Morgan's soldierly capabilities and he also failed to realize that he had taken on a well-nigh impossible task.

[4] *Ibid.*

[5] Grenfell to John H. Morgan, February 15, 1864, in Morgan Papers.

[6] Joseph E. Johnston, *Narrative of Military Operations* . . . (Bloomington, 1959), 273.

[7] Grenfell's letter of resignation is dated January 19, 1864, in Grenfell Papers-National Archives.

The Confederacy was no longer what it had been. It started the war with a defensive strategy by deliberate choice but now, after the defeats of 1863, it was on the defensive by necessity, and the North had the initiative which it was never thereafter to relinquish. The South's resources of manpower and materiel had shrunk disastrously. It could no longer afford military adventures, and there was enough realism in the Confederate War Department to make it unwilling to entrust precious resources to commanders who had demonstrated a lack of reliability and a chronic unwillingness to work in harness.

After Morgan's departure for Decatur near the end of January, Grenfell went to work on the peculiarly placed Kentucky delegation in the Confederate Congress—the representatives of a state whose membership in the Confederacy was the merest fiction—to persuade them to bring political pressure to bear on the administration on Morgan's behalf. He reported to Morgan that he had obtained the signatures of all but one of the congressmen to a document, supporting Morgan's case, which Senator Simms of Kentucky was to present to the secretary of war. The only nonsigner gave as the reason for his refusal that "Morgan's Men had gone against him in some electioneering matter"; even in the twilight months of a fight for independence, political grudges in the Bluegrass State were a force to be reckoned with.[8] This uncooperative congressman, whose constitutents were safely within the Union, was the subject of the first of Grenfell's recorded comments on religion. He wrote Morgan, "I found out that he was a Parson, and as all of that profession are more spiteful and revengeful than any other class, his conduct did not surprise me, so I left him alone."[9] His second observation on the subject was made a few years later. He learned that some of his sisters had left the Church of England to become Roman Catholics; the news caused him to comment: "I do not see any harm in the old maids, my sisters, becoming Roman Catholics! It is the fashion to do so nowadays, and after all, one religion is as good as another, provided one is sin-

[8] Grenfell to John H. Morgan, February 8, 1864, in Morgan Papers.
[9] *Ibid.*

116

cere. I am nothing at all at present, or if anything, a follower of the Devil." [10]

In the course of running his political errands, Grenfell had an opportunity to observe the workings of the Confederate governmental machine, which led him to form an unflattering opinion of the President and his cabinet. Davis, he thought, was too busy "obtaining the souls" of members of Congress to have time for the claims of individuals unless they happened to be his favorites, and his cabinet was made up of "poor hacks without a grain of talent or sense between them." [11]

In addition to attending to his political chores, Grenfell also called daily at the War Department. He endeavored to expedite through that harassed and overworked office Morgan's many requests for the return to him of some of his old units, requests which were strenuously opposed by commanders who now had these troops and were unwilling to part with them. He did his best also to hasten action on Morgan's requisitions for arms, equipment, and supplies. Most important of all, he tried to obtain the War Department's consent for Morgan to move his base from Decatur, where he was under General Johnston's firm thumb, to southwestern Virginia, where he could have his precious independence. Grenfell made small headway with the first two of these projects, but he was successful with the third, for on February 28, Morgan was authorized to move his headquarters to Abingdon, Virginia, where he thought he could more easily get men and horses from Kentucky, and to resume his raids into that state.[12]

Much of Grenfell's time was taken up with acting as a clearinghouse for the many applications by groups and individuals, civilians as well as soldiers, who wanted to join Morgan.[13] Service in bands of irregular cavalry, many of which had little military value and were more of a menace to the civilian population of the South than to the enemy, had a never-failing attraction for Southerners.

[10] Grenfell to Marie Pearce-Serocold, February 26, 1868, in Weaks (ed.), "Colonel . . . Grenfell," 19–20.
[11] Grenfell to John H. Morgan, February 8, 1864, in Morgan Papers.
[12] OR, Vol. XXXII, Part II, 182.
[13] Grenfell to John H. Morgan, February 8, 1864, in Morgan Papers.

Membership in such a unit provided an opportunity to fight without the irksome restraints of discipline or the strain of continuous effort, and had it not been for the rule, rigidly enforced by the War Department, that applications for transfer to Morgan's new force would be approved only if they bore the consent of the applicant's commanding officer, Morgan would soon have had more men than he could possibly use. As it was, the recruiting activities of his overzealous friends and former subordinates caused an endless amount of trouble. General Johnston complained to the secretary of war that Morgan's agents were breaking up his infantry, "enticing them to desert, and shielding deserters, as well as conscripts and volunteers out of the infantry where alone we want them." [14] General Lee was obliged to protest directly to the President; he wrote that he had heard "some days since that several men of this army mostly Louisianans that were in or passed through Richmond, were joining Genl Morgan's Command. . . . A member of my staff informs me that . . . a recruiting officer of Genl Morgan visited . . . [Jackson] Hospital, promised the men clothing and two months furlough, & that 25 or 30 convalescents . . . about to [be sent] to this army, deserted & . . . were forwarded to Decatur Geo." [15]

Morgan of course denied all knowledge of this overenthusiastic recruiting, but it was going on nevertheless. Grenfell apparently had no hand in it; he informed Morgan that he was besieged by applicants but was accepting only those whose papers were in order.[16] He was not only careful about the recruits he would himself accept, but he also took the trouble to warn Morgan about other undesirable candidates. Considering his own antecedents, it is curious to find him cautioning his chief about a Frenchman calling himself Captain Kleber: "I am assured that this is not his real name. His antecedents are very bad, the associate of chevaliers

[14] Quoted in Holland, *Morgan and His Raiders,* 301.

[15] D. S. Freeman and Grady McWhiney (eds.), *Lee's Dispatches* (New York, 1957), 131. The Morgan Papers in the University of North Carolina Library contain dozens of applications from individuals, groups large and small, and complete units, asking Morgan to accept them into his new command.

[16] Grenfell to John H. Morgan, February 8, 1864, in Morgan Papers.

d'Industrie & swindlers! I am afraid he will do you no good." [17]

Grenfell had made little progress in his negotiations with the War Department by mid-February, but he had some interesting news, which he reported in carefully guarded language. Thomas Henry Hines had been captured with Morgan in the Indiana-Ohio raid and imprisoned with him in the Ohio penitentiary. He had been the directing brain of the prison break in November, 1863, in which he himself, Morgan, and a number of his officers made their escape. Now, in February, Hines appeared in Richmond. The letter in which Grenfell tells of Hines's arrival is of great importance in its bearing on his own connection with the project Hines had come to Richmond to propose to the government: "Good information leads me to believe that Captain Hines is about to proceed upon a Mission of some importance. I wish to tell you that if you would give him some document testifying your knowledge of his honesty and requesting all well wishers of yours to assist him it would be of more importance to him than all the Secretary of Wars [sic] recommendations. This I am sure of, if as I suppose the mission be to C——a or England." [18]

On February 15, 1864, Grenfell wrote Morgan two letters. One of them, which he said, "may hereafter if they do not give you your Command have to be published," is a curious document. After explaining that he resigned his commission because of the adjutant general's refusal to let him serve under Morgan, he wrote:

> I . . . rejoined my old Command, the only one in my eyes worth serving in as a Private . . . my reduction to the ranks . . . [will not] prevent my serving you with alacrity and zeal, provided you are not held in the leading strings of some General who may be your Senior in Rank through favouritism, but immeasurably your junior in all qualities that make a distinguished soldier. I only hope General that our Rulers will profit by past experience and not again place you the first and most esteemed Cavalry Officer of the Confederacy under the orders of any Cavalry Officer be he whom [sic] he may,

[17] *Ibid.* The term *chevalier d'industrie* was much in vogue in the nineteenth century to describe a person who lived by his wits, *i.e.*, a confidence man or swindler.
[18] Grenfell to John H. Morgan, February 15, 1864, in Morgan Papers.

for I am convinced that such a course would cramp your energies and render you powerless to carry out any measure of importance with success ... if Public opinion could be expressed and acted upon, you would be placed at once in the independant [*sic*] situation which your gallant conduct has won for you, and your future deeds would continue to deserve.[19]

The obvious sincerity of this unusual letter and the flattering terms, vastly beyond his deserts, in which Morgan is referred to, suggest that Grenfell had an unexpected capacity for hero worship. If the letter had been published as Grenfell intended and, especially if it had been published in an antiadministration newspaper, it would have helped Morgan not at all. Grenfell failed to realize that neither the Civil War nor Morgan's reputation was what it had been in 1862. It is probably just as well that the letter never saw the light of day. President Davis had demonstrated many times that he was impervious to popular clamor or political pressure in making his military appointments, and Grenfell's scathing remarks about generals who achieved rank and seniority through favoritism were not likely to sway him in Morgan's favor. In any case, the President and the War Department had a far more realistic opinion of Morgan's capabilities than had Grenfell.

Morgan's affairs made little progress in the next six weeks. With little help from the authorities, he was collecting men in Abingdon, " a few detachments of his old command, a remnant of men of Hodge's cavalry, and scores of men of questionable reputation gathered in by recruiting agents without regard for their fitness or responsibility." [20] But he lacked horses, weapons, equipment of all kinds, and even clothing for his men. Grenfell, for all his effort, was unable to obtain any of these necessities for him. If he wrote Morgan about his tribulations during this period, his letters have not survived and the frustrations he experienced are not on record.

On March 30 Grenfell wrote Morgan that on the previous day, he had made his daily visit to the adjutant general's office to press for action on Morgan's request to have his old regiments restored

[19] *Ibid.*   [20] Holland, *Morgan and His Raiders*, 310.

120

to him.[21] His previous visits for the same purpose had produced only courteous evasions, but on this occasion he was given a forthright answer—he was told that nothing could or would be done to meet Morgan's wishes in this matter. Major Melford, who interviewed Grenfell, tried to soften his refusal with conventional expressions of his personal regard for Morgan. Then he referred to Grenfell's own status; he informed him that his appointment as Morgan's assistant adjutant general had been approved, with the rank of captain, which he would be required to accept because it was against regulations for him to serve as assistant adjutant general without the rank appropriate to the post.

In the midst of the conversation, the adjutant general himself, flinty old General Samuel Cooper, "stiff as a bayonet, with a face like a nutmeg grater," as Grenfell quite accurately described him, entered the room, and proceeded to read Grenfell a lecture. Some commanding officers, the general said, had as many as six assistant adjutants general on their staffs; the department intended to curtail the number of these appointments and would see to it that only "meritorious officers" retained these posts. Grenfell concluded that the general's remarks were mere official verbiage to hide "Bragg's intention to put *the meritorious officers*' (his own tools) into all Posts of responsibility and to turn out all those or force them to resign by neglect, who do not swear by Jeff Davis and himself." Thereupon, Grenfell rejected the compulsory commission out of hand and decided then and there to quit the Confederate service forever, sell his horses, and leave for Europe.

This is the story Grenfell reported to Morgan. He added, as justification for his abrupt decision, that the wood he was made of was getting old and stiff and no longer bent as readily to the winds of fate as it had done in the past. But did Grenfell tell the whole

[21] The story of Grenfell's visit to the War Department on March 29, as told in this and the following paragraphs, his description of General Cooper, and his conclusions as to the real motive behind the general's remarks are based on, or quoted from Grenfell to Morgan, March 30, 1864, in Morgan Papers. Readers who wish to verify the accuracy of Grenfell's description of General Cooper are referred to R. U. Johnson and C. C. Buel (eds.), *Battles and Leaders of the Civil War* (New York, 1888), I, 241.

story or even the true story? There are good reasons to doubt it, and because of its bearing on his fate, the incident requires careful examination.

On the face of it, the story is plausible enough. Given his readiness to take offense and his quick temper, it might have been predicted that his struggles with bureaucracy would end in some such fashion. It would not be difficult to assume that he was driven to resign by the seeming ingratitude of the Confederate government, and the blow to his self-esteem. But having accepted a commission to serve under Wheeler, why should he have resented having to accept a commission to serve under Morgan? Why the sudden hostility to General Bragg who had always been well disposed toward him? Why the assumption that General Cooper's remarks about the oversized staffs of *some* commanding officers were aimed at Morgan and himself?

Grenfell himself has cast doubt on the credibility of his narrative by telling the story quite differently on two other occasions. He told Secretary of War Stanton two months later that *Morgan* would not allow him to serve as his assistant adjutant general without a commission. To accept the commission, Grenfell said, he would have had to take "the oath," which he refused to do, and thereupon decided to leave the Confederate service altogether. He added that when President Davis learned of his decision, he asked him in a personal interview to stay on and offered him the post of inspector general of cavalry with the rank of brigadier general; Grenfell said that he declined the flattering offer and told Davis that it was his fixed intention to return to England.[22]

On the second occasion, two years later, Grenfell wrote: "I left the Confederate service, in which I was a colonel . . . of my own accord, and although I was offered promotion if I would remain, in consequence of a serious dispute with Mr. Jefferson Davis himself; and nothing could have induced me to serve again under a govern-

[22] *House Executive Documents*, 599. Grenfell repeated this version in a letter to the British minister in Washington on January 23, 1865. British Legation, Washington, Archives (Public Record Office, London), FO 115/448; hereinafter cited as British Legation-Archives.

ment so unjust and ungrateful." [23] One can read too much into the discrepancies in these three accounts, but it is impossible to resist the suspicion that they exist because none of the three is true. The discrepancies exist because Grenfell had to invent a justification for his departure from the Confederacy. Even Morgan could not be told the truth and as Grenfell was dealing in fiction in any case, the story varied at each telling to suit the needs of the moment.

Two facts turn suspicion into certainty. Early in 1865, while Grenfell was on trial in Cincinnati, the British consul in St. Louis visited Chicago to see if anything could be done in his behalf. While there, he interviewed Colonel Benjamin Sweet, who had been responsible for Grenfell's arrest, and asked him if at the time of the arrest Grenfell was officially a Confederate officer. Sweet replied that when Grenfell's papers were examined, a captain's commission in the Confederate army was found among them. [24] Obviously, if Grenfell had accepted the commission, then the tale of his refusal to serve because of his refusal to do precisely that, falls to the ground. And the second fact is that he did accept the commission. On March 15, two weeks before his encounter with General Cooper, Morgan submitted a request to the adjutant general for Grenfell's appointment as assistant adjutant general of his brigade with the rank of captain—and the request is unmistakably in Grenfell's handwriting. [25] Moreover, the endorsements on the request indicate that it was approved as soon as the secretary of war had satisfied himself that Morgan had enough men to constitute a brigade; and Grenfell's commission as captain was issued on March 26, three days before his interview, stormy or otherwise, with Major Melford and General Cooper. Thus, whatever may have occurred in Melford's office on March 29, Grenfell's de-

[23] Grenfell to B. H. Hill, April 6, 1866, in *House Executive Documents*, 638-39.
[24] J. E. Wilkins to J. H. Burnley, February 8, 1865, in FO-U.S.-General Correspondence, FO 5/1155.
[25] John H. Morgan to Samuel Cooper, March 15, 1864, in Grenfell Papers-National Archives. The record of Grenfell's commission as captain is in Register of Appointments, C.S.A., Confederate Archives, Ch. I, File #94, p. 156, in National Archives.

cision to leave the Confederacy was certainly not caused by the War Department's insistence that he accept a commission he did not want.

One must assume that there was a reason for these mystifications, and it is nearly certain that the answer lies in the cautiously allusive personal letter Grenfell had written Morgan on February 15, to tell him of the mission "of some importance" that Hines was about to undertake in "C——a." Grenfell's information about the mission must have come from Hines himself, and he must have known precisely what the mission was. The two men had a powerful common bond in their association with and loyalty to Morgan. They were in Richmond at the same time, and in and out of the War Department daily. Unquestionably, they met—and talked. And by this time, even the impractical Grenfell must have begun to suspect that there was little likelihood of his being able to accomplish very much for Morgan in Richmond. But merely to give up the assignment as a bad job would not have been in character. To accept an invitation from Hines to join his "mission," or more probably, to volunteer to do so, not only provided an acceptable means of escaping without discredit from an impossible situation, but in addition, opened up an irresistible prospect of novel adventures which promised to be risky enough to satisfy even Grenfell's exacting standards. And too, to join the hard-driving, positive Hines would provide relief for months to come from the increasingly heavy burden of directing the course of his life. Nevertheless, his self-respect required that there be a plausible reason for throwing up the assignment which he had accepted from Morgan in January; and because neither Morgan nor the War Department could be told the truth, he had to go through the charade of fierce indignation at poor General Cooper's no doubt quite casual and impersonal remarks. The indignation, probably carefully rehearsed beforehand, served another purpose. If, as is more than likely, Hines had already reached an understanding with Grenfell, it would naturally occur to that wily conspirator that it would be well for Grenfell to be able to claim, with a surface appearance of truth, that he had irrevocably broken with the Confederacy in anger and disgust.

Grenfell remained in Richmond until May 9 to sell his horses and wind up his affairs; three days later he sailed from Wilmington, North Carolina, for Nassau aboard the blockade-runner *Helen*.[26] A week before, the Army of the Potomac under Meade, the western armies under Sherman, the armies of Crook and Sigel in the Shenandoah Valley, and the Army of the James under the ineffable Benjamin Butler, began the concerted movement planned by Grant that was to destroy the Confederacy. Before Grenfell sailed from Wilmington, he could have read in the newspapers the tale of the bloody fighting in the Wilderness and at Spotsylvania Court House. And his enemy of a few months before, Jeb Stuart, mortally wounded in the fight at Yellow Tavern with Sheridan's Union cavalry, died at perhaps the very same hour in the evening of May 12 when the *Helen* dropped down the Cape Fear River toward the Federal blockade ships and the open sea. At the same time also, John Morgan at the head of three small brigades was about to depart on the last of his raids into Kentucky. Undertaken without orders, disgraced by wholesale looting and robbery, this sorry enterprise ended with rare poetic justice in the smashing of Morgan's undisciplined mob of a command in a second battle of Cynthiana, as needless as the first. In his first fight at Cynthiana two years before, Morgan had Duke and Grenfell at his side, and he handled his enthusiastic troopers with self-confidence and energy. In the second fight, the self-confidence and energy were gone, and neither Duke nor Grenfell were there to supply the drive and leadership Morgan no longer possessed. He was finished, and it was a kind fate that led him to his death at Greeneville, Tennessee, a few months later.

Grenfell's cavalier attitude toward mere facts is typified by his accounts of his voyage on the *Helen*. On three different occasions, he gave Nassau, Bermuda, and Havana as the destination of the blockade-runner. He planned, he said, to take ship from Nassau

[26] *House Executive Documents*, 599.

(or Bermuda or Havana) to Halifax and to sail thence to England. Upon disembarking from the *Helen,* he learned that he had just missed the mail steamer to Halifax and would have to wait two or three weeks for the next sailing; however, a ship was about to sail for New York and having no desire to spend two or three weeks on "that miserable island," he took passage in it.[27] This was an abrupt end of his professed desire to return to England, but quite in order if, as is nearly certain, he had no such intention to begin with. On landing in New York, he called on the military governor, General John A. Dix, and requested permission to remain in the North, notwithstanding his previous service in the Confederate army. Dix declined the responsibility of acting on Grenfell's request and directed him to address himself to the War Department in Washington. Grenfell arrived in the capital on June 13 and had an interview with the military governor of the District of Columbia, Colonel M. N. Wiswell, who decided that the case was sufficiently novel and important to require submission to the secretary of war. Accordingly, Grenfell returned to the War Department two days later and after a brief discussion with the assistant secretary, Colonel James A. Hardie, had an interview with the redoubtable secretary himself.[28]

Nearly a year later, Sir Frederick Bruce, the British Minister in Washington, ended a letter to his Foreign Office about Grenfell's affairs, with the plaintive query, "What madness can lead men like him . . . to put themselves in the tiger's jaws when they are out of his reach?" [29] The question is apt, but like so many others suggested by the erratic course of Grenfell's life, it cannot be answered with any degree of assurance. It would not have been out of the ordinary, in an age when national allegiances were much more casual than they have since become, for a British subject who had fought for the Confederacy to wish to visit the North while the war was still going on, without having to entertain serious mis-

[27] *Ibid.,* 63.
[28] *Ibid.*
[29] Sir Frederick Bruce to E. Hammond, n. d. (received in London May 10, 1865), in FO-U.S.-General Correspondence, FO 5/1155.

givings about the kind of reception he was likely to receive. Also, why should anyone have questioned the abrupt decision of a rootless individual like Grenfell, to whom one place was as good as another, to go to New York instead of to England, for no better reason than that he did not choose to wait for two or three weeks for a ship to take him where he originally intended to go? No doubt this is precisely the impression Grenfell intended to create, but his apparently erratic proceedings were clearly part of a carefully thought out plan. To play his part in Hines's project, he had to have official sanction for his status of an innocent visitor to the North who had nothing more important in view than sightseeing, hunting, and fishing. The sole object of the sequence of interviews with General Dix, Colonels Wiswell and Hardie, and Secretary Stanton, was to get on record his *bona fides* as one who had cast from himself the Confederacy and its works. If he had simply come North without ado and gone about his hunting and fishing without all these interviews with authority, he could have enjoyed his favorite sports and no one would have paid the slightest attention to him or to his movements.

To make Stanton a participant in this scheme was to play a dangerous game indeed. For the secretary, with his well-deserved reputation as the ogre of the War Department, was not a man to trifle with. He was a very complex human being, intelligent, shrewd, tough, ruthless, and vindictive. Fanatically devoted to the Union, he hated with equal fervor Southerners who fought against it in the open and Northerners who were, or appeared to be, undermining it from within or were merely lukewarm in its defense. For Stanton, there were no gradations of guilt, and he had a long memory; there was no mercy in his heart for anyone who tried to mislead or deceive him. This is exactly what Grenfell did and he was to pay a bitter price for it.

No doubt Grenfell had his interview in Stanton's notorious reception room, the Secretary standing behind his high bookkeeper's desk, glowering at his visitor through his steel-rimmed glasses.[30]

[30] It is possible that Stanton knew something of Grenfell before they met. Colonel Fremantle's book and the translation of the Prince de Joinville's book on

127

Grenfell should have taken warning from the presence at Stanton's elbow of a War Department clerk, taking down in shorthand every word he said, but he did not. He told first a not entirely candid story of his service in the Confederate army and of the circumstances which, he professed, led to his departure from the South. Then he proceeded to give Stanton a farrago of truths, half-truths, and outright lies about the Confederate armies. In a letter he wrote three years later, he confessed that he "did lie once to Mr. Stanton, most egregiously," but he claimed that he did so in a fit of indignation because Stanton tried to pump him for information: "He had no right to question me, he knew that I had been a Southern soldier and wished me to betray the cause for which I had fought and bled. Although I had left the S[outhern] service in disgust, I was not the man to betray my old Comrades. Stanton was humbugged[,] he believed my statements and acted upon them." [31]

The stenographic record of the interview, produced in evidence at his trial, does not indicate that Stanton asked any questions about the southern armies.[32] Indeed, Frederick Hall, the clerk who took down the interview and transcribed his shorthand notes immediately afterward, testified that Grenfell volunteered his information and "expressed a perfect willingness to explain all in his power to the government." [33] If Hall's testimony was truthful, and there is no reason whatever to doubt it, and Grenfell volunteered his information in order to prove the finality of his severance from the South or to ingratiate himself with the secretary, he overacted his part, in a probably superfluous effort to make sure that he would be allowed to travel in the North. But if he gave his information in answer to Stanton's questions, he was guilty of an error of judgment. Had he declined to answer on the ground that he

the Army of the Potomac had been published before Grenfell appeared in Stanton's reception room. Stanton may well have read one or both books.

[31] Grenfell to S. L. M. Barlow, January 13, 1868, in S. L. M. Barlow Papers, Henry E. Huntington Library and Art Gallery, San Marino, California; hereinafter cited as Barlow Papers.

[32] *House Executive Documents*, 598–600.

[33] *Ibid.*, 64.

"was not the man to betray [his] old Comrades," it is most unlikely that Stanton would have pressed the issue; by the summer of 1864, the War Department had ample sources of information about the southern armies, and Stanton was shrewd enough to discount the value of any information he might have been able to extract from Grenfell under duress. The slight value he placed on the information Grenfell gave him is demonstrated by the absence from the *Official Records* of any indication that the "facts" revealed by Grenfell were ever communicated to General Grant or made use of in any other way, as they assuredly would have been had Stanton considered them important.

When Grenfell had his interview with Stanton, Lee's Army of Northern Virginia had, in six weeks of fighting, been pressed back to within nine miles of Richmond, at a cost of sixty thousand Union casualties. In the West, Sherman was in the midst of his Atlanta campaign and was about to reach Marietta. In both major theatres, in Virginia as well as in Georgia, the Union commanders faced Confederate armies which to all appearances were just as strong and just as full of fight as they had ever been. Victory for the North seemed as distant and uncertain as ever, while its financial and manpower resources were becoming more and more attenuated and the political prospects of the Lincoln administration more and more bleak. To try to hoodwink Stanton would have been risky at any time; to make the attempt at this moment of stress was doubly foolhardy.

Grenfell told Stanton that the number of troops Beauregard had brought to Petersburg to protect the right flank of Lee's forces was "estimated" at from twenty-five thousand to thirty thousand, not counting General George Pickett's division of from eleven thousand to twelve thousand.[34] Beauregard's actual strength was just short of eight thousand. Stuart's cavalry, according to Grenfell, numbered eight thousand; after six weeks of hard campaigning, it probably numbered less than five thousand. His wildest misrepresentation, however, concerned Lee's army. He told Stanton

[34] This and the other statements made by Grenfell to Stanton are taken from the transcript of the Grenfell-Stanton interview. *Ibid.*, 598–600.

that it "was in fine health and spirits and will fight well," which, as Stanton already knew full well, was true enough, for only ten days before, Lee had repulsed the full might of the Army of the Potomac at Old Cold Harbor and inflicted seven thousand casualties upon it in the process. But then he said that Lee "drew rations for one hundred and thirty thousand," which certainly deserved the adjective "egregious" which he later applied to it, for Lee's actual strength in the field at this time was less than forty-five thousand, backed by the Richmond garrison of about seventy-four hundred which he could draw upon in an emergency.[35] Grenfell then added that the "south side of Richmond was defended by hardly any works. . . . It was much the weakest. . . . By cutting the railroads south they would be entirely deprived of supplies." This was potentially the most damaging of his revelations; its value was indicated by the fact that Grant had already reached the same conclusion and was acting upon it at the very time that Grenfell was having his interview with Stanton. Moreover, the immediate cause of the fall of Richmond in the following April was the cutting of the Southside Railroad by Sheridan's cavalry. Lastly, Grenfell informed Stanton that General Forrest had "entirely given up his command." As Stanton already knew, but Grenfell did not, just five days before, Forrest had won the greatest victory of his entire career at Brice's Crossroads in Mississippi, defeating and utterly routing a Union force twice the size of his own.

According to Grenfell, Stanton closed the interview by proposing that he enter the Union army, an offer which he declined.[36] But Frederick Hall told a different story on the witness stand. Grenfell, he said, remarked to Stanton that he "did not in any way hold himself bound to the confederate government; that he was perfectly willing to enter the service of the federal government . . . [and] that he was willing to take the oath of amnesty." [37]

[35] Freeman, *R. E. Lee*, III, 397.
[36] Grenfell to "His Excellency The British Ambassador to Washington," April 4, 1865, in British Legation-Archives, FO 115/448.
[37] *House Executive Documents*, 63.

Granting that Hall gave a truthful report of Grenfell's offer to change his allegiance, historical truth requires that the fact be recorded. To explain it, much less to extenuate it, is impossible. It must stand as the blackest mark on Grenfell's record. How Stanton reacted to the offer has not been reported; no doubt it gave him Grenfell's measure, and it is clear from the sequel that it left him with an ineradicable impression that Grenfell was capable of any baseness. He certainly did not accept the offer; the day when the Union had need of the services of foreign soldiers of fortune was long past. And so Stanton allowed Grenfell to go his way. As a British subject, and on his promise—which must be carefully noted —to give no further aid to the Confederacy, he was told that he was free to travel where he pleased, without supervision and without having to report to the military authorities wherever he happened to be, and he was probably not asked to take the amnesty oath.[38]

The interview over, Grenfell walked out of the War Department, doubtless congratulating himself on having duped the secretary to the hilt. Three years later, he was in the habit of entertaining his guards and fellow prisoners with the story of his interview with Stanton. He dwelt with much complacency on his success in misleading the gullible secretary by supplying him with false information.[39] The complacency was badly misplaced, for this interview with Stanton proved to be the costliest "triumph" of Grenfell's life.[40]

[38] Grenfell stated on two occasions that he had taken the amnesty oath: in a letter of April 6, 1866, to General B. H. Hill (*House Executive Documents*, 639); and earlier, in a letter of April 4, 1865, to the British "Ambassador" in Washington, in British Legation-Archives, FO 115/448.

[39] "A. O'D.," "Thirty Months at the Dry Tortugas," *Galaxy*, VII (February, 1869), 287.

[40] Grenfell later claimed that before leaving Washington, he called on Secretary of State Seward and on President Lincoln—for example, in a letter of July 18, 1864, to his daughter, Marie, in Weaks (ed.), "Colonel . . . Grenfell," 11. He may well have done so, for both the secretary of state and the President made themselves accessible to the public. The account of the Grenfell-Stanton interview, as shown by the contemporary record and as given by Hall in his testimony at Grenfell's trial, is so explicit that it is impossible to credit the statement made by Hines and Castleman twenty years later that it was Secretary Seward who "agreed

131

Grenfell and Fitzgerald Ross met again in Washington and went on together to Baltimore, where they called on the British consul, Frederic Bernal. After a brief stay, they proceeded to New York, and then joined a party of sportsmen with whom they wandered about in the Saratoga-Adirondacks region on a leisurely hunting and fishing excursion which took them in early July to Niagara Falls, where they crossed to the Canadian side and put up at the Clifton Hotel. Ross wrote that they found at the Falls "a number of Morgan's men who were delighted to see their old colonel again." [41] Grenfell and his friends were at Niagara Falls when Horace Greeley conducted his farcical "peace negotiations" with Clement C. Clay, one of the Confederate commissioners in Canada, and it was probably here that Hines and Grenfell again met.

After the foreordained collapse of Greeley's peace conference, the participants and spectators went their various ways. Grenfell left the Ross party and went to Montreal, where he arrived on July 15 or 16, and after a stay of a few days, went west again, to fish at Collingwood on Georgian Bay. Before leaving Montreal, he wrote his daughter, Marie: "You will not see me in England for the present. There is still work to be done and I am awaiting events." [42] The significance of these cryptic sentences is underscored by a brief note he sent from Collingwood two weeks later. The note is addressed to Hines under the alias "Hunter" which the latter used in a somewhat puerile effort to cover up his conspiratorial activities. Grenfell wrote "Hunter" that he was about to try the fishing further west, at Thornbury and Owen Sound, and closed with the meaningful request, "If any news, write immediately." [43]

---

that [Grenfell] should not be arrested on his pledging himself to give no further aid to the Confederate cause." Thomas Henry Hines, "The Northwestern Conspiracy," *Southern Bivouac*, N.S., II (March, 1887), 571.

[41] Ross, *Cities and Camps*, 227.

[42] Grenfell to Marie Pearce-Serocold, July 18, 1864, in Weaks (ed.), "Colonel . . . Grenfell," 9.

[43] Grenfell to "Hunter," (Hines), July 31, 1864, in Hines Papers.

Chapter VIII

IT IS NOW NECESSARY to digress from the story of Grenfell's life in order to recount the background and history of the Northwest Conspiracy, in which he became involved with tragic consequences for himself.

The breakup of the traditional habits and customs of the western world by the American and French revolutions and by the long turmoil of the Napoleonic Wars prepared the way for a yeasty flood of novel ideas and emotions. All areas of thought, all fields of human endeavor, all facets of the relations of men with each other and with the world about them were affected. New ideologies and systems filled the air with confident promises of an instant and inevitable millennium. "Progress" became the magic word. The human spirit, infinitely powerful, was about to create a perfect world. All existing institutions were about to be reformed or, better still, replaced. The word "impossible" lost its meaning, and a host of self-intoxicated enthusiasts, each with his own magic key to a flawless world, clamored for attention.

In this feverish time, churning with new ideas, there were scores of charlatans and feather-brained zealots abroad in the land for every true prophet. The United States especially, with its fluid and self-conscious society, became a paradise for quacks of all kinds and the home of exalted "movements" on all conceivable subjects. Every day saw the foundation of a new society dedicated to the improvement of something or the eradication of yet another evil. New cults, religious sects, brotherhoods, communities flourished, and no self-anointed prophet, however questionable his credentials and however absurd his nostrums, lacked a band of devoted disciples.

One of the strangest of the new breed of prophets was Dr. George Washington Lamb Bickley.[1] A native of Virginia, who had already published a well-written history of his home county and a luridly romantic novel, he moved to Cincinnati and became a professor of its Eclectic Medical Institute. Teaching three subjects at the institute and attending to his medical practice absorbed only a portion of Bickley's superabundant energies. He edited a literary periodical, wrote medical texts, contributed articles to and helped edit the *Eclectic Medical Journal*, lectured on forensic medicine to law students, made known his views on the questions of the day in a barrage of letters to the local newspapers, speculated in land, and maintained a lively interest in many of the fraternal organizations which flourished at the time. In 1853 he founded a fraternal organization of his own, the Wayne Circle of the Brotherhood of the Union, dedicated, he said, to fostering a constitutional Union, perpetuating American history, and furthering the dignity of labor.

The year 1859 saw the start of the great work of Bickley's career. Inspired by the filibustering activities of another medical man, William S. Walker, he founded the Knights of the Golden Circle.[2] Ever since the close of the Mexican War, the doctrine of Manifest Destiny had been one of the shibboleths of the Democratic Party. Southern Democrats, who dominated the party, convinced that slavery had to expand to survive and faced with the unsuitability of the West for an economy based on slave labor,

[1] The résumé of Bickley's career which follows is based on Ollinger Crenshaw, "The Knights of the Golden Circle," *American Historical Review*, XLVII (October, 1941), 23–50.

[2] *Ibid.*, 26. Another authority on the history of subversive organizations during the Civil War states that Bickley founded the KGC in 1854. Mayo Fesler, "Secret Political Societies in the North During the Civil War," *Indiana Magazine of History*, XIV (September, 1918), 190.

held that in order to increase slave territory, the United States had to take over the huge territory between the Rio Grande and the Isthmus of Panama, with Cuba thrown in for good measure; the more hot-blooded believers in Manifest Destiny favored the annexation of all of South America as well. Any Central or South American country that had the lack of vision and the bad judgment to resist absorption into the United States was to be "Texasized." The Knights of the Golden Circle was to be the vehicle for accomplishing this grand design.

A Cincinnati newspaperman, clearly not one of Bickley's admirers, wrote that the effervescent doctor proposed to march into Latin America "carrying the Bible, the pocket-pistol, negro slavery and other blessings of civilization" in his train.[3] Bickley himself claimed that his objectives were in the best American tradition. He pointed out: "We commenced the filibustering at Plymouth Rock . . . and under the leadership of the Pilgrim Fathers . . . we filibustered the red men out of their ancestral domain."[4]

In keeping with the spirit of the times, Bickley provided the Knights with an elaborately symmetrical constitution, as well as a ritual replete with oaths and secrets. All Southerners of good character were eligible for membership. They were to advance in the order through three degrees or divisions, each of which was to consist of two "classes." One class of the lowest, or military degree, was named the "Foreign Guard," to be made up of "such worthy and eligible men who wish to participate in the wild, glorious and thrilling adventure of a campaign in Mexico." The order was to have its own army, whose organization and equipment, down to the last gaiter button, were carefully prescribed, and whose commander was to be none other than Bickley himself, his doctorate transmuted into the rank of major general.

For a generation preceding 1859, slavery in its moral aspects, and the vastly complex problems associated with it, had been absorbing an ever-greater share of national attention, and the debates

[3] Crenshaw, "The Knights of the Golden Circle," 33.
[4] Bickley to Edwin M. Stanton, January 16, 1865; quoted in Fesler, "Secret Political Societies," 193.

on these issues had been growing more and more acrimonious. The South deemed itself threatened. It became convinced that its long dominance of the national government was being eroded and that it faced a destruction of its way of life. Many Southerners, living in an uneasy atmosphere of what they conceived to be menace from without, were ready to respond to almost any Pied Piper who seemed to offer a way out of their predicament. The grandiloquent, plausible Bickley was in complete harmony with the times. His fuzzy doctrines were pure moonshine, but the audience to which they were addressed was short on discrimination and scepticism, and so, for a time, Bickley and his dizzy gospel flourished like the green bay tree. His "program" was well received, especially in the more recently settled sections of the South. He promised that the conquest of Mexico alone would produce the perpetual domination of national affairs by the South. Even his most esoteric pronouncements, for example, his solemn declaration that all civilization was the product of war, were widely publicized in the southern press and met with enthusiastic acquiescence.[5] What dissent there was, was silenced in 1860 when Bickley broadened his goals by advocating secession; he announced in April, 1860, that "the KGC may find its Mexico in the District of Columbia."[6] He boasted in the same year, and apparently with justice, that there were sixty-five thousand Knights, including the "brains" of the South, all but three of the slave state governors, and several members of President Buchanan's cabinet.[7]

Bickley's prewar following was not by any means confined to the South. While he was still beating the drum for Manifest Destiny, his doctrines won him a considerable following in the North also, especially in Ohio, Indiana, and Illinois. These three states contained large blocks of settlers who (or whose immediate forebears) had migrated there from the South, as had Bickley himself. The 1860 Census listed 179,000 residents of Illinois, 161,000 of Indiana, and 134,000 of Ohio as born in the slave states; indeed, it

---

[5] Crenshaw, "The Knights of the Golden Circle," 33.
[6] Fesler, "Secret Political Societies," 195.
[7] Crenshaw, "The Knights of the Golden Circle," 40.

has been estimated on the basis of the same census that fully 40 percent of the inhabitants of the midwestern states were of southern birth or parentage.[8] These people were largely Democratic in politics and southern in their sympathies and attitudes.

The South did not possess a monopoly of the "addiction to oaths, grips, passwords, secret signs of recognition and hidden meeting places" so popular in the middle years of the century.[9] Many organizations of a political tinge, dedicated to exalted programs of varying degrees of absurdity, were in the field and provided an outlet for such tastes. The KGC was the largest and most active of these societies, and there probably was truth in its claim of a membership of many thousands in Ohio, Indiana, Illinois, and the contiguous Border States before the outbreak of the Civil War.[10]

Among large groups of people in Ohio, Indiana, and Illinois, the "Abolition War," or "Nigger Crusade," as they called it, was intensely unpopular from the start. These dissidents were welcomed as recruits by the KGC, whose "castles" were a ready-made nucleus of disaffection and a haven for all those opposed to the war. Laying aside the advocacy of Manifest Destiny and capitalizing on antiwar feeling and increasingly bitter opposition to the Republican administration, the KGC formed new castles and enlisted members throughout this area, and with such success that in some counties of Illinois and Indiana all local officials were members of the order. Nor was it very long before some, and perhaps many, of the Knights crossed the indistinct line that, in a civil war, separates legitimate partisanship from treason. To abet insubordination in and desertion from the northern armies, to discourage volunteering, resist the bitterly hated draft, impede the collection of taxes, shelter deserters and bushwhackers, aid es-

[8] Wood Gray, *The Hidden Civil War: The Story of the Copperheads* (New York, 1942), 21.

[9] George Fort Milton, *Abraham Lincoln and the Fifth Column* (New York, 1942), 65.

[10] Reference will be made later in these notes to the views of Professor Frank L. Klement, who holds that there were no castles of the KGC in the northern states.

caped Confederate prisoners of war, circulate disloyal publications, supply the enemy with arms, medicines and information, and thwart the national government and the northern war effort in every possible way became the objects of the organization and of its members.[11] In areas in which they were in a safe majority, guerilla bands of Copperheads, as they came to be called, terrorized their loyal neighbors by methods successfully imitated by the Ku Klux Klan after the war.[12]

Officially, the Knights claimed, and no doubt many of its members believed, that, as an organization, they had no objectives that were not wholly legal, to wit, to protect the rights of Democrats, to uphold the liberties of the citizen against the encroachments of a dictatorial government, and to "preserve the freedom of the ballot against the tyrannical Republicans and their gendarmes."[13] The KGC had its share of the persecution complex that is a common characteristic of minority groups professing unpopular views, and the repressive measures of the administration provided the more radical elements in the KGC with an excuse to intensify their illegal and treasonable activities. The castles met in secret, in woods, barns, abandoned buildings and quarries; quite naturally, their secretiveness created exaggerated notions of the numbers and power of the KGC. Unquestionably, the Knights were responsible for a certain amount of violence, especially in resistance to the draft; enrolling officers were killed from ambush, enrollment papers were destroyed, and those subject to the draft were encouraged to resist or escape, but the Knights were also blamed unjustly for much unorganized spontaneous resistance to the war.[14] Nonetheless, there is little doubt that their activities

[11] Judge Advocate General Joseph Holt to Edwin M. Stanton, October 8, 1864, in Office of the Judge Advocate General, General Courts-Martial, 1812–1938, MM-2185, Boxes 675-7, War Records, National Archives. See also Milton, *Lincoln and the Fifth Column*, 87.
[12] Edward Conrad Smith, *The Borderland in the Civil War* (New York, 1927), 341.
[13] Bethania Meradith Smith, "Civil War Subversives," *Journal of the Illinois State Historical Society*, XLV (1952), 222.
[14] Fesler, "Secret Political Societies," 210.

were a source of embarrassment to the national government and a hindrance to the northern war effort.

Lacking a strong central organization and leadership, the KGC lost much of its effectiveness by the summer of 1863, and a new, more aggressive organization, named the Order of American Knights, came into being to serve as a vehicle to what may be called the underground opposition to the war. The OAK was the brainchild of Phineas C. Wright, a St. Louis lawyer and newspaperman, who had migrated there from New Orleans. When it came to getting his hands on Confederate subsidies for his Copperhead newspapers, Wright was practical enough, but he was as much of a mystical romancer and as greatly addicted to ritualistic flummery as Bickley himself. A sample of his efforts in this line is the sign of recognition he provided for members of the OAK. The sign, as described by a former member,

> was made by standing erect on both feet, placing the heel of the right foot in the hollow of the left, with the arms folded. . . . A member of the order noticing me in this posture . . . would place himself in the same position, and challenge me. He would extend his right foot to meet mine, and use the following colloquy: I would say "nu" he would answer "oh" I would reply "lac." . . . In the first degree the sign of recognition was the same except that the index finger of the left hand was placed on the right arm when the arms were folded. We were instructed that this meant State rights and State sovereignty.[15]

It will be noted that the three syllables used in this remarkable performance were the name "Calhoun," spelled backward.

A candidate for initiation was presented to the assembled brethren in the following words:

Q: Who cometh? Who cometh? Who cometh?
A: A Man! We found him in the dark ways of the Sons of Folly, bound in chains and well nigh crushed to death beneath the iron heel of the oppressor. We have brought him hither, and would fain clothe him in the white robes of virtue, and place his feet

[15] *House Executive Documents*, 233.

in the straight and narrow path which leads to Truth and Wisdom.[16]

Far more serious than these exalted idiocies was the oath prescribed for initiates into the second degree of the order:

> At all times, if needs be, to take up arms in the cause of the oppressed—in my country first of all—against any monarch, prince, potentate, power or government usurped, which may be found in arms and waging war against a people or peoples who are endeavoring to establish or have inaugurated a government for themselves of their own free choice in accordance with and founded upon the eternal principles of Truth.[17]

It is inconceivable that men of even average intelligence could fail to grasp the full import of this oath. However, two years of a bloody war, the endless casualty lists, the arbitrary acts of the government, and the first steps in the direction of emancipation increased the bitterness of the opposition, and the OAK had no difficulty in attracting members. Many came into the order as it absorbed castles of the moribund KGC; others were attracted by the militancy of the new order.

Unlike the KGC, the OAK had a hierarchy of command. The activities of the local "temples" were controlled and directed, at least in theory, by state councils, each headed by a grand commander. At the peak, and directing the entire movement, was the supreme council. On Washington's birthday, 1864, this body met, and elected Clement L. Vallandigham as supreme grand commander. Vallandigham had been a member of the House of Representatives from Ohio. His unmeasured denunciations of the war had brought about his expulsion from Union territory in the summer of 1863; running for governor of Ohio *in absentia* in the same year, on a peace-at-any price platform, he was defeated by an ominously narrow margin. He was the very symbol of antiwar, antiadministration sentiment, and a logical choice to head the OAK.

Vallandigham was to proclaim in his speeches, and was also to

[16] Benn Pitman (ed.), *The Trials for Treason at Indianapolis, Disclosing the Plans for Establishing a North-Western Confederacy* (Cincinnati, 1865), 297.
[17] *Ibid.*, 330.

testify under oath, that he accepted command of the OAK only after being assured by its leaders that the organization had no ties with the Confederate government and no objectives which were not "legitimate and lawful." [18] The mere fact that he thought it necessary to ask for this assurance suggests that the activities and aims of the order were open to question. Having protected himself, as he was always careful to do, with this show of rectitude, Vallandigham agreed to lead the OAK. The only credible motive for this action was an intention to use the order, together with any other means that came to hand, to force the national government to end the war. His object, he said and evidently believed, was to preserve the Constitution in its pristine purity. The war, in his view, was unconstitutional and had to be halted, if necessary on terms that in effect conceded southern independence. With the distorted logic of a fanatic, Vallandigham was prepared to assist in the destruction of the Union in order to preserve its constitution. Eventually, a due regard for his own safety, or perhaps a belated realization of the only possible outcome of his program, made him draw back from the brink of treason. In the meantime, however, his consent to serve as supreme grand commander gave the OAK a leader of national prominence.

Coincident with the election of Vallandigham, the supreme council, seeking to enhance the popular appeal of the order, changed its name to the more democratic-sounding Sons of Liberty. Moreover, and most significantly, the constitution and bylaws were revised and the order was reorganized along paramilitary lines, a major general being placed in command of each state in which the order was active, and a brigadier general in command of each congressional district.

In the end, all the activity, the turgid ritual, the elaborate constitution, the highly charged indignation, the violent oratory led to precisely nothing. Intemperate language there was in abundance. The Reverend Henry Clay Dean, known to his admirers as "Dirty Shirt" Dean, described President Lincoln as "the monster usurper . . . a felon . . . traitor and tyrant," who had "perjury

[18] James L. Vallandigham, *A Life of Clement L. Vallandigham* (Baltimore, 1872), 373.

141

and larceny . . . written all over him," and whose "cry . . . [was] for ever more blood." [19] Yet when the day came for the Sons of Liberty to make good with deeds on the principles they proclaimed so vociferously in the safety of their temples and meetings, they proved to be as sounding brass or a tinkling cymbal. In certain areas of Indiana and Illinois, where they were in local control and could operate in the safety of numbers, Union men had to sleep with rifles within reach and their houses barricaded for the night.[20] But the courage of the Sons of Liberty was found wanting when the risks became greater. Nevertheless, before they demonstrated that they did not have it in them to translate treasonable talk into overt rebellion, the truculence of their oratory and the carefully fostered exaggerations of their strength made them appear to be a serious menace; actually, they were never more than a noisy, cowardly, squalid nuisance.

With the benefit of hindsight, it is difficult to understand how anyone could have taken the Sons of Liberty seriously. Indeed, some historians dismiss it and other organized manifestations of antiwar, pro-southern sentiment as a myth, invented for their own profit by detectives and *agents provocateurs* in the employ of the government, by partisan, or merely gullible, state governors, and by army officers eager for promotion.[21] It is reasoned that because the average member of the KGC or the OAK or the Sons of Liber-

[19] Frederick F. Cook, *Bygone Days in Chicago* (Chicago, 1910), 84.

[20] Fesler, "Secret Political Societies," 239.

[21] This, basically, is the thesis of Frank L. Klement in *The Copperheads of the Middle West* (Chicago, 1960), a point of view which, with the greatest respect for Dr. Klement's scholarship, the author is unable to accept. Cf. Richard A. Curry, "The Union as It Was: A Critique of Recent Interpretations of the 'Copperheads,'" *Civil War History*, XIII (1967), 25–39; Stephen Z. Starr, "Was There a Northwest Conspiracy?" *Filson Club History Quarterly*, XXXVIII (1964), 323–39. It may be noted also that Klement gives a different account from that in the text of the genesis of the Sons of Liberty. He believes that it was founded in April, 1863, by Harrison H. Dodd, an Indianapolis printer and politician, to serve as a secret auxiliary of the Democratic Party "to 'defend' the Constitution, to preserve civil and individual rights, [and] to win elections." Dr. Klement believes that the organization found "few recruits" and "existed more on paper than in practice"; he holds that the OAK, founded by Wright, was an entirely distinct, unrelated organization. Klement, *The Copperheads*, 161–69.

ty was a harmless paterfamilias, a bleating sheep masquerading in wolf's clothing, the entire movement was nothing more than a somewhat exaggerated manifestation of ordinary political partisanship. Nothing could be further from the truth. Their members were driven by hatred of the war and a pathological fear of the Negro-miscegenation is an ever-recurring theme in Copperhead speeches—and the Sons of Liberty were potentially a serious threat to the survival of the Union. On February 16, 1864, the grand commander of the OAK in Indiana, spoke thus to the state convention of the order:

> Ours is the noble work of preserving the States from ruin and the races from intermixture. . . . I will not agree to remain passive under usurped authority. . . . Shall men be coerced to go to war for emancipation, miscegenation and confiscation? . . . The day is rapidly approaching in which you can make good your promise to your country. The furnace is being heated that will prove your sincerity; the hour for daring deeds is not distant.[22]

The strength of antiwar, antiadministration sentiment in the "Old Northwest" was beyond question; three months after the Union victories at Gettysburg and Vicksburg, Vallandigham received 39 percent of the votes cast in his race for governor of Ohio; and in Indiana and Illinois, opponents of the war were relatively even stronger. The question was how large a segment of this opposition was legitimately political in its motivation and aims, and how much of it teetered on the ragged edge of treason. Beyond this, there were two further questions: whether the Copperheads had the determined leadership to complement their numerical strength, and how far their leadership was willing to go in the direction of outright armed rebellion.

In the winter of 1863, with the war about to enter its fourth year, the national government, on the basis of the information it then had, believed the OAK and the Copperheads generally to be a formidable menace; it could not then know that the entire

---

[22] Pitman, *Trials for Treason*, 317-18.

movement would prove to be a hollow shell.[23] The means the Confederate government had for assessing the extent and force of Copperhead sentiment were even less trustworthy; moreover, the conclusions that it was able to draw from the information it had were colored by a great degree of wishful thinking. Therefore, when Thomas Henry Hines, former cavalry captain, director of a spectacular prison escape, a man with extensive contacts with the disaffected elements in the Northwestern and Border States, arrived in Richmond in February, 1864, with a letter of introduction from Morgan to President Davis and what appeared to be a well-considered plan for utilizing northern opposition to the war for the advantage of the Confederacy, the Richmond authorities were prepared to give him an attentive hearing. After a year of disastrous defeats, with all hope of foreign recognition gone, facing the exhaustion of its resources for carrying on the war, the Confederate government was eager to believe reports crediting the OAK with several hundred thousand members ready and willing to follow their leaders in any enterprise aimed at ending the hated Abolition War; the Davis administration was prepared to support any program that promised to set the spark to what seemed to be an explosive situation in the very heart of the Union.

President Davis, Secretary of War Seddon, and Secretary of State Benjamin, all of whom met repeatedly with Hines, had been informed by Confederate agents in the North that the leaders of the OAK, or Sons of Liberty, as it now became, had a plan that would end the war and confirm southern independence. The Copperheads, it was reported, were planning an armed insurrection to take over the state governments in Ohio, Indiana, Illinois, and Missouri; the new governments would then join to form a Northwestern Confederacy, withdraw from the war, and separate from the Union. The logic of geography and economics would then force Michigan, Wisconsin, Minnesota, Iowa, and Kansas to withdraw from the war also and join the new "nation."

[23] In the report cited in note 11 above, Judge Advocate General Holt credited the OAK with a membership of 500,000. We know now that Holt's estimate was far too large, but the important fact is that he and his superiors believed the 500,000 figure to be accurate and acted on that belief.

The idea of a Northwestern Confederacy was not new. It had been discussed sixty years before by Aaron Burr's follower, Harman Blennerhassett.[24] In 1859, in one of his most eloquent speeches, Vallandigham prophesied that the secession of the South would lead to the formation of a confederation of the northwestern states; in his last speech in Congress, after the war had already begun, he expressed the conviction that

> if you from the East, who have found this war against the South, and for the negro, gratifying to your hate or profitable to your purse, will continue it till a separation be forced between the . . . States, then, believe me, . . . the day which divides the North from the South . . . decrees eternal divorce between the West and the East . . . we will not remain, after separation from the South, a province . . . of the East, to bear her burdens and pay her taxes; nor, hemmed in and isolated as we are, and without a sea-coast, could we long remain a distinct confederacy.[25]

Vallandigham thus voiced more than the threat of a second secession; he foreshadowed the possibility that the Northwest, having followed the South into secession, would eventually join with it to form a union of agrarian states. Without going quite so far, numerous editorials in Democratic newspapers and resolutions adopted by local Democratic organizations in the northwestern states in 1863 and 1864, rang the changes on the same theme, in a peculiar combination of antiwar feeling and economic grievances: "Our interests and our inclinations will demand of us a withdrawal from political association in a common government with the New England States, who have contributed so much to every innovation upon the constitution, to our present calamity of civil war, and

[24] In 1806 Blennerhassett published a series of articles in the Marietta *Ohio Gazette* to explain that the federal government, controlled by the commercial East, exploited the agricultural West through its land, taxation, and trade policies. He proposed a separation of the sections as the only practicable remedy; he wrote that the western states had as much right to redress their grievances by means of such a separation as did the thirteen colonies when they separated from England. Thomas Perkins Abernethy, "Aaron Burr at Blennerhassett Island and in Ohio," *Bulletin of the Historical and Philosophical Society of Ohio*, XII (1954), 3–16.
[25] Speech of January 14, 1863, quoted in *Biographical Memoir of Clement L. Vallandigham, by his Brother* (New York, 1864), 60.

145

whose tariff legislation must ever prove oppressive to our agricultural and commercial pursuits." [26]

The Confederacy too had had the same happy (from its point of view) inspiration. One of the hopes, no more illusory than the others on which secession was based, "was the separation of the northwestern States from the Union and either the organization of these States into a Northwest Confederacy in alliance with the South or their admission into the Southern Confederacy." [27]

In the light of the Confederacy's grim prospects at the beginning of 1864, the plans of a Copperhead uprising as they were understood in Richmond, seemed attractive indeed. Even if the rising failed to bring about the creation of a Northwest Confederacy, a widespread insurrection in the heartland of the Union and the withdrawal from the field of the military forces needed to deal with it, would paralyze the northern war effort and would render impossible the prosecution of the war for months and perhaps forever; at the very least, the Confederacy would gain a desperately needed breathing space. Moreover, any such insurrection, even if ultimately unsuccessful, would dishearten and demoralize the troops from the northwestern states, the only component of the Union armies that the South believed had done any real fighting in the war. And if there were a second secession, one which did not carry the stigma of being based on a desire to perpetuate slavery, the moral advantage which the North enjoyed in the eyes of the world would be utterly destroyed. The greatly wished-for recognition of the Confederacy by the European powers and the irretrievable collapse of the northern effort to reconstitute the Union by force of arms would then inevitably follow.

Hines undertook to supply the one ingredient needed to make certain the success of the Copperhead plan, an idea that he said had

[26] Resolution of the Brown County, Indiana, Democratic convention, quoted in Gray, *The Hidden Civil War*, 125. Similar resolutions, so like each other as to suggest a common origin, were passed by at least fifteen other counties of Indiana in January, February, and March, 1863. William C. Cochran, "The Dream of a Northwestern Confederacy," *Publications of the State Historical Society of Wisconsin, 1916* (Madison, 1917), 242.

[27] Fesler, "Secret Political Societies," 241.

first occurred to him in December, 1863.[28] Between thirty thousand and fifty thousand Confederate prisoners of war were confined in northern prison camps, the largest of which were located in Illinois, Indiana, and Ohio—that is, in three of the four states where the Copperheads were strongest and in which they intended to raise the flag of rebellion. Hines proposed to go to Canada to collect and organize into an effective force the hundreds of Confederate officers and soldiers, mostly escaped prisoners of war and many of them former members of Morgan's command, who had found sanctuary under the British flag. With this force as a spearhead and with the armed help of the Sons of Liberty, he would free the prisoners of war in Illinois, Indiana, and Ohio. The liberated prisoners could readily be armed and equipped from the contents of captured Federal depots and arsenals located in these states; they would then be ready either to remain in the North to assure the success of the Copperhead revolt or to march South, doing all the damage possible on the way, to become a major accession of strength for the attenuated Confederate armies facing Grant and Sherman. If Hines succeeded in accomplishing only a part of what he promised, the effect on the fortunes of the South would be incalculable. The potential rewards were tremendous, and the risks, from the Confederate standpoint, negligible.

Hines is not the sole claimant to the distinction of having had the inspiration to combine into a single project the freeing of prisoners of war and a Copperhead uprising. An article written thirty years after the war states that the idea occurred in early 1864 to someone in the Army of Tennessee.

Who first conceived the plan is not known, but someone suggested that if there could be a release of prisoners in the Northwest, and an uprising simultaneously of the Northern friends of the Confederacy, Sherman would never reach the coast. . . . The more daring officers thought it might be possible, and among them was Colonel Vincent Marmaduke . . . one of the most dashing officers of the Southern service. The matter was discussed with General Hood,

[28] Thomas Henry Hines, "Autobiographic Notes on the North Western Conspiracy." MS. in Hines Papers.

and the end was that General Hood told Marmaduke that he would send him to Richmond . . . to confer with Jefferson Davis and his Cabinet. . . . Marmaduke at once made a visit to the Confederate capital. At first the undertaking was not favorably looked upon . . . but . . . [Davis] agreed to consider it. . . . He conferred with his Cabinet and . . . gave his consent to the venture, at the same time directing the Secretary of War to give the Colonel all requisite authority for the northern trip.[29]

One of the many riddles of what came to be known as the "Chicago Conspiracy" is the nature and extent of Marmaduke's participation in it and of his relationship to Hines, but it is at least certain that the role given him in the above account is incorrect. General Hood did not become a corps commander in the Army of Tennessee until March 1, 1864, and if he sent Marmaduke to Richmond with this plan, Marmaduke did not get there until three weeks or more after Hines, as Grenfell reported to Morgan, had already been charged with the project. Thus, the priority clearly belongs to Hines, and insofar as the records indicate, he was the only one formally authorized by the Confederate government to act on the plan.

After exhaustive discussions of the ways and means, Secretary Seddon gave Hines written instructions on March 16. He was ordered to proceed to Canada,

for the purpose of collecting there the men of General Morgan's command. . . . In passing through the United States . . . [he] will confer with the leading persons friendly or attached to the cause of the Confederacy, or who may be advocates of peace, and do all in [his] power to induce our friends to organize and prepare themselves to render such aid as circumstances may allow. . . . [He] will likewise have in view the possibility, by such means as [he] can command, of effecting any fair and appropriate enterprises of war against our enemies.[30]

By the very nature of his assignment, Hines could be given neither specific objectives nor precise directions as to the means he was to

[29] Stanley Waterloo, "The Chicago Conspiracy," *Nickell Magazine*, VII (1897), 133–34.
[30] MS. copy in Hines Papers. See also Hines, "Autobiographic Notes," in *ibid*.

employ to achieve them. In dealing with an uncertain situation, the Confederate government had to rely for success on Hines's ability to use whatever tools came to hand and on his resourcefulness and readiness to take advantage of every opportunity that came his way. To obtain the funds he needed, Hines had to arrange to sell in the North two hundred bales of cotton that were assigned to him to finance his operations. With the proceeds in greenbacks in his pocket, he crossed the Potomac at night; he reached Toronto about April 20 by way of Washington, Cincinnati, and Detroit and set to work at once to make contact with the Copperhead leaders in the Northwest.

Within a month of his arrival in Canada, Hines learned that he was not to have a free hand in carrying out his project. Near the end of May, a Confederate "Commission," consisting of Jacob Thompson, former United States senator from Mississippi and secretary of the interior in President Buchanan's cabinet as chairman, and another former United States senator, Clement Clay of Alabama, arrived in Montreal; the third commissioner, James P. Holcomb of Virginia, was already there. It is not without significance that Thompson and Vallandigham were good friends.[31] Thompson was given his instructions by President Davis himself; they were never entrusted to paper but were evidently the political counterpart and, in a sense, the diplomatically respectable front for Hines's assignment.[32] Under the cloak of a scrupulous, if only outward, respect for British neutrality, the commissioners were to establish relations with the disaffected elements in the northern states in order to help crystallize antiadministration and antiwar feeling towards finding an active expression in the form of an armed insurrection and the establishment, with the aid of the

[31] Robin W. Winks, *Canada and the United States: The Civil War Years* (Baltimore, 1960), 272.

[32] Thompson's commission, signed by President Davis, read: "Confiding special trust in your zeal, discretion and patriotism, I hereby direct you to proceed at once to Canada, there to carry out such instructions as you have received from me verbally, in such manner as shall seem most likely to conduce to the furtherance of the interests of the Confederate States of America which have been intrusted to you." Quoted in Wilfrid Bovey, "Confederate Agents in Canada during the American Civil War," *Canadian Historical Review*, II (1921), 47.

prisoners of war freed by Hines, of a Northwestern Confederacy. The large sum of $800,000 in greenbacks was given the commission to finance its operations, and Hines was ordered to work under Thompson's supervision and direction.[33]

The moment for initiating these activities was well chosen. The Union victories of the summer of 1863 had been succeeded by reverses which weakened northern morale and damaged the prestige of the government. After a winter of inaction, military operations resumed at the beginning of May, but the high hopes with which the spring campaigns began ended in disappointment and discouragement. Sherman seemed unable to bring to bay Johnston's Army of Tennessee, barring the road to Atlanta. Grant sustained enormous losses but failed to destroy Lee's greatly outnumbered army, and he could not even prevent him from detaching Jubal Early's corps for a campaign that brought the Confederates to the outskirts of Washington. Crook's, Sigel's, and Butler's campaigns were ignominious failures. The toll of casualties grew larger day by day. Lincoln called for a draft of 500,000 more men. With military victory as distant as ever, the North was in the grip of war weariness and despondency. Bitter resentment was aroused by emancipation, the flouting of civil rights by the government, the draft with its commutation clause favoring the rich, and the enlistment of Negroes in the Union army.

The Border States were on the verge of open revolt. In Kentucky, where the President had to suspend habeas corpus and declare martial law, outbreaks of armed violence were an almost daily occurrence; Missouri was about to be invaded by General Sterling Price, in the expectation of powerful Copperhead support. Throughout the North, the advocates of peace at any price, the pro-southern elements, the uncompromising opponents of the war, and those whose partisan bitterness made them willing to accept disunion as preferable to a victory won by a Republican administration, took heart. Even the unquestionably loyal now seemed receptive to the idea of ending the war on some basis short

[33] James A. Seddon to Thomas Henry Hines, April 27, 1864, in Hines Papers.

of a northern victory, perhaps by the recognition of southern independence or by the negotiation of a year's armistice during which a settlement acceptable to both sides might be hammered out. An ominous movement to replace President Lincoln with General Frémont seemed to be gathering support, and the President, not easily given to discouragement, was shortly to write: "This morning, as for some days past, it seems exceedingly probable that this administration will not be reelected. Then it will be my duty to so cooperate with the President-elect as to save the Union between the election and the inauguration; as he will have secured his election on such ground that he cannot possibly save it afterward." [34]

[34] Carl Sandburg, *Abraham Lincoln: The War Years* (New York, 1939), III. 213. Lincoln's note is dated August 23, 1864.

Chapter IX

I T WAS IN this atmosphere, so ominous for the future of the Union and so auspicious for the success of his project, that Hines began to shape concrete plans.

When Stephen A. Douglas died in June, 1861, he left as a part of his estate a large block of land about three miles south of the center of Chicago and about two hundred yards west of Lake Michigan. In the early months of the war, the land had been used as a "camp of rendezvous and instruction" for newly enlisted Illinois regiments, and was named Camp Douglas in honor of its illustrious owner. When Grant captured Fort Donelson in early 1862 and the North had its first large catch of prisoners, a sixty-five-acre portion of the land was set aside for use as a prisoner of war camp.[1] Five thousand of the Fort Donelson captives were shipped to Chicago and confined at Camp Douglas within the dubious security of a flimsy wooden fence and under the custody of a detail of Chicago police. Barracks to house the prisoners were constructed on six-foot-high piles to prevent tunneling; the original fence was replaced by a sturdy stockade of thick oak boards thirteen feet high and garnished with a parapet for sentries; and soldiers, usually paroled prisoners awaiting exchange, replaced the

[1] The camp was located near the intersection of what are now Thirty-fourth Street and Cottage Grove Avenue, a short distance north of the University of Chicago campus.

police guard.[2] The prisoner population varied from five to twelve thousand; in the summer of 1864, it stood at about eight thousand, guarded by a poorly armed garrison of between eight hundred and a thousand soldiers of the Eighth and Fifteenth regiments of the Veteran Reserve Corps, mostly men who had been incapacitated for service in the field by wounds or illness.[3]

A century later, it is difficult to picture the squalor of a prisoner of war camp of the Civil War era. An inspection of Camp Douglas in October, 1863, revealed that the prisoners' clothes and persons were filthy—three hydrants were the sole source of water for the nearly 7,100 prisoners and guards then in the camp.[4] The unheated, jerry-built barracks were in a ruinous condition. The 6,085 prisoners, 1,200 of whom were without blankets, were huddled together in accommodations built to house 4,500. The grounds, swampy and undrained, were in a "simply filthy" condition. The sanitary facilities were indescribably bad. In the following summer, because of the energetic work of a new camp commandant, major changes for the better were effected. The grounds were cleaned and drained, the barracks were rebuilt and whitewashed, additional water lines were laid, and weekly inspections were instituted. Notwithstanding these improvements, the incidence of sickness and the mortality rate were shockingly high; in September, 1864, well before the onset of winter, in a total prisoner population of 7,402 there were 123 deaths and 1,357 were on the sick list.[5] It is not surprising that the unfortunate prisoners were "restive and inventive in an uncommon degree." [6]

Since most of the Camp Douglas prisoners were from the western armies of the Confederacy, a high percentage of them were Kentuckians, Texans, and Tennesseans, including a large sprinkling of Morgan's former troopers. Hines was confident he could count on these men, especially the ex-Morgans, to join any enterprise,

[2] E. B. Tuttle, *The History of Camp Douglas* (Chicago, 1865), 5 ff.; *cf.* Cook, *Bygone Days*, 43.
[3] *OR*, Series II, Vol. VII, 187.
[4] *OR*, Series II, Vol. VI, 372–73.
[5] *OR*, Series II, Vol. VII, 954.
[6] *Ibid.*, 681.

however desperate, that offered them a hope of freedom. Hines's belief was fully justified, for Morgan's men were almost always the ringleaders in the chronic disciplinary difficulties in the inadequately guarded camp and in the frequent escape attempts, many of which were successful.[7]

These facts, well known on the outside, made Camp Douglas the obvious choice as the first camp to be attacked. Another important fact pointed in the same direction. The Copperhead movement appeared to be more widespread and stronger in Illinois than in any other state, with the possible exception of Indiana. The Sons of Liberty claimed to have a large membership in Central and Southern Illinois, and Chicago itself was a hotbed of Copperhead sentiment; thousands of Kentuckians had migrated to the rapidly growing city, and they, and the Irish immigrants in Chicago, had joined the Sons of Liberty in large numbers.[8] It was said that the order had five thousand members in the city, well organized, well armed, and well led, and the down-state lodges could supply large reinforcements easily and quickly.

The third fact pointing to Chicago as Hines's best target was its status as a relatively large city, a center of transportation and commerce, where the arrival of large numbers of strangers would go unnoticed. And here Hines had a fortunate coincidence handed to him ready made; 1864 was a presidential year and the Democratic National Convention was to be held in Chicago starting on July 4. Thousands of delegates and visitors would converge on the city for the convention, and the arrival at the same time of a few dozen Confederates from Canada and of several hundred, or even several thousand, Sons of Liberty from down-state Illinois would cause hardly a ripple. Thus, Chicago was the logical choice as the place, and the beginning of July as the time for the opening move in Hines's project, and his decision on these two points was practically made for him.

[7] *OR*, Series II, Vol. VI, 637–38, and Vol. VII, 104, 595.
[8] Fesler, "Secret Political Societies," 240–41. Buckner S. Morris, second mayor of Chicago and one of Grenfell's co-defendants in the Cincinnati trial, was a native of Augusta, Kentucky.

Next in importance was to arrange for the participation of the Sons of Liberty. Hines determined to start at the top and on June 9, he had a preliminary interview with Clement Vallandigham, at the latter's place of exile in Windsor, Ontario. Vallandigham's response to Hines's proposals must have been encouraging, for two days later a full-fledged council of war was held, Jacob Thompson and Hines representing the Confederacy, and Vallandigham, assisted by several leaders of the Sons of Liberty, acting as spokesman for the Copperheads. Thompson and Hines were told that the order had 300,000 members, 85,000 in Illinois, 50,000 in Indiana, and 40,000 in Ohio, many of whom, having served out their terms of enlistment in the Union army, were trained soldiers. All of them, Vallandigham said, were ready to participate at his command in an armed uprising to take over the governments of their respective states as a first step toward the establishment of a Northwestern Confederacy.[9] All that was lacking was money for arms and miscellaneous expenses.

Unlimited self-assurance, the certainty that they possessed a huge and devoted following eager to go into action at their command, and an unfortunate lack of funds have been characteristic of political exiles everywhere and at all times, and it is therefore easy to fault Thompson and Hines for placing complete faith in Vallandigham's claims. Indeed, Hines wrote some years later that Thompson "was inclined to believe much that was told him, trust too many men, doubt too little and suspect less," but it is clear enough that he was no more disposed to question the Copperhead leaders' grandiose claims than was Thompson.[10] His plans were based on his own exaggerated estimate of Copperhead capabilities, and he was expressing *ex post facto* wisdom when he later wrote that he saw through their leaders from the start, but hoped to

[9] Hines, "The Northwestern Conspiracy," 502–506. This series of articles was actually written by John B. Castleman and W. W. Cleary, on the basis of Hines's papers and with his collaboration; Cleary had been secretary of the Confederate commission in Canada. *Cf.* Jacob Thompson to Secretary of State Benjamin, December 3, 1864. *OR,* Vol. XLIII, Part II, 930–31.
[10] Hines, "The Northwestern Conspiracy," 502.

compromise them into overt rebellion.[11] His contemporary letters clearly indicate that he shared Thompson's confidence in the ability of Vallandigham and his associates to make good on their promises of effective support.

At all events, the conferees came to an understanding without difficulty. It was settled that there was to be an uprising, and that it was to take place in Chicago on July 4. Charles Walsh, the brigadier general of the Sons of Liberty in Chicago, undertook to have ready for the day a well-armed force of two thousand of his most reliable followers, backed by a large number of down-state members of the order to be brought to the city to assist. The rank and file were to be told that they were being assembled to protect the Democratic convention from interference by Federal troops. The attack on Camp Douglas was to be led by Hines and spearheaded by about a hundred Confederate soldiers brought in from Toronto. Confederate Captain Charles H. Cole was to investigate the feasibility of capturing the gunboat *Michigan*, so that its guns could be used to support the attack on the camp.[12] As a diversion, John Castleman was to lead a second group of Confederate soldiers from Canada to free the prisoners of war in the camp at Rock Island, Illinois, and, simultaneously with the attacks on the two camps, the Copperheads were to seize the machinery of state government in Illinois, Indiana, and Ohio.

Upon his return to Toronto from the June 11 meeting, Hines sent Secretary Seddon a full report of the plans that had been agreed upon and announced, on a premature note of optimism, that "we hope to make a certainty of releasing the prisoners." [13] Not until twenty years later did he write—or realize—how much of the program, that should have been worked out in the most minute detail, had been settled only in vague generalities or not settled at all.[14]

[11] This, essentially, is the thesis of the truncated account (it stops short with the failure of the August 29 uprising) of the conspiracy. *Ibid.*

[12] *Ibid.*, 567.

[13] Thomas Henry Hines to James A. Seddon, July 1, 1864, quoted in a second report by Hines to Seddon dated December 15, 1864, in Hines Papers.

[14] Hines, "The Northwestern Conspiracy," 507.

The first hitch in these plans came with the announcement that the Democratic convention was to be postponed from July 4 to August 29. The postponement was decided upon by the leadership of the Democratic Party in the belief that the war was going so badly for the Union and antiadministration feeling was growing so steadily, that it would be advantageous to hold the convention as late as possible. As soon as the postponement was announced, the Copperheads notified Hines and Thompson they wished to defer the uprising until August 29 also. Hines, who had convinced himself that the Copperhead rank and file were eager "to precipitate the conflict" and was rightfully impressed with "the absolute necessity of taking some steps to prevent the threatened advance of Gen. Sherman into the heart of the Confederacy," made a valiant effort to persuade the Sons of Liberty not to wait until August 29, and it appeared that they agreed to his suggestion of July 20 as the starting date.[15] Hardly had they done so, however, when they sent him word that they could not be ready so soon. Thereupon, a meeting was held in Chicago to resolve the situation and, after much discussion, Hines had to accept August 16 as the starting date. It was agreed also that a series of mass meetings was to be held "to prepare the public mind" and that these meetings were to culminate, and the signal for the uprising given, at monster peace meetings in Indianapolis and Chicago on August 16.

The sketchy and none too reliable records that have survived do not permit a reconstruction in precise chronological order of the numerous conclaves of Hines and the Copperhead leadership, or of the sequence of decisions reached in these meetings. It would appear that no sooner had the August 16 date been settled, than the Copperheads decided that this did not allow sufficient time for the extensive preparations they had to make and requested another postponement. On July 22, a meeting was held at St. Catharines, Ontario, to grapple with the problem once more. The Copperhead leaders expressed their willingness to go forward with the "peace meetings," but the uprising was something else again; they now "expressed the fear that unless there was such a movement by

[15] Hines to Seddon, December 15, 1864, in Hines Papers.

157

Confederate forces into Kentucky and Missouri as would occupy the attention of the Federal military authorities, troops would be immediately employed . . . to suppress any action attempted." [16]

To expect in the summer of 1864 a Confederate invasion of Kentucky and Missouri, and to make it a precondition of an uprising, was to deal in absurdities. By this time, the Copperheads may have accepted the opinion of the official leadership of the Democratic Party that dissatisfaction with the administration was growing at such a rate as to justify the expectation that a Democratic President and Congress would be elected in November, which in turn would create the possibility of ending the war without the desperate expedient of an armed rebellion. The repeated requests to postpone the uprising may well have been a subterfuge to avoid action, but without shutting off the flow of Thompson's greenbacks.[17] If these tactics aroused Hines's or Thompson's misgivings, if they caused the two Confederates to question the good faith of their reluctant allies, neither of the two has left his suspicions on record. Thompson may have been too credulous and Hines too confident of his persuasive powers to become discouraged, or perhaps they felt that to accomplish their purpose, they had to go forward on the off chance that the Copperheads could somehow be brought to the point of action.

Because the meeting at St. Catharines failed to produce an agreement, another meeting was held in London, Ontario, on August 7 to try to break the impasse. There is no record of the arguments Hines used to persuade the Copperheads to go forward, but after a lengthy discussion, they agreed, or seemed to agree, to do so. It was settled that the uprising was to take place on August 29. Hines, knowing that these delays militated against the possibility of effective action, stipulated that there could be no further postponements and the Copperheads agreed.

Vallandigham did not attend these meetings in July and August. After the June 11 meeting in Windsor, he evidently decided that

[16] Hines, "The Northwestern Conspiracy," 507.
[17] Hines alone disbursed $68,051 in gold and greenbacks, and Thompson's disbursements were far greater.

158

affairs were taking an ugly turn. His well-developed instinct for survival told him that he would be safer under the "Lincoln tyranny" than in the clutches of a determined desperado like Hines, and on June 14, he donned a puerile disguise, slipped across the border, and returned to his home. His avowed reason for returning was "to prevent, if possible, any act of insurrection by the Sons of Liberty." [18] Actually, there is reason to think that his objective was to provoke the government into proceeding against him and thereby to precipitate a crisis; if so, he was to be disappointed, for the administration took the prudent course of ignoring him altogether.

Well before the August 7 meeting in London, another factor had already jeopardized Hines's venture. The Copperheads' great reluctance to act did not stop them from boasting to all and sundry of what they intended to do. They were not alone in this, for Hines's associates in Canada also had an ample quota of talkers. Moreover, the ranks of both groups were riddled with traitors and undercover agents. As early as the middle of June, within days of Hines's and Thompson's meeting with Vallandigham, the Federal authorities knew not only that the Sons of Liberty in concert with the Confederates in Canada were up to something important, but also that Camp Douglas was the point on which their plans were focused.

Colonel Benjamin Jeffrey Sweet, who was to play an important role in these events, was born in northern New York State in 1832, the eldest in a family of fourteen children.[19] His father's health broke down when Benjamin was nine years old and from then on the youth was the principal breadwinner of the constantly increasing family. In 1848 the Sweets moved to Wisconsin. Young Benjamin had to get his education on a catch-as-catch-can basis; nevertheless, he managed to have a year at Appleton College, after which he read law, was admitted to the bar and interested himself in politics, being elected to the Wisconsin senate in 1859 as a

[18] Edward N. Vallandigham, "Clement L. Vallandigham—Copperhead," *Putnam's Monthly*, II (1907), 598.

[19] This sketch of Sweet is based on William A. Bross, *Biographical Sketch of the Late Gen. B. J. Sweet* (Chicago, 1878), 6–12.

Republican with strong abolitionist convictions. On the outbreak of war, he entered the service as a major in the Sixth Wisconsin Infantry. He returned to Wisconsin in 1862, raised two new regiments, and was commissioned colonel of one of them. Heavily engaged at the battle of Perryville, his regiment sustained three hundred casualties, Sweet himself being badly wounded. He recovered but lost the use of his right arm; incapacitated for active service, he was appointed to the Veteran Reserve Corps and on May 2, 1864, was given command of the Military Post of Chicago, with headquarters at Camp Douglas.

The camp rules allowed each prisoner to write his family once a month on a single sheet of paper.[20] In mid-June, it is said, Colonel Sweet learned that a suspiciously large percentage of the prisoners' letters covered only a small part of the allotted sheet. Then he discovered, entirely by accident, that the seemingly blank paper was in many cases covered with messages written in invisible ink, hinting at desperate doings planned for July 4.[21] This melodramatic tale purports to explain how Colonel Sweet learned that an attack on his camp was being planned.

The sequel makes it evident that the true story is far more prosaic. As early as November, 1863, there had been rumors that the Confederates in Canada were hatching an attack on one or another of the prisoner of war camps in Illinois and Ohio.[22] Immediately after he took over the Chicago command in the following May, Sweet was warned by the Federal commissary general of prisoners that "from circumstances which may soon occur more than ordinary vigilance will be required from the troops in charge of prisoners" and was cautioned to be prepared for any

[20] Tuttle, *Camp Douglas*, 16.
[21] Anonymous, "The Chicago Conspiracy," *Atlantic Monthly*, XVI (1865), 110. This article, published anonymously, was written by James Roberts Gilmore, who used the pen name "Edmund Kirke." It will be cited hereinafter as Kirke, "Chicago Conspiracy." Hines kept among his papers a copy of the article, which he annotated copiously in the margins. After identifying the author, he added the comment: "Many things here are wholly false, many others entirely omitted. The only point in which the truth is closely approached is in the magnitude of the undertaking." Hines Papers.
[22] *OR*, Series III, Vol. III, 1008, 1012, 1013.

emergency.[23] Colonel Sweet's subsequent conduct justifies the belief that the warning was superfluous. He may well have inherited a corps of stool pigeons from his predecessors; if not, it is more likely that, having the responsibility of guarding several thousand restless prisoners, he made sure that he was kept informed of what they were up to. Of necessity, Hines and his Chicago collaborators had to take some of the prisoners into their confidence. In the enforced intimacy of the prisoners' barracks, their plans were bound to become common knowledge and were promptly reported to Sweet by his spies. Leaving nothing to chance, Sweet also arranged to have Thomas H. Keefe, chief of detectives in the Northwest of the War Department secret service, sent to Toronto to learn what he could of the Confederates' plans as well as the names of their allies in Chicago.[24] He also persuaded I. Winslow Ayer, a medical quack, vendor of patent medicines, and all-around scoundrel, to join the Chicago temple of the Sons of Liberty and keep him informed of its activities and projects.[25]

A report of Colonel Sweet's, dated August 12, shows clearly that by that time, he had a reasonably accurate knowledge of what was afoot. He wrote that "the supposed organization in Toronto . . . was to come here in squads, then combine and attempt to rescue the prisoners of war at Camp Douglas. . . . there is an armed organization in this city of five thousand men . . . the rescue of our prisoners would be the signal for a general insurrection in Indiana and Illinois." [26]

At about the same time, another officer of the Union army learned of the conspiracy in a more dramatic fashion.[27] Lieutenant Colonel Bennett H. Hill, assistant provost marshal general for Michigan, received a letter bearing a Toronto postmark from an

[23] William Hoffman to Benjamin J. Sweet, May 6, 1864, in OR, Series II, Vol. VII, 123–24.
[24] Thomas H. Keefe, *The Great Chicago Conspiracy* (Chicago, n. d.—probably 1896), 10.
[25] Milton, *Lincoln and the Fifth Column*, 299.
[26] Kirke, "The Chicago Conspiracy," 110.
[27] The story of Colonel Hill's dealings with the mysterious Confederate major is told in *ibid.*, 111–12.

individual who wrote that he had been a major in the Confederate army. This person offered to reveal the details of a plot against the United States in exchange for permission to take the oath of allegiance and a monetary reward commensurate with the value of the information in his possession. Hill paid no attention to the letter and he also ignored a second letter he received from the major a short time later. One evening, not long after the arrival of the second letter, the major himself appeared in Colonel Hill's office in Detroit and volunteered enough information to enable Hill to send a fairly comprehensive report about the conspiracy to department headquarters. On the night of August 15, the major again visited Hill, who had in the meantime satisfied himself about the informer's *bona fides*. The report he now sent his superiors, based on the officer's further revelations, left nothing to be desired, either in completeness or in accuracy. Hill wrote that the major had told him

> that about two hundred picked men, of the Rebel refugees in Canada, are assembled in . . . [Toronto and] are armed with revolvers and supplied with funds and transportation-tickets to Chicago. . . . That he . . . and the balance of the men are waiting for instructions from Captain Hines, who is the commander of the expedition; that . . . the general plan is to accomplish the release of the prisoners at Camp Douglas, and in doing so, they will be assisted by an armed organization in Chicago. After being released, the prisoners will be armed, and . . . will proceed to Camp Morton . . . and there accomplish a similar object in releasing prisoners. That for months, Rebel emissaries have been traveling through the Northwest; that their arrangements are fully matured.[28]

The informer, whose identity Hill did not reveal, said he was to be a member of the contingent from Canada that was to accompany Hines to Chicago. At Hill's suggestion, the traitor agreed to communicate with Colonel Sweet when he got to Chicago. However, nothing more was ever heard of him after his second visit to Detroit. In 1865 a sensational magazine article implied

[28] *Ibid.,* 111–12. (Camp Morton was located at Indianapolis.)

that the major's treason was discovered and he was done away with.[29]

Colonel Hill's reports, together with the information turned in by Sweet's stool pigeons and the detective he had sent to Toronto, were only a part of the extensive dossier on the conspiracy in the hands of the Federal authorities. Two years earlier, Colonel Henry B. Carrington, mustering officer for Indiana, had concluded that the Copperheads were responsible for the wave of desertions from Indiana regiments. To confirm his suspicions, he persuaded Felix Stidger, a Kentuckian of Unionist sympathies, to become a government detective and to join the OAK as an undercover agent. The harmless looking Stidger did much more than merely join the order; he managed to insinuate himself into the confidence of its leaders. He became the trusted associate of Dr. William A. Bowles, "Major General" of Indiana, and of Judge Joshua Bullitt, head of the organization in Kentucky. Through the influence of the latter, Stidger was elected grand secretary of the Sons of Liberty (as it had become) in Kentucky.[30] Dr. Bowles had served as colonel of the Second Indiana Volunteers in the Mexican War and was responsible for the shameful rout of the Indiana troops at the battle of Buena Vista. In 1863 and 1864, with no one shooting at him, he was the bravest of the brave, the most vociferous of the Copperhead leaders in urging instant, violent action—and the most talkative. As the recipient of the doctor's confidences and as a member of the inner directing circle of the order, Stidger was able to supply Carrington with full information about the plans and progress of the conspiracy.

Armed with Stidger's reports, Carrington acted. The August 7 meeting in London was held under the watchful eyes of his agents and as the Copperhead leaders returned to their homes each of

[29] *Ibid.*, 112. On the other hand, Hines (who, if anyone, would have known the story at first hand) noted opposite this passage in the Kirke article: "This person was at that time *thought* to be a *traitor*, and as he had acquired some information that might be used to our injury, it was decided best (at the suggestion of Capt. JBC[astleman]) to take him fully into our confidence & employ him in an important capacity. By the sacrifice of his life, in the discharge of the duty assigned him, was demonstrated the wisdom of our course." Hines Papers.
[30] Fesler, "Secret Political Societies," 238.

163

them, without knowing it, was shepherded on his way by Carrington's detectives. On August 20 he had most of the Indiana leaders rounded up. In the Indianapolis print shop of the Indiana grand commander, the arresting officers found 132,000 rounds of ammunition and 400 revolvers, packed in boxes labeled "Sunday School Books" and "Bible Tracts." [31] Judge Bullitt had already been arrested on his return to Louisville from the July 20 meeting in Chicago; Jacob Thompson's drafts, drawn on Montreal and Toronto banks, were in his wallet, and his carpet bag was full of the greenbacks Thompson had given him to purchase arms for his followers.

While these events were taking place, Grenfell was enjoying a summer idyll of hunting and fishing along the shores of Georgian Bay. He kept Hines informed of his whereabouts, so that he could be recalled to Toronto when Hines was ready to go into action. For, let it be said now, Grenfell, for all his later protestations of innocence, was not only deeply involved in the conspiracy but, as was inevitable, was to play a leading role in the attack on Camp Douglas. [32]

Grenfell had taken pains to establish for himself the identity of an English gentleman of leisure and means, traveling in North America for his own recreation and pleasure and indulging his fondness for hunting and fishing. But he was ready for action as soon as Hines needed him. However, no one was less of a plotter and, quite wisely, he stayed, or was kept, clear of the conspiracy until it reached the stage where his special talent for the kind of action that called for desperate courage could come into play.

[31] Smith, "Civil War Subversives," 236.

[32] In anticipation of the question of Grenfell's guilt or innocence, attention should be called to an editorial written by Hines and printed in the Memphis *Appeal* on December 23, 1866: "Few persons believe Col. Grenfell guilty of the charges preferred against him . . . while all know that the tribunal before which he was tried has no sanction, either in law or in precedent. . . . The guilt or innocence then of Col. Grenfell is not a question which enters into the consideration of the justness or legality of his imprisonment" (Clipping in Hines Papers). Hines's noncommittal language is highly significant; had he known Grenfell to be innocent, surely he would have said so. Cf. John W. Headley, *Confederate Operations in Canada and New York* (New York, 1906), 264.

Grenfell had another important qualification for the role he was to play in Chicago: a genuine devotion to the cause of the South. He had written his daughter, Marie, from Montreal a few weeks earlier: "What bloody work has been going on in Virginia! . . . Nobly are my friends defending themselves, and gallantly will they fight their way out, I feel assured! . . . It is impossible to give a safe opinion upon what may take place in the South within the next three months, but they cannot subjugate it, never, never!" [33] And so, when Hines's summons came, he packed his gear and joined his friends at the Queen's Hotel, in Toronto.

In the intervals between his negotiations with the Copperheads, Hines selected, from among the Confederate officers and soldiers who had congregated in Canada, sixty men who were to make the expedition to Chicago.[34] He was assisted in this task by John Castleman, his second in command. Picked not only for courage— that was taken for granted—but also for intelligence and reliability, the chosen sixty were to provide the trained military leadership for the attack on Camp Douglas and were thereafter to organize and command the liberated prisoners. The majority of those selected had served under Morgan; they were men whom Hines and Castleman knew and thought they could depend upon. Each man chosen was given pistols, ammunition, railroad tickets to Chicago, and money for expenses.

In addition to his other duties, Hines also assumed the responsibility for working out the tactical plans for the attack on the camp. Charles Walsh, who was to command the Chicago Copperheads, lived within a third of a mile from Camp Douglas; there were only a few houses scattered between his home and the camp. On one of his numerous visits to Chicago, Hines used the Walsh house as an observation post for a careful reconnaissance of the camp and its surroundings. To obtain a detailed description of the arrangements inside the camp presented no difficulties whatever.

[33] Grenfell to Marie Pearce-Serocold, July 18, 1864, in Weaks (ed.), "Colonel . . . Grenfell," 9–11.
[34] Hines, "The Northwestern Conspiracy," 570. Castleman says that fifty-eight were chosen to go to Chicago. Castleman, *Active Service*, 154.

Many of Morgan's former troopers in the camp had relatives or friends among the Kentuckians who had migrated to Chicago before the war.[35] Passes to visit the camp were granted freely and favored prisoners were allowed to go into the city on a variety of errands; one prisoner, it is said, was permitted to visit Chicago regularly to court an attractive widow of rebel sympathies. Thus, there was a steady flow of information from within the camp to the world outside.

Based on his own observations and the data that filtered out of Camp Douglas into the city, Hines drew an accurate map of the camp and its approaches and planned the attack upon it as a textbook military operation. The assault from the outside was to be aimed at three of the four sides of the camp; as soon as it started, the prisoners were to attack the guards from the rear. The Canadian group was to be armed with pistols; Walsh, using money supplied by Hines, had accumulated a veritable arsenal of weapons and ammunition in his house and barn for arming his followers; additional weapons would of course become available when the garrison was disarmed. To effect maximum surprise, the attack was to be made at night, and to prevent the dispatch of Union reinforcements to the city, the telegraph lines leading out of Chicago were to be cut beforehand. As soon as Camp Douglas was secured, Castleman was to lead a column of liberated prisoners to Rock Island, to free the eight thousand Confederates held there and to capture the Rock Island Arsenal; Hines had already spent two thousand dollars to bribe railroad employees to transport Castleman and his men from Chicago to Rock Island.[36] Colonel Sweet later stated officially, and the government claimed, that Hines also planned to burn all the railroad stations in Chicago, destroy all the bridges and grain ele-

[35] The wife of Buckner S. Morris said that she had paid frequent visits to the camp to distribute money and clothing to the prisoners, and that she "received letters from Captain J. B. Castleman . . . and sent verbal messages in return." Cincinnati *Daily Gazette*, February 14, 1865. Brigadier General W. M. Orme, one of Colonel Sweet's predecessors in command of the Military Post of Chicago, reported in December, 1863, that "a prisoner of war, once beyond the camp lines, finds in . . . [Chicago] so many active friends and sympathizers as to render his recapture almost impossible." *OR*, Series II, Vol. VI, 861.
[36] Horan, *Confederate Agent*, 128.

vators, and loot all the banks and gunsmith shops in the city, but there is no hint in Hines's surviving papers of these subsidiary operations.[37]

Grenfell returned to Toronto in late August, presumably in response to a summons from Hines. When the latter and Castleman wrote their story of these events, Grenfell had been dead for many years. Nevertheless, out of regard for the good name of their comrade, whom they regarded as one of the martyrs of the Lost Cause, they doctored the record in his favor. They knew that as a condition of being allowed to travel undisturbed in the Northern states, he had pledged his word to "give no further aid to the Confederate cause." A truthful account of his journey to Toronto and of his actions thereafter would have revealed the fact that he had broken his solemn promise. Thus, Hines and Castleman wrote that Grenfell "astonished . . . [them] by his appearance on the scene"; Hines of course told him of his plans, whereupon Grenfell commented: "I see that in all this lives will be sacrificed. I can not take part in it, but I will go along and witness the executions."[38] If Grenfell did indeed make this equivocal remark, he must have done so tongue in cheek. Nothing could have been less in character than for him to stand aside as an idle observer when such game was afoot, nor would Hines have willingly done without the active assistance of the tried and proven soldier whom he considered to be "one of the bravest . . . men of that period."[39] Grenfell's note of July 31 to "Dr. Hunter," quoted previously, is alone sufficient to destroy Hines's and Castleman's loyal attempt to absolve him of complicity in the conspiracy. No doubt Grenfell attended the meetings in which Hines explained his plans to the chosen sixty, each of whom was given a particular task to perform, and all of whom were asked to maintain absolute silence about the expedition and admonished that "any careless word might be fatal."[40]

[37] OR, Vol. XLV, Part I, 1078.
[38] Hines, "The Northwestern Conspiracy," 570–71.
[39] Ibid., 570.
[40] Horan, Confederate Agent, 124.

Unfortunately for the fate of the project, the admonition came much too late. There had already been more than enough talk, some by deliberate traitors and some by the merely garrulous, to ruin what little chance for success the conspiracy might have had. Too many knew of the project, and most of those who did had nothing to do from one day to the next but sit in hotel lobbies, bars, and rooming houses, and talk. These tyros in the art of conspiracy were exiles and Southerners, and hence gregarious by definition, and much too free with their confidences to fellow exiles, real or bogus. Commissioner Thompson was himself talkative—"his subordinates were kept in constant apprehension lest he compromise their efforts by indiscreet confidences"—and many of the others were equally incapable of keeping a secret.[41] Moreover, as Thompson wrote later: "The bane and curse of carrying on anything in . . . [Canada] is the surveillance under which we act. Detectives . . . stand at every street corner." [42]

One of these detectives was Thomas Keefe, Colonel Sweet's envoy to Toronto. More than thirty years were to pass before he wrote of his part in these events and, for all his protestations that "I have told only what I personally know or did," he not only had a poor memory but he also wrote the story of these events because he had "a wife and family to provide for" and hoped that his recital would persuade Congress to grant a long-delayed recompense for efforts which, under the circumstances, he was not likely to minimize.[43] Hence his account is a tissue of exaggerations, distortions, inventions, obvious errors, anachronisms, and outright lies.[44]

[41] Hines, "The Northwestern Conspiracy," 502.

[42] Jacob Thompson to Judah P. Benjamin, December 3, 1864. OR, Vol. XLIII, Part I, 932. Hines himself was guilty of gross carelessness. He used for his messages the relatively simple Confederate code which the Federals had long since broken and made the decoding of his letters even simpler by "making numerous errors . . . marking the notes with symbols to mark the beginning of new encryption cycles, inserting plain text words, and using a straight alphabet based on a simple moveable wheel." Winks, Canada and the United States, 277.

[43] Keefe, The Great Chicago Conspiracy, 31, 35.

[44] Keefe had a curious career as an author. In March, 1897, the Stanley Waterloo article entitled "The Great Chicago Conspiracy" (previously cited) was published in Nickell Magazine. Three years later, in January, 1900, Everybody's Magazine printed an article by Keefe under the title "How the Northwest Was Saved." The

He claimed, for example, that one of the leaders of the conspiracy whom he came to know best when he visited Toronto was "Major General St. Leger Grenfell." Actually, when Keefe was in Toronto, Grenfell was still happily fishing in the clear blue waters of Georgian Bay. Notwithstanding the promotion to major general which the detective bestowed upon him, Grenfell would hardly have acknowledged the man's friendship, for Keefe also wrote that "Grenfell had a black record. His treatment of Union prisoners who fell into his hands was diabolical. He owned a bull dog, with which he 'baited' his prisoners of war. At Selma, he was the man who advocated raising the black flag and giving no quarter to Union soldiers." [45] As will be seen later it was Keefe who arrested Grenfell, and the high rank and grisly record with which he endowed him in retrospect were doubtless intended to enhance the importance of the capture and the size of the hoped-for gratuity from Congress.

Notwithstanding the general lack of reliability of Keefe's recollections, there is no reason to doubt that he did spend some time in Toronto, and that he became acquainted with some of Hines's associates and learned a good deal about their plans. And there were other Federal detectives besides Keefe haunting the hotels and bars of Toronto and buying confidences with money, whiskey, or mere sociability. As a result of all the loose talk, Colonel Sweet and the Federal officials generally knew as much about the conspiracy as did the conspirators themselves.[46]

Keefe article is in the main a plagiarism of the Waterloo paper, the only changes of substance being additions to inflate and glorify Keefe's own role. It is quite obvious that Keefe published *The Great Chicago Conspiracy* before the Waterloo article appeared, but he made more than full use of the latter in writing "his" article for *Everybody's Magazine.*

[45] Keefe, *The Great Chicago Conspiracy*, 13–14. The story of Grenfell's supposed brutality to prisoners and of his advocacy of the "raising of the black flag" by the Confederacy was to crop up during his trial, repeatedly during his imprisonment, and many times after his death. The present writer has been unable to trace these stories to their source or sources. As far as the "raising of the black flag" is concerned, in view of Grenfell's intemperate language on other occasions, Keefe's attribution of the remark to him cannot be dismissed as impossible.

[46] For the knowledge of the War Department in Washington of what was afoot, see Henry W. Halleck to Samuel P. Heintzelman, August 28, 1864, and

169

And so, when Hines assembled his men in Toronto for a final briefing a few days before the end of August, his project was already doomed. The caution and optimism of the heads of the Democratic Party, the fecklessness and cowardice of the Copperheads were partly responsible for the failure of his plans, but the inability of his own associates and followers to keep from talking, and the outright treachery of some of them were equally accountable. The story of Colonel Hill's mysterious visitor suggests that Hines must have known, or at least suspected, that his plans were known to the Federal authorities. Nonetheless, he went ahead. He was willing to risk his own neck and the lives of his followers in a confident gamble on his own powers of last-minute improvisation.

It is worthy of note that in the voluminous reports, letters, and memoranda Hines wrote during and after the war about this project and his own part in it, there is never a hint that he thought of it as anything other than a legitimate enterprise of war. He was convinced that there was nothing in what he tried to do "that was not thoroughly consistent with an obligation of the strictest sense of honor." [47] What Grenfell may have thought of it is not on record; more than likely, he never gave the question a moment's thought. His was not a mind given to theoretical speculations.

Heintzelman to Halleck, September 3, 1864, in *OR*, Vol. XXXIX, Part II, 312, 341–42.

[47] Hines, "The Northwestern Conspiracy," 437.

Chapter X

EVERYTHING THAT had to be done in Toronto before the departure of the Confederates to Chicago had by now been attended to. Each man had his assignment; all had their guns, ammunition, railroad tickets, and money. The men were to journey to Chicago in small groups by a variety of routes. This was a superfluous precaution, for August 27 had been chosen as the date of departure and, by then, every Chicago-bound train was crowded with delegates to the convention, politicians, newspaper people, the curious, and the idle. Every member of the expedition was assigned to predesignated quarters in Chicago. The leaders and many of the men were to put up at the Richmond House, located at the corner of Lake Street and Michigan Avenue, the hotel that also served as headquarters for the peace-at-any-price Democrats; Vallandigham held frequent meetings and receptions there while the convention was in session.

When the entire group met to receive final instructions just prior to their departure from Toronto, Hines and Castleman discovered to their consternation that their little army had increased substantially in numbers. Without consulting either of them, Thompson and his fellow commissioners had invited between a dozen and twenty men to join the expedition.[1] Much was to be made later of

[1] Castleman, *Active Service*, 154.

the unreliability of these unwelcome reinforcements but their presence did not affect in the slightest the outcome of Hines's project.

Grenfell left Toronto with one of the groups of Confederates late on the evening of August 26 and arrived in Chicago two days later.[2] The guest register of the Richmond House showed that he checked in on the twenty-eighth, and was assigned to the "gentlemen's parlor." [3]

Maurice Langhorne, one of the leading witnesses for the government at the Cincinnati trial, was a member of the party with which Grenfell traveled to Chicago. He testified that Grenfell had his sporting guns and his dog with him on the train and wore a suit of Confederate gray for the journey. When Langhorne twitted him about his clothes with the remark, "Colonel, if you go in those clothes to Chicago, they will arrest you; you will not live there five hours," Grenfell replied, "No . . . this is an old uniform that was worn in an English battalion I once belonged to . . . I have my English papers, and my gun and my dog, and if they ask me what I am doing, I will say I am going hunting." [4]

On his way from Richmond to New York in early May, Grenfell had sent to England a box containing spare uniforms and other

[2] There is something of a mystery about the date and circumstances of Grenfell's departure for Chicago. Horan, in his sensational account of Hines's role in the many conspiracies hatched by the Confederates in the last desperate year of the war, states: "After a conference with Thompson, Hines sent Grenfel [sic] to Chicago to contact Walsh and arm Walsh's 'two regiments' with the thousands of rifles and revolvers hidden throughout the city." Horan, Confederate Agent, 121. However, James Maughan, a resident of Windsor, Ontario, whom Thompson used as a courier to maintain contact with Hines in Chicago, stated that he saw Grenfell in Toronto between August 26 and 30, and Maurice Langhorne explicitly testified that he was a member of the group with which Grenfell left Toronto for Chicago on the evening of August 26. Maughan: House Executive Documents, 175; Langhorne: ibid., 82. Because Horan does not indicate the source of his statement, it must be assumed that Maughan's and Langhorne's statements were accurate. Horan, relying probably on House Executive Documents, regularly spells Grenfell's name with a single l and states that "Grenfell's name is usually spelled with two l's. But he signed his name with one l." But Grenfell, who may be assumed to know the correct spelling of his own and his family's name, invariably wrote it with two l's.
[3] House Executive Documents, 471.
[4] Ibid., 82.

personal belongings, including a thirty-two-star American flag that Morgan's men had captured from a Kentucky Home Guard unit in 1862 and given him as a keepsake.[5] Before leaving for Chicago, he stripped down to campaigning gear and left his nonessential belongings with the proprietor of the Queen's Hotel for safekeeping.

On the eve of the opening session of the Democratic convention, Chicago swarmed with thousands of strangers.[6] Hines and his men had arrived without incident; many of them were installed in the Richmond House in a block of rooms marked with a sign identifying them as the "Missouri Delegation." On Sunday evening, August 28, Hines, Castleman, and Grenfell met with the Copperhead leaders in what was expected to be nothing more than a routine meeting to put the last-minute touches to the program for the next day's uprising. The arms needed for the assault on the camp had been assembled and the prisoners organized and warned. It only remained to learn how many Copperheads were available for the attack, and to assign them to their places.

But within moments from the start of the meeting, the three Confederates learned there was to be no uprising the next day. Charles Walsh had spent, or said he had spent, with a lavish hand the money Hines had given him "to get the boys organized," but his two thousand devoted and eager followers were not ready for action, for the good and sufficient reason that they existed only in his imagination.[7] The thousands of down-state Copperheads who were to be in Chicago, armed and organized, had not even been notified that they would be needed on the twenty-ninth, and the few who had drifted into the city on their own initiative were wandering about, looking for someone who could tell them what

[5] The flag still exists. It was presented to the Filson Club of Louisville, Kentucky, by A. H. Packe, Grenfell's great-grandson.
[6] In a paper read to the Chicago Historical Society in 1878, William A. Bross, author of a brief biography of Colonel Sweet, described the delegates and visitors to the Democratic National Convention in the following terms: "The whole city seemed alive with a motley crew of big-shouldered, blear-eyed, bottle-nosed, whiskey-blotched vagabonds—the very excrescence and sweepings of the slums and sinks of all the cities of the nation." Unidentified and undated newspaper clipping in Hines Papers.
[7] *House Executive Documents*, 80.

173

to do.[8] It was apparent that the Copperhead high command, so brave and confident in Canada when the day for action lay comfortably far in the future, had failed in every particular. They had been sufficiently glib with lavish promises and grandiose statements of their objectives ("We must look to bigger results than the mere liberation of prisoners. We should look to the grand end of adding an empire of Northwestern States.") and, of course, always eager for more of Hines's gold and greenbacks.[9] Veritable lions in the security of a Canadian hotel room, their resolution had evaporated long before August 29.

It has been asserted that the uprising was not aborted by a failure of nerve on the part of the Copperhead leaders, but rather that it was vetoed by the heads of the New York delegation to the convention, who did not want a riot while the convention was in session nor any "demonstration which might turn against the party the votes of the 'War Democrats,' or create any sentiment that would redound to the discredit of the Democratic party of the North."[10] It has been suggested also that the Illinois Copperheads lost their nerve because of the rounding up of their Indiana colleagues by Colonel Carrington on August 20 and the news that the Camp Douglas garrison had been reinforced.[11] A much simpler and more probable explanation of the fiasco is that these were

[8] Milton, *Lincoln and the Fifth Column*, 303. Typical of the general unreliability of Keefe's narratives is his statement: "There were now in Chicago, as was subsequently ascertained, about 2,000 armed Confederates, awaiting the signal to make the place a pandemonium." Keefe, "How the Northwest Was Saved," 85. Even if Keefe intended the term "Confederates" to include both Hines's men from Canada and the Chicago and down-state Copperheads, his 2,000 figure is a wild exaggeration. Hines says that only about "two hundred Copperheads reported for duty." Hines, "Autobiographic Notes," in Hines Papers.

[9] Quoted from a letter addressed by the Sons of Liberty leaders to the Confederate Commissioners in Canada, in Fesler, "Secret Political Societies," 250.

[10] Waterloo, "The Great Chicago Conspiracy," 138.

[11] Kirke, "The Chicago Conspiracy," 112. Colonel Sweet had received twelve hundred reinforcements, all of them hundred-day volunteers of dubious military value. Rumor, which the Copperheads were only too ready to believe, placed the number of reinforcements at seven thousand. Hines and Castleman, who had accurate information, tried in vain to convince the Copperheads that the seven thousand figure was a gross exaggeration. Hines, "The Northwestern Conspiracy," 573.

convenient excuses for evading the fulfillment of commitments which the Copperhead leaders never had the ability or the courage, or quite possibly even the intention, to live up to.

The disappointment and disgust of the Confederates, who had already risked much and were ready to risk more, can be imagined. But to save the Confederacy called for desperate measures and they were determined to go forward; however, to mount a successful attack against the camp was beyond the powers of seventy or eighty men, however brave and dedicated they may have been. They had to have Copperhead help. By this time, even Hines must have lost his illusions about Copperhead capabilities. Had he been older and more experienced, or less of an optimist, or perhaps if he had not sent such confident assurances of success to Richmond, he might well have given up as hopeless his plans for the attack, there and then. But he did not do so. He reasoned, or perhaps he rationalized later, that if some overt act, however trifling, could be committed with obvious Copperhead participation, they would be so compromised that they would have no choice but to go forward to save their own skins; that, in other words, if they could not be induced to fight for their convictions like men, they might be trapped into fighting like cornered rats.[12] Hence, after listening patiently to their excuses and explanations, he proposed that an effort be made overnight to collect and organize as many as possible of Walsh's followers and their down-state brethren; if only five hundred could be assembled, he said, he was ready to proceed. To make the enterprise seem less desperate and more palatable to his costive allies, he told them that he would forego the attack on Camp Douglas and would attack instead the much more lightly defended prison camp and arsenal at Rock Island.[13] The meeting ended on the understanding that the Copperheads would get busy forthwith to collect the five hundred men Hines had asked for.

Meanwhile, Colonel Sweet, against whom all this activity was aimed, was giving a demonstration of the value of an aggressive defense. He knew that Camp Douglas would be the prime target of

[12] Castleman, *Active Service*, 147–48.
[13] Fesler, "Secret Political Societies," 255.

any uprising in Chicago. A minimum of intuition would have told him, even if his spies, stool pigeons, and detectives had not done so, that the attackers would assemble under cover of the Democratic convention and that the assault on the camp would probably be launched while the convention was in session.[14] And now he was informed that Thomas Hines, the brains and moving spirit of the conspiracy, had arrived in Chicago at the head of "150 to 200" Confederate desperadoes.[15]

At the beginning of August, Sweet had disposed of a camp garrison of eight to nine hundred, of whom not more than a third were on duty at one time, to guard between eight and nine thousand prisoners and to repel any attack from the outside.[16] After receiving Colonel Hill's report of his second interview with the turncoat major, Sweet began to bombard department headquarters in Columbus, Ohio, with urgent pleas for reinforcements. The North had been stripped bare of troops to build up the armies in the field, and reinforcements were nearly impossible to find, but Major General Samuel P. Heintzelman, the department commander, eventually scraped together about twelve hundred nearly untrained hundred-day volunteers and shipped them off to Chicago.[17] With two thousand men to hold the stockade and keep the prisoners in check, Sweet felt reasonably secure, but he decided that he should do more than merely wait to be attacked. In the conviction that a show of force would overawe the Copperheads, he sent out large patrols to tour the downtown streets. The patrols made their rounds amidst a chorus of Copperhead jeers and catcalls, but they

[14] As early as August 27, the Chicago *Tribune* reported: "The city is full to overflowing already with the gathering clans of Copperheads, Butternuts, OAK's, Sons of Liberty, . . . [and] gentlemen from Canada." Quoted in Fesler, "Secret Political Societies," 253; cf. *OR*, Vol. XXXIX, Part II, 312.

[15] Sweet to Provost Marshal General James B. Fry, Nov. 23, 1864, in *OR*, Vol. XLV, Part I, 1077.

[16] There is confusion about the number of prisoners and guards at Camp Douglas in August. The Adjutant General's office credited the camp with 4,377 prisoners and 1,664 guards, the latter increased to 2,974 by the reinforcements rushed to the camp in late August. The Adjutant General's figures are quoted in Hines, "The Northwestern Conspiracy," 570. The figures given in the text are those of Colonel Sweet in his testimony in Cincinnati. *House Executive Documents*, 188–89.

[17] *House Executive Documents*, 188.

also had the effect Sweet intended; they were a demonstration that the Federals were in strength and alert, and they helped to confirm Walsh and his friends in the belief that an uprising would be a very risky venture indeed.

On Monday evening, August 29, Walsh and his associates returned to the Richmond House to give an account of their efforts to round up five hundred of their followers. Judged by the result, one may well doubt the earnestness of their efforts. Walsh reported that his followers had been rendered extremely cautious by Sweet's patrols, and he confessed that no more than twenty-five Sons of Liberty were willing to join the project.[18] The grand program of liberating the Union from the Lincoln tyranny and of creating "an empire of Northwestern States" had come to this; the regiments of Sons of Liberty, the tens of thousands of Copperheads ready to risk their lives for their beliefs, had shrunk to a miserable squad of twenty-five.

There was much more talk, a repetition of the facile assurances Hines had already heard many times, promises, if he would agree to make one more try, of better organization, more strenuous efforts, more careful preparation, and the suggestion that the uprising be planned for Election Day, November 8, which, in the opinion of Walsh and his colleagues, would be the ideal occasion for it. The subsequent course of events makes it evident that in spite of everything that had already happened, Hines did not lose faith in his ability to bring off an uprising. He agreed to the Copperheads' suggestion.

For the moment, nothing more could be done in Chicago. At the conclusion of the meeting with the Copperheads, Hines assembled his men, explained the situation, and offered them the choice of staying with him in the North, returning to Canada, or going South. The majority chose Canada or the South, but Hines, Castleman, and twenty-two Rebels went to Marshall and Mattoon, Illinois, to conduct a campaign of sabotage and to rally Copperhead support for the November uprising. Grenfell decided to carry

---

[18] Hines, "The Northwestern Conspiracy," 574; *cf.* Brown, *The Bold Cavaliers,* 282.

on in the role of the British sportsman; he would stay on quietly in the Richmond House for a few days and would then take the train to Carlyle, Illinois, and hunt prairie chickens until his presence was again needed to hunt bigger game in Chicago.

A curious footnote, entirely apocryphal, to Grenfell's presence in Chicago during the sessions of the convention is found in a history of Kansas in the 1860s. The author, Samuel J. Crawford, whose fierce pro-Union and pro-Republican bias is evident throughout the book, declares that the Rebels sent scores of "ambassadors" North in the summer of 1864 "to help organize and discipline the Anti-war Democrats, knights of the Golden Circle, Sons of Liberty, Copperheads, Bounty-jumpers and other similar characters," in order to unite "their dupes and sympathizers under the banner of Democracy, with a view of electing a President who would take down the American flag, call home the Federal troops, dissolve the Union, and let the slave-holding States go their way in peace." The stage was thus set for the convention. One of its sessions was addressed by a New Jersey Democrat, who, Crawford said, "proceeded to shake the rafters with his eloquence . . . he was ready to storm the gates of Camp Douglas and send home eight thousand Confederate gentlemen who had been ruthlessly torn from their beloved . . . homes by . . . Lincoln's army." [19] This oratory was clearly to the taste of the delegates, who "shrieked for vengeance, and were clamorous to be led against Camp Douglas—'the Black Hole of Calcutta,' as they called it. [Horatio] Seymour, their presiding officer, tried to call the rabble to order, but . . . [the] more they were called to order, the louder they roared, until finally Colonel Grenfell (of the staff of John Morgan, the Rebel raider) . . . stepped to the front and ordered them to be quiet." In a further passage, Crawford identifies Grenfell as one of several Confederate officers who were delegates to the convention.[20] One wonders what twisted recollection of newspaper stories read many years before,

[19] This and the following quotations are from Samuel J. Crawford, *Kansas in the Sixties* (Chicago, 1911), 186.
[20] *Ibid.*, 188.

178

and what odd association of ideas, caused Crawford to identify Grenfell as a delegate and a sergeant at arms at the convention.

On August 31, before leaving Chicago, Grenfell wrote to England, not to one of his daughters, but to William Maynard, chief clerk of Pascoe Grenfell and Company, the firm which his grandfather founded and which was headed by his uncle, Pascoe, until the latter's death in 1838. Addressing Maynard as an old friend, he told him enough of his activities to lay at rest any possible doubt about his involvement in the Chicago Conspiracy or about the existence of the conspiracy itself. He asked Maynard to:

> Tell the girls I am alive and well, although engaged in rather dangerous speculations, which you will know more of, probably, bye and bye. . . . The North West states are ripe for revolt. If interfered with in their election they will rise. All this is in favor of the South. If anything happens to me, the little property I have is in the hands of the proprietor of the Queen's Hotel, Toronto. . . . A letter addressed to Col Thompson . . . might or might not reach me. We are on the eve of great events. Abe Lincoln will either have made peace, or made himself a military dictator, within the next two months. In the latter case, the N. W. . . . . [States] secede, and there comes a row.[21]

The "Col Thompson" mentioned in this letter is, of course, Commissioner Jacob Thompson; obviously, Grenfell expected to remain in touch with him, either directly or through Hines, who would know where Grenfell was, and could forward to him any letters that Thompson's couriers brought to him from Toronto.

---

[21] Grenfell to William Maynard, August 31, 1864, in Weaks (ed.), "Colonel . . . Grenfell," 11. Reference has been made previously to Frank L. Klement's opinion that the treasonable plans of the KGC, the OAK, and the Sons of Liberty were the invention of detectives, Republican politicians, and ambitious army officers and had no existence in fact. He holds that the Chicago Conspiracy was a myth, concocted by mercenary detectives like Keefe, small-time *agents provocateurs* like "Dr." Ayer and army officers on the make like Sweet. Hines and Castleman, Klement believes, use the writings of these people to concoct fictitious "postwar tales of adventure and wartime activity." Klement, *The Copperheads,* 250. Leaving aside the probative value of Hines's and Thompson's contemporary notes and reports, surely Grenfell's letter of August 31, not published until nearly a century after these events, cuts the ground from under Klement's conclusion. The failure of the conspiracy is not proof that the conspiracy never existed.

Grenfell's letter to Maynard ends with the cheery assurance, "I am well and hearty." Evidently, the weeks of leisurely hunting and fishing after his departure from the depressing atmosphere of Richmond had restored his normal vigor and spirits and made him ready once again to risk his life with complete equanimity. It speaks volumes for his capacity for enthusiasms untempered with a particle of shrewdness or realism, that only a few days after his direct exposure to Copperhead futility, he could still express complete faith in the eventual success of the conspiracy. His confidence is an indication also of the powerful hold that Hines, with his "firmness, zeal and persistence," had on his associates, and of Grenfell's readiness to place his fate in the hands of the younger man.[22]

The letter Grenfell had written his daughter, Marie, in March, brief and rather uncommunicative as it was, nevertheless shows that he remained on cordial terms with at least one of his daughters. It shows also that by 1864, Grenfell had learned enough about himself to have no illusions about his ability to fulfill the role of a parent or of a stable member of society, for he wrote, "I know you often think of me when my unfortunate wandering propensities prevent my occupying myself about you."[23] But the letter to Maynard strikes a new and unexpected note of wistfulness; he tells Maynard, "I have not heard from you all for a long time. I was going to say from home, but I forget I have no home."[24]

In 1864 Carlyle, in Central Illinois, where Grenfell went to hunt, was a typical prairie settlement of a few dozen houses, situated about forty miles east of St. Louis, on the highway to Louisville. Grenfell described it as a "horrible hole," but it was probably no worse than hundreds of other midwestern hamlets in a region which had been at the edge of the settlements only a little more than a generation earlier.

[22] Jacob Thompson to Judah P. Benjamin, December 3, 1864, in OR, Vol. XLIII, Part II, 934. Cf. Headley, *Confederate Operations in Canada*, 294.

[23] It is of course possible that Grenfell also wrote to his daughters Caroline and Blanche, but if he did, his letters have not survived. Grenfell to Marie Pearce-Serocold, March 18, 1864, in Weaks (ed.), "Colonel . . . Grenfell," 9.

[24] *Ibid.*, 11.

When the August 29 meeting with the Copperheads made it obvious that there was to be no uprising, Grenfell went to Maurice Langhorne's room in the Richmond House and remarked, so Langhorne said, that all that was left for the Canadian contingent to do was "to go to south Illinois and drill copperheads." [25] Whether or not Grenfell actually made the remark, it is at least certain that in the two months he spent in Carlyle, he drilled no one. John Kendall, whose house in the village was next to that of Grenfell's host, an Englishman named Baxter, saw Grenfell arrive some time between September 5 and 10, and saw him daily thereafter. Kendall swore that Grenfell went out with Baxter nearly every day to hunt, that he had no visitors and never discussed politics, and that he did not at any time drill Copperheads.[26] Kendall's testimony was supported by that of the village doctor, J. D. Knapp, who lived across the street from Baxter and saw Grenfell nearly every day. Dr. Knapp made the telling point that in a small, isolated village like Carlyle, it would have been impossible for anyone, especially a stranger as conspicuous as Grenfell, to be engaged in drilling Copperheads without everyone knowing about it; "any such transaction would have fired them up in a few hours," Dr. Knapp said.[27]

There was, in any case, no reason why Grenfell should have done anything more than spend his time as agreeably as possible until it was time to return to Chicago. And, loving field sports as he did, what occupation could have been more to his taste than to hunt grouse in the open prairie, in the bracing autumn air? But the hunting did not make him happy or even contented; notwithstanding his claim of being hale and hearty, he was apparently not in good health, and indeed his Carlyle acquaintances thought he looked unwell.[28] No doubt the strain of waiting and the uncertainty, neither of which he could tolerate for very long, contributed to

[25] *House Executive Documents*, 81.
[26] *Ibid.*, 355–56 and 359.
[27] *Ibid.*, 356–58. A third witness, who lived in the next house but one from Baxter's, corroborated Kendall's and Knapp's testimony. *Ibid.*, 358–59. When asked on cross-examination if he belonged to any secret organization, he replied, "Yes, sir; I belong to the 'Licensed Victuallers.'"
[28] *Ibid.*, 357.

his physical distress. Whatever the cause, it was from Carlyle that he wrote the most resigned and most introspective of his letters: "I am well, and have been too long used to discomfort, to consider comfort as being at all necessary to existence. Most people would consider it a great misfortune to be condemned to live in this horrible hole among hogs and hoosiers. . . . Not that I think it necessary to make myself miserable; bien au contraire. I make the best of everything, and am as jolly in a poor way as circumstances will permit." [29] And he ended with a sardonic postscript: "you must not expect interesting descriptions or details. These 'tarnation Yankees open everything they suspect, and I have to send this round and round again to get a chance of it reaching you. Vive la Liberté et la République."

When Grenfell wrote this letter, it was nearly time for him to return to Chicago. The fiasco in August and the patent unreliability of Copperhead promises had not deterred Hines from resolving to try once more to stage the oft-postponed uprising. As has been mentioned, Election Day, November 8, was to be the time, and Chicago the place. This time, there was not to be a failure; money was made available to the Copperhead chiefs in seemingly unlimited amounts, and even they agreed that the two months from the end of August to November 8 were ample to organize the large numbers of down-state Sons of Liberty who were to be brought to Chicago during the weekend preceding Election Day.[30] The pretext on which these men were to be induced to go to Chicago, and which Walsh would use to rally his followers in the city, was that the polls and the right of Democrats to vote had to be protected from interference by armed Republican thugs.

Grenfell was to be back in Chicago about ten days before Election Day. Taught some degree of caution by the August failure,

---

[29] Grenfell to Marie Pearce-Serocold, October 11, 1864, in Weaks (ed.), "Colonel . . . Grenfell," 12. The balance of this letter has been quoted on page 41.

[30] In addition to monies given previously, Hines gave the Sons of Liberty, just before November 8, $13,950 for arms and $12,000 to bring Southern Illinois Copperheads to Chicago. E. McK. Coffman, "The Civil War Career of Thomas Henry Hines" (M.A. thesis, 1955, University of Kentucky), 95.

Hines decided that Grenfell, who was the least likely to arouse suspicion and whom he could trust, should check on the state of Copperhead preparations far enough in advance of November 8 to leave time to do whatever might still be necessary to perfect the arrangements for the uprising. Hines himself visited Chicago on October 9, probably for the same purpose.[31] But just before he was due to leave Carlyle, Grenfell was taken seriously ill; he was forced to remain in town a week longer than he intended and did not reach Chicago until November 5.[32] He had planned his departure for a date that would make it possible for him to claim, in case of need, that he had stayed in Carlyle until the end of the hunting season, and he could account for his presence in Chicago because it was on the direct route to Toronto, where he intended to pick up his baggage on his way back to England.[33] On his arrival in Chicago, he again went to the Richmond House; he signed the register as "G. St. Leger Grenfell, Great Britain," and was given room 64.[34] Hines and his men, about a third as many as he had in August, had preceded Grenfell to the city. There was, however, a serious gap in their ranks, for John Castleman had been arrested a short time before by Colonel Carrington's detectives and was lodged in an Indianapolis jail. One may surmise, although there is no evidence on this point, that in Castleman's absence, Grenfell acted as Hines's second in command.

The program for the November uprising was a greatly watered-down version of the August plans. There was no more talk of a Northwestern Confederacy. Farragut's capture of Mobile, Sheridan's victories in the Shenandoah Valley, and, above all, Sherman's telegram of September 4, "Atlanta is ours and fairly won" had put the quietus on what little substance there had ever been

[31] Hines diary, entry for October 9, 1865: "One year ago today, I spent the day at Mrs. Morris' in Chicago, Ill.", in Hines Papers.
[32] *House Executive Documents*, 359, 471. The copy of the guest book entry from the Richmond House, placed in evidence at Grenfell's trial, gives November 15 as the date of his arrival in Chicago, an obvious error on the part of the court stenographer or the printer; by November 15, Grenfell had already been in prison for eight days.
[33] *Ibid.*, 639.
[34] *Ibid.*, 471.

in that dream. In addition, Colonel Carrington's arrests in mid-August had effectively scotched any possibility of a Copperhead takeover of any state government.

The political trimmings of the conspiracy were thus quite thoroughly eliminated, and Hines had to lower his sights on the military phase as well. The key operation was still to be the attack on Camp Douglas. Four separate groups of Copperheads, each under Confederate leadership, were to deliver a simultaneous assault on the four sides of the camp. As Hines undoubtedly knew, the chances of a successful attack had been considerably improved by the withdrawal of the reinforcements which had been sent to the camp in August, leaving Colonel Sweet with his regular garrison of just under eight hundred.[35] The prisoners, outnumbering the guards about ten to one, were to take advantage of the confusion created by the attack from the outside to attack the garrison from the rear. According to Detective Keefe, as melodramatic as always: "A signaling system had been devised, consisting of red, white and blue toy balloons, to be sent up at night, carrying lights by which the Confederates outside were to warn those inside . . . when to cooperate."[36] He does not bother to explain why balloons of different colors were to be used at night, or, indeed, why so wild a scheme should have been thought necessary to signal the start of the attack to the prisoners, who could hear and see the hundreds of guns being fired by the attackers.

As soon as the Camp Douglas guards had been overpowered and the liberated prisoners armed from the wagonloads of guns and ammunition that were to follow each of the attacking columns, one group was to go west to liberate the prisoners at Rock Island and another southeast to do the same at Camp Morton in Indianapolis. Meanwhile, squads told off for the purpose were to cut the telegraph lines leading out of Chicago, empty the gunsmith shops, and generally create as much havoc and confusion as possible. Af-

[35] Colonel Sweet stated that on November 6, "the whole number of men for duty, in and about Chicago, was 796, rank and file." *House Executive Documents*, 189.

[36] Keefe, "How the Northwest Was Saved," 89.

ter the prisoners at Rock Island and Indianapolis had been freed, the three groups, totaling better than 25,000, were to meet and march to a rendezvous with Nathan Bedford Forrest somewhere on the Ohio River in southern Indiana.

But after all his planning and hard work, after all the danger, all the frustrations and delays, Hines was to be deprived once more of his moment of glory. There was no uprising on Election Day and this time the Copperheads could not be blamed for the failure. The final collapse of Hines's project was due to Confederate treachery and to the energy and foresight of Colonel Sweet.

By the evening of November 5, three days before the date set for the uprising, Colonel Sweet knew that large numbers of suspicious-looking individuals, mostly from Fayette and Christian counties in South-Central Illinois, were arriving in the city.[37] The exact sequence of events in the next three days cannot be established with certainty, but it would appear that by the evening of the fifth, Sweet had also learned of the presence in Chicago of Hines, Grenfell, and the other Confederates. During the night of the fourth or the afternoon of the fifth, he was visited by a "stranger" who introduced himself as a colonel in the Confederate army and revealed the whole story of the forthcoming attack.[38] The informer was Maurice Langhorne, formerly an artillery sergeant in Morgan's command; Hines described him as "the infamous traitor who sold his comrades for 'blood money,'" a completely accurate and, if anything, too mild a characterization.[39] A year earlier, Langhorne, the possessor of numerous aliases, had reached Canada under circumstances which make it practically certain that he was a deserter and not an escaped prisoner of war. Being short of cash, he helped to put together the program for an imaginary Confederate raid on Detroit from Windsor and then

[37] *OR*, Vol. XLV, Part I, 1078.
[38] Kirke ("The Chicago Conspiracy," 114) is responsible for the statement that the "colonel," that is, Maurice Langhorne, called on Colonel Sweet on the night of November 4. Sweet, however, stated (*House Executive Documents*, 192) that Langhorne visited him for the first time in the afternoon of the fifth.
[39] Hines's marginal notes on the Kirke *Atlantic Monthly* article, in Hines Papers.

offered to sell the secrets of the pretended plot to the commandant of the army garrison in Detroit.[40]

Langhorne had had no luck with his confidence game in Detroit, but he had better wares to sell in Chicago and Colonel Sweet
was a more receptive prospect. Before launching into his story
about the conspiracy, the turncoat salved what little self-respect
he had by explaining that when he learned the details of Hines's
plans, he was so appalled that "though he was betraying his friends
and the South which he loved, the humanity in him would not
let him rest till he had washed his hands of the horrible crime." [41]
He neglected, however, to explain why his "humanity" had not
caused him to reveal the plot, which he knew all about in August,
until November.

The only full account of Langhorne's interview with Sweet is
that published by "Edmund Kirke" in the *Atlantic Monthly*.[42]
Kirke's story abounds in improbabilities and impossibilities, all of
which he relates with an equal assurance and with the same melodramatic trappings, but he claims that it is based on a five-hour interview with Langhorne, and a fourteen-page statement the turncoat wrote out for him. Since Colonel Sweet has left no record of
the interview, it is not possible to determine whether the obvious
flaws in Kirke's report reflect the author's irresponsible tampering

[40] *House Executive Documents,* 91–92; see also Coffman, "The Civil War Career
of Thomas Henry Hines," 102.
[41] Kirke, "The Chicago Conspiracy," 115. One may question if a shabby villain
like Langhorne would have bothered to stage the cheap comedy of self-justification with which Kirke credits him. It would have been much more in character
for him to get right to the point and negotiate the best possible price for his
treachery.
[42] After a successful career in business, "Kirke" (James Roberts Gilmore) went
into journalism. He became coeditor of a monthly devoted to antislavery propaganda and also formed an association with Horace Greeley, who sent him to
Tennessee to size up General Rosecrans' qualifications to replace Abraham Lincoln
as President. Later, Gilmore persuaded President Lincoln to let him go with
Colonel James Jaques, a religious fanatic from Illinois, on an absurd "peace
mission" to Richmond in the spring of 1864. "The reasons for the despatch of
any peace mission at all are partially concealed by the inconsistencies and in-
credibilities of the various narratives which Gilmore has given. The earlier ones
. . . are sheer propaganda. The later accounts have the defects of recollections.
Their chronology is confused and the citation of documents is often inaccurate."
Edward Chase Kirkland, *The Peacemakers of 1864* (New York, 1927), 90n.

with the truth or are an accurate recital of Langhorne's lies and exaggerations. There are ample grounds for doubting the veracity of both worthies.

Having finished his breast-beating about humanity, his friends, and the South, Langhorne came to the point. He told Sweet that twelve hundred "bushwhackers" from southern Illinois and Missouri were about to gather in Chicago to attack Camp Douglas on the night of November 8, that Hines was in overall charge, but that the military phase of the operation was to be led by Grenfell, assisted by Colonel Vincent Marmaduke and "a dozen other Rebel officers," all of whom he named.[43] These, he said, were already in Chicago, awaiting the arrival of the twelve hundred Copperheads. He also told Sweet of an arsenal collected at Walsh's house to arm the attackers, and although there is no mention of it in Kirke's account, he probably also told Sweet that some of the Confederates were to put up at the Richmond House.

Colonel Sweet now had to determine his course of action. With a garrison of 796, rank and file, and no possibility of getting reinforcements before the eighth, his most prudent course would have been to take the offensive at once. However, instead of moving immediately to forestall the attack by rounding up as many of the Confederates and Copperheads as he could find, and thereby frightening off the rest, he decided to wait two days, until Monday the seventh, in the expectation that the delay would enable him to locate and apprehend all the Confederate leaders and their henchmen. He planned also to use these two days to gather as much additional information as possible about the plot, in a form that could eventually be used in evidence against the conspirators.

One of the prisoners of war at Camp Douglas was a Texan, John T. Shanks. Of all the sordid characters Grenfell had met, or was still to meet, in the course of his chequered life, none was more abject than Shanks. He had no redeeming features and no excuses for his villainy. He was a forger, thief, traitor, spy, liar, perjurer, and a coward; in Hines's words, "a blacker-hearted villain never

[43] Kirke, "The Chicago Conspiracy," 114–15; *cf.* Coffman, "The Civil War Career of Thomas Henry Hines," 102.

187

lived." [44] Before the war, he had been a clerk in the Texas land office in Austin; shortly before 1861, he was tried for forging land warrants and was convicted. After his father had failed to have him pardoned, he managed his own release from the penitentiary by enlisting in the Confederate army. [45] Wholly in character was his assertion later that he was actually devoted to the Union, but had been *forced* into the rebel army, and that he had taken the oath of allegiance to the Confederacy only after entering a verbal protest against having to do so. [46] The ex-jailbird served under Bragg for a time and then with Morgan; he was among the captives sent to Camp Douglas when Morgan's Indiana-Ohio raid was broken up. Because of the shortage of army personnel, much of the clerical work in the camp was done by prisoners; Shanks was one of those chosen to perform such duties, and for some time before November, 1864, he had been a clerk, first in the post surgeon's office and then in the office of the camp commandant. [47]

Shanks was to play a key role in settling the fate of the conspiracy. There are several accounts to choose from for the tale of his movements and activities from November third to the night of the sixth. As usual, the version in Kirke's *Atlantic Monthly* article is the most lurid. He tells a touching tale to explain how Colonel Sweet came to select Shanks for a task so much better suited to his character and talents than the shuffling of papers in the camp headquarters office. It appears that Shanks was one of the favored prisoners who enjoyed (or bought) the privilege of leaving camp from time to time to visit the fleshpots of Chicago, and indeed he was the prisoner who used these holidays from captivity to pay his addresses to the pro-Rebel widow. Knowing this, Kirke writes, Sweet called Shanks into his office and offered him a harrowing choice: he could either become a spy for the government or he would be deprived thenceforth of the joys and comforts of the widow's society. His delicate sense of honor

[44] Hines's marginal notes on the Kirke *Atlantic Monthly* article, in Hines Papers.
[45] *House Executive Documents*, 67–68; 396; 459–62; 478–80.
[46] *Ibid.*, 43.
[47] *Ibid.*, 31.

touched to the quick by the colonel's proposal, Shanks exclaimed, "But I shall betray my friends! Can I do that in honor?" Prompted by his love for the widow, he answered his own rhetorical question in the affirmative after the briefest of hesitations and agreed to serve the colonel.[48]

This is the melodramatic confrontation as recorded by Kirke. The true situation was obviously quite different. With the fate of his command at stake, Sweet could take no chances. He needed a spy, someone who had been a member of Morgan's command and therefore knew, and was known by, the conspirators, and it had to be someone whose willingness to perform any filthy job for favors granted or promised had been thoroughly established. However lax the administration of the camp may have been, it is not likely that Shanks would have been granted his extraordinary privileges without a *quid pro quo*. Doubtless he had long since established a position as a reliable informant. In fact, within a month after assuming the Chicago command, Sweet had approved and forwarded Shanks's application to be allowed to take the amnesty oath, on the ground that Shanks "had given . . . the best evidence that he was a loyal man, and disposed to serve the government of the United States"—surely a most revealing statement and as clear an indication as one could wish that as early as June, 1864, Sweet was satisfied with Shanks's dependability as a stool pigeon and spy.[49] The Texan was thus an obvious choice for the job Sweet now wanted done. He was undoubtedly promised a reward in the form of freedom and money, both of which he received on December 5, when he was permitted to take the amnesty oath and was given a job at the camp at a wage of a hundred dollars a month and one ration.[50]

Another version of the Shanks saga was told by Thomas Keefe, with the detective himself as the inevitable hero of the tale.[51] He had become acquainted with Shanks some time before, says Keefe,

[48] Kirke, "The Chicago Conspiracy," 115.
[49] *House Executive Documents*, 191.
[50] *Ibid.*, 57.
[51] Keefe, *The Great Chicago Conspiracy*, 17–19.

but does not explain how the acquaintance had come about. Keefe knew that the conspirators were in Chicago and decided that they should be shadowed. He could not do it himself, inasmuch as they had met him in Toronto and would become suspicious if they now saw him in Chicago. Therefore, he thought of Shanks, a "reliable man," for the job and proposed to Colonel Sweet that the Texan he permitted "to join the conspirators." Sweet was opposed to the idea at first but allowed himself to be persuaded. As to Shanks himself, there were no problems: "When I broached the subject to him, Shanks said that I had treated him nice and pledged himself to serve me faithfully and honestly, if I secured him liberty and he be allowed to go back home to Virginia." [52] It is quite possible that the phrase "home to Virginia" was not a slip of Keefe's pen; after his sojourn in the Austin penitentiary, Shanks may not have been eager to claim Texas as "home."

Shanks's own account of the way in which he was recruited to act as a spy is quite matter of fact and differs from both Kirke's and Keefe's accounts. He testified that Lieutenant Colonel Lewis C. Skinner, commandant of the garrison, selected him for the job on November 3.[53] Since Shanks had no reason for not telling the truth on this point, his version is probably correct. Colonel Skinner may well have been acting for Sweet in this matter and doubtless knew, as did his superior, that Shanks was just the man for the assignment.

From this point onward, the chronology of Shanks's movements is inextricably confused. According to Kirke, on the evening of the fifth Shanks acted out the scenario devised by Colonel Sweet, of an escape from the camp. It required Shanks to hide among the other offal in a wagon that removed the day's accumulation of rubbish and garbage from the camp.[54] One is tempted to believe the story, if for no other reason than that it endows Colonel Sweet with an unexpectedly apt sense of humor, but there was no reason to

[52] *Ibid.*, 18–19.
[53] *House Executive Documents*, 69.
[54] Kirke, "The Chicago Conspiracy," 115. Shanks himself never made any mention of his supposed escape.

stage such an escape, and no doubt this story, like that of the invisible ink, is merely a product of Kirke's overheated imagination. Moreover, unless Shanks's own memory was greatly at fault, it was on November 3, and not on November 5, that his spying activities began.[55]

Before his departure from the camp, in the rubbish wagon or otherwise, Shanks was instructed to go directly to the home of Judge Buckner S. Morris. He was to present himself as a prisoner just escaped from Camp Douglas looking for a place to hide, and was to ask "whether there were not some escaped prisoners secreted in the city which Judge or Mrs. Morris knew about." [56] The judge was one of the leaders of the Sons of Liberty in Chicago, and his wife was active in the distribution of clothing, medicines, money, and gifts from home among the Camp Douglas prisoners. The pro-southern sympathies of husband and wife alike were undisguised and notorious. Sweet, Skinner, and Keefe evidently suspected that the conspirators might be in touch with the Morrises and could be located through them. Shanks went to the Morris home as directed and told a convincing tale of his supposed escape. Mrs. Morris responded by urging him to leave at once for Kentucky; she gave him one of her husband's suits to wear in place of the Confederate uniform he had on and also gave him, by a wholly appropriate coincidence, hallowed by biblical precedent, the sum of thirty dollars.[57]

Every step Shanks took after he left the camp was shadowed by Keefe and another detective, assigned to that task by Colonel Sweet, whose faith in the stool pigeon's reliability was evidently not unlimited.

Shanks's visit to the Morris home had effectively entrapped the judge and his wife but had failed in its object of discovering the hiding places of Hines and his men. The records do not show how Shanks spent his time after calling on Judge and Mrs. Morris until, on Sunday afternoon, November 6, he appeared in the lobby of

[55] *House Executive Documents*, 69.
[56] *Ibid.*
[57] *Ibid.*, 34.

the Richmond House, with the ever-faithful Keefe discreetly in the background, "for the purpose of ascertaining if there were any confederate officers stopping at the house." [58] Keefe asserts that Shanks went to the Richmond House on his instructions and implies that he himself had discovered that some of Hines's men were staying there. Actually, Grenfell was the only member of the group who was staying at the Richmond House; his presence at the hotel and the likelihood that others of the conspirators could at times be found there were probably revealed to Colonel Sweet by Langhorne, and Shanks's movements were directed accordingly.

[58] *Ibid.*, 35.

Chapter XI

T HE BIOGRAPHER of George St. Leger Grenfell must at
times rely on speculation and intuition because of a total lack
of records on lengthy periods of his life, and at other times must
dig out the truth from an overabundance of contradictory reports
covering brief episodes. The crowded hours and events in and
about the Richmond House on the typically raw, rainy November
evening and night of the sixth are in the latter category. The
biographer's problem here is to filter out of the collection of fanci-
ful, spurious, tendentious, and sometimes absurd stories of the
participants, a residue of definite, or at least probable, facts.

Thomas Keefe, Colonel Sweet's detective, had been at John
Shanks's elbow or at his heels ever since the latter left Camp Douglas, with or without the aid of the rubbish wagon. Having already
taken credit for the happy thought of sending Shanks to the Richmond House, Keefe also asserts that he instructed him to register
under the alias of George Brown. Typical of the difficulty of arriving at the truth of these events is the fact that even on a minor
point like this, no two stories agree, for Shanks himself said that
he registered as John Thompson.[1] Neither he nor Keefe bothered
to explain why he should have registered at all, or why an alias
should have been thought necessary to enable him to locate men
whom he knew and who knew him.

[1] *House Executive Documents,* 35.

Having signed the register and checked into his room, Shanks walked down a corridor, and according to Keefe, was

> approached by a tall, spare man, who accosted him with: "Why, Shanks, what in h__ are you doing here?" "Keep still," said Shanks in a low voice. "My name isn't Shanks . . . I've just escaped from Camp Douglas." "Come up to my room, then," said the tall man, and Shanks accepted the invitation . . . the tall, lean man . . . was . . . Grenfell. When Grenfell got Shanks up to his room, Shanks met Capt. Hines. To them Shanks told of his "escape" . . . and that he was waiting for money . . . to . . . get out of Chicago. . . . His story was accepted by Grenfell and Hines. They drank freely and became very communicative. . . . Capt. Hines opened up to Shanks the whole plot . . . [and] gave [him] a suit of civilian clothes. Shanks remained with Grenfell until about half past 12 o'clock midnight.

Having learned the secrets of the conspiracy, Shanks made his way to the room that Keefe had taken at the Richmond House, and told the detective that

> the conspirators had a list of all the banks in Chicago . . . they also told him that in addition to the force they could rely on to participate in the revolution, they knew of more than 500 bushwhackers who had just arrived . . . who only needed the signal agreed upon to rise, arm themselves, set free the prisoners in Camp Douglas, rob the banks, burn and sack the city, and march to other points to do the same . . . Grenfell stated to him that the plot would culminate on Nov. 7.[2]

This is a narrative straight out of late-nineteenth century melodrama, and it is difficult to see how its penny-dreadful quality could have been improved upon. Kirke, however, managed to do just that; his version is more lurid than Keefe's. Being in his own fashion a writer, Kirke fabricated a yarn that could have served without the change of a syllable, as the opening scene of a fourth-rate, blood-and-thunder Italian opera.

Shanks, according to Kirke, went first to Judge Morris' house and then, with a change to the dramatic present,

[2] Keefe, *The Great Chicago Conspiracy*, 22–25.

194

he goes to the private door of a public house, speaks a magic word, and is shown to a room in the upper story. Three low, prolonged raps on the wall, and—he is among them. They are seated about a small table, on which there is a plan of the prison. One is about forty-five, a tall, thin man, with a wiry frame, a jovial face, and eyes which have the wild, roving look of an Arab's. . . . In battle he is said to be a thunderbolt—lightning harnessed and inspired with the will of a devil. . . . It is . . . Grenfell. At his right sits another tall, erect man, of about thirty, with large, prominent eyes, and thin black hair and moustache. He is of a dark complexion, has a coarse, harsh voice, and a quick, boisterous manner. His face tells of dissipation and his dress shows the dandy. . . . This is the notorious Captain Hines. . . . [He] and Grenfell spring to their feet and grasp the hand of the Texan. He is a godsend—sent to do what no man of them is brave enough to do—lead the attack on the front gateway of the prison. So they affirm, with great oaths. . . . The banks will be robbed, the stores gutted, the houses of loyal men plundered, and the railway stations, grain-elevators and other public buildings burned to the ground. . . . Chicago will be dealt with like a city taken by assault, given over to the torch, the sword and the brutal lust of a drunken soldiery. . . . It is a diabolical plan, conceived far down in hell amid the thick darkness.[3]

The description of Grenfell in this turgid balderdash is lifted almost verbatim from Colonel Fremantle's book; that of Hines is not too far off the mark as a portrait of Marmaduke but is a ludicrously inaccurate representation of Hines.

One aspect of Shanks's participation in the events of the evening and night of November 6 is beyond comprehension. One of Hines's marginal notes on his copy of Kirke's *Atlantic Monthly* article declares that Shanks "was employed for many months as a spy to watch the movements of his comrades." This was true without question. Hines adds that when Shanks visited the Morris residence, he himself was hidden there, "& saw the traitor enter. He was then known to be a 'Spy' & was received as such." Grenfell, according to Hines, "knew the character of Shanks. Not an hour before meeting (*sic*) S[hanks] Grenfell had called upon me for definite in-

---

[3] Kirke, "The Chicago Conspiracy," 117–18. The present writer has tried assiduously to produce "*prolonged* raps," but so far without success.

structions as to the manner of attack, and I had spoken to him of the Spy Shanks & warned him to be on his guard." [4] Warnings were well enough, but it is evident from the sequel that neither Hines nor Grenfell had any idea of how to handle Shanks. Had they been more experienced in cloak-and-dagger work, they would have known how to protect themselves, and had they been as ruthless as their project required them to be, Shanks would have been enticed out of the hotel on some pretext and quietly but finally disposed of. They did nothing. This is difficult enough to account for, but Grenfell's subsequent conduct toward a man whom he knew to be a spy is incapable of any rational explanation.

Shanks told his story of the events of this night on the witness stand at Grenfell's trial, in which he appeared as the star witness for the prosecution. [5] Apart from the fact that his testimony bears all the earmarks of having been carefully rehearsed beforehand, it is a reasonably straightforward and convincing recital of his encounter with Grenfell. Shanks said that the first thing he did on arriving at the Richmond House was to look at the register, in which he found Grenfell's name. As has been mentioned, Grenfell went openly to the hotel and made no attempt to hide his identity, unlike the other conspirators, who either used aliases or avoided hotels entirely and hid in the homes of Confederate sympathizers.

Having found Grenfell's name in the guest book, Shanks sent a note to his room. He reminded Grenfell that they had met in December, 1862, while they were both in the Confederate army, and requested an interview. Receiving no response, Shanks went to Grenfell's room himself. Grenfell did not recognize him and did not recall their brief and casual acquaintance of two years before. Shanks identified himself, told the story of his "escape" from Camp Douglas, and asked for money so that he could leave Chicago. Grenfell replied that he was willing to help an "old comrade" but was short of cash himself and would have to telegraph for some.

---

[4] Hines's marginal notes on the Kirke *Atlantic Monthly* article, in Hines Papers.
[5] Shanks's testimony, recounting the events of the night of November 6–7, is in *House Executive Documents*, 35–41, 54–56, and 59.

There was some conversation, as was only natural under the circumstances, about conditions in Camp Douglas, the attitude of the prisoners, and their willingness to cooperate if an attempt were made from the outside to liberate them. It is significant that in reciting this exchange on the witness stand, Shanks could not recall if Grenfell had asked whether the prisoners could be counted upon to cooperate if an attack were made on the camp from the outside; it may be taken for granted that Shanks himself brought up the subject in an attempt to draw out and entrap his host. The conversation, however, was brief, and Shanks left with the understanding that he was to return later in the evening.

When Shanks returned at half-past nine, Grenfell had two other men in his room. One was a "Mr. Ware," not otherwise identified, whom Shanks mentioned two or three times as being present; he then disappears from the record. The other was J. B. Fielding, the alias of Confederate Lieutenant John J. Bettersworth.

One of the stock characters of fictional conspiracies is the well-intentioned fool or weakling whose role it is to betray associates to whom he is sincerely devoted; he cannot help himself—his treason is the result of stupidity or a flaw of character. This, to all appearances, was Bettersworth's role on the night of November 6. His weakness was an irresistible urge to talk when he was in his cups. Shanks's recital of what occurred in Grenfell's room in the course of this second visit makes it appear that the conversation that ensued was entirely between himself and Bettersworth; while they talked, Grenfell paced up and down and listened but did not participate in the talk. It must be observed, however, that even this passive role was sufficient to make him legally guilty of conspiracy.

"Something was said," according to Shanks, about releasing the Camp Douglas prisoners, and Bettersworth had asked him to estimate the number of men that would be needed to make a successful assault on the camp. He replied, Shanks said, that with two hundred men, he could carry the main gate and the artillery positioned immediately behind it. Then Shanks nearly forgot his lines. He testified that he was told by Bettersworth that "attacks

197

would be made on the city at the same time" that the camp was attacked, whereupon Judge Advocate Henry L. Burnett pointedly asked, "Who said that?" Shanks recovered quickly, and replied: "I think it was Grenfell; it was in his presence. Grenfell was to be in charge of the attack upon the city. The banks were to be taken charge of, railroad depots were to be burned, and the telegraph wires cut; . . . the prisoners were to be released and turned loose upon the city. This was said in the conversation, but whether by Fielding or Grenfell, I could not say; it was with the sanction of both parties." [6] Thus, within the space of a few confused sentences, Shanks attributed the disclosure of the plan to sack Chicago first to Bettersworth and then to Grenfell; then he admitted he could not recall which of them had spoken of it, and finally, remembering the coaching he had had before testifying, he made the legally improper and inadmissible statement that it had been said "with the sanction" of both of them. Read with a knowledge of the kind of evidence the prosecution had to offer to prove Grenfell's complicity in a treasonable plot, it is not at all difficult to detect the artful phraseology in which Shanks had been carefully rehearsed beforehand.

After the conversation between Shanks and Bettersworth had gone on for some time, Grenfell remarked that he was feeling rather unwell, whereupon his two guests bade him good night and went to Shanks's room. Shanks produced a bottle and plied Bettersworth with brandy. In a short time, his wits befuddled by the alcohol and his tongue further loosened, Bettersworth told Shanks everything about the conspiracy that he had not already revealed. The spy now had all the information he had been directed to obtain; he knew the plan and the time of the attack on the camp, the strength of the attacking force, the names of the principal conspirators, their aliases, and their hiding places in the city.[7]

There is, of course, not a word about Bettersworth's maudlin betrayal of the plot in Keefe's narrative. The detective either knew nothing of it, or what is more likely, deliberately omitted all

[6] *Ibid.*, 36.
[7] *Ibid.*, 38–40, 77.

mention of it, lest it detract from the glory of his own achievements. Kirke too fails to speak of it, either because he was unaware of the incident, or because it does not fit his thesis that the plot was revealed by Confederate soldiers of lofty principles after a hard struggle between their southern patriotism and the claims of a humanitarian conscience. Nor is it at all surprising that the conversation with the drunken Bettersworth in Shanks's room is greatly played down in the latter's testimony. The plot was aborted before Grenfell had committed any overt act of rebellion; hence, to obtain his conviction, the prosecution had to show that in all essentials, the plans of the conspiracy were revealed to Shanks in Grenfell's presence and hearing.

The survival of old letters is a chancy thing, and it is a strange quirk of fate that a letter has been preserved in which Bettersworth himself described the events on November 6 in Grenfell's and Shanks's rooms. When the conspiracy blew up, Bettersworth escaped to Canada. In the spring of 1865 Jacob Thompson told him that Hines held him responsible for the failure of the plot. Hines was convinced, Thompson said, that Bettersworth had been the source of all Shanks's information. In March, Bettersworth wrote Hines a seven-page letter to protest his innocence. He could not deny that he was present when Shanks visited Grenfell the second time, but, he wrote,

> it was plain to me at that time that S[hanks] knew everything in connection with the affair. . . . I knew the man with whom I was dealing. . . . I frequently made suggestions as to the manner of attack, but never did I say one thing until I was entirely convinced he knew more of the affair than I. G[renfell] frequently requested S[hanks] to either leave his room or change his theme. Said G[renfell] I have, as you know[,] been in the CSA but am now out of it, and do not wish the conversation to continue relative to an attack on C[amp] D[ouglas].[8]

Of course, Bettersworth was careful to say nothing of going on to Shanks's room and drinking with him.

[8] John J. Bettersworth to Thomas Henry Hines, March 12, 1865, in Hines Papers.

Hines was not at all impressed with this attempt at self-justification. He sent the letter on to his wife with the comment: "B[ettersworth] attempts to justify his conduct . . . & in my opinion makes his case worse. . . . It grieves me much to say it but my conviction is firmly established that Mr. B.—did reveal the whole plan to Shanks while under the influence of liquor." [9] In a sense, Hines's comment is unfair. Bettersworth had done more than enough talking while he was still sober. His drunken babbling to Shanks merely added frosting to the cake. And in any case, Colonel Sweet knew enough, several hours before Bettersworth went to Shanks's room, to be able to scotch the conspiracy. Bettersworth's revelations added only useful but not essential details; the chief value to the government of his loose tongue was that it added corroborative evidence on the existence of the plot and on Grenfell's involvement in it.

It was past one A.M. on the seventh when Bettersworth left Shanks. As soon as his guest was gone, Shanks hurried with the tale of his discoveries to Colonel Sweet, who at some time on Sunday set up his headquarters in the city to be in closer touch with developments.[10]

Even before he was in possession of the additional information Shanks gave him, Sweet had decided to change his plans. Having learned late in the afternoon of the sixth that more Sons of Liberty from southern Illinois were arriving in the city, he came to the conclusion that it would be too risky to wait another day to round up the conspirators and decided to act that night.[11]

This was Sweet's explanation of his reason for moving to the attack on the night of the sixth. One may suspect that he had a far more persuasive motive, but one which he could not very well avow. If the arrests were to be made, why not make them at once, so that news of the "Copperhead Conspiracy" would be in the newspaper on the seventh—the day before the election? The "crimes

[9] Undated note, in *ibid.*
[10] *House Executive Documents*, 40. It will be recalled that in Keefe's version, Shanks came to him with the story, and he in turn informed Colonel Sweet.
[11] *Ibid.*, 195–96.

of the Copperheads" had been a potent electioneering weapon in the hands of the Republicans in 1863, and Sweet himself was a Republican stalwart. Might not a well-timed and well-publicized exposure of another Copperhead plot, worse than any that had gone before, be an important factor in deciding the outcome of the presidential election? Was it not safe to assume that revelations so beneficial to the Republican Party would prove equally beneficial to the officer whose alertness and energy had uncovered the dastardly plot and foiled it at the eleventh hour?

Whatever his total motivation may have been, Sweet sent a messenger by train to Springfield, Illinois, at 8:30 in the evening to General John Cook, in command of the Military District of Ilinois, with a dispatch which he said he was afraid to entrust to the telegraph.[12] The message stated:

> The city is filling up with suspicious characters, some of whom we know to be escaped prisoners, and others who were here from Canada during the Chicago convention, plotting to release the prisoners of war at Camp Douglas. I have every reason to believe that Colonel Marmaduke, of the rebel army, is in the city under an assumed name, and also Captain Hines, of Morgan's command; also Col. G. St. Leger Grenfell, formerly Morgan's adjutant-general, as well as other officers of the rebel army. . . . I am certainly not justifiable in waiting to take risks, and mean to arrest these officers if possible before morning.[13]

It is to be noted that this dispatch was on its way to General Cook an hour before Shanks made his second visit to Grenfell's room, and before he met Bettersworth.

After sending this dispatch, Sweet organized his forces for the night's operations. Colonel Skinner was given fifty men and ordered to raid the home of Charles Walsh. Captain Pettiplace, whose patronymic is misspelled even more frequently than Grenfell's, was to proceed to the Richmond House with a mixed force of soldiers and detectives to arrest Grenfell and any other Confederate officers found in the hotel. A third detachment of a hundred

---

[12] *Ibid.*, 190.
[13] *OR*, Vol. XXXIX, Part III, 678.

soldiers under Captain Strong was to patrol the center of the city to preserve order. His men were to round up as many of the "bushwhackers" as they could lay their hands on; the bushwhackers were to be identified by their "general kind of wolfish aspect." [14]

Soon after midnight, the three groups of soldiers sallied from the camp. Colonel Skinner's men had the shortest way to go and were the first in action. They forced their way into the Walsh home and found two of Hines's men, George Cantrill and Charles T. Daniel, hiding on the roof and took them into custody. In the house itself, they found a store of arms consisting of 142 double-barreled shotguns loaded and capped, 349 Joslyn revolvers also loaded and capped, 13,412 ball cartridges, and 344 boxes of caps.[15] Walsh himself and his son were arrested also, and they and the two Confederates were marched off to Camp Douglas.

When Captain Pettiplace and his soldiers and detectives arrived at the Richmond House, they posted guards all arround the building, and then the captain himself with a numerous escort went to Grenfell's room. Grenfell had not yet gone to bed. He was seated, fully dressed, before the fireplace, his dog asleep on the floor at his feet, when Pettiplace knocked on the door. On the table next to his chair was a slip of paper bearing the message, "Colonel—you must leave tonight. Go to Briggs House." The note was signed "J. Fielding." [16] Not so far gone in drink as to fail to see what he had done, and in a panic for his own fate, Bettersworth had found the wits to dash off a warning and send it to Grenfell's room before he himself disappeared into the night. But why did Grenfell make no move to save himself? Did he decide that as a British subject he had nothing to fear? Did he weigh his chances of escape and conclude that the effort would be hopeless? Did he dismiss

[14] *House Executive Documents*, 195; the phrase is Colonel Sweet's.

[15] *OR*, Vol. XXXIX, Part III, 1079. A search a few days turned up 47 additional shotguns, 30 Allen's carbines, and one Enfield rifle in Walsh's barn. Colonel Sweet testified that "about 354 revolvers, about 200 shot-guns, double-barreled, and about 30 cavalry carbines" as well as "fourteen or fifteen thousand rounds of cartridges" were found in Walsh's house and barn. *House Executive Documents*, 194.

[16] Horan, *Confederate Agent*, 196; *cf.* Bettersworth to Hines, March 12, 1865, in Hines Papers.

the idea of escape altogether and decide to brazen it out? Or was his failure to heed Bettersworth's warning due to an abdication of a will to act, a passive acceptance of fate? There is unfortunately no way of discovering what thoughts passed through his mind as he sat quietly in his hotel room in the dreary hours of a November night, waiting for the Federal officers to come for him.

It was nearly three o'clock in the morning when Grenfell heard Captain Pettiplace's knock. He called out, "Who is there?" and the resourceful Keefe answered, "Boy with a telegram." Grenfell came to the door and found himself looking into the muzzles of more than a dozen pistols in the hands of as many soldiers, detectives, and policemen. The sardonic streak in him should have been amused and his vanity flattered by the size of the force the Federals deemed necessary to capture him. He was told, rather unnecessarily under the circumstances, that he was under arrest. He offered no resistance, nor, contrary to Keefe's gaudy account, did he "rage like a lion," although it may be taken for granted that he protested energetically at the indignity of an innocent traveler's being arrested as a common criminal.[17] The heroic Keefe looked into the room and noticed Grenfell's dog; remembering that he had been told that "he was a fierce and savage beast, and would 'do a man up' in short order," Keefe threatened to shoot the unoffending animal unless Grenfell tied it up forthwith.[18] Grenfell obliged and, thus reassured, Keefe took the dog to the police station, "from which he was subsequently taken to and exhibited at a [sanitary] fair that was being held in Bryan[t] Hall, on Clark Street." Just as Grenfell had been promoted to major general, so his harmless hunting dog was promoted to a fierce bloodhound; placards were posted throughout the city and advertisements appeared in the newspapers, to notify the public that Grenfell's "bloodhound" could be viewed by the curious for an admission charge of twenty-five cents.[19]

[17] Keefe, *The Great Chicago Conspiracy*, 27; Waterloo, "The Great Chicago Conspiracy," 148.
[18] Keefe, *The Great Chicago Conspiracy*, 27.
[19] *Ibid.*, 27–28; *cf. House Executive Documents*, 100.

Grenfell himself was taken, not to a police station, but to Trinity Church, on the corner of Wabash Avenue and Jackson Street, which had been designated beforehand by Colonel Sweet as the collection depot for prisoners taken in the city. Shanks, who had been "arrested" also, was likewise taken to Trinity Church, doubtless in the expectation that by posing as a prisoner, he could pick up additional tidbits of information from his fellow captives that could later be used in evidence against them. They were joined shortly by Judge Morris, Vincent Marmaduke, and Benjamin Anderson, the two latter being the only Confederates caught besides Cantrill, Daniel, and Grenfell. Hines, Bettersworth, and all the others escaped. The bushwhackers did not fare equally well; twenty-seven of them, all armed, were rounded up in the Fort Donelson Hotel, sleeping six to a bed, according to the Chicago *Tribune;* another lot, also armed, was arrested in a "den on North Water Street"; and all through the day, groups of them, large and small, were picked up by patrols of police and soldiers "in hotels, grog-shops, boarding-houses, streets, alleys, and under the sidewalks, and wherever . . . men of this character and description" could be found.[20] Eventually, a total of about 150 of them were arrested, on nothing more than suspicion.[21]

Sweet's reports and dispatches, and the report in the Chicago *Tribune* of the events of November 6 and 7, make it evident that in Hines's absence, and possibly in order to gloss over his escape, Grenfell was given prominence as the prize catch. The first story of the arrests in the *Tribune* declared that "Col. G. St. Leger Grenfell is, as his name implies, a Southern aristocrat."[22] This statement was later corrected, but neither Sweet nor the newspapers thought it necessary to mention that when Grenfell's baggage was searched, not a scrap of evidence was found to connect him with

[20] Chicago *Tribune,* November 8, 1864; *House Executive Documents,* 190.
[21] The figure of 150 was given by Sweet in his testimony in the Grenfell trial (*House Executive Documents,* 190); however, in his official report (*OR,* Vol. XLV, Part I, 1079) to the provost marshal general, he stated that 106 "bushwhackers, guerillas and rebel soldiers" were arrested.
[22] Chicago *Tribune,* November 8, 1864.

204

the conspiracy.[23] Oddly enough, the defense did not bring out this fact at Grenfell's trial; the first and only reference to what might have been considered a telling point in his favor was in a hostile brief prepared by Judge Advocate General Joseph Holt, two months after the trial had ended.

At some time during November 7, all the prisoners were taken from Trinity Church to Camp Douglas. Grenfell was placed in a cell which he described as six feet long by four feet wide.[24] His bed was two and a half feet wide; thus there was not enough space left to allow him to walk about, and he was not permitted to leave the cell for exercise. There was no heat and the cell was not only bitterly cold but, in addition, its atmosphere was poisoned by the nearly unbearable stench of the latrines over which it was located. After fifteen days of confinement, Grenfell wrote, one of his fellow prisoners was on the point of death and another was out of his mind. Grenfell himself, suffering from one of his recurrent attacks of dysentery, aggravated by bad food, lack of exercise, and the foul air, was taking four grains of opium daily on the orders of the prison doctor. When he asked for some mush in place of the unvarying daily diet of salt pork and soggy bread which he said would kill him, the officer in charge of the prison said, "Then let him die, God damn him, he deserves nothing else." [25] This was the first demonstration of the persistent hostility of which he, alone among the prisoners, was the object. There were probably two reasons for it: the fact that he was a foreigner certainly counted heavily against him, but more important was the general belief that his role in the uprising was to be in command of the sack

[23] *House Executive Documents*, 649.

[24] Grenfell to Acting British Ambassador, January 23, 1865, in British Legation-Archives, FO 115/448.

[25] *Ibid.* Grenfell was somewhat prone to exaggerate the hardships he was made to endure by callous or actively hostile Federal officials, but there seems little doubt that conditions in the prison at Camp Douglas were atrociously bad. William L. Felton, one of the Chicago Copperheads arrested on the night of November 6, testified that he was kept in the Camp Douglas prison for thirty-one days in the cold of a Chicago winter without a blanket or an overcoat. (*House Executive Documents*, 468–69.

205

of Chicago, when the city was "given over to the torch, the sword and the brutal lust of a drunken soldiery." [26]

The newspapers reported that Charles Walsh's bravery, so much in evidence when all he needed to do was to pocket Hines's greenbacks, evaporated as soon as he was arrested. He became eager to tell the authorities everything he knew about the conspiracy, into which, he said, he had been led by designing persons who had used him as a cat's-paw.[27] Grenfell, on the other hand, maintained silence, although efforts were made to get him to talk. Langhorne offered him his freedom if he agreed to become a witness for the government. When confronted with this at Grenfell's trial, Langhorne resorted to the standard disclaimer of the police spy; what he had actually proposed, he said, was "that if he would . . . confess the whole matter and implicate those concerned . . . I would use my influence to see that he was let loose." [28] He undoubtedly did propose to Grenfell that he too turn informer and promised him his freedom if he would do so; the only question is whether he did this on his own initiative or whether he was performing Colonel Sweet's dirty work. Langhorne was equally capable of either, but it is difficult to believe that he would have been granted access to Grenfell and to Walsh, to whom he made the same offer, had he not been acting with the sanction, if not the instigation, of Colonel Sweet.

Indeed, there is a suggestion, so strong as to amount to a near certainty, that Sweet's activities in this affair were not motivated by disinterested patriotism alone. Obadiah Jackson, who had the ill fortune to become president of the Chicago temple of the Sons of Liberty just in time to be arrested on November 7, testified that Sweet told him that "if things were all right, he expected to be made a brigadier." [29] The colonel certainly left no stone unturned to make certain that "things" would be "all right." On the other hand, it must be said in his favor that, to all appearances, he sin-

[26] Kirke, "The Chicago Conspiracy," 118.
[27] Chicago *Tribune*, November 8, 1864.
[28] *House Executive Documents*, 97.
[29] *Ibid.*, 451.

cerely believed that his prisoners were guilty; he ended his official report of the events of November 7 with the recommendation that the prisoners "be tried before a military commission and punished." [30] If the omission of the phrase "if found guilty" from the colonel's stern suggestion does not quite square with Anglo-Saxon ideals of justice, it must be remembered that the report was written in time of war.

Entertaining these feelings, and believing that the aims of the conspiracy constituted a flagrant violation of the laws of civilized warfare, Sweet could not be expected to ameliorate the conditions of Grenfell's imprisonment, especially after the latter's refusal to bear witness against his fellow-conspirators. Nevertheless, Sweet was well aware of the fact that Grenfell had no value to the government unless he remained alive long enough to be tried and convicted. Hence toward the end of November, there was a slight easing of the hardships of his imprisonment. He was permitted to leave his cell for a short time each day to stretch his legs and to warm himself at the stove in the guardroom, and, shortly afterwards, he was moved from his tiny, noisome cell to a larger, airy room, where he had space in which to move about.[31] Here he remained until the end of December, when he was taken to Cincinnati to stand trial.

Grenfell had been in prison for twenty-seven days before he was allowed to communicate with the outside world. By that time, the government had decided to try him before a military commission in company with Anderson, Cantrill, Daniel, and Marmaduke, as well as Judge Morris, Walsh, and R. T. Semmes, the last three being the only Copperheads of the 150-odd arrested whom the government thought it worthwhile to prosecute. The government's choice of a military commission to try the prisoners was in keeping with the practice initiated by Secretary of War Stanton,

[30] *OR*, Vol. XLV, Part I, 1080.

[31] Grenfell to Acting British Ambassador, January 23, 1865, in British Legation Archives, FO 115/448. In a later letter, Grenfell decreased the width of the cell to 3½ feet and said that he had been "without fire, bed, or blankets, the thermometer 10 degrees below zero." Grenfell to British Ambassador, April 4, 1865, in *ibid.*

of trying anyone accused of actions which the War Department considered seditious before a military commission rather than a civil court. Stanton's announced aim of respecting "individual rights as far as it might be consistent with public safety and the preservation of the Government," reinforced by a presidential order that anyone accused of disloyal practices be tried by a military court and denied the protection of habeas corpus, in effect suspended traditional civil rights for the duration of the war.[32] Justified or not—and the merits of the case were argued with great heat by contemporaries and are still the subject of debate among scholars and political theorists—the Stanton-Lincoln method of dealing with real or supposed disloyalty gave the government all the cards, as Grenfell was to learn shortly.

On November 8 and again on November 12, I. Edward Wilkins, the British consul in St. Louis (Chicago was not large enough in 1864 to justify the presence there of a British consulate) had his brother, a resident of Chicago, inquire of the authorities if any British subject had been arrested by Colonel Sweet. The reply each time was in the negative and Grenfell was held incommunicado until December 2.[33] He was not given the opportunity to retain counsel, he was not arraigned, he was not notified formally of the charges on which he was being held, and, of course, there was no chance whatever that he should be admitted to bail. In all this he shared the common fate of everyone who had the misfortune to fall into the clutches of military justice in the last two years of the war.

At last, nearly a month after being arrested, Grenfell was allowed to send a note, which he datelined "Cell No. 3, Camp Douglas," to the "British Consul, Chicago," in which he asked to communicate with the consul to obtain the means for his defense and to inform his friends in England, "who are powerful and influential," of his predicament.[34] The note was forwarded to Wil-

[32] Thomas and Hyman, *Stanton*, 249.
[33] I. E. Wilkins to J. H. Burnley, January 18, 1865, in British Legation-Archives, FO 115/552.
[34] Grenfell to British Consul, Chicago, December 2, 1864, in *ibid.*, FO 115/442.

kins in St. Louis. In the absence of instructions from his superiors in Washington and heedful of his delicate position as the representative of a neutral power, Wilkins replied that because Grenfell held a colonel's commission in the "Army of the so-styled Confederate States," and was "in custody on the charge of being connected with the plot to release the prisoners of War at Camp Douglas," he could not with priority intervene on his behalf.[35]

Within a few days after December 2, Grenfell was also allowed to retain counsel. How he made his choice is not known, but he settled on Judge Robert S. Wilson and Edward G. Asay, both members of the Chicago bar, to defend him. Wilson and Asay were already representing Walsh, and Grenfell may have chosen them simply for that reason. Asay, according to Consul Wilkins, was "well known as entertaining strong political views adverse to the . . . administration," a reputation that was not likely to benefit any client of his in a case with strong political overtones.[36] At some time during the trial, Robert Hervey, one of the corps of three attorneys representing Judge Morris, began to act for Grenfell also, but there is nothing in the records to indicate why or how he came to do so. Perhaps it came about as a result of Grenfell's and Hervey's common British origin. Hervey was of Scottish birth; he had practiced law in Canada before moving in 1852 to Chicago, where he formed a law partnership with Judge Morris.[37]

On December 5 Wilson and Asay informed William Maynard, chief clerk of Pascoe Grenfell and Company, that they had agreed to defend Grenfell; they wrote that: "The Government intimate that he will be tried by Court Martial, but we are anxious to secure a trial before the Civil Courts as he will stand on a better footing there. We will do everything in our power to obtain his discharge as we believe him innocent, but it is a critical and dangerous charge and very difficult to manage. Any influence his friends at home can bring to bear upon our Government ought to be had for him,

---

[35] I. E. Wilkins to Grenfell, December 6, 1864, in *ibid.*

[36] Wilkins to J. H. Burnley, February 8, 1865, in FO-U.S.-General Correspondence, FO 5/1155.

[37] Robert Hervey obituary (1903); Chicago Historical Society.

and without delay." [38] On the same day, Grenfell also was given permission to write to Maynard. He informed Maynard that, being without funds, he had drawn a letter of credit upon him for £50 to cover in part the cost of his defense. [39] The letter of credit was undoubtedly honored but, so far as can be determined, this was the only occasion prior to his conviction that Grenfell received any financial aid from his relatives in England. The expenses of his defense were in the main met by Hines, on the basis of Jacob Thompson's instructions to use for the conspirators' legal expenses the sum of between $4,000 and $6,000 remaining in his hands of the money he had been given to finance the uprising. [40] Additionally, Judge Morris had in his possession nearly $10,000 that Thompson had given him, which he apparently used for his own defense, and perhaps some of this money also went to help his fellow prisoners. [41]

After mentioning the letter of credit, Grenfell wrote Maynard: "If my cousin Charles [Grenfell] would use his influence with Lord Lyons it might be of use to me. I cannot say more at present. I know not a soul here nor have I a friend. In case of accident, I have property at the Queen's hotel, Toronto, which will be delivered to your order, and to your order only." [42] And he added in a postscript, "I leave it to you to inform my girls of my situation or not just as you like." It is a curious and a sad circumstance that even in the desperate straits in which he now found himself, Grenfell should have found it advisable to address his plea for help to an employee of his cousin's firm, rather than to Charles

[38] Robert S. Wilson and Edward G. Asay to William Maynard, December 5, 1864, in FO-U.S.-General Correspondence, FO 5/1155.
[39] Grenfell to Maynard, December 5, 1864, in *ibid.*
[40] Jacob Thompson to Thomas H. Hines, n. d., in Hines Papers. Hines informed Thompson that he had written to all the defense attorneys to assure them that they "shal [sic] not want for reasonable fees." Hines to Thompson, March 19, 1865, in *ibid.*
[41] Thompson to Hines, n. d., in Hines Papers.
[42] Grenfell to William Maynard, December 5, 1864, in FO-U.S.-General Correspondence, FO 5/1155. Lord Lyons, or, more accurately, Richard P. B. Lyons, Earl Lyons, was British minister to the United States.

Grenfell himself or to any other of his numerous clan of close relatives.

Within two weeks from the date of these letters, Charles Grenfell called on Under-Secretary of State for Foreign Affairs Austen Henry Layard to solicit the help of the British government for his cousin.[43] The case was handled with remarkable dispatch. On December 31, instructions were sent with the approval of the foreign secretary, Lord John Russell, to J. Hume Burnley, chargé d'affaires in Washington, to make official inquiries about the case and to do whatever could be accomplished through diplomatic channels to help Grenfell.[44]

Given the mood of the administration in Washington and of the North generally during the last winter of the war, it is more than doubtful that the British legation could have given Grenfell any effective help under any circumstances; nevertheless, it was unfortunate that at a critical moment in his affairs, Lord Lyons, the British minister, was absent from his post, and the task of looking after his interests fell to a diplomat of junior rank. Conceivably, Lord Lyons might have found the means through his personal friendships and influence with the leading members of the administration to help Grenfell. Burnley had none of Lord Lyons' prestige. His first response to London to the instructions he had received, held out no hope whatever; he wrote that he was "convinced that it will be impossible to do anything for . . . [Grenfell] as everything seems to militate against him. The United States Government with every show of right look upon him as an incarnate enemy . . . and will act accordingly." [45] Clearly, Burnley

[43] Layard, a Victorian in the Renaissance tradition, had learned his trade as a diplomat in company with John Drummond Hay at the British embassy in Constantinople. In the course of his generous periods of leave, he located and began to excavate the ruins of Nineveh and later identified the ruins of Babylon.

[44] E. Hammond (Foreign Office) to J. H. Burnley, December 31, 1864, in FO-U.S.-General Correspondence, FO 5/1155. It is significant that these instructions were transmitted to Burnley in the form of a private note, rather than as an official dispatch. Hammond closed his note with the comment that "it seems rather a doubtful matter."

[45] Burnley to Foreign Office, January 16, 1865, in *ibid*.

did not indulge in excessive optimism and because he obviously agreed with the opinion of the United States government that Grenfell was an "incarnate enemy" of the Union, there was little chance that he would exert himself unduly on his behalf. He instructed Wilkins "to make some few inquiries" about the case on a wholly unofficial basis. Such tepid instructions were not calculated to elicit an extraordinary effort on the part of the consul, especially as they were coupled with a repetition of Burnley's doubt "whether under the circ[umstanc]es anything can be done for . . . [Grenfell] as the U. S. w*d*. very properly look upon him as a decided enemy." [46] Wilkins, however, did what he could within the strictly circumscribed limits of his authority, and despite the wording of orders which he would have been justified in interpreting in the sense that his official superior was quite content to let Grenfell suffer the consequences of his own folly.

[46] Burnley to I. E. Wikins, January 16, 1865, in *ibid*. Burnley closed with the sentence: "You seem to be on such good terms with the Authorities that I dare say you may be able to effect something privately when I sh*d* most likely fail officially.

Chapter XII

MEANWHILE, Grenfell and his seven fellow prisoners had been transferred to McLean Military Prison (McLean Barracks) in Cincinnati. Sometime between Christmas and New Year's, heavy leg irons were fastened to Grenfell's ankles, and he was taken to Cincinnati by train in the custody of a military guard. After spending a night and a day without food on the train, he passed his first night in his new prison still without food and had to sleep without blankets on a bare, dirty floor. His leg irons were removed the following morning and replaced by a ball and chain weighing sixty pounds which he had to wear for the next six weeks, except when he was in court or on his way there and back.[1]

The government's decision to try the eight "Chicago Conspirators" before a military commission was based on the theory that their alleged criminal acts had been committed within "the military lines and theatre of military operations of the army of the United States, at a period of war and armed rebellion."[2] The prisoners to be tried, besides Grenfell, were, as has been mentioned, George Cantrill, Charles Travis Daniel, Charles Walsh, Judge Buckner S. Morris, R. T. Semmes, Benjamin M. Anderson

[1] Grenfell to "British Ambassador, Washington," January 23, 1865, in British Legation-Archives, FO 11/448.
[2] *House Executive Documents*, 22.

and Vincent Marmaduke.[3] The prisoners were to be tried on two principal charges: first, that "in violation of the laws of war," they had conspired "to release the prisoners confined . . . at Camp Douglas"; and second, that they had conspired "to lay waste and destroy the city of Chicago." [4]

By having the prisoners tried by a military commission, the government greatly increased the odds in favor of a conviction. There was only a minimal chance that in time of war, a tribunal of army officers would consider such a case with complete impartiality; moreover, in a trial before a military commission, the prisoners would lack the protection of many of the procedural safeguards which would have been theirs in a trial before a civil court. However, it is open to question whether at that moment, they could have received an entirely fair trial even in a civil court; the "crimes of the Copperheads" had been one of the prominent issues in the presidential election only two months before and were still vivid in the public mind. Finally, by trying the eight men as a group on a charge of conspiracy, the prosecution gained the immense advantage that whatever evidence was offered against any one of them would to some degree operate to the prejudice of the other seven.

The trial was to take place in Cincinnati, the headquarters of Major General Joseph Hooker, commanding the Northern De-

[3] Marmaduke's role in the conspiracy is one of its many mysteries. He was involved in some way, but no evidence has survived to show the nature or extent of his participation. Hines wrote that "Marmaduke knew nothing until two days prior to the intended movement. *He had no command* as I had assigned him *no* duty up to this time." Hines's marginal notes on Kirke's "The Chicago Conspiracy," in Hines Papers. Stanley Waterloo credited Marmaduke with the leadership of the conspiracy under the authority granted him by President Davis. Waterloo, "The Great Chicago Conspiracy," 133-34. This, at least, is clearly erroneous. Marmaduke's father had been governor of Missouri, and his brother, John S., was a Confederate general. Vincent Marmaduke was born in 1830, graduated from Yale, and was farming in Missouri when the war broke out. Arrested for disloyalty, banished to the Confederacy, his gallantry in the battle of Corinth won him promotion to the rank of colonel. Later, he was sent to Europe by President Davis to purchase arms and munitions. Grace Marmaduke Sharp, "The Marmaduke and Some Allied Families," *William and Mary College Quarterly Historical Magazine*, XV (1935), 151-72.
[4] *House Executive Documents*, 22-23.

214

partment of the Union Army. On December 29 Hooker issued orders constituting the military commission which was to sit in judgment on the conspirators.[5] Nine officers, several of whom were lawyers in civil life, were appointed to the court. Four held the rank of colonel, three were lieutenant colonels and two were majors. Six of the judges were volunteer officers and three were regulars.[6] The presiding officer, Colonel Charles D. Murray of the Eighty-ninth Indiana Infantry, and two of his associates, Colonels Benjamin Spooner and Richard P. DeHart, had been members of the military commission which a month before had convicted Dr. William Bowles, Lambdin P. Milligan, and the other leading Indiana Copperheads of conspiring to overthrow the United States government, afford aid and comfort to the rebels, and incite insurrection.[7]

Grenfell was to characterize the court as "that packed and perjured commission," an "assassination commission," and its members as "those mercenary and subservient wretches." [8]

The prosecutor, or judge advocate, was to be Henry Lawrence Burnett. Born in Youngstown, Ohio, in 1838, Burnett decided at the age of fifteen that he wanted a better education than was obtainable at his birthplace, and with forty-six dollars in his pocket and a bundle of clothing over his shoulder, walked a hundred miles to enroll in Chester Academy in Pennsylvania. Subsequently he read law, was admitted to the bar in 1859, and began to practice in Youngstown. On the outbreak of war, he enlisted in the Second Ohio Cavalry and was elected captain of one of its companies. He saw active service with the regiment in Missouri and Kentucky. In September, 1862, he was a candidate for the colonelcy of the regiment, and was actually elected to the post, but for reasons which are not in the records, his election was nullified. The

[5] *Ibid.*
[6] *Ibid.,* 3.
[7] Pitman, *Trials for Treason,* 9.
[8] Grenfell to James A. McMaster, June 7, 1866; in University of Notre Dame Archives, Notre Dame, Indiana; Grenfell to S. L. M. Barlow, December 5, 1867; in Barlow Papers; quotation from Grenfell's Fort Jefferson prison diary (now lost), entry for October 22, 1865, in T. P. McElrath, "Annals of the War . . . Story of a Soldier of Fortune," Philadelphia *Weekly Times,* May 3, 1879.

explanation may be a note in the diary of a member of the regiment: "Officers and men full of wine and champagne at Burnett's expense." [9] In 1863 Burnett was appointed judge advocate of the Department of the Ohio, and filled the post with such success that when the government prepared to try the Indiana Copperheads, Governor Oliver P. Morton of Indiana requested that he be assigned to conduct the prosecution.[10] The conviction of the Copperheads made Burnett a marked man, and it was almost a foregone conclusion that he would be given charge of the prosecution of the Chicago conspirators. He had not only earned the assignment as a professional reward but also, because the government had to prove the complicity of the Copperhead organizations and their leaders in the Chicago affair, it was obviously advantageous to have the prosecution in the hands of someone who was already thoroughly posted on the subject of these organizations and their activities.

It will be seen that the twenty-seven-year-old Burnett's work in Cincinnati fully justified the confidence of the War Department in his qualifications and competence. He conducted a slashing, aggressive prosecution. His tactics were frequently questionable, particularly his harassment of witnesses for the defense and the use, for his own side, of witnesses whose worthlessness he was far too intelligent not to recognize. But if the test of a prosecutor's competence is a remorseless determination to obtain a conviction at almost any cost, Burnett was an ideal choice for the job.[11]

The commission held its first session at 2 P.M. on Monday, January 9, 1865. Because of the political connotations of the case, it had been decided that the trial should be open to the press and the public. The lurid accounts of the conspiracy in the Chicago newspapers, widely reprinted, as well as the recently concluded trial of the Indiana Copperheads, with its sensational revelations, had created a great public interest in the case and in the person-

[9] Luman Harris Tenney, *War Diary, 1861–1865* (Cleveland, 1914), 31.
[10] *Dictionary of American Biography* (New York, 1929), IX, 181–83.
[11] Burnett had a civilian assistant, J. P. Jackson, of the Cincinnati law firm of Jackson and Johnson, but he himself examined all the witnesses for the prosecution and cross-examined nearly all the witnesses for the defense.

alities of the prisoners. There was, too, a special curiosity to see the notorious British soldier of fortune, the bloodthirsty Colonel Grenfell. The room assigned to the commission, in a downtown office building, proved entirely too small to hold the judges, the prisoners and their numerous attorneys, the witnesses—many of whom, especially those called by the judge advocate, were permitted to attend sessions of the court and hear each other's testimony—the press, and the many curious who tried to gain admittance. On the second day, the commission removed to the grand jury room in the handsome Greek Revival county courthouse. This room also proved to be too small, and for its third session, the court moved once again, this time to the courthouse rotunda, a roomy, glassed-in enclosure located in the center of the building on the second floor. The rotunda was large enough to accommodate nearly all who wished to get in, and the spectators for whom there was not room inside could view the proceedings through the windows which enclosed it on all sides; they could, said the reporter for the Cincinnati *Daily Gazette*, "see the pomp and circumstance of a military court, and look upon distinguished specimens of the bold and desperate men who have plotted evil to our government and the people of our sister city." [12] It will be observed that the reporter was not troubled by doubts about the guilt of the prisoners; he did concede, however, that they had the appearance of "gentlemen of respectability, education and some degree of refinement."

Each day that the commission sat, the prisoners were marched the seven squares between McLean Barracks and the courthouse. They made the journey on foot in all weathers, handcuffed together in pairs, except for Judge Morris, who, as the Nestor of the group, was permitted to walk with the sergeant in charge of the military escort as his partner. General Hooker ordered the court to hold its sittings "without regard to hours," instructions which the commission chose to interpret in a liberal spirit, for its sessions normally did not begin until 11 A.M. [13] Moreover, and

[12] Cincinnati *Daily Gazette*, January 19, 1865.
[13] *House Executive Documents*, 3.

217

much to General Hooker's annoyance, the court also recessed periodically for a day or two, sometimes with little excuse for doing so.

On January 12, the commission having completed the formalities of organization and having found a permanent home, the defense attorneys were introduced to the court and the charges against the prisoners were read. The defendants were then instructed to plead to the charges. Now ensued the first trial of strength between the prosecution and the defense. The prisoners declined to plead and challenged the jurisdiction of the court, contending that under the law and the Constitution, it had no authority to try them. The brief submitted on Grenfell's behalf, typical of all of them, stated that

> not being and never having been in the military or naval service of the United States nor in any other capacity which renders him subject to the articles of war or the jurisdiction of a military tribunal, and not having been within the lines of any military camp nor within the sphere of any military operations . . . and the offenses charged not being infractions of any of the articles of war, he is not amenable . . . to the jurisdiction of this military tribunal . . . the civil courts of the United States are open and wholly unobstructed and . . . the administration of the laws of the United States within . . . the State of Illinois . . . is unimpaired in the said courts . . . which have full jurisdiction, and power, and authority under the laws . . . to hear and determine the matters charged . . . and that he is amenable solely to the authority and jurisdiction of the circuit courts of the United States . . . [in] Illinois, where he can have legal process to enforce the attendance of witnesses on his behalf.[14]

These arguments, solidly grounded on the common law, statutes, and the Constitution, were further buttressed by the following points: 1. Ordinarily, a military court may try only those whose status made them subject to military law, such as members of the armed forces, spies, and the like. 2. A military court may try civilians only if "by reason of the existence of an armed insurrection, the courts of law are . . . powerless, and the military have

[14] *Ibid.*, 10–11.

possession of a place and have assumed the administration of justice." 3. The acts which the defendants were charged with having committed constituted treason, and by statute, the Federal courts had sole jurisdiction over cases of treason. 4. The fact that the defendants were arrested by the military did not in itself give the military the right to try them.[15]

The judge advocate's elaborate reply to this challenge of the jurisdiction of the commission covered 119 pages of legal foolscap, and required two entire sessions to read. Burnett defended the jurisdiction of the commission mainly on the ground that "martial law obtained throughout the United States . . . during the continuance of the War," and he contended also that by conspiring to sack and destroy a city occupied by units of the Union army, the defendants were planning to commit a breach of the laws of war, and offenses against these laws were properly triable before a military tribunal.[16]

At the close of the session of January 17, the court, to the surprise of no one, rejected the contentions of the defense and upheld those of the judge advocate.[17] This ruling set the pattern which was to prevail throughout the trial; the pleas and objections of the defense were with few exceptions overruled, while those of the prosecution were almost invariably sustained. A ruling of the court on the eighteenth is typical of its attitude—one is strongly tempted to call it its hostile attitude—toward the defendants and illustrates the nearly hopeless handicap it imposed upon the defense. Counsel for Marmaduke moved on behalf of all the defendants that they be furnished with a list of the witnesses the prosecution intended to call to the stand.[18] The mere fact that the defense had to request the aid of the court to get this essential information is indicative of the spirit in which the prosecution was

[15] *Ibid.*, 17–18.

[16] Burnett's lengthy statement does not appear in the printed record of the trial (*House Executive Documents*), but it is a part of the official transcript preserved in Office of the Judge Advocate General: General Courts Martial, 1812–1938, MM2185, Boxes 675–77, War Records, National Archives.

[17] *House Executive Documents*, 20.

[18] *Ibid.*, 24.

conducted. To give the other side advance notice of the witnesses to be called was so customary and so eminently fair, as to constitute virtually a legal obligation.[19] Burnett had not seen fit to observe this custom, and objected to the defense motion "at the express instance and desire of several of the witnesses, who assured him that their lives would not be worth an hour's purchase in this or other cities if known." [20] If this gravely prejudicial statement had been made in a civil court within the hearing of the jury, it would have been grounds for declaring a mistrial; here, on the other hand, not only was the remark allowed to remain in the record, but the court also ruled "that the judge advocate should furnish the accused with a list of witnesses, so far as in his judgment it would not interfere with the interests of the service; but believing it to be a matter within his discretion, they declined to make any order in the premises." [21] Not until the following day, only twenty-four hours before Burnett was to begin the presentation of evidence on behalf of the prosecution, did he give the defense a list of those of his witnesses whose names "he deemed it expedient to present"; the list contained the names of only thirteen of the twenty-four witnesses he was actually to call.[22] Needless to say, his fears on behalf of his witnesses proved to be quite groundless; all twenty-four survived the trial in robust health.

After the dispute over the jurisdiction of the court had been settled in the judge advocate's favor, the prisoners were instructed to plead to the charges. All of them answered Not Guilty, but Grenfell did so with a characteristic flourish of ill-timed bravado; having made his plea, he turned to the judge advocate and gave him a mocking salute.[23]

The preliminaries which had taken up the first ten days of the

---

[19] Stephen Vincent Benet, *A Treatise on Military Law and the Practice of Courts-Martial* (New York, 1862), 62.

[20] *House Executive Documents*, 24; Cincinnati *Daily Enquirer*, January 19, 1865.

[21] *House Executive Documents*, 24.

[22] *Ibid.*, 28.

[23] Cincinnati *Daily Enquirer*, January 19, 1865.

trial had now been concluded.[24] The prosecution was about to call its first witness, and when the court assembled on the morning of January 20, a large audience was present. On hand were several Cincinnati judges, many of the most distinguished attorneys of the city, prominent citizens of every sort, and a "fair representation of ladies." [25] Burnett's strategy became evident as soon as he called his first witness; he had obviously concluded not only that he had a strong case against Grenfell, but also that as a foreign soldier of fortune, Grenfell was the most vulnerable of all the defendants. By leading off with the evidence against him, Burnett intended in the first place to prove the existence of the conspiracy, and secondly, by presenting Grenfell as an amoral, unscrupulous mercenary, to surround the conspiracy with an aura of cold-blooded villainy. The tone of the trial would thus be set, and anyone who could be shown to have been involved in the conspiracy in any way would share to some degree the Englishman's carefully highlighted iniquity.

It was thus that the audience assembled in the rotunda on the morning of the twentieth had the doubtful privilege of hearing the testimony of Burnett's prize exhibit, the shameless villain John Shanks. It must be said for the man that he made an excellent witness. The Cincinnati *Daily Gazette* described him as "a gentlemanly-looking individual, about thirty-five years of age; hair and eyes black; countenance a little fierce, but intelligent and thoughtful, and his language and manner indicate an average of culture." [26]

[24] Among these preliminaries was a motion for a separate trial made by each of the defendants. All the motions were denied, except George Cantrell's; he was granted a severance "on [the] ground of his evident inability to be present during the . . . trial." *House Executive Documents*, 24. The nature of his "evident inability" was nowhere explained; perhaps he was the prisoner whom Grenfell reported as having been driven out of his mind by the hardships of his imprisonment at Camp Douglas. On January 19, J. O. Broadhead, counsel for Marmaduke, moved on behalf of all the defendants that "the publication of the testimony . . . be excluded from the public papers until all the witnesses have testified," on the ground that the witnesses, who "may be of such character as not to be very reliable," should not have the opportunity to learn through the newspapers what others had testified. Broadhead's motion was denied by the court. *Ibid.*, 28–30.
[25] Cincinnati *Daily Gazette*, January 21, 1865.
[26] *Ibid.;* Shanks was actually thirty-three years old.

221

He told his carefully rehearsed story in a straightforward way, as Burnett, on direct examination, led him through a recital of his enlistment in the Confederate army, his capture in Ohio in 1863, his life in Camp Douglas, and the events in Chicago on the night of November 6.[27] Burnett took special pains to draw the sting of the obvious line of attack on Shank's credibility by having him admit that, a month before the trial began, he had been permitted to take the amnesty oath and was given a paid job in the camp, and that for months prior to November, 1864, he had been the recipient of special privileges and favors.

Burnett used all of one session and part of a second for the presentation of Shanks's testimony. The most damaging part of it, from Grenfell's point of view, concerned Shanks's conversation with Bettersworth about the forthcoming attack on the camp and the sacking of Chicago, first in Grenfell's room and then in Shanks's. Over the objections of the defense, which were of course overruled, Shanks was permitted to testify that what Bettersworth had said on those subjects in Grenfell's presence was spoken with the latter's "sanction," but he was not asked to explain in what manner Grenfell had indicated his approval of Bettersworth's statements. He was also permitted to repeat what Bettersworth had said when Grenfell was not present, on the convenient theory, advanced by Burnett, that "the acts or speech of any man who was connected with this conspiracy after we have connected Grenfell . . . with it is just as much evidence against him as though he himself did the thing or uttered the word." [28] This proposition left out of account the obvious fact that the only proof offered to connect Grenfell with the conspiracy, up to the point where Shanks told of his conversation with Bettersworth, was the very evidence that the defense objected to in vain.

When Shanks finished answering Burnett's questions on direct

[27] Shanks's testimony on direct examination will be found in *House Executive Documents*, 30–41.

[28] *Ibid.*, 37. Burnett's argument was legally valid, but he chose to overlook the equally well-established principle: "Proof of the plot or combination must precede proof of the declarations . . . of the accused parties." Benet, *Military Law*, 288.

examination, the defense had its chance to have a go at him. For two full days and part of a third, he was cross-examined, first by Robert S. Wilson on Grenfell's behalf and then by Robert Hervey for Judge Morris. Shanks had little trouble holding his own against Wilson's not especially adroit or effective questioning—the *Gazette* reported that he kept "far cooler or more collected than the Counsel"—and retained his composure even when Hervey began to expose his Achilles' heel by asking searching questions about his life in Texas before the war. Hervey put the question, "Were you, Mr. Shanks, ever arrested, tried, convicted and sentenced for the crime of . . . [forgery] in Texas?" [29] The question, although an entirely proper attack on the credibility of the witness, was objected to by the judge advocate as illegitimate and immaterial and, as a matter of course, his objection was sustained. Shanks was thus relieved of the necessity of answering; but with the self-possession of a congenital liar, he asked permission to reply and said with complete aplomb, "I never was." [30]

This exchange and indeed Shank's presence on the witness stand raised a number of fundamental problems. It should be said at the outset that Shanks *had* been "arrested, tried, convicted and sentenced" for forgery in Texas, and that he perjured himself by denying it. It was a well-established principle of military law that: "The conviction of an infamous crime, followed by judgment, disqualifies a person from giving evidence . . . and persons rejected for this cause, are said to be incompetent on account of the infamy of their character. . . . *Thus, a conviction of forgery will disqualify.*" [31] It would be an insult to Major Burnett's intelligence and ability to suppose that he was unaware of Shanks's past when he called him as a witness; it is, however, a sad commentary on his integrity that, with full knowledge of the man's criminal record and knowing him to be debarred thereby from

[29] *House Executive Documents,* 68. The word "forgery" has been substituted in the text for the word "felony" appearing in *House Executive Documents,* 68; the latter is a printer's error for the word "forgery," which appears in the handwritten transcript of the trial record.

[30] *Ibid.,* 68.

[31] Benet, *Military Law,* 232; italics mine.

testifying before a military court, he nevertheless used him as his principal witness in a case which might well lead to death sentences for the defendants.

But Burnett's disregard of what one can properly term an elementary rule of fair play did not stop at the mere use of an incompetent witness. One cannot resist the suspicion that Shanks's request that he be allowed to answer Hervey's question was a clever maneuver carefully prearranged by the prosecutor. The weight of authority held that a witness in court-martial proceedings was not bound to answer questions "tending to degrade his character," but that, if he chose to do so, the party asking the questions was bound by the witness' answer and could not subsequently introduce evidence to rebut it.[32] Northwithstanding this rule, the defense prevailed upon the court at a later stage of the trial to allow a succession of witnesses to prove beyond the shadow of a doubt that Shanks lied when he denied that he had been convicted of forgery in Texas. One of these witnesses, a cheerful and colorful rascal named Davis, a gambler by profession, testified that he and Shanks had been cellmates in the Texas penitentiary. When Burnett summed up for the prosecution at the close of the trial, he knew that he had to try to rehabilitate the character of his chief witness. He had to concede, he said,

> that Shanks had been seriously contradicted and impeached. . . . Shanks denied that he had been imprisoned, tried and convicted at Austin, Texas; he was so heartily ashamed of that passage of his life that in seeking to hide it, he lied about it. . . . You will remember, gentlemen, the bearing of Shanks on the witness stand; he is a fearless man and certainly a man of courage, and I cannot for myself avoid associating, to a considerable extent, courage with truthfulness.[33]

To claim, as Burnett in effect did, that the testimony of a brazen liar is "to a considerable extent" worthy of belief, whereas that of a nervous liar might not be, is somewhat lacking in logic. There is no way of knowing how much weight this absurd argument

[32] *Ibid.*, 314.
[33] *House Executive Documents*, 580–81.

carried with the members of the court; however, the entire course of the trial makes it only too plain that they were quite prepared to believe Shanks's evidence, notwithstanding his blatant perjury and that Burnett's effort to prop up his credibility was quite superfluous.

Three years later, long after Grenfell's codefendants had gone free and Hines was enjoying in peace and comfort all the rights and privileges of a loyal citizen of the United States, Judge Advocate General Joseph Holt, chief law officer of the War Department, was still contending that because Grenfell was clearly guilty, it made no difference that the principal witness against him should not have been allowed to testify at all and was an arrant perjurer besides. No doubt the nine military judges, prejudiced against Grenfell to begin with, held similar views. The result was a miscarriage of justice of a peculiar character. Without question, there had been a conspiracy and Grenfell had been a willing and active participant. Facts which were not and could not be known to the court, some of which did not come to light until many years later, prove his guilt beyond a doubt. But as a matter of abstract justice, he should not have been convicted of a capital crime, as he actually was, mainly on the testimony of such a man as Shanks.

The defense could not impeach or contradict Shanks's testimony on the one issue that mattered, namely the truth or falsity of his recital of what had been said to him or in his presence at the Richmond House on the night of November 6. Bettersworth's apologetic letter to Hines makes it abundantly clear that Shanks's evidence on this point was essentially truthful, but it might have been shown to be incorrect in so many particulars as to destroy the impact of his total testimony. But, in keeping with the practice of courts-martial in 1865, Grenfell could not take the stand to testify on his own behalf.[34] And Bettersworth, the only other participant

[34] Benet stated the rule in the following words: "With regard to the competency of parties defending in criminal prosecutions, as they are generally most strongly interested in the event, it seldom happens that they can be called as witnesses." Benet, *Military Law*, 236–37.

in the conversation, had disappeared without a trace and could not be called as a witness; if by chance he had come forward to testify for the defense, Burnett would have had him in the prisoners' dock, his testimony discredited in advance as that of a rebel and a conspirator. The judge advocate's heart was hardened against rebels, unless they had shown their return to righteousness by becoming paid spies and perjurers. Burnett was to demonstrate more than once in the course of the trial that he did not hesitate to deal harshly with witnesses for the defense. For example, a character witness for Walsh admitted in the course of his testimony that he had been a member of the OAK. When he left the stand, and while he was still in the courtroom, Burnett had him arrested; called to task by the defense, he declared to the court:

> On finding an avowed enemy of the government in this room, in discharge of my duty, I ordered his arrest. . . . The witness, by his own admission . . . avows his connection with an organization at enmity with the government, and his participation with the enemies of the government in bringing men into Chicago in violation of the laws. I therefore ordered his arrest; and I will act in like manner towards any other witnesses as fast as they reveal their guilt.[35]

The arrogant intimidation of witnesses could not well be carried much further.

The cross-examination of Shanks was completed on January 24, after an interruption to allow Frederick Hall, the War Department clerk who had made the stenographic record of Grenfell's interview with Secretary Stanton, to testify on that subject. Hall's calm recital of what Grenfell had said on that occasion, the information he had given about the strength of Lee's, Stuart's, and Beauregard's forces, his offer to take the amnesty oath, his expressed willingness to enter the service of the Union were he not restrained from do-

---

[35] *House Executive Documents*, 301. Another witness for the defense, Patrick Dooley, who had been arrested on November 15 and later released, testified that Burnett told him "if you in any way assisted the defense in getting witnesses to throw light upon these transactions you would be thrown back into prison." In a merciless cross-examination, Burnett was unable to shake Dooley on this point. *Ibid.*, 433–38.

ing so by "his fear that his position would be misunderstood by the confederate authorities" all placed Grenfell in the worst possible light.[36] It gave the court ample justification to regard him as an unprincipled mercenary, capable of changing his allegiance to suit his momentary convenience. Moreover, it branded him with the stigma of a double traitor; it was shown that after buying by his betrayal of the South the right to move about freely in the North, he proceeded to betray the Union, whose undeserved favor had just been extended to him, by engaging in a conspiracy aimed at its destruction.

After Shanks left the stand, the second renegade, Maurice Langhorne, had his turn. The Cincinnati *Daily Gazette* reporter who had been favorably impressed by Shanks's appearance and manner, found Langhorne's even better, and described him as "evidently a man of intelligence and mental culture, about thirty years old, and disposed to tell the whole truth, whether it made for or against the prosecution." [37]

Langhorne's testimony ranged over a wide area. He implicated Walsh, Anderson, and Marmaduke in the conspiracy. He told of his conversation with Grenfell in the train from Toronto to Chicago in August (quoted earlier). He went on to give a rather muddled account of another conversation with Grenfell at the Richmond House on August 29, which occurred when the latter came to his room "and said he could not find anybody, either Hines or Marmaduke, who could tell him what to do, or what was the next thing on the programme." [38] It was at the conclusion of this conversation that Grenfell supposedly remarked that "all they had now to do was to go to South Illinois and drill Copperheads."

Langhorne too was subjected to a vigorous cross-examination and was forced to admit that he had participated in the forging of documents which were to be used to lend an appearance of authenticity to the story of the nonexistent plot to raid Detroit, the

[36] *Ibid.*, 63. The full transcript of Grenfell's statement to Stanton was introduced in evidence and appears in *ibid.*, 598–600.
[37] Cincinnati *Daily Gazette*, January 26, 1865.
[38] *House Executive Documents*, 81.

secrets of which he tried without success to sell to Colonel Hill.[39] Wilson's questions about this sorry affair were objected to by Burnett as immaterial and irrelevant and, in routine fashion, his objection was sustained. Nevertheless, in his summation, he thought it advisable to whitewash Langhorne, after performing the same rather thankless service for Shanks; Langhorne, he said, "was an enterprising, energetic man, of nervous temperament, and had great pride of character. . . . In Canada, being idle and restless . . . is it at all surprising that he should have assisted in organizing raids across the border?" [40]

Langhorne's testimony did, however, include one redeeming sentence. In response to the question asked him on cross-examination, "Have you any bad feeling towards Colonel Grenfel[l]?" he replied, "No, sir; I entertain the highest respect for him; I think he is the best soldier I ever saw, without exception." [41]

The exchanges between Burnett and Robert S. Wilson about the part Langhorne had played in getting up the Detroit Conspiracy led to a clash between the press and the court. The Cincinnati *Daily Gazette* reported that the witness had "tried to sell Col. Hill a fake Detroit conspiracy. Judge Wilson spoke at considerable length on this point, and with much shrewdness and plausibility damaged the reputation of the witness." [42] One of the members of the court took exception to the laudatory terms in which the *Gazette* had referred to Wilson, and "submitted that this was a violation of the order of the commission which permitted reporters to be present to report the testimony of witnesses and argument of counsel; but that they had no right to express their own convictions or opinions as to witnesses or their testimony during the progress of the trial." [43] Having voiced his conception of the meaning of freedom of the press, the learned military judge (who is not identified in the records) moved that reporters be forbidden thenceforth to publish their opinions and conclusions. The

[39] *Ibid.*, 90–92.
[40] *Ibid.*, 582.
[41] *Ibid.*, 96.
[42] Cincinnati *Daily Gazette*, January 26, 1865.
[43] *House Executive Documents*, 92.

motion was adopted, but as any civilian judge would have known, the press had the last word. The next day, the *Gazette* reported the incident in lavish detail, and ended its account with the tongue-in-cheek comment: "By avoiding any reference to the learned disputations between Judge Advocate and counsel, hereafter, we will perhaps happily escape both censure and praise." [44]

Far more serious from Grenfell's point of view was the inability of the defense to refute those portions of Langhorne's testimony which related to him. His presence in Chicago on August 28 and 29 and November 5 was clearly established. Frederick Hall's testimony had so blackened his character that the court could readily believe him capable of committing the crimes with which he was charged. The uncontradicted testimony of the two turncoats, Shanks and Langhorne, linked him with Hines, Castleman, Marmaduke, and the other principals in the conspiracy; it was the final link in the chain of evidence showing his complicity. The inability of the defense to meet this evidence head on and to disprove it left Grenfell's fate hanging on the illusory hope that the judges would disregard Shanks's and Langhorne's testimony entirely because of the shady past and generally unsavory charactory of the two witnesses.

A few days before Langhorne took the stand, the Cincinnati newspapers were permitted to print a letter which the wife of Buckner Morris had sent to General Hooker. She had been arrested on December 11 and after a comfortable stay at Camp Douglas, in an "apartment" that had been fitted up for her and her husband, was brought to Cincinnati and incarcerated in McLean Barracks. Wisely, the prosecution did not place her on trial. It would have been difficult to connect her with the conspiracy, and Burnett may also have feared that any sympathy she would arouse among the more sentimental and susceptible members of the court would benefit her husband and the other prisoners. She was, however, permitted to be present at the trial as a spectator, and, as the reporter for a Chicago newspaper had it, "she was the observed of some hundreds of observers." The same

[44] Cincinnati *Daily Gazette*, January 27, 1865.

reporter noted also: "As Mr. Shanks, the witness who has testified against her husband . . . entered the Court room . . . he was greeted with a look from Mrs. Morris very much less gracious than when she befriended him at her door as an escaped rebel prisoner." [45]

In her letter to General Hooker, Mrs. Morris admitted that on several occasions, she had aided escaped Confederate prisoners, including Shanks, with gifts of money and clothing. She had done this, she said, without her husband's knowledge and without the least suspicion that by aiding prisoners of war to escape, she was violating any law. Nor had she realized, she said, that in having Hines and Castleman, both of whom she knew to be in the Confederate service, as guests in her home on numerous occasions, she was doing anything improper. She now threw herself on General Hooker's "clemency and mercy"; she begged to be released from prison, and promised to conduct herself thereafter "as a truly loyal woman." [46] One cannot suppose that this disingenuous letter was permitted to reach the newspapers without Burnett's prior knowledge; one may even credit him with having engineered a clever coup. He could not put Mrs. Morris on the stand to testify against her husband, but by allowing her letter to General Hooker to be published or, more probably, seeing to it that it *was* published, so that it could be read by the military judges, he got for the prosecution the full benefit of her story, including an authentication of portions of Shanks's and Langhorne's testimony. It may be added that Mrs. Morris was well advised to throw herself on the mercy of the gallant General Hooker. Her punishment was light indeed. She was sentenced to exile in "the so-called Southern Confederacy," but in consideration of her voluntary confession and her promise of future good conduct, the sentence was remitted, and she was given permission to reside with her father in Kentucky, so long as she continued to behave herself.[47]

The presentation of evidence by the prosecution went on, day

[45] Unidentified and undated newspaper clipping, in Hines Papers.
[46] Cincinnati *Daily Gazette*, February 14, 1865.
[47] Cincinnati *Daily Enquirer*, February 15, 1865.

230

after weary day. Witness followed witness, to offer testimony in which Grenfell had no interest, implicating Walsh, Morris, and the others in the conspiracy. A vast amount of evidence was produced to show that the Sons of Liberty was a disloyal organization and that its objectives were treasonable, to persuade the court that those of the prisoners who had been prominent in the order were *ipso facto* guilty of conspiracy to commit treason. Numerous sessions of the court were devoted to the presentation of evidence to show that the Walsh home was an arsenal. The proceedings, usually tedious in the extreme, became sporadically interesting when a witness appeared whose testimony was important, Colonel Sweet, for example, or whose personality made him an object of interest; prominent among the latter was the patent medicine vendor, "Dr." I. Winslow Ayer, well qualified to be one of Colonel Sweet's triumvirate of spies and informants, whose blatant rascality and congenital inability to tell the truth shone through every word he spoke.[48]

Only two more of the twenty-one witnesses for the prosecution who followed Langhorne offered testimony relating directly to Grenfell. One was George W. Hull, former member of the Second Kentucky Cavalry. Hull testified that he had been told in October, 1864, by Benjamin Anderson, one of the prisoners, "that there was an Englishman who was capable of taking charge" of all the prisoners of war in Camp Douglas as soon as they were released.[49] Hull did not identify the Englishman on direct examination, but distinctly implied it was Grenfell. This was clearly hearsay evidence, inadmissible in a civil court and equally so in a court-martial, but here it was admitted nonetheless. A clumsily worded question on cross-examination gave Hull the opportunity to identify the Englishman as Grenfell.[50] The second was Absalom

---

[48] For Colonel Sweet's testimony, see *House Executive Documents*, 188–96; for Ayer's, *ibid.*, 196–230. Stanley Waterloo writes that while Sweet was in Cincinnati, he was fired on in the street, the bullet passing through his hat. There is no mention of the incident in the trial record, in contemporary newspapers, or in Bross's biography of Sweet. Waterloo, "The Great Chicago Conspiracy," 149.
[49] *House Executive Documents*, 115.
[50] *Ibid.*, 117.

B. Moore, formerly colonel of the 104th Illinois Infantry. He could have had only one motive for appearing as a witness against Grenfell: a bitter hatred of everyone and everything connected with John Morgan, for they had witnessed his incompetence and his cowardly surrender at Hartsville in December, 1862. Moore testified that after his surrender, he overheard a conversation between Grenfell and one of Morgan's officers, in which "one or both said if he could have his way they would raise the black flag and exterminate the whole Yankee force." [51] Here was the mysterious black flag story once again. Unaccountably, the defense made no effort on cross-examination to pin Moore down to a definite statement as to whether it was Grenfell or the other officer who made the black flag remark.

At the conclusion of the session on Friday, February 3, the court adjourned until the following Wednesday, "on account of sickness in the family of one of the members," and the prisoners and their attorneys had a few days' rest. But the adjournment drew upon the court the wrath of General Hooker; as soon as he heard of it, he issued orders that no member of the court was to leave Cincinnati and that no more adjournments would be tolerated in the future.[52]

[51] *Ibid.*, 269.
[52] Cincinnati *Daily Gazette*, February 4, 1865.

Chapter XIII

COLONEL MOORE was the last but one of the witnesses for the prosecution, and on February 15 Burnett announced that the presentation of evidence by his side had been completed. Counsel for Semmes and Marmaduke thereupon submitted the cases of their clients to judgment by the commission on the plea that the evidence offered by the judge advocate to link them to the conspiracy was too weak to require the presentation of testimony to prove their innocence. After considering the matter for nearly two hours, the court found Semmes guilty on all counts and sentenced him to three years' imprisonment at hard labor; Marmaduke was acquitted and discharged from custody.[1]

After these verdicts had been announced, counsel for the remaining defendants moved for a two-week adjournment "for the purpose of preparing the defense and procuring testimony." [2] Burnett objected to an adjournment of more than one week, on the ground that "the military power above would not sanction it" and reminded the court that it would be his duty to make a report to General Hooker if a recess of more than three days were taken.[3] One of the judges thereupon observed that in matters of duty he did not recognize any power above his own conscience except

[1] *House Executive Documents,* 272–73.
[2] *Ibid.,* 273.
[3] Cincinnati *Daily Gazette,* February 16, 1865.

God. This placed the question of adjournment on the highest possible plane but the other eight judges preferred caution. The result was a compromise between judicial independence and military subordination; an adjournment of eight days was granted.

When the court reconvened on the afternoon of February 23, Burnett had to make the mortifying announcement that one of the defendants, Charles Travis Daniel, had escaped. On the fifteenth, while the judges debated the question of adjournment, he walked out of the courtroom in the custody of a sergeant of the guard, gave him the slip, and disappeared.[4] Another prisoner, Benjamin Anderson, committed suicide in prison during the recess.

Grenfell too was absent from the February 23 session. He had become ill a few days earlier. On the twentieth, he was examined in his cell by the assistant medical director of the department, in the presence of one of General Hooker's staff officers. The doctor reported that Grenfell had a mild case of rheumatism, that he was not "paralyzed," as he claimed to be, and that he would be as comfortable in his cell, under the care of the prison medical officer, as he would be in any Cincinnati hospital. Hooker's staff drew the obvious conclusion that Grenfell was shamming illness, and the prison commandant was warned to be on his guard: "Look out that Grenfell is not playing some sharp game to escape. I have no confidence in him. Be sure and not give him a chance to escape."[5] The warning, however, was unnececssary. Grenfell was in no condition to attempt an escape; he was not only not shamming but his illness became steadily worse. On the day the court reassembled, he was examined by the prison medical officer, who reported that he had a severe case of inflammatory rheumatism, "from which he has suffered very much for several days past. In my opinion he is unfit to appear in court, and from present appearances and condition I do not think he will be able to leave his bed

[4] The Cincinnati *Daily Gazette* reported on February 28 that Daniel was recaptured near Millersburg, Kentucky, by a detachment of the Forty-fifth Kentucky Infantry, but he escaped again and made his way back to Canada by way of Virginia. *Cf.* Daniel to Thomas Henry Hines, May 9, 1865, in Hines Papers.
[5] C. H. Potter to Captain Booth, February 20, 1865, in Grenfell Papers-National Archives.

for several days, so as to be safely taken from the Barracks." [6] Grenfell was not sufficiently well to attend court until the twenty-eighth; in the meantime, the trial proceeded without him.

The letters Grenfell wrote in January and February make it evident that he was receiving mail from England, presumably from William Maynard and perhaps from members of his family as well. He knew that instructions to help him had been sent by the Foreign Office to the British legation in Washington. To make certain that the chargé d'affaires, J. Hume Burnley, was fully and correctly informed of his situation, Grenfell sent him a long letter on January 23, of which the portions describing the hardships of his imprisonment in Camp Douglas and of his transfer to McLean Barracks, have already been quoted. Grenfell wrote the letter shortly after Shanks had testified, and when he was in two minds about the possible impact of the renegade's testimony. He was hopeful that reliance on such witnesses as Shanks would do the prosecution more harm than good, but he realized that he might well be indulging in optimism in that respect: "[Shanks's] invention is most fertile, he sticks at nothing, one tenth part of his assertions if true would be sufficient to hang me . . . I expect other men of the same class to follow, daily instructed by the Judge Advocate what to say and having free access to all each others evidence . . . what chance have I or any other man against such witnesses backed by all the influence of Government?" [7]

This was a remarkably realistic appraisal of the situation. Of course Grenfell protested his innocence of the crimes with which he was charged and asked the rhetorical (and quite disingenuous) question whether, having declined to serve the Confederacy as inspector of cavalry with the rank of brigadier general, it was likely that he should place himself "under the orders of lawless unscru-

[6] Report of Dr. E. B. Stevens, February 23, 1865, in *ibid.*
[7] Grenfell to "British Ambassador, Washington," January 23, 1865, in British Legation-Archives, FO 115/448. Grenfell's statement that the witnesses for the prosecution had "free access to each other's evidence" was certainly true in the case of Shanks and Langhorne. It was brought out in the course of the trial that they shared a room in a Cincinnati hotel while they were in the city to testify. *House Executive Documents*, 54.

pulous subaltern officers or of cowardly deserters from the South?"
—hardly a flattering or even accurate description of his friends
Hines and Castleman.[8] He recognized that as a foreigner and a
former officer in the Rebel army, he could expect little mercy.
Nonetheless, he seemed genuinely shocked by the judge advocate's
tactics, and with a naivete surprising in one who had seen so much
of the world, he wrote,

> All I ask for is fair play, an impartial trial[,] an honest upright
> Judge, not a Judge Advocate who openly announced in court his
> conviction of our guilt before a single witness had been examined,
> a Judge Advocate whose chance of promotion depends upon his
> procuring our conviction and who tortures the law into every form
> that can militate against us, whilst he is backed in his illegal op-
> pression by a Servile Court and favored by the pressure of Govern-
> ment influence.[9]

One of Grenfell's more curious traits was his invariable reaction
of hurt surprise, of which the above passage is an example, whenever one of his ill-considered or unconsidered actions ended in
disaster and he had to face the prospect of having to pay the piper.
Contemptuous of the rules in his dealings with others, he was
quick to cry Foul when the rules were violated by others to
his detriment.

Burnley was not to be diverted from the posture of cool official detachment that he had thought it proper to adopt by anything Grenfell had to say and, indeed, he was careful not to reply
to this letter. Instead, he wrote to Consul Wilkins in St. Louis
to express his desire "to convey in some sort of way that it may
reach . . . [Grenfell] and not be read by the prison officials . . .
that it would be quite indecorous on my part to interfere officially about a prisoner who there is no question must be looked upon
as an enemy of the U.S., that if anything can be done privately I
should be happy to assist him but even in this way I do not see

[8] Grenfell to "British Ambassador, Washington," January 23, 1865, in British
Legation-Archives, FO 115/448.
[9] *Ibid.*

what can be effected." [10] It would have been bitter comfort to a man on trial for his life to learn that the diplomatic representative of his country thought it "indecorous" to do anything for him, and Burnley himself evidently decided on further reflection that he was carrying diplomatic reserve to an indefensible extreme. He asked Wilkins in a later dispatch to use the occasion of a trip he was about to make to Chicago on other matters, to look into the case and find out if anything could be done for Grenfell. [11]

When Wilkins carried out Burnley's instructions a short time later, he was careful to emphasize the unofficial nature of his inquiries, lest he arouse the latent Anglophobia of the American officials with whom he met. He interviewed Colonel Sweet among others and found him convinced of Grenfell's guilt and of the probability that he would be convicted and sentenced to death. Asay, one of Grenfell's lawyers, happened to be in Chicago while Wilkins was there, and the consul called on him also. Asay made it clear that Grenfell was greatly disappointed by the failure of the British officials in Washington to do anything for him. He spoke hopefully of the eventual success of his attack on the jurisdiction of the military commission, an optimism Wilkins was shrewd enough not to share. [12]

Burnley, for his part, waited until nearly the end of February or early March to deliver to Secretary of State William Seward a collection of papers on the case, including a bowdlerized copy of Grenfell's letter of January 23 to himself, from which all references to the ill treatment to which he had been subjected and all animadversions against United States officials were carefully deleted. Burnley called attention to the disreputable character of the witnesses against Grenfell, but with a caution that might have been deemed excessive even in a diplomat, he did so not in his own words, but indirectly, by including in the dossier a copy of a letter from Charles Grenfell to the British Foreign Office, in which

[10] J. H. Burnley to I. E. Wilkins, January 30, 1865, in *ibid.*, FO 115/445.

[11] Burnley's instructions to Wilkins were "private" and have not survived; they must have been sent January 31, 1865, or a day or two later.

[12] Wilkins' report to Burnley of his visit to Chicago is dated February 8, 1865. FO-U.S.-General Correspondence, FO 5/1155.

this point was emphasized.[13] A far less hardheaded secretary of state than Seward could have deduced from this fact alone that the British government was not vitally concerned about Grenfell and probably did not intend to make a major issue of his fate.

Two weeks later, on March 15, Burnley at last made a direct appeal to Seward, but did so in writing: "If you could use your influence in any shape or way that you may deem most suitable or proper in procuring . . . [Grenfell's] release or at any rate mitigate his punishment should the decision of the Court Martial be adverse to him, I shall feel much indebted to you." [14] The representatives of Great Britain used far different language in the nineteenth century when they really meant business—and Seward knew it. There is nothing to indicate that he concerned himself about the case or that he did anything in response to Burnley's polite solicitation, beyond forwarding his letter to the judge advocate general. Two weeks later, the latter informed Seward that the record of the trial (which was then still in progress) had not been received in Washington. Seward sent this information on to Burnley and this, for the time being, ended his involvement in the case.[15]

It is worthy of mention that the British consul in Portland, Maine, in the early months of 1865 was none other than Henry John Murray, who had been vice-consul and acting consul general in Tangier when Grenfell was driven out of that city by the Moorish government, nearly twenty years before. His posting to

[13] Burnley's communication to Seward is not in the records. In his March 15 letter to Seward, cited below, Burnley refers to it as having been sent "a few days ago." Charles Grenfell's letter calling Shanks and Langhorne "unworthy of credit" is dated February 22 and was forwarded to Burnley by the Foreign Office the next day. FO-U.S.-General Correspondence, FO 5/1155. Grenfell's letter of January 23 was apparently edited for the copyist by Burnley himself. Whole sentences and paragraphs, including the paragraph cited in note 9 above, are crossed out, and Burnley's instructions to the copyist to omit those parts appear on the back of the letter. Charles Grenfell was keeping posted on the progress of the trial by means of letters from his cousin's attorneys and the Cincinnati newspapers, which he received regularly.

[14] J. H. Burnley to William H. Seward, March 15, 1865, in British Legation-Archives, FO 115/441.

[15] Seward to Burnley, April 8, 1865, in *ibid*. In this letter, Seward gives March 31 as the date of the judge advocate general's report to him.

a diplomatic backwater like Portland suggests that his career had not prospered. The Chicago Conspiracy had achieved nationwide notoriety and no doubt the Portland papers carried articles about the Cincinnati trial. One wonders if Murray recognized George St. Leger, his enemy of Tangier days, under his proper name of Grenfell, and if he did, whether he derived any satisfaction from the evidence that the pitcher had gone to the well once too often.

In February, Grenfell wrote to Frederic Bernal, the British consul in Baltimore, with whom he had struck up a friendship on his way north from Washington the previous summer.[16] The letter was written under a handicap; "The very fact of my writing at all brings the eyes of Uncle Sam's detectives about me to see what I am going to do with my letter." Nevertheless, Grenfell was on the crest of a wave of optimism when he wrote the letter, for he declared, "My friends in England are *awake*, and our Ambassador duly instructed. The whole will end, as far as I am concerned, in a disgraceful expose of Government officials." And, as he had already done several times, and was to continue doing, he proclaimed his complete innocence of the charges against him.

Once more before the end of the trial Grenfell attempted to enlist the active help of the British legation. More than two months had passed since he wrote his first letter to Washington, and he had still seen no sign that the diplomatic representatives of his country had any interest in his fate. His letters had not been answered. He heard from London that his relatives were continuing to bring pressure on the Foreign Office, but so far as he could tell, they had not succeeded in overcoming the inertia of the legation in Washington. He had assumed and expected that, as a British subject, he would receive the protection of his government under any and all circumstances, and he professed to be unable to understand why, having aided the South disinterestedly "in its gallant attempt to liberate itself from thraldom," he should fail to receive that protection, while "those estimable citizens who were engaged by thousands in supplying the Confederate Government with Iron Clad

---

[16] Grenfell to Frederic Bernal, February 12, 1865, in Packe Papers.

239

Ships, Arms, ammunition and every article for carrying on the War . . . and not from any sympathy with a high souled People, quivering under the attack of a powerful enemy, but from sordid hopes of gain alone," were enjoying all the advantages and benefits of British citizenship.[17] He also paid his respects to Colonel Sweet and Major Burnett without actually naming them—and quite unfairly, since both officers had seen active service—by describing the trial then in progress as "a disgraceful cruel farce; got up by Federal officers desirous of promotion and too cowardly to seek it where Men of Honor gain [it,] on the Battle Field."

Grenfell ended his letter with the comparatively modest request that the legation intercede with President Lincoln to allow him to be freed on parole or on bail until the end of the trial, on the ground of ill health. He explained that he had just recovered from a severe attack of rheumatic fever that nearly deprived him of the use of his right arm, and he complained of the general deterioration of his health caused by five months of imprisonment. The request was hopelessly visionary. It is difficult to believe that Grenfell actually expected to be freed, either on bail or on parole, especially after Daniel's escape. He was on trial on a capital charge, Kentucky with its large pro-southern population was only the width of the Ohio River away, his activities following his interview with Stanton justified the belief that his word was not to be relied upon, and, for better or worse, he had a reputation for reckless bravery. There was no chance whatever that such a plea would be granted, even if Burnley had been so ill advised as to make it.

Grenfell remained in McLean Barracks except when he was in the courtroom, which, after three months, must have seemed nearly as severe a hardship as his imprisonment. For a time during March, continuing illness made his court attendance quite irregular. However, the trial crept forward, the time of the court being taken up with an interminable procession of witnesses for the defense, members, many of them, of the Sons of Liberty or of the Democratic Party, who testified to the loyalty and good repute

[17] Grenfell to J. H. Burnley, April 4, 1865, in British Legation-Archives, FO 115/448.

of Charles Walsh and Judge Morris. Had the trial not been a dead-ly serious affair, Grenfell might have found amusement in the veritable Saint Patrick Day's parade of Hibernian worthies—Dris-coll, Comiskey, Tehan, Dunn, Dooley, Lorregan, O'Hara, and many more—all of whom solemnly swore that Walsh was a gener-ous, humane, kindhearted man, albeit somewhat impulsive and excitable. An equally lengthy series of witnesses declared that Judge Morris, while much addicted to violent language, was really a peaceable citizen of unexceptionable loyalty and that, being the owner of a great deal of valuable Chicago real estate, it was un-thinkable that he should aid and abet a plot to burn the city and his properties with it.

Only at rare intervals did anything occur to relieve the monotony of the trial. On February 23 Walsh's three daughters came into court, and a scene "of a deeply affecting and interesting char-acter" ensued, which unquestionably had the emotional impact on the members of the court that it was intended to have.[18] It was a great pity that Grenfell's three daughters were too far away to render him a similar service. On March 8 John Kendall, Dr. J. D. Knapp, and James Mullen gave their evidence about Gren-fell's stay in Carlyle. Morris S. Davis made his sprightly contribu-tion to the proceedings on March 13, when he testified about his acquaintance with Shanks "under very unpleasant circumstances" while they shared a cell as guests of the penitentiary at Austin.[19] Recalled to the stand ten days later to identify Shanks, who had not been in the courtroom on the thirteenth, Davis gave an even better performance. He was asked, "Do you recognize that man as John T. Shanks?" and answered, "Yes, sir; this is Mr. Shanks; (approach-ing him with a smile of recognition, which was not returned) and

[18] Cincinnati *Daily Enquirer*, February 24, 1865. In an effort to counteract the effect of the Walsh girls' appearance in the courtroom, Burnett said in his summation: "I am truly sorry that . . . [Walsh] should have permitted his daughters to come here . . . to testify to that which we cannot believe. No one who has been present during this trial but must have noticed their affectionate attachment to their father. Their affection, their bias, has affected their testimony, and the cause of the accused is injured rather than benefited by their testimony." *House Executive Documents*, 590.
[19] *Ibid.*, 396.

John knows me as well as I know him; he is the same man of whom I testified." [20]

Since Davis' first appearance on the stand, the judge advocate had investigated his past and had ready for his second appearance some questions that would have embarrassed most people, but not the jovially unrepentant Davis. The following colloquy took place on cross-examination: Q. What were you doing in Texas? A. I was keeping a millinery store there. Q. Did you sell the bonnets? A. I sometimes did; when I did not, a lady who passed herself as Mrs. Davis did. Q. Were you living with her as your wife? A. Yes, sir. Q. How many times have you married? A. Three. Q. How many are living? A. All three.[21] Other witnesses, not so colorful as Davis but of considerably better repute, were produced by the defense to prove beyond the shadow of a doubt that Shanks had in fact been in prison in Texas for forgery, and had therefore committed perjury when he went out of his way to deny that fact under oath.[22]

On March 29 Clement Vallandigham was called to the stand as a witness for the defense. It was known in advance that he was to testify that day and his appearance on the stand was expected to provide the great dramatic climax of the trial. Hence, when the session opened on the twenty-ninth, there was "an immense attendance in the Court, the number exceeding that of any single day since the commencement of the sessions." [23] Nor was the audience disappointed, for Vallandigham gave them a virtuoso per-

---

[20] Cincinnati *Daily Gazette*, March 23, 1865. The official trial record uses less picturesque language to describe the scene: "Q. Do you recognize that man as John T. Shanks? A. Yes, sir. I know him perfectly well and he knows me; he is the same man of whom I testified, and with whom I slept in the Austin, Texas jail." *House Executive Documents*, 471.

[21] *Ibid.*, 471–72.

[22] *Ibid.*, 459–62 (Wesley Johnson); 466–67 (Richard Leek); 417–19 (John Phelps); 478–80 (A. Banning Norton).

[23] Cincinnati *Daily Enquirer*, March 30, 1865. The *Enquirer*, a paper of strongly Democratic, not to say Copperhead, sympathies, printed nearly complete transcripts of the trial at the beginning; as the trial progressed and the testimony became more and more monotonous and repetitious, the space it devoted to the trial gradually shrank to a half column. But Vallandigham's testimony was reported verbatim in four columns of exceedingly small type.

formance.[24] Many of his answers to questions asked him on direct examination were orations. Much of the testimony was a tissue of half-truths, but by a clever manipulation of words, he avoided direct perjury. His chief function as a witness was to deny authoritatively, as former supreme grand commander of the Sons of Liberty, that the order had any subversive or treasonable aims and to assert that it was in fact a legitimate political organization. Typical of the tenor of his entire testimony was his reply to the question, "Was the release of the confederate prisoners of war one of the objects contemplated by this order?" He answered, "It never was. I never heard that subject alluded to at any meeting . . . of the organization, nor by any member of the organization to me." [25] Of course he was quite safe in answering in the negative the question as it was worded, for it was certain of the leaders, and not the Sons of Liberty as such, who participated in the planning of the liberation of the Camp Douglas prisoners; nor was it these leaders, but Hines, Thompson, and other Confederate agents in Canada, who discussed these plans with him. Equally smooth and equally false was his denial of any "knowledge, intimation or suspicion" of the payment of money by the Confederate commissioners to any of the Indiana Copperheads; he made no mention of the Illinois Copperheads, and he was careful not to speak of Barrett, the Missouri Copperhead, to whom money had been given in his presence, and indeed at his direction, after the money had been offered to himself. On cross-examination, when his opportunities for verbal gymnastics and evasions were more circumscribed, he was forced to resort to more direct perjuries.

April 1 was the fifty-sixth day of the trial. The appearance on the stand that day and the next of the ex-grand commander of the Sons of Liberty in Illinois completed the presentation of testimony by the defense. On the three following days, the judge advocate presented rebuttal evidence, dealing principally with the circumstances of the raid on Walsh's house on the night of Novem-

---

[24] For Vallandigham's testimony on direct examination, see *House Executive Documents*, pp. 502–10; on cross-examination, *ibid.*, 510–18.
[25] *Ibid.*, 505.

243

ber 6. At the close of the sixtieth session, on April 6, all the evidence was before the commission, and the case was ready for the closing arguments of the attorneys for the defense and the judge advocate.

As the trial drew to its close, in Virginia and the Carolinas, 500 miles away, the Confederacy was in its death throes. Sherman's army, cutting a swath of destruction northward from Savannah, Georgia, had reached Goldsboro, North Carolina. On March 2 Sheridan had wiped out the pitiful remnant of Jubal Early's army at Waynesboro, Virginia; the clearing of the Shenandoah Valley of rebels was complete, and Sheridan marched to join Grant before Richmond. Lee, with what was left of the Army of Northern Virginia, its ranks riddled by casualties, sickness and desertion, was trying desperately to prolong what had now become a hopeless fight in the trenches before Petersburg and Richmond. The failure of the Confederate attack on Fort Stedman on March 25, at the cost of nearly five thousand casualties, the virtual destruction of George Pickett's force at Five Forks six days later, and the breaching of the main Confederate defense system before Petersburg at last forced Lee to order the evacuation of Richmond. On April 3 the capital of the Confederacy was occupied by the Union army and when the news was released from Washington, the entire North went wild with joy.

When the last witness to come before the court left the stand on the afternoon of the sixth, the defense attorneys were granted a three-day recess to review the evidence and prepare their closing arguments. Thus it came about that it was on Monday afternoon, the day following General Lee's surrender at Appomattox Court House, that Robert Wilson, the first of the defense attorneys to speak, addressed the court on behalf of Charles Walsh. After all the other attorneys had spoken, Robert Hervey made his speech for Grenfell on Wednesday morning, April 12.

The closing arguments of defense counsel are not included in the official trial record, and the Cincinnati newspapers, which for three months had carried a remarkably comprehensive daily account of the proceedings, had no space in that week of delirium for anything but stories dealing with the triumphant ending of the long war. Only a few lines were devoted by one of the newspapers to E. G. Asay's summation on behalf of Walsh, delivered in the presence of a large audience. "Nothing finer," the newspaper said, "in the way of an impassioned appeal, was ever . . . heard before any tribunal, than the scathing invective of Mr. Asay. The perjured spies and Government detectives, not less than . . . Colonel Sweet, who, it was claimed, had manufactured this plot, so far as it had any existence, were attacked as with a blade of Damascus steel in the hands of a skilful antagonist, terribly in earnest." [26]

On the morning of April 18, the court met to hear the judge advocate sum up on behalf of the prosecution.

A good trial attorney, like an actor who becomes for the time being the character he portrays, identifies himself so completely with the cause he represents that he becomes the first convert of his own advocacy. Justice and the cause of his client become identical. Detachment and objectivity are not the virtues of an advocate, and Burnett was without doubt an able member of the profession. His clients were the Union and the American people. The trial record cannot reproduce the tones of his voice, his gestures, the changes in his expression, but even in print, his words speak with a passionate conviction. It would be wholly beside the point to question if he was sincerely satisfied in his own mind and conscience of the guilt of the three men whose lives and freedom he was about to place in jeopardy by the use of every resource of his considerable oratorical talents.

In keeping with the forensic convention of his day, Burnett began by invoking divine assistance: "I ask only that the Omnipotent, who rules the wills of men, and who commands their destinies, may guide me, so that I may do no man wrong, and say no word that will prejudice these accused in your minds; that I may do my duty to my country this day, in her hour of sore affliction, God giving me help." [27] After a few paragraphs devoted to a reiteration of his belief that the commission had jurisdiction over the case, he turned

[26] Cincinnati *Daily Enquirer*, April 12, 1865.
[27] *House Executive Documents*, 576.

245

to a consideration of the evidence. He reviewed and commented on the salient points elicited from his witnesses. Quite naturally, he emphasized the points most favorable to his side and then dwelt at length on the weak and vulnerable aspects of the evidence presented by the defense. He did his best to explain away the questionable antecedents of his two principal witnesses, Shanks and Langhorne, and even attempted the nearly impossible task of clothing the ineffable Dr. Ayer in a few rags of respectability.

Grenfell, however, was excluded from the benefit of the convenient, if illogical, standards of credibility applied by Burnett to his own witnesses, and to Shanks in particular. He had given it as his conviction that Shanks, being a man of courage, was necessarily also a man of truth. But not so Grenfell.

> The entry of Grenfell's full name on the registry of the Richmond House has been adduced as confirmatory of the fact that no concealment was sought on his part. . . . But, . . . this is not the first instance, in the annals of crime, in which openness and frankness have been the most effective means of averting suspicion. It is not the first time that an open and brazen effrontery has been mistaken for integrity of purpose. Grenfell remained in obscurity and quiet so long as it served his purpose; when the time for action came, he was in Chicago at his post . . . ready, when the storm should burst, to follow, or direct, the whirlwind that should sweep out of existence that devoted city, and extend desolation over the North.[28]

After several more paragraphs of analysis of the evidence, Burnett reached his peroration. He dealt compassionately with Walsh: "The evidence is as you have seen it . . . I would not say one word that would take from this family their father; but if this man was guilty of this crime, or has aided and abetted this conspiracy, you have but one duty to perform."[29] This was amazingly, even suspiciously, lenient treatment of the truculent brigadier general of the Sons of Liberty, the man whose house was an arsenal and the hiding place of Daniel and Cantrill. But Judge Morris fared nearly as well: "As for Judge Morris, for his white hair and old

[28] *Ibid.*, 585.
[29] *Ibid.*, 593.

age I have only respect. For all that is worthy in him as a citizen I do him reverence; but if this white haired old man has engaged in a conspiracy against my nation and my country, I turn to the other side, and see white-haired patriots who mourn in sadness because such as he have done these evil deeds—and I remember justice!" [30]

It was for Grenfell, and Grenfell alone, that Burnett reserved the utmost virulence at his command and the most damaging flights of his eloquence. A portion of his denunciation of Grenfell, as an unprincipled soldier of fortune to whom the morality of the cause for which he fought meant nothing, has already been quoted. But even this was not the most damning thing Burnett could find to say against him. "He is not true to the cause he espouses," the judge advocate declared: "When in Washington, he went to the Secretary of War and betrays the very people with whom he had been fighting; tells all he knows of the strength, position and designs of the confederates. He said he proposed to leave immediately for England, but he breaks his faith, proceeds to Canada, and is found among the conspirators." [31] And Burnett ended his oration with a sweeping burst of eloquence:

> I say, then, to the learned counsel, while you plead for these accused with an eloquence that must move all hearts that have human sympathy, I must plead for my people; I plead for the soldier who has perilled his life to save his country; I plead in behalf of the memory of those who have sealed their patriotism with their life's blood; I plead for their wives and their orphaned little ones; and I plead in behalf of my country that they would divide and destroy. Mercy has her claims and justice hers.[32]

The court, as has been indicated, found Walsh guilty and sentenced him to five years' imprisonment. Judge Morris was acquitted. Grenfell was found guilty and sentenced to death by hanging. And finally, in a strange reversal of its earlier decision, the

[30] *Ibid.*
[31] *Ibid.*, 594.
[32] *Ibid.*

court recommended that the sentence of three years' imprisonment it had previously meted out to Semmes be remitted.[33]

On the day following the handing down of these verdicts and sentences, the commission sent General Hooker a recommendation that he pardon Walsh, in consideration of "his long confinement . . . the fact of his services to the United States prior to his arrest and the fact of a very numerous family requiring his aid and support." [34]

In keeping with the normal practice of courts-martial, only the verdicts were announced in open court on the evening of April 18; the sentences were to remain officially secret until approved and confirmed by higher authority. On April 27 General Hooker approved the findings and sentences of the commission and forwarded the trial record to Washington, where the War Department and the President had to pass on the death sentence meted out to Grenfell.

Thus, the result of the abortive conspiracy, of the many arrests and of the lengthy trial, was that many of those most deeply implicated—Thomas Henry Hines, for example—escaped entirely; of those arrested, numbering well over one hundred, eight were held for trial and the rest released; of the seven actually tried—six of whom, if they were guilty at all, were guilty of disloyalty and treason against the government and country whose citizens they were—one committed suicide, two were acquitted, one escaped, two were found guilty but pardoned, and only the seventh, the foreigner, George St. Leger Grenfell, was convicted and given the maximum sentence.

[33] *Ibid.*, 573–74.
[34] *Ibid.*, 574–75. The recommendation that Walsh be pardoned was signed by seven of the nine judges.

Chapter XIV

THE LETTERS Grenfell wrote after his conviction make it evident that he had found or purchased the means of smuggling uncensored letters out of McLean Barracks, for it is inconceivable that even the most lenient of censors should have passed them as they stand. The day after the close of the trial, still smarting from the violent and, in his view, grossly unfair attack Burnett had made upon him, and bitter about his conviction, Grenfell sent the editor of the influential *Harper's Magazine* an offer to write an article about the conspiracy and the trial. He proposed to set forth the facts about the conspiracy that had come to his notice, including "the Canadian intrigues" and the names of "the real movers in the Conspiracy." He would, he wrote, "expose certain nefarious transactions which it will be to the public interest to have ventilated" and "give a lie to some extraordinary facts connected with . . . [the] trial which have hitherto baffled curiosity." He wanted to write partly to pass the time, and partly "as a means of sustaining . . . [himself] in prison" and to provide the funds he needed to buy the comforts which, at his age, were "almost necessary to keep body and soul together." [1]

This letter was not one of Grenfell's better efforts. It is nearly incoherent and shows every sign of having been written under

[1] Grenfell to Editor, *Harper's Magazine*, April 19, 1865, in Grenfell Papers-National Archives.

stress. No doubt he had the notion of writing the article to avenge himself upon Burnett, Sweet, Shanks, Langhorne, the judges, and perhaps even Hines; it would not have been at all strange if he had felt that he had been abandoned, that he had been made the scapegoat for the entire conspiracy, and had been exposed to the full rigor of the government's vengeance by the passivity of his erstwhile friends. Possibly he did not know that all or nearly all of the expenses of his defense had been met by Hines on Jacob Thompson's instructions. It is quite unlikely that he knew that in January, Hines in Toronto gave "gold checks" drawn on a Chicago bank to a shadowy individual named B. P. Churchill, a Cincinnati Copperhead; the proceeds, amounting to the large sum of $1,686, were "to be used for the release of Col. G. St. Leger . . . confined in prison in Cincinnati." [2]

The result of Grenfell's letter to *Harper's Magazine* was far from what he expected or hoped, and the proposed article was never written. *Harper's* was firmly and ostentatiously pro-Union. The editor, Alfred H. Guernsey, knowing the ways of the War Department with hostile publications and their editors, was not minded to have his magazine suppressed and himself imprisoned in Fort Lafayette—a singularly unsuitable name for the military prison in New York Harbor in which hundreds of political prisoners were housed during the war—for publishing an article which promised to be violently critical of the administration. Hence he directed his reply, to which he attached Grenfell's letter to himself, to the commandant of McLean Barracks and explained in a covering note his sense of the impropriety of communicating with a prisoner except with the knowledge and consent of his jailers. He left it to the discretion of the prison commandant to deliver or not, as he thought best, the following sanctimonious missive to Grenfell:

---

[2] Receipt, signed "Churchill," dated January 22, 1865, in Hines Papers. Churchill agreed that if the money was "not used for this purpose to return immediately after the trial to Capt. Hines." It is evident from the context that the money was to be used to finance Grenfell's escape from prison, by means of bribery or otherwise. Churchill's name appears in the Cincinnati *City Directory* for 1865, but the author has been unable to find any other information concerning him.

I am in receipt of your note of the 19th. I can not consider it . . . a "confidential" communication. I could not properly receive any confidential communication from one who occupies the position of a public enemy. . . . In respect to the subject of your note I can only say that no paper the aim or effect of which is to weaken the confidence of the people in the Government . . . can by any possibility find a place in Harper's Magazine. If the paper you propose . . . throughs (*sic*) light upon any nefarious transactions which it will be of public benefit "to have ventilated" it would quite likely be available for the Magazine. . . . Should such a paper reach me it will receive my attention . . . [but] I do not wish to receive such a paper except through the Commanding officer of the prison, or . . . with his knowledge and sanction; and should such a paper reach me I should hold myself at liberty to communicate it . . . to the proper authorities. . . . Also, should I find the paper generally available, I should consider myself at perfect liberty to omit any passage the publication of which appeared to me to be objectionable.[3]

Having discharged himself of this epistle, and displayed for all to see his devotion to the Union, the patriotic editor turned, no doubt with relief, to deal with the less dangerous contributors to his magazine.

The effect of Guernsey's letter on the prison commandant and his officers may readily be imagined. Whether the letter was shown to Grenfell is not known, but it may be taken for granted that he had to listen to a pointed lecture on the iniquity of smuggling letters out of prison, and no doubt he was told in unequivocal terms that any venture of his into authorship along the lines of his proposal to Guernsey would not be looked upon with favor. The entire correspondence was then forwarded to General Hooker with the shamefaced admission that "the Letter written by Col[.] Grenfell was taken out of this Barracks and was mailed undiscovered to the officers and was not examined by them."[4] Two days later, Captain William Mahon, in command of the prison, was directed by headquarters "to observe the greatest vigilance in the case of the prisoner . . . Grenfell to prevent communications or any

[3] A. H. Guernsey to Grenfell, April 24, 1865, in Grenfell Papers-National Archives.
[4] William Mahon to Captain Booth, April 27, 1865, in *ibid*.

article which might aid him in attempting to escape being secreted to him and that all his letters pass through your hands."[5]

Meanwhile, Grenfell had written once again to the British legation. The post of minister was now held by Sir Frederick Bruce, who was to occupy it until his sudden death in 1867. Sir Frederick's father was the Earl of Elgin and Kincardine who had acquired and removed to England portions of the Parthenon frieze and other classical Greek carvings known since as the Elgin Marbles. The son followed in the father's footsteps as a career diplomat and before his selection to succeed Lord Lyons, had held posts in Hong Kong, Newfoundland, Egypt, and China. Theoretically, his presence in Washington gave Grenfell an advantage he did not possess before; whatever representations might be made thenceforth on his behalf by the British would be made by the chief diplomatic representative of Great Britain in the United States, and not by a chargé d'affaires of temporary status and modest prestige. On the other hand, Bruce, for all his experience and tact, was a newcomer in Washington and had not been there long enough to establish the personal relationships with members of the government that, in a case like Grenfell's, might well have provided a more effective basis for favorable action than any amount of official representations.

Grenfell wrote his letter to the legation to ask if he had "anything to hope for from the protection of the British Government."[6] He said little about the trial, except to voice once again his indignation over the way Burnett had singled him out for attack in his summation, which Grenfell called a "furious diatribe." A few days later, Robert Hervey also wrote to Bruce, to assure him of his own sincere belief in Grenfell's innocence and to express his conviction that the verdict of the commission had been based on evidence "of the most unreliable character."[7] Another letter came from Wilkins, who had followed the progress of the

[5] Booth to Mahon, April 29, 1865, in *ibid*.
[6] Grenfell to Sir Frederick Bruce, April 20, 1865, in British Legation-Archives, FO 115/448.
[7] Robert Hervey to Bruce, April 25, 1865, in *ibid*.

trial through the newspapers, and who wrote that he was satisfied that no testimony had been presented to "justify the additional severity of Mr. Grenfell's sentence beyond that passed on the other convicted prisoners, all of whom are American Citizens." [8] Three days later, Wilkins expressed the same view more explicitly; he wrote the legation that he knew, on the basis of "undoubted evidence," that Grenfell's nationality had been an important factor in producing the commission's verdict of guilty. [9] Then came another letter from the energetic and devoted Hervey, offering to visit Washington to discuss the case face to face with Sir Frederick. [10]

Thus bombarded, and perhaps not too well pleased with the course of ultracautious inaction Burnley had seen fit to adopt, Bruce set vigorously to work to help Grenfell. Secretary Seward was absent from his office, recovering from the wounds Lewis Paine had inflicted upon him on the night President Lincoln was assassinated, and Bruce had to deal with Acting Secretary Hunter. The minister realized that the popular "indignation felt against raiders from Canada" and the pressure of public opinion in favor of severe punishment for those who had been caught would be too powerful for the new President to resist, especially in Seward's absence. He gave it as his opinion that under these circumstances, "Justice, not mercy, is the utmost . . . [he could] hope to obtain." Nevertheless, he made the best of an unpromising case; in a conversation with Hunter on April 29, he complained about the excessive animus Burnett had displayed toward Grenfell; he spoke also of the untrustworthy character of the witnesses for the prosecution and asked Hunter to call these points to the judge advocate general's attention. [11]

[8] I. E. Wilkins to Bruce, April 25, 1865, in *ibid.*, FO 115/443. In the same letter, Wilkins wrote that he had heard "from a private source" that Grenfell had been sentenced to be hanged.

[9] Wilkins to Bruce, April 28, 1865, in *ibid.*

[10] Robert Hervey to Bruce, April 29, 1865, in British Legation-Archives, FO 115/448.

[11] Bruce to E. Hammond, "30 May, 1865"; as the report is marked as received in London on May 14, the date in the caption is probably an error for 30 April, 1865; FO-U.S.-General Correspondence, FO 5/1155.

Bruce was quite pessimistic about the chances of a successful intervention on Grenfell's behalf. He reported to London that "the bitterness felt against the conspirators and raiders is so great that no appeal to mercy will be listened to, and official interference would only insure the utmost rigor of the law being enforced against . . . [Grenfell]." [12] In a private note to Foreign Secretary Lord John Russell, he gave an unflattering description of the state of civil liberties in the United States at that moment; as the comment of an unbiased observer on a matter that is commonly treated with a great deal of bias, it deserves quotation in full:

> There is no relaxation of arbitrary power in this country. The Govt., acting through the military authority, arrests anyone it pleases, brings him to trial or not as it suits it, and detains him as long as it pleases. Witnesses are kept in prison till required to give evidence . . . without being admitted to bail; and as the jurisdiction of the State Courts is overridden, there is no appeal except to the War Department. . . . In fact personal liberty is at an end throughout the Northern States, and as long as the War Party, which is in the ascendant, professes and considers this power necessary to the National safety, there is no reason to suppose it will terminate . . . individual rights have no foundation here except in the Will of the Majority. . . . If, as is likely, the feelings of the North and South become more embittered, the future condition of residents, foreign and native, will be far worse than it has hitherto been.[13]

A week later, in another private note to the foreign secretary, Bruce explained why he could not be hopeful about Grenfell's prospects:

> All I can do at present is to try and effect the release of British subjects who on various pretexts have been seized by the Military Authorities . . . I try to have their cases enquired into by the War Dept. in the hope that any favorable circumstances may be considered and lead to their release. But it depends entirely on the humor of the officer referred to what is done in these cases, for Martial Law as administered here is really no Law at all, and the feeling

[12] Bruce to Hammond, n. d. (received in London, May 10, 1865), in *ibid.*
[13] Bruce to Lord John Russell, April 20, 1865, in Russell Papers (Public Record Office, London), PRO 30.22/38; hereinafter cited as Russell Papers.

against foreigners who have served . . . in the South is so strong as to make a fair trial almost hopeless. Their cases require great delicacy in handling, for to insinuate unfairness on the part of the officers composing these Military Commissions would render the execution of a sentence only the more certain. The certainty now felt of suppressing the insurrection inclines the people against leniency where a foreigner is concerned, and the Govt. will not openly thwart the popular sentiment in that respect. I feel much apprehension on Grenfell's account. What madness induced him to return to the United States? [14]

Notwithstanding these gloomy auguries, Bruce used the resources of diplomacy on Grenfell's behalf as often as he thought it opportune to do so and in any quarter where help might be looked for. On May 7 he wrote Stanton to ask that Hervey be permitted to meet with Judge Advocate General Holt to discuss those facts about the evidence and the witnesses which would justify executive clemency for Grenfell. His request was denied, but he was told that Hervey might submit a written brief within a "reasonable time." [15] This was at least a minor victory, for any delay was likely to work in Grenfell's favor, and Bruce at once notified Hervey.[16] Ten days later, Hervey was badly frightened by a newspaper report that Grenfell's death sentence was about to be carried out. The story was erroneous but it caused Hervey to hurry on the completion of his brief, and he sent it off to the War Department by express on May 25.[17] A copy went to Sir Frederick, who in turn had copies made for Secretary Seward and Lord John Russell. The latter, as soon as his copy reached him, sent Bruce official instructions

to lose no time in urging the American Government to deal leniently with the Prisoner, and at all costs to spare his life. The United States Government might surely, now that the Civil War was brought to an end, abstain from inflicting the penalty of death

[14] Bruce to Russell, April 27, 1865, in *ibid.*
[15] Edwin M. Stanton to Bruce, May 7, 8, 1865; Holt memorandum, May 8, 1865, in British Legation-Archives, FO 115/448.
[16] Telegram, Bruce to Robert Hervey, May 8, 1865, in *ibid.*, FO 115/445.
[17] Hervey to Bruce, May 17, 23, 25, 1865, in *ibid.*, FO 115/448.

... in a case which rests entirely as it would seem on the credibility of untrustworthy witnesses ... it will in all probability appear hereafter that the worthless wretches who bore evidence against him perjured themselves for the sake of pecuniary reward.

P. S. State the substance of this despatch if necessary to Mr. Seward.[18]

There was no need for anyone to urge Sir Frederick on to greater exertions.[19] He was already doing a yeoman job. His private letters to Lord John Russell, even more than his official dispatches, show that he worked devotedly and hard for Grenfell. In June, while the trial record was being studied in Holt's office, he described for Lord John's benefit the political situation which made his task so difficult:

The upholder of Mr. Stanton and his Reign of Terror are the Black Republican party. . . . This party are conscious that their policy and ideas are repugnant to the great majority of the American people both in the North and in the South. Partly from fanaticism, partly from love of power, these men are ready to stifle free expression of opinion and to suppress the constitutional guarantees of liberty. . . . In the North they seek to justify the continuance of martial law by bringing forward witnesses who swear to the continued existence of plots and conspiracies to burn Northern cities and assassinate Northern statesmen.[20]

In the hope of gaining support for his efforts on Grenfell's behalf, Bruce cultivated friendly relations with everyone in the War Department whose active help or passive good will might prove useful. In speaking of the case to these officials, he was careful not to become entangled in discussions of its legal or constitutional aspects and based his appeals for leniency entirely on considerations of humanity and abstract justice. Nor did he fail to

[18] Lord John Russell to Bruce, June 17, 1865, in FO-U.S.-General Correspondence, FO 5/1155.
[19] On May 8, R. S. Wilson had written Bruce: "There was not a particle of reliable evidence against [Grenfell]. If his life should be taken upon the evidence given against him it would . . . be a disgrace to humanity." British Legation-Archives, FO 115/448.
[20] Bruce to Lord John Russell, June 18, 1865, in Russell Papers.

follow up any line of attack suggested to him by Hervey and R. S. Wilson, who wrote to him almost daily to call to his notice every slight circumstance that might be used in Grenfell's favor. The two attorneys used all their resources to obtain the help of every public figure they could reach who had any influence in Washington and might be convinced to use it on behalf of their client. They persuaded John Purcell, the Roman Catholic archbishop of Cincinnati, to ask William Dennison, the postmaster general and former governor of Ohio, to intercede for Grenfell.[21] At their suggestion, Bruce called on Dennison and had a long discussion with him about the case, in which he laid special emphasis on the questionable evidence on which Grenfell had been convicted. Dennison, whom Bruce described as "moderate and well-disposed," appeared to be won over and promised to convey the minister's arguments to the President. Henry Burnett happened to be with the postmaster general when Bruce called. Sir Frederick did not mention in his report to London Burnett's reaction to his strictures on the character of the evidence the judge advocate had seen fit to rely on. He did inform Lord John Russell, however, that Burnett had told him he had "accompanied his Report of the case with the observation that he did not think the [death] sentence ought to be carried out."[22]

Hervey and Wilson also obtained letters to the President from two members of the commission, Colonel M. N. Wiswell and Major W. C. Macrae, urging that Grenfell be pardoned. Colonel Wiswell, who was on friendly terms with the President, not only wrote him but, on the occasion of a visit to Washington, called on Andrew Johnson and in a confidential conversation about the case, repeated the points in Grenfell's favor that he had previously brought out in his letter.[23] It will be recalled in this connection that while the commission was unanimous in finding Grenfell guilty, only six of the nine judges voted for a death sentence.

[21] Robert S. Wilson to Bruce, June 27, 1865, in British Legation-Archives, FO 115/448.
[22] Bruce to Lord John Russell, June 27, 1865, in Russell Papers.
[23] Robert Hervey to Bruce, July 18, 26, 1865, in British Legation-Archives, FO 115/448.

Grenfell himself remembered that in November, 1863, he had tired to protect the property of John Minor Botts from the depredations of Stuart's troopers and had spent two weeks as a guest in Botts's home. It occurred to him now that Botts might be willing to help him. This was a happy inspiration, for the story Botts could tell would go a long way to counteract the picture of Grenfell as a bloodthirsty mercenary, eager to "raise the black flag" against the North, that Burnett had painted at the trial; moreover, Botts's record was such that anything he chose to say or do for Grenfell would carry a great deal of weight. A Virginian by birth, he had been admitted to the bar at eighteen, after studying law for a mere six weeks. A successful farmer and lawyer—the latter in spite of his fixed rule of accepting a case only if he were sure that justice was on the side of his client—he was a prominent Whig member of Congress in the years before the war. Convinced that the Democrats were engaged in an unholy conspiracy to bring about secession in order to prevent control of the national government passing from the South to the North, he fought them tooth and nail. In the spring of 1861 he was in the forefront of the fight to keep Virginia in the Union. When the war began, he retired to his farm. In the spring of 1862, he was arrested by the Confederate authorities on suspicion of disloyalty and kept in prison for two months. After his release, he bought a farm near Culpeper, Virginia, and was living there, preyed upon alternately by both armies, when Grenfell met him.[24] Grenfell now wrote him: "If the slight services I was enabled to render you . . . are fresh in your recollection as the kind hospitality you tendered me is in mine, I am sure I may calculate upon your using all your influence to assure the President that, so far from being the bloodthirsty, reckless being my accusers make me out to be, I was, while in the Confederate States service, the protector of everyone, irrespective of politics, against the lawless depredations of our troops."[25]

Botts responded to Grenfell's appeal with a letter to Judge

[24] *Dictionary of American Biography,* I, 472–73.
[25] Grenfell to John Minor Botts, May 19, 1865, in *House Executive Documents,* 636.

258

Advocate General Holt, in which he described the circumstances under which he and Grenfell had become acquainted and spoke highly of the guest that an accident of war had brought to his home; "During the fortnight he remained under my roof he impressed me with the conviction that he was not only the most rigid disciplinarian in the service of the confederacy that I had met with, but that he was a gentleman of too much elevation of character ever to engage in such a conspiracy as that with which he has been charged and convicted." [26] True to the principles which had guided him in the practice of law, he concluded with a statement as creditable to the man who wrote it as it was to the man about whom it was written:

> I can, and do, say that . . . I should require the most conclusive and unimpeachable testimony of his guilt before I would subject him to punishment for such an offense as he stands charged with . . . I offer this statement as a simple act of justice to a gentleman of whom I had formed a good opinion; and in the absence of all knowledge of the facts resting upon this case, I must hope and believe he is not guilty of the foul crime of which he stands convicted.

Unfortunately, Holt and the War Department were convinced that there *was* "conclusive and unimpeachable testimony" of Grenfell's guilt.

Obtaining the intercession of Archbishop Purcell, Colonel Wiswell, Major Macrae, and Postmaster General Dennison, and keeping Sir Frederick Bruce up to the mark did not represent the sum total of Wilson's and Hervey's accomplishments. They did the seemingly impossible by getting and forwarding to Bruce on June 27 a letter to President Johnson from none other than Colonel (now Brigadier General) Sweet, recommending executive clemency for Grenfell.[27]

[26] Botts to Joseph Holt, June 17, 1865, in *ibid.*, 638.
[27] Robert S. Wilson to Sir Frederick Bruce, June 27, 1865. Wilson refers to General Sweet's letter to the President as "enclose[d] herewith," but neither the original nor any copy of it have survived. British Legation-Archives, FO 115/448. The original letter was given by Bruce to the President. Bruce to Lord John Russell, July 10, 1865; FO-U.S.-General Correspondence, FO 5/1155.

Wilson and Hervey considered at this time that the best course for Bruce to follow was to bring pressure on the President not to confirm the sentence of the military commission; this failure to confirm would, they hoped, operate as a "pocket veto" and would result in Grenfell's liberation. Bruce, however, favored another tactic, which he thought was safer. Being on the firing line in Washington, he was more aware than were the Chicago lawyers, of the strength of official hostility toward anyone charged with complicity in a Confederate-inspired conspiracy. He evidently thought that, given the circumstances of the moment, it would be best to settle for a presidential confirmation of the commission's verdict, coupled with a commutation of the death sentence to one of imprisonment for a term of years; he reasoned that if Grenfell's life could be spared in this way, there would be an opportunity later on, after the wartime bitterness and the popular feeling aroused by Lincoln's assassination had begun to die down, to obtain a full pardon.

President Johnson had been heard to remark more than once that "treason is a crime and must be made odious." [28] Bruce was undoubtedly right in assuming that it would be next to impossible to persuade him that he would be justified in granting Grenfell a full pardon. The letters of Botts, General Sweet and the members of the court, and the personal intercession of Seward, Dennison, Colonel Wiswell, and Montgomery Blair (whose help had also been enlisted) would no doubt be helpful in inclining Johnson toward some degree of leniency, but the determining factor, next to the President's own predilections, would be the attitude taken in the matter by the War Department.

The secretary of war was at this time the most powerful member of Johnson's official family, and had the greatest influence on the President. Stanton's personal hostility toward Grenfell could be taken for granted, and his vindictiveness toward anyone who had earned his enmity was notorious. The Cincinnati trial would

[28] Ulysses S. Grant, *The Personal Memoirs of U. S. Grant* (New York, 1885–86), II, 638.

have refreshed his recollection of his interview with Grenfell less than a year before, and he was not the man to boggle unduly over questions of legality or constitutionality in dealing with anyone who *might* have been guilty of conspiring against the Union. On the question of the preservation of the Federal Union, and even that of winning the war, Stanton had operated from the beginning on the premise that it was better that ten innocent should suffer than that one guilty escape. Nor was it in Stanton's nature to allow the victory of the North to cast a mantle of forgiveness over those who had done anything to jeopardize or delay that victory.

Next in importance to Stanton, as far as Grenfell's fate was concerned, was the chief law officer of the War Department, Judge Advocate General Joseph Holt. Holt, a Kentuckian by birth, had earned a competence as a lawyer by the time he was thirty-five, and he retired from active practice to devote himself to politics. He was as equally as successful in his second career as he had been in the first. He became postmaster general and later secretary of war under President Buchanan, and he was one of the three members (Stanton and Secretary of State Jeremiah Black were the others) of the cabinet of that much harried individual who were unswerving in their determination to keep their wavering chief on a pro-Union course. In March, 1861, Holt returned to Kentucky and exerted himself to keep his native state in the Union. In 1862 he was rewarded by appointment as judge advocate general of the army, a post created by Congress shortly before and charged with the responsibility of reviewing and recording the proceedings of courts-martial. In Holt's hands and with the backing of Stanton (and, it must be said, of President Lincoln also) the office became something quite different from what Congress had intended. Holt conceived it to be his duty to extend the jurisdiction of military commissions to embrace persons and offenses not normally subject to cognizance by courts-martial, and particularly to what would now be called security cases, in which the nature of the offense or the weakness of the evidence made it unlikely that the government could obtain convictions in a civil court.[29]

By its very nature, this method of dealing with what were essentially political offenses, was subject to misuse and abuse, and Holt, a ruthless, credulous, and unscrupulous pro-Union fanatic, deliberately fostered and aggravated the evils of an inherently vicious system. His attitude in such matters was well exemplified by his conduct of the case against the Lincoln conspirators. Not only was the prosecution of Dr. Samuel Mudd, whose only crime was that he set John Wilkes Booth's broken leg after the assassination, a flagrant abuse of power and of the judicial process; but, in addition, Holt was accused, and was unquestionably guilty, of suppressing evidence that might have aided the defense and of withholding from the President the military commission's recommendation of mercy in the case of Mrs. Surratt.[30] Moreover, convinced that he "had a God-given mission in life to avenge Lincoln," Holt spent many thousands of dollars of government money to finance the operations of three arrant crooks, Sanford Conover, Richard Montgomery, and Dr. James E. Merritt (shades of Shanks, Langhorne, and Dr. I. Winslow Ayer!) who were easily able to persuade him of their ability to produce evidence linking Jefferson Davis and other members of the Confederate government to the plot to murder Lincoln.[31] Every word of the evidence purchased by Holt was manufactured and perjured, and the judge advocate general had to write a memorandum that occupies fifteen closely printed pages of the *Official Records* to explain to Stanton how he had been hoodwinked.[32]

This, then, was the man on whose sense of fairness and justice Grenfell's fate was largely to depend.

On June 29 Holt had completed his review of the trial record and his report on the case was delivered to the White House.[33] It began with the flat assertion that the existence of a conspiracy

[29] *Dictionary of American Biography*, IX, 181–83.
[30] *Ibid.*
[31] Thomas and Hyman, *Stanton*, 442.
[32] *OR*, Series II, Vol. VIII, 931–45.
[33] Holt's report to the President is in *House Executive Documents*, 645–49.

to release the Camp Douglas prisoners and "to destroy and sack" Chicago had been proven beyond a doubt by the evidence presented in the Cincinnati trial. It then asserted that "the evidence which tends to fasten upon Grenfell a knowledge of and participation in the plot is of such a nature as to satisfy this bureau of the correctness of the conclusions of the court." As Holt had demonstrated with Conover, Montgomery, and Merritt, his standards of credibility in conspiracy cases were not excessively strict. The record made it clear that it was primarily Shanks's testimony that linked Grenfell to the conspiracy; the crux of the case, therefore, was Shanks's credibility and it was to this issue that Holt addressed himself. The first hurdle he had to get over was Shanks's self-evident perjury in denying that he had been convicted of forgery in Texas. Holt did not try to go over the hurdle—he went around it, evading this key issue on strictly legalistic grounds. After stating that Shanks had denied his criminal past "in the most positive manner"—the doubtless unintended implication being that perjury committed in a "positive manner" stood on a different footing from perjury committed in a manner less than positive—Holt declared:

> It is a well-settled rule of law that the answer of a witness to a question put him in cross-examination . . . and with a view to injure his credibility, must be taken as final. Evidence in rebuttal cannot be legally admitted afterwards to show the falsity of his answer. And though considerable testimony was subsequently introduced by the defence to show that Shanks had been convicted and punished for forgery . . . yet his denial of this accusation . . . is legally decisive of the matter, and renders the admission of rebutting testimony . . . wholly unjustified . . . .[34]

Even as a matter of law, this statement rests on a shaky foundation. The most authoritative work available in 1865 on the rules of evidence in courts-martial stated that "there is no fixed rule" on the point Holt claimed to be well settled; the same authority stated, however, that the "weight of authority" seemed to favor Holt's

[34] *Ibid.*, 647.

position.[35] A more generally authoritative work, 98 *Corpus Juris Secundum,* under the rubric "Witnesses," Sec. 516, states: "If a witness is cross examined as to a particular fact not material to the issue, his answer concludes the questioning party, except that the commission of a crime may, if denied, be proved by the record." It will be noted that to prove the commission of a crime in this situation, the record of the conviction—in other words, documentary evidence—is required. It is an elementary rule that the "best evidence" of a documented fact is the document itself and, normally, a court will require that the document itself be offered in evidence; however, this rule is subject to numerous exceptions, and in many cases, when the documentary evidence has been destroyed, or, as a practical matter, is not obtainable, verbal, or "parole" evidence may be admitted in its place.[36] This was the case in the present instance. When the defense placed John Phelps, the first of the witnesses to testify to Shanks's criminal record, on the stand, Burnett objected on the ground that his testimony was not the best evidence; but when the defense pointed out that the documentary evidence of Shanks's conviction was "within the lines of the enemy" and hence unobtainable, he withdrew his objection and the witness was permitted to testify.[37]

Even if Holt's contention on this issue is accepted as legally valid, it is obvious nonetheless that he knowingly evaded the real problem. The military commission may have erred as a matter of law in admitting the evidence proving Shanks a perjurer, but the evidence had in fact been admitted, and it demolished Shanks's credibility as a witness. He was shown to be a convicted forger and a perjurer, and the issue before Holt was therefore not one of law but of elementary equity and morality—namely, whether there could be any justification for confirming a conviction and a death sentence based principally on the testimony of a proven perjurer. If Holt had been writing an impartial review of the record

[35] Benet, *Military Law,* 314.
[36] Benet states the rule as it is to be applied in courts-martial, as: "The [best evidence] rule is satisfied by the production of the best *attainable* evidence." *Ibid.,* 266.
[37] *House Executive Documents,* 418.

for the President's guidance, rather than a brief for the prosecution, and if he had been guided by considerations of justice as he should have been, he would have conceded that the main prop supporting Grenfell's conviction had been destroyed.

Holt's second problem was to deal with the evidence presented by the defense to show that Shanks had a generally bad reputation in Texas. There may be some extenuation of the manner in which he handled the problem of Shanks's perjury; believing that it was his duty to plead a case for the government, he had the right, perhaps, to claim the benefit of any principle of law that tended to support his position, and to close his eyes to the moral aspects of the case. But there can be no possible extenuation of the way he handled the second problem; in this instance, he was guilty of a deliberate falsification and suppression of evidence. Holt stated to the President that the witnesses through whom the defense proved Shanks's bad reputation, "were themselves Texans, sharers in the rebellion against the institutions of their country, and, therefore, deserving of little credit, when testifying . . . in the interest of one who had shared in their sympathies, and whose punishment, for crimes common to him and to themselves, they are anxious to avert." [38]

It is perhaps only in the aftermath of a bitter civil war that a high law officer of the government, a man of respectable antecedents, can advance the proposition that the evidence of a forger and perjurer, a bought stool pigeon and turncoat was to be preferred to that of respectable individuals whose only crime was that they had been residents of a seceded state. Had Holt done no more than this, his position might be understandable, however difficult it would be to excuse it. But he went much further. He made this statement in the face of the fact, clearly stated in the trial record before him, that of the five witnesses who testified about Shanks's past, only one was a Texan. The not entirely respectable Maurice Davis was a resident of Ohio; John Phelps, Wesley Johnson, and Richard Leek were residents of Illinois; these four had visited or stayed in Texas for brief periods before the war

[38] *Ibid.*, 647.

for business reasons; "business" in the case of Davis was gambling and the sale of millinery, but even by the hospitable standards of the Lone Star State, none of the four could have been called a Texan. A. Banning Norton, the only Texan of the five, voted against secession as a member of the Texas legislature, edited a pro-Union newspaper in Austin, and was forced to leave Texas "in consequence of that country becoming too hot a place for a Union man." [39]

Holt's report, which neither Bruce nor Grenfell's attorneys had the opportunity to study or to rebut, was the basis on which the President had to decide whether to confirm or overrule the findings of the military commission. It must be said, but hardly as a point in Holt's favor, that he concluded his report with the grudging suggestion that some mitigation of Grenfell's punishment might be in order. He did this in churlish fashion, not out of regard for justice, but as an act of mercy Grenfell did not deserve:

For the accused . . . the subject of a foreign power at peace with our government, and who, without pretence of provocation or wrong, united himself with traitors and malefactors for the overthrow of our republic in the interests of slavery, an institution abhorred by his country and people, there can be neither sympathy nor respect. In the altered condition of public affairs, however, growing out of the overthrow of the rebellion and the arrest or flight of its leaders . . . it may be that the President will feel justified in sparing even so unworthy and dishonored a life as that of the accused is shown to be. If the death sentence is commuted, it is believed that the punishment substituted should be severe and infamous.[40]

[39] For John Phelps, see *House Executive Documents*, 417–19; for Johnson, *ibid.*, 459–62; for Leek, *ibid.*, 466–67; for Davis, *ibid.*, 396–99, 426, 471–72; for Norton, *ibid.*, 478–80.
[40] *Ibid.*, 649.

Chapter XV

SIR FREDERICK BRUCE had an appointment on June 26 to see the President about the Grenfell case. He intended to ask Johnson to take no formal action until he (Bruce) had had an opportunity to present his observations on the credibility of the evidence on which Grenfell had been convicted. It appears that Bruce had learned unofficially that Holt's report was about to be delivered to the White House, and he sought the interview to forestall, if possible, the effect of what he knew, or had reason to suspect, would be a prejudicial and damaging document. Johnson, however, became ill just before the twenty-sixth and had to cancel the appointment. Bruce waited a few days to make a new appointment but as the President's indisposition continued, he decided to plead Grenfell's case in writing and did so on July 1: "Your Excellency has already pardoned Walsh, the person who according to the opinion of Colonel Burnett . . . was the most seriously implicated in the alleged plot. I think I can bring forward strong reasons for extending the same favor to Mr. Grenfell, and I trust before confirming the sentence against him, Your Excellency will allow me the opportunity of laying before you the circumstances . . . which are favorable to him." [1]

While waiting for the President's response, Bruce continued to

[1] Sir Frederick Bruce to Andrew Johnson, July 1, 1865, in British Legation-Archives, FO 115/448.

bring pressure on Secretary Seward in personal interviews and by letter, and spoke again to Postmaster General Dennison about the case.[2] Eventually, on July 19 to 20, he was able to see Johnson also. Bruce did not make a formal report to the Foreign Office of this interview and referred to it only briefly in a personal note to Lord John Russell: "I took the occasion of my interview with the President to recommend Grenfell's case to him. He said the facts should be carefully looked into, and that he trusted he would be able to deal with it as I wished."[3] Coming from the normally blunt and forthright Johnson, a vague half-promise like this was the height of diplomatic evasiveness and Bruce no doubt knew it.

Meanwhile, as the season changed from spring to the oppressively hot summer of the Ohio Valley, Grenfell continued to languish in his Cincinnati prison. Since the middle of April, he no longer had even the distraction of the trial and the daily journey to the courthouse to break the monotony of his confinement. He was receiving mail from England with some regularity and was permitted to correspond with his attorneys in Chicago. He was even allowed to receive an occasional visitor. On June 1, two ladies, Mrs. McCabe and Miss Estep, were given passes to visit him for one hour; it is to be feared that their call was motivated not by a concern for his temporal welfare but for his immortal soul, a subject in which Grenfell showed a minimum of interest, then or at any other time.[4] A short time before Judge Thomas M. Key of Cincinnati had also been allowed to visit him.[5] Key, an attorney and Democratic politician, had served during the war as judge advocate on the staff of General George B. McClellan and was reputed to have written the notorious Harrison's Landing Letter, in which McClellan undertook to lecture President Lincoln on the proper discharge of his duties; some months before committing that gross impertinence, McClellan had sent Key to Kentucky to learn if there was any truth in the rumor that Brigadier General

<hr/>

[2] Bruce to Robert Hervey, July 3, 1865, in *ibid.*, FO 115/445. *Cf.* Bruce to Lord John Russell, July 10, 1865, in FO-U.S.-General Correspondence, FO 5/1155.
[3] Bruce to Lord John Russell, July 20, 1865, in Russell Papers.
[4] Pass dated June 1, 1865, in Grenfell Papers-National Archives.
[5] Passes dated May 19 and July 19, in *ibid.*

William Tecumseh Sherman was insane. Key reported that this was indeed the case and that, in his considered judgment, Sherman was unfit to command an army.[6] Now back in civilian life, Key decided to take an interest in Grenfell and volunteered to assist him. The two men had several interviews but no documents have survived to show what, if anything, Key did to fulfill the hopes he may have aroused.

Generally, however, Grenfell had very little to occupy his mind and his time. If one may judge from his surviving letters, he never read a book after his school days were over and, apart from the newspapers and the letters he received and sent, he had no resources to relieve the monotony of his days and weeks in prison. He made a casual effort to keep a diary but his entries were made at irregular intervals. For the most part he vegetated, brooding over his bleak situation. The weeks followed each other in weary succession, but as yet he knew only that the records of the trial had been forwarded to Washington for review. He had no official information, only rumor, about the severity of the sentence pronounced by the court. His letters to the British legation had gone unanswered and, while he received periodic assurances from Hervey and Wilson that everything possible was being done for him, he persuaded himself, as was only natural under the circumstances, that these efforts were either inadequate or had already failed and that the truth about his situation and prospects was being kept from him.[7]

Grenfell shortly was to receive a blunt confirmation of his fears. Orders were issued on July 20 to the commandant of McLean Barracks to have him taken to Columbus under military guard and there delivered for safekeeping to the state penitentiary.[8] Two days later, after making the ninety-mile journey to Columbus, he was turned over to the warden of the penitentiary, who receipted for him in due form: "Received of Capt. Wm. Mahon, the following

[6] For Judge Key's wartime career, see Anonymous, *History of Cincinnati and Hamilton County* (Cincinnati, 1894), 160.
[7] Robert Hervey to Sir Frederick Bruce, July 24, 1865, in British Legation-Archives, FO 115/448.
[8] Orders dated July 20, 1865, in Grenfell Papers-National Archives.

named prisoner, to wit:—*G. St. Leger Grenfell* . . . John A. Prentice, Warden." [9]

The surviving records do not indicate why Grenfell was transferred to the state penitentiary. The warnings that had been given to Captain Mahon to guard him with the greatest viligance suggest that the authorities were concerned about the proximity of his friends in Kentucky, and wanted him kept in a prison which offered greater security than the somewhat sketchy safeguards available at McLean Barracks. Nor is there any indication in the records as to why that precise moment was chosen to move him to a prison "where the surroundings . . . [were] so very much more degrading" than those in the military prison in Cincinnati.[10] It will be seen that the presidential order confirming the verdict of the military commission is dated July 22, the day when Grenfell arrived at the peniteniary. This coincidence of dates is probably not accidental. Doubtless Johnson made his decision, and informed Stanton of it, some days earlier, whereupon the War Department decided to remove Grenfell to Columbus prior to the formal announcement of the President's decision, to forestall any desperation attempt on his part to escape, or on the part of his friends to liberate him. If these assumptions are correct, a curious light is shed on Johnson's assurances to Bruce. It is quite probable, indeed, that the President had already made up his mind on the case when he fobbed off the British minister with the half-promise to dispose of it in accordance with the latter's wishes.

When John Morgan, Thomas Hines, Basil Duke, and a number of other officers of Morgan's cavalry were taken to the Ohio State Penitentiary after their capture in 1863, their "first experience of convict life was to be stripped and ordered into water barrels where they were brushed vigorously with horse brushes. After these rough baths they were seated in barber chairs, and beards and hair were close-shaved." [11] One may hope that in consideration

[9] Receipt dated July 22, 1865, in *ibid.*
[10] Robert Hervey to Sir Frederick Bruce, July 24, 1865, in British Legation-Archives, FO 115/448.
[11] Brown, *The Bold Cavaliers*, 238.

of his age, Grenfell was spared these indignities and was permitted to keep his hair, moustaches, and beard. Nonetheless, he was keenly conscious of the humiliation of losing the relatively honorable status of a military prisoner and being confined with common criminals in a penitentiary.

On July 22, President Johnson appended his signature to the following document:

> The proceedings and findings in the case of G. St. Leger Grenfell are hereby approved; but in consideration of the recommendation of members of the court, and of the successful progress of the government in suppressing the rebellion, and in accordance with the suggestion of the Judge Advocate General, the sentence is hereby commuted to imprisonment for life, at hard labor, at the Dry Tortugas, or at such other place as the Secretary of War may designate.[12]

The President's decision was a victory of sorts for Sir Frederick Bruce and for the lawyers who had worked untiringly on the case; that Grenfell's life had been spared was indeed something but it was hardly a triumph of justice. It must be said in Johnson's favor, however, that the Grenfell case had received much notoriety and that he had to act on it a scant four months after the end of the war, long before the spirit of forgiveness began to replace the bitterness the war had engendered. Lincoln, had he lived, might well have found it in his heart and would have had the political courage to pardon Grenfell on condition that he left the United States forever. In that event, Grenfell's life might have been prolonged by a few years. He might have lived for some time longer on the charity of his family, to die, as he had written his daughter, Marie, at his appointed time, either in a four-poster bed, or more likely before a firing squad or in a ditch in some out-of-the-way part of the world. But Johnson was not Lincoln, and in any case, Holt's damaging report, on which he had to base his decision, was such as to make even the sparing of Grenfell's life appear to be an undeserved act of mercy.

Not until August 19, nearly a month after Johnson had acted on the case, was Bruce informed officially by Secretary Seward

[12] *House Executive Documents*, 652–53.

271

that Grenfell's death sentence had been commuted to life imprisonment.[18] Two days later, the minister sent a message to London to report on the outcome of the case, and added,

> While the case was under consideration I called on Mr. Seward and pressed upon him the considerations mostly in Grenfell's favor. . . . Not having seen the evidence in the case, I thought it better not to enter into the question of his innocence, as soon as I saw that Mr. Seward treated him as guilty. Two circumstances specially affecting Mr. Grenfell have mainly contributed to this severe sentence. He served some time with Morgan's Force, who is looked upon as a mere raider and partisan leader. When he left the South, he was favourably received by this Government and his joining subsequently in a plot against it is considered a gross breach of faith and honour. . . . I did not seek an interview with the President as I found that such a proceeding would have done no good as far as the President was concerned, and would have been distasteful to Mr. Seward, who is very touchy in his relations with the diplomatic body—Mr. Stanton, I knew from himself, took the most unfavourable view of Mr. Grenfell's conduct, and I felt the only hope for the unfortunate man was to endeavour to enlist Mr. Seward on the side of leniency.[14]

This was an accurate statement of the difficulties with which Bruce and Grenfell's lawyers had to contend; especially significant is the reference to Stanton's hostile attitude, for at this time the secretary of war's influence with the President was all powerful. But Bruce's statement that he "did not ask for an interview with the President" is rather puzzling, in the light of his earlier report to Lord John Russell that he had had a conversation with Johnson about the Grenfell case; it may well be that the conversation he spoke of had occurred informally, on an unofficial, social occasion.

Sir Frederick was evidently satisfied to minimize the effectiveness of his representations in bringing about the commutation of

[18] William H. Seward to Sir Frederick Bruce, August 19, 1865; FO-U.S.-General Correspondence, FO 5/1155.

[14] Bruce to Lord John Russell, August 21, 1865, in *ibid.* On September 9, Austen Layard informed Charles Grenfell of the President's decision; three days later, Lord John Russell directed Bruce to take no further action in the Grenfell case until instructed otherwise from London. Layard to C. P. Grenfell, September 9, 1865, and Lord John Russell to Bruce, September 12, 1865; both in *ibid.*

Grenfell's death sentence. Nonetheless, it was popularly believed at the time that it was the diplomatic pressure he exerted on behalf of his government that saved Grenfell from death by hanging.[15]

Up to mid-August, Grenfell was without any official information about his fate, although it is quite likely that he had some intimation of it through the prison grapevine. Some days prior to August 19, Hervey heard from "various sources" that Grenfell had been granted a full pardon and had already been released from prison; the news of the supposed pardon had in fact appeared in the Chicago papers. Also, Hervey was told by "a gentleman from Cincinnati" that he had seen Grenfell "in the streets of that city."[16] The false news that Grenfell had been freed came to Secretary Stanton's attention on the nineteenth, and he had the adjutant general's office telegraph to Colonel Burnett, who happened to be in Cincinnati at the time, that: "The Secetary of War desires to know if Grenfell is at large, and if so, you will please communicate to the proper Commander the order of the Secretary of War that he be immediately arrested and held in confinement. Report receipt and action taken."[17] Grenfell, of course, was not free. He was still in the penitentiary in Columbus, but the baseless rumor that he had been released was enough to stir the War Department into prompt action to have him placed beyond the possibility of escape through an administrative error or otherwise. The President's order commuting Grenfell's sentence to life imprisonment, which had been in Stanton's office for nearly a month, was endorsed the same day, "Referred to the Adjutant General to execute the President's order. The Dry Tortugas designated."[18] Orders were at once telegraphed to department headquarters to arrange for Grenfell's transfer to Fort Jefferson. The telegram was followed by written orders three days later, "to send the prisoner G. St. Leger Grenfell, under charge of a commissioned [officer]

[15] *House Executive Documents*, 650.

[16] Robert Hervey to Sir Frederick Bruce, August 19, 1865, in British Legation-Archives, FO 115/448.

[17] Telegram signed by General E. D. Townsend, in Grenfell Papers-National Archives.

[18] *House Executive Documents*, 652.

273

with a sufficient guard to the Dry Tortugas, Florida . . . where he will be delivered to the commanding officer of the post, who is hereby ordered to confine said Grenfell at hard labor during the period designated in his sentence." [19]

Major General E. O. C. Ord, commanding the department, wired the necessary instructions to the army post in Columbus. However, the Ohio capital was far enough removed from Washington along the chain of command for the urgency of the numerous telegrams of August 19 and 20 about Grenfell to become thoroughly dissipated; and not until three weeks later was Lieutenant E. Wigman of the Fourth United States Infantry given orders to take Grenfell in charge for transportation to the Dry Tortugas.[20] On September 19 Wigman and an escort of enlisted men went to the penitentiary and the prisoner was delivered to them. The party then proceeded by train to New York, where Grenfell was deposited for safekeeping in Fort Wood, to await the sailing of the ship that was to take him to Florida. On September 28, in company with a dozen other "graduates of military commissions," he was placed on board the transport *John Rice* and after a ten-day journey, arrived at the Dry Tortugas on October 8 and had his first glimpse of the prison in which he was to spend the last twenty-six months of his life.[21]

What Grenfell saw before him on that October morning fully justified his comment, "I cannot say that the appearance of the Dry Tortugas is very inviting." [22] The Florida Keys are the above-water portions of the long coral reef which curves in a two hundred-mile arc southwestward from the tip of Florida into the Gulf of Mexico. The main chain of keys begins at Key Largo and ends at Key West. Twenty-five miles west of Key West lies the small cluster of islands named Marquesas Keys. Nearly fifty miles farther west, at the very end of the great Florida Reef, is a group of islets, covered with thick brushwood, mango, and prickly pear; sandy, deserted, none of them are more than five feet above high

[19] *Ibid.*, 654.
[20] Orders dated September 13, 1865, in Grenfell Papers-National Archives.
[21] McElrath, "Annals of the War."
[22] *Ibid.*

water. These are the Dry Tortugas, discovered and named by Ponce de Leon in 1513. The light, whitish-blue waters of the Gulf of Mexico are to the north of the islands and the deep blue water of the Gulf Stream is to the south. The Tortugas got their name from the huge loggerhead turtles, *tortugas* in Spanish, thousands of which dig their nests and lay their eggs in the sandy surface of the ten islands which make up the group. The largest island, with an area of about sixteen acres, is Garden Key; others, large enough to be named, and all lying within an area of ten square miles, are East Key, Middle Key, Sand Key, Long Key, Bird Key, and Loggerhead Key.

Shortly after Florida was admitted to statehood, the national government decided to erect a major fort in the Tortugas to guard the entrance by way of the Florida Straits into the Gulf of Mexico and to protect the passage of American shipping from New Orleans into the Atlantic.[23] In 1846 construction began on Fort Jefferson on Garden Key, on the basis of plans drawn by Lieutenant Montgomery C. Meigs, who was to become the very able quartermaster general of the Union army in the Civil War. In charge of construction was Lieutenant Horatio G. Wright, who, risen to major-general, was to defend Washington at the time of Jubal Early's raid in 1864, and who tried without much success to prevent President Lincoln from exposing himself to enemy gunfire.

To build anything on the soft coral and shell sand of Garden Key, and especially fortifications on the great scale Meigs' plans called for, was an immensely difficult task. All the workmen and artisans, slaves hired from their masters in Florida and Irish laborers brought down from the North, all their food, every one of the millions of bricks, every trowelful of cement, every plank and nail, and even the topsoil for the parade ground, had to be brought to the site from the mainland, the bricks from Pensacola, cement from New York, lumber and iron from Mobile, stone from the quarries in New Hampshire.[24] Construction went on for thirty

[23] Albert Manucy, "The Gibraltar of the Gulf of Mexico," *Florida Historical Quarterly*, XXI (1943), 305–306.
[24] *Ibid.*, 310.

years, but the "Gibraltar of the Gulf" was never completed. The fort was an irregular hexagon with a half-mile perimeter. Its brick walls were immensely massive, sixty feet thick at the base and fifty feet high. A huge bastion was located at each of the six corners, and there were embrasures in the walls and bastions for five hundred large-caliber guns mounted in three tiers. In the area enclosed by the walls, barracks were built for six companies of artillerymen; another large building was erected to house the officers and their families. A chapel, hospital, commandant's quarters, and storehouses were constructed "on a scale of liberality for comfort and elegance." [25] The parade ground within the fort was planted with Bermuda grass; around it, and among the buildings, evergreen mangoes, cottonwoods, cocoa and date palms, fig trees, gum and banana trees, and castor bean plants were set out in large clusters to provide shade from the glaring sun, and the buildings were festooned with jasmine, Thunbergia, cypress and morning-glory vines.

The walls and bastions, as one approached the island, seemed to rise straight from the sea. Those who saw the fort for the first time regularly described it as riding like a ship on the Gulf waters. Actually, to protect the brickwork from the pounding of the waves, a low stone wall was built at the water's edge, and between it and the walls of the fort proper was a lagoon or moat sixty feet wide. The stone wall, or breakwater, was pierced at intervals for iron pipes, through which the seawater could circulate in and out of the moat with the changes of the tide. The nearby waters teemed with sharks and after September, 1861, when the government began to avail itself of the obvious advantages of Fort Jefferson as a prison for military criminals, the garrison amused itself by catching sharks and setting them free in the moat, where they swam up and down, their dorsal fins cutting the surface of the water, as a warning to would-be escapees. These sharks were jokingly called provost marshals. The only entrance to the fort was the sally port, reached by a drawbridge over the moat and pro-

[25] J. B. Holder, "The Dry Tortugas," *Harper's Magazine*, XXXVII (1868), 262.

tected by heavy gates, and it was through these that Grenfell entered his new home.

Apart from the isolation, which caused the military and civilian inhabitants of the fort to feel that they were inhabiting another planet, there were certain compensations to living on Garden Key, especially for those who had eyes for some of the more unusual manifestations of nature. The Tortugas lie on one of the major flyways from North America to Cuba and South America, and in season, myriads of migratory birds fly over the islands or drop off to rest, and each year thousands upon thousands of sooty terns settle on the Tortugas for their nesting season. Countless pelicans and seagulls make their permanent home on the islands. The shallows teem with tropical fish and every form of marine life. Storms wash up rare shells and drive schools of porpoises into the lagoons surrounding each of the keys. The sunsets are surpassingly beautiful. And the islands were not cut off completely from the outside world. When Grenfell was a prisoner there, two schooners from Key West made weekly trips to the fort and a steamer from New Orleans came every fortnight. These ships brought in replacements for the garrison, new prisoners, supplies of all kinds, and what prisoners and garrison alike considered most important of all, the mail and newspapers. Occasionally, a boat came up from Cuba with a cargo of watermelons, pineapples, bananas, and fresh vegetables to sell to the garrison at outrageously high prices.

The advances in naval ordnance and the advent of the ironclad warship immediately before and during the Civil War rendered Fort Jefferson virtually obsolete. It was the Gibraltar of the Gulf no longer and from the close of the war until 1869, it was used as a maximum-security prison, the Alcatraz of its day. It was said in army circles that Fort Jefferson was mainly useful as an adjunct of yellow fever to speed up promotion in the artillery branch of the service, which supplied the garrison for the fort. The number of prisoners fluctuated widely; at times there were several hundred but usually not so many. The normal garrison consisted of five companies of heavy artillery, but when Grenfell arrived, the garri-

277

son was a Negro regiment, the Eighty-Second United States Infantry—a "detested and abominable negro regiment," Dr. Samuel Mudd of Maryland called it—but it was replaced by white artillerymen a month later.[26] The prisoners were housed in the casemates, singly or in small groups, in rooms of various sizes, the smallest measuring about ten feet by fifteen. Each room or cell had a window to the outside; there were no bars on the windows, nor were bars necessary, for these openings were V-shaped vertical slits let into the wall high above floor level, narrowing from a width of two feet on the inside to four or five inches on the outside.

Two weeks after his arrival at Fort Jefferson, Grenfell began a new diary. His opening entry was anything but cheerful:

> My journal, which I left in Cincinnati, was brought up to the 21st of July—unhappy day—when I received the order to proceed to the penitentiary at Columbus to await the promulgation of my sentence. What a farce! I was condemned by these mercenary, subservient wretches of the military commission to be hung. Why did they not hang me at once? Far better for me had they done so than to endure all the misfortune which I have since gone through, and still have to go through. It would appear that every change I make is for the worse, and when I think I am at the bottom of the pit the ground suddenly gives way under me and precipitates me still lower.[27]

Except for the apparent hopelessness of his prospects, Grenfell's situation, especially during the first two weeks in his new prison, was not so cheerless as his far from contrite and somewhat melodramatic diary entry would suggest. He arrived at the Tortugas after the worst of the summer heat was over, and at first he was lodged in a large, comfortable cell. He was allowed the luxury of a daily bath, and in consideration of the state of his health,

[26] Nettie Mudd (ed.), *The Life of Samuel A. Mudd* (New York, 1906), 139.
[27] McElrath, "Annals of the War." The existence of the diary and the quotations from it in "Annals of the War" are accepted on the faith of Captain McElrath's narrative. When Grenfell escaped from Fort Jefferson, he left his papers behind. His diary was among them and came into McElrath's possession. McElrath evidently had the diary when he wrote "Annals of the War" in 1879. The present writer's efforts to trace McElrath's descendants and to locate the diary have proven fruitless.

which showed the effect of eleven months' confinement, the post surgeon excused him from the hard labor which his sentence required him to perform. Indeed, his situation was quite tolerable, except for the loss of freedom, and in that respect, the officers and men of the garrison and the officers' families were hardly better off than he was.

This relatively mild regime ended when Grenfell was moved into a cramped cell that he had to share with four other prisoners, Dr. Samuel Mudd, Samuel Arnold, Michael O'Laughlin, and Edward Spangler. These four had been convicted by a military commission for their connection with John Wilkes Booth in the assassination of President Lincoln and were serving out their sentences in the Tortugas. Mudd was a blameless country doctor when fate brought Booth with his broken leg to his door. Arnold, an unemployed clerk and farmhand, and O'Laughlin, a feed salesman and livery-stable roustabout, had been schoolmates of Booth's in Maryland and had been recruited by him to help kidnap the President. Spangler was a carpenter and stagehand at Ford's Theatre, and held Booth's horse in the alley behind the building while the actor committed his demented deed.

Two days after Grenfell became a member of this group of "political prisoners," the five were moved to a dungeon on the ground floor, a small, damp, airless room in which they were "herded together like so many cattle." [28] Two weeks later, heavy leg irons and chains were fastened to their ankles, to be worn while they were at work during the day; the irons were removed only when they were locked up in their cell for the night.[29] They were given no official reason for this severe treatment, but they heard from their guards that strict orders had come down from the secretary of war himself that the most stringent precautions were to be taken to prevent their escape. The regiment of guards, the sixty-foot-thick walls, the moat patrolled by sharks, and the seventy-five miles of water between the Tortugas and Key West or

[28] Samuel Arnold, "The Lincoln Plot," New York *Sun*, December 14, 1902.
[29] Mudd, *Samuel Mudd*, 139.

279

the ninety miles of open sea between the islands and Cuba were not considered adequate deterrents.

Dr. Mudd must have been heartily tired of the uninspiring society of Arnold, O'Laughlin, and Spangler by the time Grenfell joined them, and correspondingly pleased with the addition of a newcomer to the group. He struck up a congenial and be it said to his credit, a compassionate relationship with Grenfell. He wrote his brother that,

> Colonel Grenfell is quite an intelligent man, tall, straight, and about sixty-one or two years of age. He speaks fluently several languages, and often adds mirth by his witty sarcasm and jests. He has been badly wounded and is now suffering with dropsy, and is allowed no medical treatment whatever, but loaded down with chains and fed upon the most loathsome food, which treatment in a short time must bring him to an untimely grave. You will confer an act of kindness and mercy by acquainting the British Minister in Washington . . . of these facts.[30]

Grenfell's constitution was much tougher, his spirits more resilient, and his will to live more tenacious than Dr. Mudd gave him credit for.

Grenfell and his new companions had in common something more than the shared miseries of their imprisonment. All five were the victims of Henry Burnett's skill as prosecutor. No doubt they whiled away many a long hour comparing notes on their respective trials, and on the kind of evidence—"extorted, perverted, and when necessary, manufactured"—on which they had been convicted.[31]

[30] *Ibid.*, 140-41. Grenfell was actually fifty-seven. There is no evidence, apart from this remark of Dr. Mudd's, that Grenfell suffered from dropsy, and if he was ever "badly wounded," it was not during the Civil War. However serious the wound may have been, it was not disabling and Grenfell himself never referred to it. Mudd's comment on the loathsomeness of the food served to the prisoners is amply borne out by Samuel Arnold's report: "Coffee was brought over to our quarters in a dirty, greasy bucket, always with grease swimming upon its surface; bread, rotten fish and meat, all mixed together." Arnold, "The Lincoln Plot."
[31] Margaret Leech, *Reveille in Washington* (New York, 1941), 411.

Grenfell's doleful diary entry reflected a passing mood. Actually, neither his life sentence, nor the eleven months he had spent in prison, nor indifferent health, nor his advancing years, nor the hardships he was undergoing at Fort Jefferson could break his spirit. Nor, for that matter, had all his misfortunes been sufficient to teach him prudence or the ability to curb his temper. Within two weeks after his arrival at Fort Jefferson, he made the following entry in his diary:

> Yesterday a one-horse lieutenant insulted me most grossly without any cause. He told me, for no reason at all, that I was not a man of honor. I told him that I had more honor than he had, and that he must be a coward to insult an unoffending prisoner who could not resent it. He went away and I have heard nothing of it as yet, although I expected to be ironed and hung up by the thumbs—a common punishment here for the most trivial offenses.[32]

However gross the provocation may have been, Grenfell's blunt response was not calculated to gain him the good will of his new masters. A few weeks later, when a soldier who had contracted smallpox was placed in a casemate near his cell instead of being isolated in a remote section of the fort, he obtained a large board, "and upon it in large letters inscribed 'Small-Pox Hospital,' directing all persons to shun it. . . . Col. Grenfell was severely reprimanded for his action and sternly commanded to take in the board and to be very careful in his actions in the future." [33]

However, Grenfell's situation was about to change, and greatly to his advantage. At the end of October, a new commanding officer reported for duty at the fort. In one of the strange coincidences of Grenfell's life, this was the same colonel—now brigadier general by brevet—Bennett Hill who, as assistant provost marshal for the state of Michigan in 1864, was visited in Detroit by the mysterious Confederate major whose disclosures about the Chicago Conspiracy he passed on to Colonel Sweet. Hill was an 1837

---

[32] Quoted from Grenfell's diary in McElrath, "Annals of the War," the second sentence, as Grenfell actually wrote it, was: "He told me, *apropos de bottes* that I was not a man of honour."

[33] Arnold, "The Lincoln Plot," New York *Sun*, December 15, 1902.

graduate of West Point, a classmate of Bragg and Hooker.[34] Assigned to administrative duties during the war, he had had no opportunity to distinguish himself. A man of kindly instincts, he took a friendly interest in Grenfell and tried in various ways to help him. Perhaps he was motivated to some extent by the knowledge that his prisoner had been convicted partly on the testimony of the same Maurice Langhorne who had tried to sell him the "secrets" of the nonexistent "Detroit Conspiracy."

Disturbed by the pointless cruelty of keeping a man of Grenfell's age in leg irons and chains, he asked the War Department for instructions about the treatment that was to be accorded him. He was informed that Grenfell was a "State Prisoner" and was to be treated as such, which meant that he had to wear leg irons and chains during the day and had to be locked up for the night with the "Lincoln Conspirators." [35] Nevertheless, all five men were now to be released from their cell daily to perform the hard labor that their sentences had prescribed. This gave them the benefit of fresh air, sunshine, and exercise and, for the most part, the work they were required to perform was anything but demanding. They were set to cleaning old brick, a dirty and tedious occupation, but Dr. Mudd reported on one occasion that he "worked hard all day and came very near finishing one brick." [36] It may be supposed that Grenfell worked no harder than his medical friend. When the supply of old brick ran out, they were given the task of sweeping and sanding the six bastions every day, Sundays and holidays excepted, a job that required a minimum of time or exertion. They also had to help the soldiers unload the ships that brought supplies to the fort from Key West and New Orleans.

The bad drinking water, the unwholesome diet, utterly unsuited to the climate, consisting almost entirely of salt pork and salt beef (only rarely was fresh meat issued as often as every third day), bread and coffee, the lack of fresh vegetables and fruit, the

[34] G. W. Cullum, *Biographical Register of the Officers and Graduates of the U.S. Military Academy* (Boston, 1891), I, 676.

[35] War Department to B. H. Hill, December 3, 1866; in Grenfell Papers-National Archives.

[36] Mudd, *Samuel Mudd*, 121.

mosquitoes and vermin with which the island was infested, the "torpid monotony" of their life were hardships which had to be endured by everyone in the fort, and were hardly more severe for the prisoners than they were for the garrison.[37] Prisoners were permitted to send and receive letters and to use the prison library, which was fairly well stocked with books, periodicals, and New York newspapers; and when they had performed the trivial daily tasks assigned to them, they were free to fight the boredom of their dull existence in whatever way they wished, within the limits of the scanty recreational facilities available. Whenever a shipment of fruit or vegetables arrived, the prisoners received a share and after General Hill took command, each prisoner was given a monthly credit of three dollars with the sutler, with which he could buy food, tobacco, stationery, and notions. The three dollars did not go very far—Grenfell complained that a toothbrush cost seventy-five cents—but it helped. And shortly before Christmas, the prisoners learned that they were to have the same delicacies for their holiday dinner as the garrison, namely "canned roast turkey, sausage, oysters, preserves, fresh peaches, tomatoes, etc." [38] At the end of January, other changes for the better occurred. The "political prisoners" were relieved of their shackles, moved from their damp, unwholesome dungeon into a larger, airier cell and their diet was greatly improved.

In his letters to his daughter, Marie, in England and to an extensive list of correspondents in America, Grenfell rang the changes on the miseries of his life in prison. He was pleading for sympathy and freedom and perhaps should not be blamed for stretching the truth in describing the hardships he had to endure. Nevertheless, in some instances he exaggerated to the point of outright falsification. Dr. Mudd's letters clearly indicate that from February, 1866, on, Grenfell received humane and even considerate treatment. He was a prisoner, of course, and for a man of his disposition and habits, the mere fact of confinement to one place for an indefinite future was unquestionably a severe hardship. In addition, he managed to

[37] "A. O'D," "Dry Tortugas," 284.
[38] Mudd, Samuel Mudd, 150.

convince himself that he was completely innocent of the charges on which he had been convicted, and the belief that he was the victim of a miscarriage of justice turned inconveniences into major grievances and real grievances into intolerable outrage. He was blinded by self-pity to the many evidences of what appears to have been a real desire on the part of the officers to lighten the burden of his imprisonment. General George D. Ramsey, former chief of ordnance, visited the fort and saw Grenfell in the spring of 1866; he told Sir Frederick Bruce that Grenfell was "a favorite of the officers, and . . . they do all in their power to alleviate his situation." [39]

Grenfell was particularly unjust to General Hill, whom he called "a bad old man," a description the General certainly did not merit.[40] In May, 1866, Hill wrote to Mrs. Vyvyan, one of Grenfell's sisters, "He seems to be in vigorous health and cheerful. His employment, which is of his own seeking, is the charge of a small garden, in which he takes great interest. In reply to an enquiry of mine, why he did not write to his friends, he stated that he did not wish to hear from them, as it only unsettled his mind, and made him discontent[ed] and unhappy. I do not know that he is in want of anything. . . . His friends may rest assured that he is kindly treated." [41]

The garden assigned to Grenfell's care was a small area, surrounded by a picket fence, along one edge of the parade ground, "in which a suspicion of soil partially concealed the coral sand of the island." [42] Captain T. P. McElrath, Fifth United States Ar-

[39] Sir Frederick Bruce to E. Hammond, June 8, 1866, in FO-U.S.-General Correspondence, FO 5/1155.

[40] Grenfell to Marie Pearce-Serocold, June 30, 1867, in Weaks (ed.), "Colonel . . . Grenfell," 13. General Hill, whom Grenfell called a bad *old* man, was actually his junior by several years.

[41] Hill to Mrs. Vyvyan, May 26, 1866; in Packe Papers. A few months earlier, when a British visitor to the United States asked Sir Frederick Bruce to obtain the War Department's permission for one of Grenfell's sisters to send him "some conveniences in the way of bedding, wearing apparel, books, etc.,—as he seems in terrible plight," the request was denied. John H. Kennaway to Bruce, December 13, 1865, in British Legation-Archives, FO 115/461; Holt to Bruce, January 2, 1866, in *ibid*, FO 115/455.

[42] McElrath, "Annals of the War."

tillery, in the course of a visit to the fort, saw Grenfell tending the garden, and described him thus:

> He was dressed in Confederate gray and surmounted by a high straw hat squeezed to a conical point at the crown and destitute of a ribbon, giving him the general appearance of respectability peculiar to the average native Southern planter of the early reconstruction days ... to all appearances [he] performed the duties of his position with earnestness and zeal. . . . [The garden] never proved productive, but for a long time it gave its captive superintendent agreeable and healthful recreation.[43]

There were times when Grenfell was able to view his situation with detachment and even humor, as he did when he described his new occupation to a friend in Kentucky: "Be it known to you that they have turned my sword into a shovel & a rake and I am at the head of my profession here. What I say or do (horticulturally) is law!" [44] But he was also capable of unreasoning anger and bitterness and on at least two occasions vented on his garden his resentment of real or fancied grievances. Once he sprinkled the growing vegetables with sea water, which caused them to shrivel and die. Another time, having been given a stock of seed to plant, he secretly roasted the seed before planting it and was apparently highly pleased with the disappointment of the officers over the failure of the seed to germinate.[45]

General Hill allowed Grenfell to write and receive as many letters as he pleased. As the general had indicated to Mrs. Vyvyan, there were times when Grenfell chose not to take advantage of Hill's indulgence; whether out of contrariness or a desire to punish himself, he went for weeks without writing to his relatives or friends. At other times, he abused the privilege. In letters which he was permitted to send out uncensored, he made manifestly untrue statements about his life in prison. Thus, he wrote his daughter, Marie, in June, 1867, that he "was worked very hard in the

[43] *Ibid.*
[44] Grenfell to H. L. Stone, January 15, 1868; in Stone Papers, Kentucky Historical Society, Frankfort.
[45] McElrath, "Annals of the War."

285

chain gang from 6 till ½ past 5," that he was "dying by inches from inanition," and that on General Hill's orders, he was "ten times worse treated than any other prisoner on the island." [46] These statements may be contrasted with a letter Hill had written Mrs. Vyvyan only a short time before:

> Your brother was in excellent health when I left Fort Jefferson. . . . His duties are of a very light character and food and clothing are ample. On a previous occasion when you expressed a wish to send him some articles that you thought would add to his comfort, I mentioned the subject to him and suggested . . . that he write to you . . . [to] let you know what he required; but his reply was that he wanted nothing and that the supplies issued to him by the government were ample. [47]

Actually, far from being treated worse than other prisoners, Grenfell appears to have been treated with unusual indulgence. With the exception of one incident, to be mentioned later, there is nothing in Dr. Mudd's numerous (and apparently uncensored) letters to his family to suggest that Grenfell was mistreated in any way. When he was punished, as he sometimes was, it was because of his own injudicious or refractory behavior, and the punishment was not nearly so severe as his letters and diary would lead one to believe.

In April, 1867, when he had been at Fort Jefferson for eighteen months, Grenfell submitted a petition for executive clemency, which General Hill sent to Washington with a generous endorsement: "In forwarding it, it is but just to add that his strict and cheerful attention to [his] duties has attracted the special notice of the officers of the fort." [48] Judge Advocate General Holt did not allow Hill's praise of the prisoner to arouse his compassion or to weaken his hostility toward Grenfell. He did forward the petition to the President, but did so with a characteristically peevish comment: "This bureau has heretofore expressed the conviction

[46] Grenfell to Marie Pearce-Serocold, June 30, 1867, in Weaks (ed.), "Colonel . . . Grenfell," 13.
[47] Bennett H. Hill to Mrs. Vyvyan, March 28, 1867, in Packe Papers.
[48] *House Executive Documents*, 638.

that the prisoner Grenfell . . . should be made to expiate his crime by suffering the penalty imposed. . . . The bureau does not feel justified in submitting any favorable recommendation." [49] One can only speculate on the degree or quantity of the expiation that would have been sufficient to satisfy Holt's desires. Clearly, he did not intend maudlin considerations of forgiveness, pity, or charity to affect his determination to do what he conceived to be his duty.

General Ramsay, who had evidently taken a liking to Grenfell, returned to Washington while the petition for clemency was still in the hands of the War Department. Entirely of his own volition, he exerted himself to persuade his army friends to take a favorable view of the Grenfell case. But, as he informed Sir Frederick Bruce, "He found . . . that there is too great a prejudice against him in that quarter to allow of any steps being taken with effect on his behalf. Besides the charge of having virtually broken his parole, they have a story against him which does not sound at all probable, of having acted with great harshness towards some Federal prisoners. They will get witnesses enough to swear to it." [50] In the face of this official hostility and Holt's adverse recommendation, President Johnson declined to grant the petition and his decision was communicated to Grenfell on June 8.[51]

[49] *Ibid.*, 640.
[50] Sir Frederick Bruce to E. Hammond, June 8, 1866, in FO-U.S.-General Correspondence, FO 5/1155.
[51] *House Executive Documents*, 651.

Chapter XVI

IN APRIL, 1866, Grenfell's prospects for regaining his freedom were brightened considerably by the announcement of the decision of the United States Supreme Court in the habeas corpus proceedings brought by Lambdin P. Milligan.[1] One of the Indiana Copperhead chieftains, Milligan had been arrested in 1864 and tried by a military commission on charges of conspiracy, affording aid and comfort to the rebels, inciting insurrection, disloyal practices, and violation of the laws of war. After a trial which made Henry Burnett's reputation as a prosecutor, Milligan was convicted and sentenced to death. Just before the date set for his execution, his attorneys applied for a writ of habeas corpus. The case went to the Supreme Court on the question of whether the military commission had jurisdiction to try Milligan. Justice David Davis, delivering the decision of the court, stated thus the issue raised by the case: "The importance of the main question presented by this record cannot be overstated; for it involves the very framework of the government and the fundamental principles of American liberty. . . . No graver question was ever considered by this court, nor one which more nearly concerns the rights of the whole people; for it is the birthright of every American citizen, when charged with crime, to be tried and punished according to law." The court established as facts that Milligan was a civilian, that he

[1] *Ex parte Milligan;* 4 Wallace 2-142 (1867).

288

was neither a resident of one of the seceded states nor a prisoner of war, that the state of Indiana was not in rebellion, that federal authority in that state was unquestioned and the courts open to hear and dispose of criminal cases; hence the court concluded that the trial of Milligan before a military commission was a violation of the rights guaranteed by Article III, Section 2 (3), and the Fourth, Fifth, and Sixth Amendments of the Constitution. The writ of habeas corpus was therefore granted.

In a concurring opinion, Chief Justice Salmon P. Chase held that, "whatever [Milligan's] desert of punishment may be, it is more important to the country and to every citizen that he should not be punished under an illegal sentence . . . than that he should be punished at all. The laws which protect the liberties of the whole people must not be violated or set aside in order to inflict, even upon the guilty, unauthorized though merited punishment."

This landmark decision was a complete vindication of the arguments of Grenfell's attorneys in their attack on the right of the military commission to try him. He too was a civilian, having left the Confederate army well before the commission of the crimes with which he was charged; he was neither a resident of one of the seceded states nor a prisoner of war. The acts with which he was charged had been committed in a state that was neither in rebellion nor insurrection, and at the time of his trial, grand juries met and courts sat in complete security in Illinois. It might have been argued that *Ex parte Milligan* did not help Grenfell, because he was a British subject and not a citizen of the United States; however, it is a firmly established principle of law that a citizen of a country at peace with the United States is protected in this country by the same legal and constitutional safeguards as an American citizen.

Robert S. Wilson, who retained a "deep interest" in "poor Grenfell's case," suggested to Sir Frederick Bruce, as soon as the *Ex parte Milligan* decision was announced, that it provided an opportunity to take up the Grenfell question with the President, and he offered to go to Washington if his assistance might be of use to hasten Grenfell's release.[2] Grenfell himself wrote to Bruce to point out that the Supreme Court had "finally settled the question as to the legality or illegality of [his] arrest, imprisonment, trial and sentence"; he reminded the minister that his own position was identical to Milligan's, and implored Bruce "to lose no time in *demanding* from the Secretary of War an order for my release, seeing that their own Tribunals have decided that *all the proceedings under which I now suffer are unconstitutional and illegal,* they can have no plea for detaining me any longer in this miserable fortress." [3]

Unfortunately for him, the problem was not so simple as, in his anxiety to be released from imprisonment, he imagined it to be. *Ex parte Milligan* did not automatically settle the legality of Grenfell's detention nor did it compel the Executive to set free any and every prisoner who had been sentenced by a military commission. In actual fact, in July, 1866, the War Department did order the release of all civilian prisoners condemned by military commissions who had served at least six months of their sentences, but Mudd, Spangler, Arnold, O'Laughlin, and Grenfell ("those under Sentence at the Dry Tortugas") were specifically excluded from the scope of the order.[4] Grenfell might have been freed in one of two ways. One way would have been to petition a federal court for a writ of habeas corpus on his behalf; his attorneys would then have had the task of persuading the court that his case was governed by the precedent of *Ex parte Milligan.* Or the Executive might have freed him of its own volition, conceding, as an act of grace, that in view of the Milligan decision, it did not consider itself justified in keeping him in prison. But with Stanton and Holt still at the War Department and with Andrew Johnson fighting for his political life, there was little likelihood that the second alternative would occur.

[2] Robert S. Wilson to Sir Frederick Bruce, April 7, 1866, in British Legation-Archives, FO 115/461.

[3] Grenfell to Bruce, May 17, 1866, in *ibid.*

[4] General Orders No. 46, quoted in full in a letter from Grenfell to Robert Hervey, October 30, 1866, which the latter forwarded to Bruce on November 16, in *ibid.*

Suggestions were made from time to time in the months following the Milligan ruling that habeas corpus proceedings be instituted to obtain Grenfell's release, but for reasons which the surviving documents do not reveal, this was never done. The high cost of a suit which was almost certain to be opposed by the government—and might have to be carried all the way to the Supreme Court—was apparently a factor. In November, Bruce forwarded to London an offer by former Confederate General Bradley T. Johnson to act for Grenfell if he were supplied with "a few hundred dollars to procure the release of this unhappy gentleman"; Bruce asked the Foreign Office to suggest to "Grenfell's friends" that they underwrite the cost of suing out a writ of habeas corpus.[5] The Foreign Office communicated with Grenfell's cousin, Charles Pascoe Grenfell, who declined to underwrite the cost of an action to be brought by Johnson, but stated that if Bruce wished to take the opinion of "a first rate counsel" and was advised by him to sue for a writ of habeas corpus, the family would be willing to bear the expenses.[6] This course was not followed. Apparently Bruce was influenced by the hope that through his own efforts and with the assistance of friendly intermediaries, the President could be persuaded to free Grenfell voluntarily, and he considered that as long as there was a reasonable prospect of obtaining his freedom in that way, it would not be prudent to force the Executive on the defensive by initiating court action which it was bound to oppose.

With the benefit of hindsight, it may be questioned if there was ever any real chance that the War Department and the President could have been persuaded to free him voluntarily. As far as the War Department was concerned, the answer must be an unqualified No. So long as Stanton remained at its head—and it was not until May, 1868, after the failure of the Senate to impeach Johnson, that he "relinquished" his office—there was no hope for

[5] Bradley T. Johnson to Bruce, November 6, 1866; Bruce to E. Hammond, November 14, 1866, in FO-U.S.-General Correspondence, FO 5/1155.
[6] E. Hammond to C. P. Grenfell, November 26, 1866; H. R. Grenfell to Hammond, December 17, 1866, in *ibid.*

Grenfell in that quarter. Holt's enmity toward Grenfell was, if possible, even more unyielding than Stanton's, and Holt remained glued to his post until 1875. His feelings never changed towards those tainted with rebellion; his attitude is shown by the revealing title he gave a pamphlet he wrote to defend himself against the continuing criticism of his handling of the trial of the Lincoln conspirators: "Vindication of Judge Advocate General Holt from the Foul Slanders of Traitors, Confessed Perjurers and Suborners, Acting in the Interest of Jefferson Davis." Each time one of the numerous petitions to free Grenfell or to ease the conditions of his imprisonment was referred to the judge advocate general's office for comment, it brought forth a response whose petulant tone made it evident that Holt would not be deprived of his victim. The comment on a petition from "certain inhabitants of Cornwall" for Grenfell's release, transmitted to Washington through Charles Francis Adams, the American minister in London, was typical of all of them:

> This bureau can only refer to its former report fully treating the merits of the case. The commutation of [Grenfell's] death sentence was an act of rare clemency, in granting which the President probably yielded only to the pressing intercession of the prisoner's highly respectable friends, acting through the British legation . . . That exercise of the pardoning power, rescuing him from the gallows, to which his merited punishment had consigned him, is believed to have extended the extreme measure of mercy that can be asked on his behalf.[7]

Nor was the political climate propitious to Grenfell's cause. The decision of the Supreme Court in the Milligan case was greeted by the Radical Republicans with a storm of abuse; and as is customary whenever the court hands down a landmark decision upholding the civil rights of an unpopular minority, a loud clamor arose for its reorganization. Johnson was in the thick of a bitter struggle with the Radical Republicans in Congress over his reconstruction policies. It was not reasonable to expect him to add

[7] *House Executive Documents*, 650.

to his difficulties by pardoning, over the reiterated objections of the War Department, a foreign soldier of fortune whom the country generally believed guilty of a particularly heinous crime. Had he done so, he would have handed Stanton, the head and front of the opposition, a weapon which that astute and ruthless politician would have sunk to the hilt.

The feeling in Congress may be judged by the actions of Representative John Wentworth of Chicago, who was police commissioner of that city in November, 1864, when Grenfell was arrested. On December 19, 1866, having read in the newspapers that the Illinois and Florida legislatures had adopted resolutions urging that Grenfell be pardoned, he introduced a resolution of his own in the House of Representatives requesting the President to furnish the House "copies of all the papers in his possession touching the case of . . . George St. Leger Grenfell." [8] Two weeks later, on the strength of rumors that other moves were afoot to obtain a pardon for Grenfell, he introduced another resolution, calling upon the President for "information" about the pardoning of the Chicago conspirators.[9] On January 4, he read to the House a letter he had received from Absalom B. Moore, erstwhile colonel of the 104th Illinois Infantry and the hero of the disgraceful surrender at Hartsville. The "gallant colonel" (the adjective is Wentworth's) had this to say on the subject of freeing Grenfell:

I have just read in the papers your remarks respecting the application of Florida for the restoration of Grenfell from the Dry Tortugas. I had the misfortune to fall into the hands of this infamous rebel as a prisoner of war when he was adjutant general of John Morgan's brigands. He is one of the worst men that lives

[8] *Ibid.*, 2.
[9] Wentworth introduced his resolution asking for information about the pardoning of the Chicago conspirators on January 3, 1867; a few days later, he introduced another resolution: "That the Committee on the Judiciary report what measures, if any, can be taken to prevent the Supreme Court from releasing and discharging the assassins of Mr. Lincoln and the conspirators to release the rebel prisoners at Camp Douglas . . . under color and pretense of . . . [the Habeas Corpus Act of March 3,] 1863, and also to inquire into the expediency of repealing said law." *Congressional Globe for the Second Session Thirty-Ninth Congress,* Part I, 249.

on the face of the earth, and was known as a robber and mur-
derer and most conspicuous guerilla in all the rebellion. He should
have been hung. Never allow him to be released. Keep him in the
Tortugas until he rots, is my desire for the scoundrel.[10]

After reading this effusion to the House, Wentworth added
the observation, "Now, Mr. Chairman, that is the way the mass
of our soldiers feel respecting this man." Of course no one rose
to inquire in what way Wentworth had discovered how the mass
of ex-soldiers of the Union army or indeed any of them apart from
the heroic Colonel Moore, felt about Grenfell. Moore had already
tried, by testifying against Grenfell in the Cincinnati trial, to relieve himself of the burden of his humiliation at Hartsville by causing the death of one who had witnessed it and his testimony
had helped to send Grenfell to the Dry Tortugas. His letter to
Wentworth helped to keep him there. The closing sentence, "Keep
him in the Dry Tortugas until he rots, is my desire for the scoundrel," was greeted with appreciative laughter; and Wentworth had
the respectful and sympathetic attention of the House when he
went on to advert to the steps that were being taken on Grenfell's
behalf:

> I understand that . . . with reference to [Grenfell] the usual course
> has been resorted to to get him pardoned. First, a number of *quasi*
> rebels, men too old to go to war themselves, but who sent all their
> sons and grandsons, and who now plead loyalty for damages,
> signed the petition . . . the next thing is to get some leading clergy-
> man—if possible the bishop of some diocese—to sign it. Then they
> try a few weak-backed Republicans and get their signatures, and
> finally the application, thus prepared, takes the usual course
> through the hands of well-known claim-agents and pardon-brokers.
> . . . This man Grenfell is an Englishman. . . . He was sent out by
> Davis to liberate the rebel prisoners at Camp Douglas, and after-
> ward to burn the city. Had he succeeded in that enterprise, there
> is every probability that the Davis government would have em-
> ployed him as one of the assassins of Mr. Lincoln.[11]

[10] *Ibid.*, 286.
[11] If one may believe the detective, Thomas H. Keefe, whose stories, more often
than not, strain one's credulity, this was not the first of John Wentworth's inter-
ventions in Grenfell's affairs. At some time not mentioned, he had "sent for

Unscrupulous and heartless demagoguery could not be carried much further. Wentworth's vicious diatribe and its reception by the House served to put Johnson on notice, if, indeed, any notice was needed, of the probable Congressional reaction to any leniency on his part toward Grenfell.

Nevertheless, there was no remission in the efforts to free the prisoner. He himself wrote to Lord Stanley, who was now foreign secretary, to urge that the British government offer to exchange the American-born Fenian conspirators, then being held in prison in Ireland, for himself. He accused Sir Frederick Bruce most unfairly of having promised a great deal and done nothing, and then advanced the quite impracticable suggestion: "One Word from Your Lordship to your Ambassador at Washington ordering him to take out a Writ of Habeas Corpus for me, would free an innocent man from the most irksome Slavery, and Your Lordship would confer the greatest possible obligation on an old Man now nearly worn out by two years of hard labor, close confinement and fed upon offal which Your Lordships dogs would refuse to eat." [12] Lord Stanley's somewhat starchy response was hardly calculated to cause Grenfell to revise the poor opinion he had formed of Her Majesty's Foreign Office twenty years earlier, when he was in the midst of his Moroccan difficulties. The foreign secretary directed that Grenfell be informed, "that Her Majesty's Minister at Washington has done all that was officially within his powers in your behalf. Lord Stanley is however in communication with your friends in this country and any further instructions to

---

[Keefe] to come to Washington and had [him] relate [his] experiences and tell the Departments of War and Justice what [he] knew of [Grenfell]." Keefe expressed the opinion that Grenfell would have been pardoned had it not been for Wentworth. Keefe, *The Great Chicago Conspiracy*, 31.

[12] Grenfell to Lord Stanley, September 18, 1866, in FO-U.S.-General, Correspondence, FO 5/1015. The letter, as appears from a "Note" in Grenfell's handwriting appended to it, was not mailed until some time after October 28. It was submitted to Lord Stanley in mid-December. In a covering note, Hammond wrote the foreign secretary, "I believe [Grenfell] is a bad subject and has given his family much trouble." E. Hammond to Lord Stanley, December 18, 1866, in *ibid.*, FO 5/1155.

Sir Frederick Bruce with reference to your case will be made in concert with them." [13]

Robert Hervey remained in close touch with Bruce, kept him informed of his own activities, and called to his attention every legal and political development that offered the smallest morsel of hope. [14] On his own responsibility, he instructed A. J. Peeler, an attorney in Tallahassee, Florida, to apply for a writ of habeas corpus on Grenfell's behalf, a course which, he said, had been suggested by the President himself. [15] This allusion implies that one or another of Grenfell's friends had spoken to Johnson about the case and was told, or urged, to have recourse to the courts to effect his release. This may have been an evasion on Johnson's part, or the result of a frank recognition that political considerations made it impossible for him to exercise executive clemency in the case. So far as can be determined, the application for the writ was not made, but Peeler, an ex-officer in the Confederate army, who had himself been a prisoner of war on Johnson's Island for two years and was a member of the Florida legislature, introduced a resolution requesting the federal government to release Grenfell. The resolution was adopted unanimously and forwarded to Washington, but its only effect was to elicit Colonel Moore's infamous letter and Congressman Wentworth's equally infamous demagoguery. [16]

The list of those whose help was solicited by Grenfell himself or by Hervey, or who volunteered their services, was a long one. Bradley T. Johnson, who had been an able and vigorous officer and a favorite of Stonewall Jackson, had met Grenfell casually during the war; now, with no other motive than a desire to help a fellow

[13] Hammond to Grenfell, December 20, 1866, in *ibid.*

[14] Grenfell to Robert Hervey, October 30, 1866; Hervey to Sir Frederick Bruce, November 16 and December 18, 1866, in British Legation-Archives, FO 115/461. Hervey did, however, commit the grievous error of forwarding to Bruce the Grenfell letter of October 30 to himself, in which the writer referred to Bruce as "that old humbug." Sir Frederick was more charitable toward Grenfell than Grenfell was toward him. So far as can be detected, this unmerited outburst made no change in his unvaryingly helpful attitude toward the prisoner.

[15] Hervey to Bruce, December 18, 1866, in *ibid.*

[16] A. J. Peeler to Grenfell, October 11, 1866, in *House Executive Documents*, 655.

soldier, he wrote, as has been mentioned, to Bruce and to Grenfell himself to offer his assistance.[17] Thomas M. Key of Cincinnati continued to work for Grenfell through his political friends in Washington. Former Postmaster General Montgomery Blair, Archbishop Purcell (no doubt the "bishop" referred to by Wentworth), and others interceded with the authorities on his behalf. James A. McMaster, editor of the New York *Freeman's Journal*, who had been a witness for the defense at the Cincinnati trial, was asked by Grenfell to use his "talent . . . courage . . . [and] influence" to help him to "escape legally from this den of misery and death." [18] McMaster was not without talent or courage, but it was naive of Grenfell to expect that a former Peace Democrat, notorious as a wartime Copperhead, would have any influence with the Johnson administration.

When General Hill received the War Department order directing the release of those who had been convicted by military commissions, he intentionally misinterpreted it and included Grenfell's name in the roster of those at Fort Jefferson who were to be freed, but his "error" did not escape the sharp eyes of the judge advocate general's underlings and Grenfell's name was promptly stricken from the list.[19] At some time during this period and as a result, apparently, of Robert Hervey's efforts, General Sweet, Colonel Burnett, and four of the officers who had been members of the court that tried Grenfell joined in a petition to the President to grant him his freedom.[20]

Friends of the Morgan days, Basil Duke, Charlton Morgan (John Morgan's brother), Thomas Hines, and others had, one by one, accepted paroles or taken the amnesty oath and returned to their homes. As recently reformed rebels, their resources and influence were minimal, but what they had of either was used freely to help their old comrade. Hines, who was studying law in Memphis and

[17] Douglas Southall Freeman, *Lee's Lieutenants* (New York, 1942), III, 549.
[18] Grenfell to James A. McMaster, June 7, 1866, in University of Notre Dame Archives. (McMaster's testimony is found in *House Executive Documents*, 519–30.)
[19] Grenfell to Robert Hervey, October 30, 1866, in British Legation-Archives, FO 115/461.
[20] Grenfell to S. L. M. Barlow, December 5, 1867, in Barlow Papers.

writing for the Memphis *Appeal,* wrote a powerful pro-Grenfell editorial for the December 23, 1866, issue of the paper, under the caption "A Victim Forgotten by the South." He wrote that

> it is the solemn duty of every southern state to exert itself for this gallant soldier, who so freely perilled his life for our liberties. . . . Few persons believe Col. Grenfell to be guilty of the charges against him . . . while all know that the tribunal before which he was tried had no sanction, either in law or precedent in this country. . . . Let the people of the South consider that this inhuman treatment of a gallant soldier who, for love of freedom, fought their battles, is not only a disgrace to the nation, but a burning, damning shame to themselves and their posterity forever.[21]

Petitions from individuals and groups in England were being forwarded to Washington by Charles Francis Adams, and every British visitor to America who had any claim on Sir Frederick Bruce's attention urged him on to greater exertions to have Grenfell freed. Thus, T. F. Maguire, member of Parliament for Cork City, used the occasion of a visit to Washington to write Bruce, "I know the subject [of Grenfell's imprisonment] has excited the very deepest interest . . . in England—and is certain to be made the occasion for discussion in Parliament; but I feel sure that your sense of what is due to the honour of the Government you so worthily represent, to say nothing of your generous sympathy with the sufferings of a gallant soldier, will induce you to make such representations to the U. S. Authorities as must be attended with a happy result." [22]

As has been mentioned, John Castleman had been arrested by Colonel Carrington's detectives in the fall of 1864. He remained in prison until the spring of 1866, when he was released on a parole, the terms of which required him to leave the country. He chose England as his place of exile and made it his business to see what he could do in London to help Grenfell. He knew of the high regard John Bright enjoyed in the United States because of his unswerving support of the North throughout the war, and decided

---

[21] Clipping in Hines Papers; portions of this editorial have been quoted earlier.
[22] T. F. Maguire to Sir Frederick Bruce, February 1, 1867, in British Legation-Archives, FO 115/471.

that Bright's intercession might well prove to be decisive. He set about obtaining it. The sequel is best told in his own words:

> With the confidence so often not justified in youth, I obtained . . . a note of introduction to Mr. Bright. Mr. Bright was so courteous, manifested so marked a personal interest in me, that I felt sure of success. I proceeded to briefly present a pathetic, condensed story, and was politely but positively met with the response: "Mr. Castleman, the government will not intervene for any British subject who has violated Her Majesty's proclamation warning her people not to take part in the War between the States." I concluded that my youthful confidence was not warranted. My experience as a diplomat was not successful.[23]

Understandably enough, all this noisy and chaotic activity, so greatly at variance with the quiet, orderly processes of diplomacy, began to disturb Sir Frederick Bruce. Maguire's letter was apparently the last straw, and the Member for Cork City received an unexpectedly sharp reply. Bruce pointed out that

> [Grenfell's] case has been latterly twice under the consideration of this Govt. . . . Most unluckily for him his Southern friends bestirred themselves at that conjuncture in his favour. The result was a most violent speech from Mr. Wentworth of Illinois agst. him in Congress, and the passage of a resolution directed agst. the exercise of Presidential clemency on his behalf. If Parliament is indiscreet enough to take up the question, I warn you . . . that the result will be most disastrous for him. . . . It wd. be better to have him released by the Executive if possible. But he is entitled to have the legality of his imprisonment tried upon a writ of Habeas Corpus, & that proceeding is open to his friends to try. But even admitting that they have a right to expect his discharge after the decision of the Court in Milligan's case, it is by no means certain that he might not be put upon his trial before a Civil Court, and no one can foretell the issue of a political trial in the North-Western States . . . the advisors of the President and especially the War Dept. uphold the justice of [his] sentence, and it is idle to expect that they will release him save on general grounds of humanity.[24]

[23] Castleman, *Active Service*, 197. John Bright was in Parliament, but not in office, in 1867.

[24] Sir Frederick Bruce to T. F. Maguire, February 1, 1867, in British Legation-Archives, FO 115/471. Bruce actually wrote that "Mr. Washburn of Illinois" made the violent speech against Grenfell. This obvious slip has been corrected in the text.

This was a basically realistic appraisal of the situation and, in view of the tangled cross-currents bearing on the issue, Bruce was undoubtedly right in urging the wisdom of a cautious approach.

Two days after writing Maguire, Bruce reported to the Foreign Office that he had called on Attorney General James Speed, who deprecated the idea of trying to free Grenfell through habeas corpus proceedings. Bruce gained the impression that Speed was convinced Grenfell would be released shortly. Nevertheless, the minister was sufficiently alive to the political bearings of the case to be certain that Johnson would not venture to pardon him while Congress remained in session. He took pains to tell his government:

> You have no idea how strong is the belief among the North-Western people that there existed a wide spread conspiracy against the Govt. in those States in the year 1864, and how bitter they are against persons supposed to have been implicated in it. . . . Grenfell's antecedents and character, combined with the general belief in the conspiracy, rather than the evidence adduced, were the grounds of his conviction, and they form the difficulty in the way of his pardon.[25]

Certain that his analysis of the situation and his choice of the course to be pursued were correct, Bruce refused to be hustled into actions he considered unwise. He did nothing when the Foreign Office sent him without comment another letter from Grenfell to Lord Stanley, in which Grenfell gave it as his opinion that Bruce viewed the problem in the wrong light and urged that his release be demanded of the American government as a matter of right and justice, rather than begged for as a favor. It must be said that the precedent he cited in support of his thesis was very much to the point. He reminded Lord Stanley that as recently as October, 1866, Secretary Seward had said to Bruce, in discussing the trial of two of the Fenian conspirators, that "the Govt. of the United States is required by the highest considerations of National Duty and Dignity and Honor to inquire into the legality, justice and regularity

[25] Bruce to E. Hammond, February 10, 1867, in FO-U.S.-General Correspondence, FO 5/1155.

of the judicial proceedings which have taken place." [26] However, tit for tat is not necessarily a safe precept to follow in diplomacy. Bruce realized, as Grenfell did not, that with the handicap of Grenfell's record, and with the British government very much on the defensive in the dispute growing out of the "Alabama" case, he was not in a position to demand Grenfell's liberation. He also knew that nothing was so well calculated to keep Grenfell in the Dry Tortugas for the rest of his life than a formal demand for his release and the publicity and the outburst of anti-British feeling that it would probably precipitate.

While all this activity involving his fate was going on, Grenfell was more or less assiduously tending his garden. But before the spring of 1867 was far advanced, he found himself in serious trouble. It all began when he became indignant over the viciously brutal punishment inflicted on one James Dunn, one of the non-political prisoners at Fort Jefferson. Dunn, together with his guards, became intoxicated while unloading stores from one of the vessels from Key West, and Samuel Arnold's description of the tortures to which he was subjected as punishment for this offense cannot be read even after the lapse of a hundred years without revulsion and horror.[27] The army used Fort Jefferson to house its worst and most intractable criminals, robbers, rapists, and murderers. The most severe discipline was thought to be necessary to keep these men in order and punishments were imposed with a heavy hand. Grenfell considered the punishment meted out to Dunn excessive and inhuman, and if Arnold's description of it is even partly correct, his reaction was fully justified. He vented his indignation by describing the incident in detail in a letter to Bradley Johnson.[28] Captain McElrath, in what may be described as the official version of the incident, expressed the opinion that Grenfell's recital contained "many exaggerated perversions of the truth"; but a literally accurate description, without a particle of exag-

[26] Grenfell to Lord Stanley, February 9, 1867 (Marked "Received in Foreign Office 15th April"; copy forwarded to Bruce, April 18, 1867), in *ibid*.
[27] Arnold, "The Lincoln Plot," December 15, 1902.
[28] Grenfell to Stone, January 15, 1868, in Stone Papers.

301

geration, would have been horrible enough.[29] Bradley Johnson, thoughtless of the probable consequences, sent the letter to the antiadministration New York *World* which promptly published it, arousing great sympathy for what the Democratic newspapers, many of which reprinted the letter, called "the helpless victims of military despotism." [30]

When word of the publication of the letter reached Fort Jefferson via the War Department, with comments by "higher authority," the nature of which can readily be imagined, and the authorship of the letter had been traced to Grenfell, as was inevitable that it should be, he was "removed from his quarters and placed within a dungeon in solitary confinement, where he was denied pen, paper or ink, reading matter of every description and all intercourse and communication with every one at the fort." [31] More serious than the actual punishment was the fact that the letter made Grenfell a marked man, and it behooved him thenceforth to step warily to avoid giving the agents of "military despotism" the slightest excuse to settle accounts with him. But it was not in Grenfell's nature to step warily, and indeed he was a prisoner at Fort Jefferson because of his constitutional inability to do so. His letter to Bradley Johnson was more creditable to his heart than to his head, and Johnson's thoughtlessness in sending it to the *World* was no more than Grenfell's usual bad luck. Nevertheless, the result was that he antagonized the officers whose good will had until then made his existence on the island fairly tolerable. And on April 8, he provided them with a perfect excuse for retaliation.

There are four accounts of what occurred that day: Captain McElrath's, Dr. Mudd's, Samuel Arnold's, and Grenfell's own. McElrath's is rather obviously the pro-Army, boys-will-be boys version. He wrote that Grenfell became "sullen and refractory" and pleaded illness to escape work. He was examined by the prison doctor, who found nothing the matter with him. He was then

[29] McElrath, "Annals of the War."
[30] *Ibid.*
[31] Arnold, "The Lincoln Plot," December 16, 1902.

302

ordered back to work but refused flatly to obey. The young lieutenant who was acting provost marshal for the day then took charge of the situation; on his orders, "a rope was passed under . . . Grenfell's body under the arms and, forty pounds of irons being attached to his ankles, he was gently lowered off the wharf into the waters of the Gulf until his health was restored, which . . . was happily effected after two or three duckings." [32]

We are given to understand that these duckings were administered in a spirit of good clean fun and were no more than an entertaining exhibition of a young lieutenant's boisterous sense of humor. Grenfell, who, unlike McElrath, actually underwent the duckings, related the incident in rather different fashion:

When still stiff and sore from overwork, I was ordered to pick up bricks off the ground, and load a lighter at the wharf. I could not stoop my back hurt me so, but offered to do any kind of work which required . . . no bending. . . . I was taken away, tied up by the wrists to an iron grating, and left there in the sun from 7 a.m. to 4 p.m. My hands were tied up over my head; my feet were fastened to a rope on the ground; devoured by mosquitoes and exposed to the rays of the tropical sun. . . . At 4 an Irish Lieutenant Robinson . . . asked whether I would carry the bricks. I told him I could not. He came back in a few minutes with some rope and a revolver, two other officers with him. They ordered the guard to take me down to the sea. I was laid down on the wharf, my hands tied savagely behind me so as to cut all the skin round my wrists, and I was thrown off into twenty-five feet of water. Unfortunately I could swim very well thus tied, so they hauled me on shore again & tied my legs. Still by great exertion I managed to float, and I was once more hauled in. . . . This time they sunk me by iron weights attached to my feet and when insensible they hauled me up again. When recovered I was asked if I would carry bricks. Upon my saying I could not, in I went. . . . This was repeated three times until . . . I fainted off entirely and was put on some blankets to recover as best I could. Every time I was brought out of the water Robinson would kick me. My ribs, elbows and hands were stripped of the skin through these kicks.[33]

[32] McElrath, "Annals of the War."
[33] Grenfell to Marie Pearce-Serocold, June 30, 1867, in Weaks (ed.), "Colonel . . . Grenfell," 12–14.

Arnold's version, nearly as detailed as Grenfell's, differs from it in only minor particulars, but it mentions a point not found in Grenfell's recital. Arnold wrote that after Grenfell had already been ducked twice and iron weights were being fastened to his ankles, he said to the three officers, "Gentlemen, if it is your intention to murder me, do it in a respectable manner, and I will thank you for the act." One of the officers answered, "Damn you, you deserve to die for the crimes you have been guilty of." Grenfell countered, "I leave God to judge between us which is worse, you, gentlemen, or I." [34]

Dr. Mudd's succinct account agrees in all essentials with Arnold's. Grenfell's version, although it omits the significant point that he had been pronounced able to work by the prison doctor and no doubt heightens the colors to arouse sympathy for himself, is not so different from the other two to be open to serious question.[35] There is little reason to doubt, therefore, that between the three, we have a generally factual report of this deplorable event. Clearly, McElrath yielded to the temptation to tone down his version in order to avoid showing his army friends and army discipline in general in an unfavorable light. Grenfell, on the other hand, by omitting the crucial fact that he had been passed as physically fit by the prison doctor, hides the essential point that by the rough and ready standards of army discipline, he was a malingerer and a stubborn one at that. Still, after every allowance is made for the suppressions and possible exaggerations in Grenfell's story, the fact remains that he was punished with great brutality. Robinson's cruelty is even harder to pardon when one remembers that, by the standards of the time, Grenfell was an old man; nor can it be pleaded in the lieutenant's favor that he probably would have punished just as harshly any other prisoner whom he considered to be insubordinate.

[34] Arnold, "The Lincoln Plot," December 16 and 17, 1902. Grenfell wrote that he was ordered to load bricks, but in Arnold's version, Grenfell was ordered to move a pile of heavy planks "which required the utmost exertion and strength of a young, much less of an old and infirm man like Grenfell."

[35] Mudd, *Samuel Mudd*, 234. Dr. Mudd corroborates McElrath's statement that Grenfell was passed by the prison doctor as fit to work.

It would appear that for some time after this incident, Grenfell remained in solitary confinement, which would indicate that the punishment Robinson had meted out to him met with the approval of the latter's superiors. In the letter describing his ducking, Grenfell wrote that he was "closely confined under guard . . . and kept in an unwholesome cell alone, and without a light, not even a match." [36] He did not indicate how long he was kept in solitary confinement. He was no longer in "solitary" when he wrote the letter at the end of June; therefore this additional punishment could not have lasted more than three months. When, however, he wrote in the following January to Henry Stone, the young trooper of Morgan's Ninth Kentucky Cavalry to whom he had lent a horse on a mountain road in Tennessee in 1862, he said that he had been shut up "in a close Dungeon for 10 months, every orifice carefully stopped up except one for air! denied speech with every one, lights, books or Papers." [37] Clearly, Grenfell is not the most reliable of witnesses on the subject of his own misfortunes and sufferings.

If as an aftermath of his encounter with Robinson, Grenfell had to undergo a period of solitary confinement, it could not have been for long. General Hill's tour of duty as commandant of Fort Jefferson ended on March 9 and, pending the arrival of his successor, the acting commandant was Major Valentine H. Stone, Fifth United States Artillery, who treated Grenfell not with mere indulgence but with much kindness. Major Stone had been the first man in Putnam County, Indiana, to volunteer for service in the Union army when the Civil War broke out. Two younger brothers followed his example. The youngest brother, Henry, saw his duty differently; he crossed the Ohio River to enlist under John Morgan. In April, 1867, Henry Stone learned that Valentine was temporarily in command at Fort Jefferson. Knowing that Grenfell was a prisoner there, and remembering his kindness of five years before, Stone wrote his brother, "to do all in his power, consistent with his duty, to alleviate the prison life of [his] old

[36] Grenfell to Marie Pearce-Serocold, June 30, 1867, in Weaks (ed.), "Colonel . . . Grenfell," 13.
[37] Grenfell to H. L. Stone, January 15, 1868, in Stone Papers.

army friend, who was, as a true soldier and gentleman, worthy of such consideration." [38] It is inconceivable that in the face of such a solicitation from his brother, Major Stone would have kept Grenfell, who had already been punished with more than sufficient severity for his inability or refusal to obey orders, in solitary confinement for three months. [39]

The mild regime of Major Stone was followed by that of Major George P. Andrews, Fifth United States Infantry, who on June 3, 1867, succeeded General Hill as post commandant. Even Grenfell, who had described General Hill as a bad old man, had to concede that Andrews was a kindly, humane officer; he wrote after Andrews had been in command for several months, "I really have not a fault to find with him." [40] Under the Andrews regime, the political prisoners had little cause to complain of their treatment. [41] Their diet of salt pork and "indifferent bread" was varied with an occasional issue of potatoes, corn, and beans, and they were permitted to use their minute "wages" to have additional supplies of fresh vegetables and fruit bought for them at Key West. Grenfell was relieved of labor considered too heavy for his years—although, as the events of the next few months were to show, he had a tougher constitution than many men half his age—and was encouraged to resume his gardening. He was allowed to receive and send uncensored letters, and his days were cheered by the arrival of messages from many friends and sympathizers. By the summer of 1867, after Jefferson Davis had been released from his two years' imprisonment in Fortress Monroe, Grenfell was the only Confederate of any prominence still in prison, and his misfortunes elicited much popular interest and sympathy throughout the South and especially in Kentucky, where he was widely known. Mrs. Walker M. Bell of Garrettsville, Kentucky, whose husband had been a captain in the Confederate army, wrote him, "my

[38] Stone, "Morgan's Men," 26–27.
[39] Grenfell wrote Henry Stone on January 15, 1868, "the heavy restrictions placed on me for no fault of mine by former commanders had been removed by . . . your brother." Grenfell to Stone, January 15, 1868, in Stone Papers.
[40] *Ibid.*
[41] Mudd, *Samuel Mudd*, 248 *passim.*

306

husband (who bears a kind remembrance of you in the War) and myself felt ashamed to sit over our happy fireside whilst his old comrade was wearing out his life in captivity and we determined to work until we obtain your liberty." [42] Such letters were a tonic. They may well have caused Grenfell, who had no home anywhere, to feel that he would find one among his old comrades in Kentucky after he was released from prison. He was especially proud of the letter Jefferson Davis sent him, expressing his sympathy and enclosing a package of tobacco and twenty dollars. General Bragg also sent a kindly note. Everyone promised help, but in 1867 veterans of the Confederate army and former officials of the Confederate government were scarcely in a position to help anyone; they had neither the resources nor the political power to match their undoubted goodwill. However, as the presidential year of 1868 opened, Grenfell wrote his daughter, Marie: "You will be glad to hear that as the Democratic Party are beginning politically to raise their heads my old Southern friends are rallying round me. Their sympathy at one time would only have injured me, and they knew it. Oh! If the Democrats come into power—then! ! ! But if the Black Republicans hold their own I am lost. Stanton . . . will never let me out." [43]

[42] Quoted by Grenfell in a letter to Henry Stone, January 15, 1868, in Stone Papers.
[43] Grenfell to Marie Pearce-Serocold, February 26, 1868, in Weaks (ed.), "Colonel . . . Grenfell," 19.

Chapter XVII

G RENFELL ENJOYED a brief Indian summer while Major
Andrews had command of Fort Jefferson. It was to be very
brief indeed and, in the curious ways of destiny, it was succeeded
by the finest, most heroic days of his wasted life. Fate had evidently decided to offer him the opportunity to redeem spectacularly
the errors and failures of nearly sixty years. And Grenfell rose
to the occasion in magnificent fashion.

The beginning of this, the grimmest episode of Grenfell's life
is foreshadowed by one of Dr. Mudd's chatty letters to his wife.
He wrote on August 25, 1867: "We have had one case of yellow
fever here since I last wrote, which proved fatal. It originated here
and was not imported. A general renovation ensued, which will
prevent its recurrence." [1] The renovation, whatever it may have
been, proved wholly ineffectual. The *Aedes aegypti* mosquito went
about its deadly work, carrying the virus from one victim to the
next. A second yellow fever case was admitted to the garrison hospital on the day after Mudd wrote his optimistic letter. Within
a week, by September 3, there had already been three fatalities, a
large number of new cases were in the hospital, and officers, soldiers, and prisoners alike were in a state of panic. Only three days
later, the majority of the whites on the island—the Negroes were
relatively immune—had been infected and were hospitalized.

[1] Mudd, *Samuel Mudd,* 255.

The prison doctor, Brevet Major J. Sim Smith, had been among the first to be stricken, and died on the night of September 7. Dr. D. W. Whitehurst, the elderly post surgeon of the Key West Naval Station, was ordered to the Tortugas as soon as news of Dr. Smith's illness reached the mainland, and arrived at Fort Jefferson the night Dr. Smith died.[2] He and Mudd then divided between them the impossible task of caring for the more than one hundred yellow fever cases then on the island. The garrison hospital had long since become filled to overflowing. Additional hospitals were improvised by setting up cots in three of the bastions. This made four hospitals in operation, and there were hardly enough of the healthy left on the island to care for the sick and bury the dead.

The first symptoms of the onset of yellow fever were nothing more ominous than a flushed face, fever, and a congestion of the mucous membranes, followed a few days later by a sharp rise in the patient's temperature, accompanied by a slow and feeble pulse; the skin turned cold and developed the characteristic yellow tint that gave the disease its name. Then came massive hemorrhages into the gastrointestinal tract, causing the vomiting of blood, the deadly symptom from which yellow fever derived its Spanish name of *vomito negro*. A complete prostration of the patient followed, terminating either in a slow recovery or, more commonly, in death; fatalities were usually well over 50 percent and sometimes in excess of 80 percent.

With the only two doctors on the island utterly unequal to the task of looking after the multitude of seriously ill patients, Grenfell appointed himself to the post of chief nurse. No one asked, much less ordered, him to do this, and it is a mere platitude to observe that in volunteering his services to care for the sick, he demonstrated the highest degree of moral courage. To take his chances of stopping a bullet in a cavalry charge in the heat and excitement of battle was as nothing compared to this. From his days in South America he knew well the sights, sounds, and smells of yellow fever. It was believed in 1867 and for many years afterward that

[2] *Ibid.*, 258.

the disease was transmitted by contact with the clothing and bedding of those who had the disease; hence Grenfell had no reason to doubt that he was risking his life by exposing himself daily and hourly to the contagion.[3] Nevertheless, he made his decision without hesitation and, having made it, he gave no sign that he was doing anything out of the ordinary. The same man who was capable of magnifying minor irritations and grievances to the point of outright falsehood, went about his self-imposed, loathsome duties of mercy at the risk of his life, without self-pity or heroics, or without ulterior motives. He expended on complete strangers, guards and prisoners alike—all the tenderness, pity, self-sacrifice, and even love, which for so many years had been without an outlet except for his devotion to his horses and dogs.

For a month, until he himself contracted yellow fever, Grenfell worked around the clock, day after day, tending the sick. He began by nursing Dr. Smith and his wife. After the doctor died and his wife had safely passed the crisis, he took complete charge of one of the four hospitals, which at one time had as many as thirty-seven patients. Besides tending the sick in his own hospital, he made the rounds, day and night, of the other three with Whitehurst and Mudd. He performed all the duties of a medical orderly and nurse without hesitation or complaint; in a period of twenty-eight days, he slept in his bed only twice.[4]

By the latter part of September, the Tortugas had become an inferno. The temperature in the improvised hospitals passed the hundred-degree mark, day after day. Sanitary facilities for the sick did not exist. The fortunate few who had escaped the contagion or were recovering moved about like ghosts under the pall of suffering, death, and fear that had settled on the fort. An officer's wife, who lived through the nightmare, wrote:

The silence was oppressive beyond description. There were no soldiers for drill or parade, and the gloom was indescribable. . . . The mercury was 104 in the hospital. . . . We seemed to be in some

[3] It was not until 1899 that Dr. Walter Reed demonstrated that yellow fever was transmitted by the *Stegomyia fasciata* (now named *Aedes aegypti*) mosquito.
[4] Grenfell to S. L. M. Barlow, December 5, 1867, in Barlow Papers.

horrible nightmare. It was terible beyond description to be hemmed in by those high, literally red-hot walls, with so much suffering. I could see the beds brought out, hoping for a breath of air to fan the burning brow and the fever-parched lips. There was nothing to brighten the cloud of despair that encompassed the island.[5]

News of the epidemic had of course reached the mainland, and the ships which normally made regular trips to the fort with supplies stopped going there. Fort Jefferson was cut off from contact with the outside world. The sick, the convalescents, and the healthy were reduced to a diet of salt pork and salt beef, and the ravages of scurvy were soon added to those of yellow fever. At one time there were nearly two hundred cases of scurvy on the island, and some who had escaped yellow fever or recovered from it died of scurvy. On September 25, a month after the yellow fever epidemic broke out, Dr. Mudd wrote his wife, "No more respect is shown the dead, be he officer or soldier, than [to] the putrid remains of a dead dog. The burial party are allowed a drink of whiskey, both before and after the burying. . . . They move quickly, and in a half hour after a man dies, he is put in a coffin, nailed down, carried to a boat, rowed a mile to an adjacent island, the grave dug, covered up, and the party returned in the best of humor, for their drinks." [6]

When Mudd wrote this letter, there were not a half dozen men on Garden Key who had not already had yellow fever or were not then in one of the hospitals with yellow fever or scurvy. Of the large garrison, not more than twenty men were fit for duty. The mortality rate, however, had been miraculously small. Before the epidemic worked itself out early in October, more than three hundred prisoners and guards had contracted yellow fever, but only two prisoners and thirty-seven officers, enlisted men, and members of their families had died of it.[7] Five of the six officers on the island when the epidemic began, including Major Stone, were

[5] Quoted in George A. England, "Tortugas Tales," *Saturday Evening Post,* CIC–II (1926), 10–11.

[6] Mudd, *Samuel Mudd,* 271.

[7] Arnold, "The Lincoln Plot," December 18, 1902.

311

among the victims. Dr. Mudd, bone-tired after six weeks of ceaseless labor, was nevertheless able to see the gruesome humor of the situation; he noted that thirty-seven officers and soldiers and their kin had died, victims at one remove of the atonement exacted of the four (now reduced to three, for O'Laughlin too was dead of yellow fever) Lincoln conspirators and Grenfell; Dr. Mudd thought that the government had paid too high a price for the pleasures of vengeance.[8]

Shortly before he too became ill, Grenfell found the time and energy to write to Henry Stone, to tell him of the death of his brother and sister-in-law.[9] When he wrote the letter, he had already spent twenty-one days and nights nursing the sick, getting what sleep he could in brief snatches. It is little wonder, constantly exposed as he was, his constitution weakened by unwholesome food and extreme fatigue, that he finally caught the contagion. The marvel is that he survived. He was fortunate in being one of the last to fall ill; by then the worst was over and he received better care than he could have had a week or two earlier. Dr. Mudd was particularly zealous in looking after him and did everything in his power to save his life. On September 30, five days after he became ill, his life hung in the balance and Dr. Mudd considered his chances of survival doubtful.[10] Grenfell himself wrote later that he had no wish to recover and hoped that he would die.[11] In spite of that, his amazingly strong and resilient constitution and his will to live, far more powerful than he realized, pulled him through; by the end of October, he was well on the way to recovery.

When he was once again able to move about, Grenfell found himself one of the favored members of the Fort Jefferson community. His heroic conduct during the epidemic made him the object of friendly admiration, and Major Andrews saw to it that he had every indulgence and privilege that could be granted him. He resumed his gardening and in time became quite proud of his

[8] Mudd, *Samuel Mudd*, 274.
[9] Grenfell to H. L. Stone, Wednesday, n.d., September, 1867, in Stone Papers.
[10] Mudd, *Samuel Mudd*, 273.
[11] Grenfell to H. L. Stone, October 25, 1867, in Stone Papers.

horticultural successes, boasting that he had "Tomatoes[,] Peppers & Melons in full bloom[,] radishes[,] Peas & Beans at maturity." [12] Like any winter vacationer in Florida of a later generation, he boasted of the climate and delighted in pointing out to his winter-bound correspondents in the North: "Whilst you are blowing your fingers ends from cold, I sleep close to an open window with one blanket only and that oftener off than on. . . . In fact, I am obliged to use sun shades from 10 to 3." [13] He even became capable once again of occasional flashes of humor; he wrote Henry Stone: "From a learned Physician Dr. Mudd has descended to playing the Fiddle for drunken Soldiers to dance to or to form part of a very miserable orchestra at a still more miserable theatrical performance. Wonders never cease but my paper does, so I will simply wish you a happy New Year." [14]

Fate was about to play the last but one of its many hoaxes on Grenfell, by holding out to him an illusory hope of a pardon and freedom. Sir Frederick Bruce died suddenly in September, 1867. Grenfell did not know of the endless amount of trouble the minister had taken to obtain his liberation, but he knew only too well that he was well into the third year of his imprisonment at Fort Jefferson. This was a sufficient indication, as far as he was concerned, that Bruce had failed to act with the requisite energy and persistence to have him freed. After an interval while Francis Clare Ford filled in as chargé d'affaires, Edward Thornton, whom Grenfell had known in Montevideo, was appointed to succeed Bruce as minister. The appointment pleased Grenfell, and he expressed the hope that his old acquaintance of South American days would be more industrious and effective in pleading his case than Bruce had been. [15]

Henry Stone had sent one or two of Grenfell's letters to newspapers in Kentucky—remembering the aftermath of the publication of his letter to Bradley Johnson, Grenfell had a momentary twinge

[12] Grenfell to H. L. Stone, January 15, 1868, in *ibid*.
[13] *Ibid*.
[14] *Ibid*.
[15] Grenfell to S. L. M. Barlow, December 5, 1867, in Barlow Papers.

313

of alarm that he might have written something that would get him into trouble once again—and the publicity given his continued imprisonment brought him many messages of sympathy and encouragement.[16] Mrs. Jefferson Davis sent him a large package containing underclothes, shirts, and a suit. The ladies of Lexington, Kentucky, "made a collection of all sorts of good things" to send him.[17] His daughter, Marie, sent him £5, a part of which he used to buy a pocket knife, toothbrush, and hairbrush from the sutler. All in all, the old warrior stood in grave danger of being spoiled by the wave of attention, kindness, and sympathy that now descended upon him.

At this time also, Joseph Eastland, a resident of San Francisco, took a hand in Grenfell's affairs. Grenfell had become acquainted with Eastland's family in Tennessee during the war. Joseph Eastland himself had never met Grenfell, but it was enough for him that his family had thought well of the Englishman, and he made up his mind to help him. There was no reason why he should have done so; his only motive was a desire to help a worthy and gallant gentleman whom he believed to be the victim of undeserved injustice. Having come to this decision, Eastland threw himself into the project with great energy. On his way to Europe in April, 1867, he called on Sir Frederick Bruce to talk to him about the case, and he also obtained from Senator Stewart of Nevada a promise to do what he could for Grenfell during his own absence in Europe. On his return to America in October, Eastland was shocked to learn that Grenfell was still in prison. Satisfied of Grenfell's innocence and feeling strongly that he had been sufficiently punished even if guilty, Eastland wrote to Francis Ford to urge him to "have the matter presented in the proper shape to the President" and to express his own conviction that "but a little effort will succeed in effecting so great an act of mercy." [18] More to the point, he persuaded his influential friend, S. L. M. Barlow of New

<hr>

[16] Grenfell to H. L. Stone, January 15, 1867, in Stone Papers.
[17] Grenfell to Marie Pearce-Serocold, February 26, 1868, in Weaks (ed.), "Colonel . . . Grenfell," 19.
[18] Joseph Eastland to Francis Ford, October 20, 1867, in British Legation-Archives, FO 115/471.

York, to take an interest in the case and informed Ford and Grenfell that he had done so.

Barlow was one of the most interesting and versatile public figures of his time. The grandson on his mother's side of Jean Brillat-Savarin, he was called to the bar in 1849 and became a successful lawyer almost overnight. His resourcefulness, sound judgment, and ability to discern the crucial point of his clients' problems made him one of the leading lights of the New York bar. His large and lucrative practice enabled him to indulge his hereditary taste for good food, to practice hospitality on a lavish scale, and to form a fine collection of books and materials on early American history. An astute politician, active in the affairs of the Democratic Party, Barlow had a large circle of friends, President Johnson and General Grant among them.[19] Having promised Eastland that he would endeavor to secure Grenfell's release, he wrote at once to Francis Ford to ask in what way he could be most helpful.[20]

Grenfell was singularly unfortunate in the matter of chargés d'affaires. Ford's reply to Barlow was sufficiently starchy to discourage the most enthusiastic volunteer: "I trust you will appreciate my motives when I tell you that I consider that any action taken in the matter except through Her Majesty's Legation might tend rather to injure than improve Col. Grenfell's position."[21] Ford had previously sent a letter in a similarly discouraging vein to Eastland.[22]

Shortly before his exchanges with Eastland and Barlow, Ford had spoken to Secretary Seward about the Grenfell case and gathered that while there was no immediate prospect of Grenfell's liberation, he would nonetheless be pardoned "sooner or later,"

[19] *Dictionary of American Biography*, I, 613–15. Barlow's most spectacular professional exploit occurred in 1872, when, in association with General Daniel Sickles, who had lost a leg at Gettysburg, he led the invasion of the headquarters of the Erie Railroad and ousted Jay Gould from control of the line; later, he accomplished the even more spectacular coup of forcing Gould to disgorge $9,000,-000 of the money he had fraudulently taken from the Erie.
[20] Barlow to Francis Ford, October 30, 1867, in British Legation-Archives, FO 115/471.
[21] Ford to Barlow, November 1, 1867, in *ibid*.
[22] Ford to Joseph Eastland, October 22, 1867, in *ibid*.

possibly in exchange for the release by the British government of one or two of the Fenian conspirators.[23] Satisfied with these assurances, and with the touchiness of a professional, Ford wanted no interference by well-meaning amateurs. The passage of time meant little to him. As a respectable diplomat, he could have had no conception of the misery of Grenfell's situation. How could he picture the effect on a man serving a life sentence, who had already spent nearly three years in prison, two of them on the Dry Tortugas, of the vague promise that he would be freed "sooner or later"?

Upon learning from Eastland of his discussions with Barlow and of the latter's willingness to be of assistance, and obviously pleased that a man of Barlow's prominence should interest himself in his case, Grenfell wrote directly to the New York lawyer. During December, 1867, and January, 1868, several letters passed between them. In each of his, Grenfell reiterated his claim of innocence. He insisted he had not been a party to the conspiracy, had known nothing of it, had never even heard a rumor of it, and knew none of the conspirators except George Cantrill, whom he had neither seen nor heard from for two years until they met in prison in November, 1864. He declared that he "scorn[ed] the idea of being one of Jake Thompson's agents," and had "nothing to do with him in any way whatever or any other Confederate Agent." [24] He also wrote, and perhaps really believed, that the actual conspirators, Marmaduke, Judge Morris, Walsh, Daniel, and others, who were either acquitted altogether or convicted but pardoned, had escaped punishment because money or influence had been used on their behalf; as there had to be a victim, he himself, a foreigner, was made the scapegoat for the real culprits.[25]

Whether Barlow completely believed these protestations of innocence may well be doubted; very likely he shared Eastland's opinion that even if Grenfell was guilty, he had already paid for his crime. As a result of his solicitations, Montgomery Blair dis-

[23] Ford to Lord Stanley, November 4, 1867, in *ibid.*, 115/466.
[24] Grenfell to S. L. M. Barlow, December 5, 1867, in Barlow Papers.
[25] Grenfell to Barlow, December 5, 1867, January 13, 20, 1868, in *ibid.*

316

cussed the case with the President; and apparently Barlow himself spoke with or wrote to Johnson about it, but the President would not allow himself to be pinned down to a firm promise to free Grenfell. He was at the crisis of his long battle with the Radical Republicans over reconstruction. He would have been guilty of gross folly if he had added to his already overwhelming difficulties by granting a pardon at this moment to someone who represented many of the things his Congressional enemies abominated. Hence his answers to Blair and Barlow were masterpieces of politic evasiveness, which everyone could interpret to suit his own fancy. To Barlow he said that he would try to pardon Grenfell, notwithstanding that there were "several *hard points* in the case." [26] Although Grenfell was usually quick to seize upon the least excuse for optimism, he realized that such vague assurances of good will were valueless. He wrote Barlow: "I have looked so long for an end to my misery that I am now almost afraid to hope; all I can do is to trust that you and other friends who are now working for me will not allow yourselves to be dejected by one or more refusals of Mr. Johnson's to liberate me but will return to the assault until you gain your point." [27] He had also come to understand what Sir Frederick Bruce had seen from the start—namely, that there was little hope of a presidential pardon for him so long as Stanton remained at the head of the War Department and was locked in battle with the President. He wrote his daughter, "it is all of no use so long as 'Mordecai' sits in the gate. Stanton must go or no releif [*sic*] for me!" [28]

Notwithstanding the discouraging outlook, Grenfell did not sit back passively to endure his imprisonment in patience until Stanton's long tenure of his post should come to an end. He continued to correspond with his friends in Kentucky, with Barlow, and with the British minister. He sent to Thornton certificates from Major Andrews and Dr. Whitehurst testifying to the value of the

[26] Grenfell to Barlow, January 13, 1868, quoting from a letter from Barlow to him dated December 21, 1867, in *ibid.*
[27] Grenfell to Barlow, January 30, 1968, in *ibid.*
[28] Grenfell to Marie Pearce-Serocold, February 26, 1868, in Weaks (ed.), "Colonel . . . Grenfell," 19–20.

services he had rendered at the time of the yellow fever epidemic.[29] Whitehurst spoke of his "generous and invaluable aid" and declared that the "unwearied and continuous service" he had rendered "night and day" had greatly contributed to "the restoration of the troops."[30] Andrews' statement was even more generous: "I state with great pleasure that the conduct of G. St. Leger Grenfell while he has been under my command has been perfectly good and that I recognize his services as nurse to the sick during the epidemic of yellow fever of last August to October as having been of the highest benefit."[31]

Meanwhile, Robert Hervey, whose concern for his erstwhile client had never ceased, also wrote to the new British minister to call Grenfell's situation to his attention and to urge him to resume the efforts, interrupted by Bruce's death, to obtain his release.[32] Thornton replied with the assurance that he was thoroughly familiar with the case and that, when circumstances were more propitious, he would not fail to do his utmost on Grenfell's behalf.[33] And Thornton repeated the same assurances in a letter he sent directly to Grenfell.

This, then, was the condition of Grenfell's affairs in the early spring of 1868. His health and vigor were back to normal after his successful battle with yellow fever. He was, and knew himself to be, the object of much solicitude among a large circle of well-wishers. The conditions of his imprisonment had been made as tolerable as he could well expect by a humane and friendly post commandant. Indeed, he had everything except freedom—but that was the one thing that mattered. He was still a prisoner, with no certain prospect of release. His inveterate enemies, Holt and Stanton, remained in power; he knew from Thornton and Barlow that their hostility was as great as ever and their influence still too powerful to overcome. Notwithstanding his occasional expressions

[29] Grenfell to Edward Thornton, February 26, 1868, in British Legation-Archives, FO 115/484.
[30] D. W. Whitehurst to Grenfell, February 22, 1868, in *ibid*.
[31] Major Andrews' endorsement on the above, in *ibid*.
[32] Robert Hervey to Thornton, February 25, 1868, in *ibid*.
[33] Edward Thornton to Hervey, February 28, 1868, in *ibid*.

of fatalism, Grenfell had never been able to resign himself for long to passivity; he was not the man to possess his soul in patience, to wait for time and the slow change of circumstances to bring about a result that might be produced by his own frequently ill-timed efforts. More often than not, his attempts to force the hand of destiny resulted in disaster, but for a man of his temperament, precedents did not exist, and past failures were not a deterrent to present action.

It would have been strange indeed, given Grenfell's daring and his gambling instincts, if the idea of escape had not crossed his mind from time to time during the two years he had spent on the Dry Tortugas. Escape looked deceptively easy and had in fact been tried many times. There were numerous boats on the island, the usually placid waters around it were empty of shipping, and with the aid of the strong current of the Gulf Stream and a favorable breeze, Cuba, lying only ninety miles to the south, might be reached in a few hours. It had been done before and with careful planning and a little luck, it might be done again. In the diary which Grenfell kept sporadically for about a year after his arrival at Fort Jefferson, there were numerous entries to show that the idea of escape was never far from his mind; the diary contained sketches of the fort, the bearings of the nearby keys, rough charts of the channels leading out of the ring of keys into the open sea, and tables of distances and compass bearings from the Tortugas to various points in Cuba, Florida, and places on the mainland as far away as New Orleans.[34]

One of the prisoners at Fort Jefferson was a desperado named Adair or Adare. As brave, or as reckless, as Grenfell himself, Adair had escaped successfully not long before Grenfell's arrival at the fort. He and a Negro prisoner had negotiated the three miles of shark-infested waters from Garden Key to Loggerhead Key on a plank; there they possessed themselves of the boat belonging to the lighthouse and rowed themselves to Cuba. Not trusting the hospitality of the Cuban government, Adair decided to go on to

---

[34] McElrath, "Annals of the War."

Europe. To raise money for his journey, he advertised for sale the Negro whose help had made his escape possible, and to enhance the value of the offer, let it be known that the man was a bargain at the asking price, in view of his proven skill as a sailor. The Negro learned of this and complained to the authorities. Adair's cynical effrontery was more than the Spanish officials could swallow; they arrested him and, in spite of the fact that there was then no extradition treaty between Spain and the United States, shipped him off to Key West and turned him over to the American authorities. Back at Fort Jefferson after his brief taste of freedom, Adair was not in the least reconciled to the prospect of staying there. A year and a half later, he tried another escape. Ever since his return to the fort, he had had attached to one of his ankles a ball and chain weighing nearly thirty pounds. Despite this handicap, he again swam the three miles to Loggerhead Key, using a plank to support the ball and chain. This time, however, he was unable to steal the lighthouse boat and, after hiding for several hours in the dense underbrush that covered the island, he was recaptured and ignominiously returned to the fort.[35]

There is nothing to indicate when and how Adair and Grenfell decided to join forces for another escape attempt. It appears likely that Grenfell was the moving spirit in this enterprise. He was in a position to supply a number of ingredients vital to a successful venture: iron nerve, sailing experience dating back to his years on the Barbary Coast, and, it would appear, money for bribery. At some point in the planning, two more prisoners, James Orr and Joseph Holroyd, were added to the escape party. Holroyd, as will be seen, was assigned an important role in the escape, but Orr was to be only a passenger; both men were probably cronies of Adair's.

If Samuel Arnold is to be believed, Grenfell had a special incentive to make a break for freedom at this moment. In temporary command of the fort when Grenfell's letter describing the punishment of James Dunn was published by the New York *World* was First Lieutenant (Brevet Major) C. C. MacConnell, Fifth United

---

[35] *Ibid.;* cf. "A. O'D.," "Dry Tortugas," 286–87.

States Artillery. When Major Andrews completed his tour of duty as commandant at the beginning of March, 1868, MacConnell succeeded him. The latter, Arnold says, "felt very bitter toward Grenfell on account of the . . . [letter] published by him, it nearly being the means of his dismissal from the service." [36] Arnold goes on to say that MacConnell, on assuming command, relieved Grenfell of his gardening duties, "and placed the old man at the heaviest work that was to be done"; thereupon Grenfell decided "that they had started . . . to kill him inch by inch, [and] determined to escape at all hazards, preferring, as he said, a watery grave to the indignities imposed upon him." Arnold's remark is borne out to some degree by Grenfell's statement to his daughter, Marie: that "our kind Commandant, Major Andrews, is about to be relieved, a great loss to us all, but to me in particular. His successors have a deadly hatred for me!" [37] We are told, on the other hand, that MacConnell had been in command "but a couple of days" when Grenfell made his break for freedom; it may be that fear of what MacConnell would do, rather than resentment over what he had already done, triggered the escape attempt.[38]

The spring of 1868 seemed a propitious time for a break for freedom. In March, there were only two companies of the Fifth Artillery on the island, the rest of the garrison having been ordered to New Orleans to deal with one of the several violent crises over reconstruction in that volatile city. Indeed, General Hill, then in command of the military post of Key West, under whose jurisdiction Fort Jefferson lay, protested to his superiors that the troops left on the island were too few to maintain an adequate guard over the prisoners.[39] Nevertheless, the difficulties in the way of a successful escape were formidable. Each evening, after the ceremony of Retreat, the prisoners were confined to their quar-

[36] This and the two following quotations are from Arnold, "The Lincoln Plot," December 18, 1902. Arnold does not mention MacConnell by name.

[37] Grenfell to Marie Pearce-Serocold, February 26, 1868, in Weaks (ed.), "Colonel . . . Grenfell," 19. In the original, the second of the two sentences quoted is in French: "Ses Successeurs m'en veulent à mort!"

[38] Report of Lieutenant Paul Roemer, April 8, 1868, in Grenfell Papers-National Archives.

[39] B. H. Hill to R. C. Drum, March 2, 1868; copy in *ibid.*

ters in one section of the casemates, from which there was only one exit, guarded by a sentinel. A second sentry was stationed at the sally port, the only exit from the fort to the island. The small fishing boats used by the garrison were secured within a wooden boom at Number One Wharf, a sentry being posted at this point also. The oars and rudders belonging to the boats were stored each night under lock and key in the guardhouse. A fourth sentry patrolled Number Two Wharf, about thirty yards from the boom within which the boats were secured and in plain view of it.[40] To make a successful escape, Grenfell and his associates had to get out of their locked quarters and out of the fort; then they had to possess themselves of a boat and its tackle. Having done all this, and evaded four sentries in the process, they had to navigate several miles of tortuous channel within range of the guns of the fort before they reached the doubtful safety of the open sea beyond the ring of keys. It is obvious, therefore, that the escape needed careful planning; barring phenomenal luck, an attempt made on the spur of the moment had practically no hope of success.

Thus, at the very time when Grenfell was conducting an extensive correspondence with Thornton, Barlow, and others, and endeavoring through their help to obtain a presidential pardon, he was also busy with plans to effect his own release in the teeth of Stanton, Holt, President Johnson and the whole power of the United States government. One can picture him savoring in advance, with a relish only less keen than his anticipation of the pleasure of freedom itself, the gratification of announcing his self-bestowed freedom to his enemies and lukewarm friends, and turning over in his mind the vigorous and scathing phrases he would use in his letters from Cuba to the British minister, the secretary of war, Joseph Holt, and others.

The key figure in the escape project was to be Private William Noreil, Fifth United States Artillery. The four conspirators had reached the self-evident conclusion that to effect a successful es-

[40] "A. O'D.," "Dry Tortugas," 26.

cape, they had to have the help of a member of the garrison. How they came to choose Noreil, what there was about the man to cause Grenfell and Adair to suspect that he could be induced to betray his trust is not known. Lieutenant MacConnell, in his report on Grenfell's escape, expressed the "belief that Grenfell had considerable money . . . by and through which he bribed [Noreil]." [41] It would have been surprising if MacConnell had not blamed Noreil's defection on bribery, but Lieutenant Paul Roemer, who was sent to Fort Jefferson to make a full investigation of the escape, agreed with him. Roemer reported that under Major Andrews' mild regime, mail addressed to the prisoners was not examined by the officers of the garrison; Roemer was told that Grenfell had received a registered letter not long before the escape and was known to be in funds. This was enough to convince him that Grenfell must have bribed Noreil.[42] Roemer also hinted that Noreil had been worked on by someone from the outside; he reported: "From a letter received at the Post subsequent to the escape . . . addressed to Pvt. Noreil . . . it appears that the matter had been plotted and planned some time previously."

Not unexpectedly, Samuel Arnold has an entirely different explanation of Noreil's defection. He says that Noreil "had received very harsh treatment and was anxious to desert" and dismisses the bribery story out of hand. Grenfell, he writes: "could have gone without a dollar, as the rule of the place was as disgusting to the soldier as it was to those confined, and help at any time would have been rendered to any who desired to escape, provided that the soldiers in doing so were not compromised." [43] However difficult it may be to reconcile this statement with Major Andrews' reputation for kindness and mildness, Arnold firmly believed that the bribery story was thought up by MacConnell to minimize his own responsibility for Grenfell's escape, and he asserted that "Grenfell did not have in his possession at the time of his escape $25."

[41] C. C. MacConnell to B. H. Hill, March 12, 1868, in Grenfell Papers-National Archives.
[42] Paul Roemer to Hill, April 8, 1868, in *ibid.*
[43] This and the following quotation are from Arnold, "The Lincoln Plot," December 18 and 19, 1902.

Whatever Noreil's reasons may have been for aiding the escape, he was scheduled to be the sentry at Wharf Number One on the night of March 6 and it was during that night that the escape attempt was to be made. At some time during the day, the oars and rudder of the Company I fishing boat—a small, open sailboat—were hidden by someone, probably Noreil, where they could be found easily during the night. It was now within a few days of the vernal equinox, the weather was unsettled, and on the evening of the sixth, a violent storm blew up. It is doubtful if the bad weather caused Grenfell and Adair to consider postponing their project; they probably welcomed the storm as an unexpected ally, especially since it blew from the north and was therefore fair for Cuba.

At 11 P.M. on the sixth, Noreil took his place at Wharf Number One (known as Sentry Post Number Two) for a two-hour tour of sentry duty. The escape was to be made between that hour and 1 A.M. on the seventh, when Noreil was due to be relieved.

The events of these two hours and the mechanics of the escape can only be surmised.[44] It would appear that as soon as the corporal of the guard, who had overseen the formalities of Noreil's taking over Sentry Post Number Two, was out of sight, Noreil left his post and entered the fort through the sally port. No doubt he gave the sentry stationed at that point a plausible reason for doing so. Now inside the fort, he went to the bastion guarding the casemate in which the prisoners were locked up for the night. To get past the sentry posted in the bastion and into the casemate, Noreil needed another plausible excuse, and no doubt he had one. He also had a key to the cell which Grenfell and Adair shared. He let the two prisoners out of their cell, and the three of them then let themselves down one by one to the ground at the foot of the wall through one of the gun embrasures, by means of a rope Noreil had brought with him. The officers of the garrison thought

[44] The account of the probable course of the escape is based on the report of First Lieutenant Paul Roemer, Fifth United States Artillery, dated April 8, 1868, in Grenfell Papers-National Archives. Roemer was sent to Fort Jefferson by General Hill to "make a thorough inquiry into the circumstances and causes of the escape." Special Orders No. 11, April 4, 1868; quoted in Roemer's report.

that the three might have had help from Joseph Holroyd in getting out of the fort. Holroyd was the cook for the prisoners' mess and slept in the mess hall on the ground floor, from which, apparently, it was not too difficult to get outside through a gun embrasure on the first floor. Orr, carrying his ball and chain, escaped from his ground floor cell by prying loose enough bricks from the thin wall separating it from the casemate next door to enable him to crawl through; after getting into the casemate, he jumped out through a gun embrasure in the southwest wall of the fort and climbed over the moat which, at the point where he crossed it, was an unfinished dry ditch.

As soon as Grenfell, Adair, Noreil, and Holroyd were outside the fortress wall, they were hidden in the inky darkness and the pouring rain, and the noise they made was obliterated by the wind and the pounding surf. They swam across the moat and were met on the other side by Orr. The hardest part of their task, but not the most dangerous, was now behind them. The five confederates then made their way to Wharf Number One, found the oars and rudder of the Company I fishing boat, lifted the boat over the boom, unseen by the sentry stationed at Wharf Number Two, and struck off into the partially sheltered waters of Garden Key harbor. Nor were they seen from the Coast Guard survey vessel *Bibb*, which had come into the harbor in the evening to ride out the storm.

To get their badly overloaded boat into open water, Grenfell and his companions had a choice of two routes. They could have gone north through the narrow channel separating Garden Key from Bush Key, and then turned first east and then southeast through the Southeast Channel. This route, however, would have taken them into the teeth of the wind for the first part of their course and broadside to it during the crucial passage over the reefs into the Southeast Channel. It is therefore probable that, with the wind blowing hard from the north, they left the harbor on a southerly course, and then turned southwest over an area of reefs and shallows to the Southwest Channel. To reach open water on this course necessitated crossing a two-mile-wide area in which the coral reefs broke up the heavy surf into steep, choppy waves, treacherous cross currents and patches of boiling water. To make this crossing on a pitch-dark night and in the midst of a storm, to navigate by instinct alone, with all landmarks blotted out, required great skill, the last ounce of the men's strength at the oars, and, above all, miraculous good fortune. One must surmise, however, that the miracle came to pass and that the passage was made good; after what must have been a tremendous struggle, the fugitives were past the surf line and headed southward into the night and the deep rollers of the Florida Channel. It could not have been much later that the small, heavily loaded open boat was caught by a flaw in the wind or an unexpectedly steep wave, causing it to broach and founder.

And so Grenfell's life ended in the midst of the storm, in the waters of the Gulf of Mexico. But he died a free man. He had made good his escape from prison, but once more, and for the last time, fate played against him with loaded dice. It permitted him to escape—into death.

Epilogue

WHEN THE CORPORAL of the guard made the rounds of the sentry posts with the 1 A.M. relief, Noreil's absence from his post was discovered and the alarm was given. A rapid check by the officer of the day revealed that the Company I fishing boat and four of the prisoners were missing. Pursuit in the storm and darkness would have been useless and, in any case, the officers were convinced that the escapees "must have been swept into eternity before they were three hundred yards from the fort." [1] Nevertheless, at first light, Captain Slott of the *Bibb* offered to go in search of the fugitives, although he made no secret of his belief that he was going on a fruitless errand, as no small boat could have ridden out the night's storm.[2] Still, he set out and while daylight lasted, the *Bibb* crisscrossed the waters south and southeast of the Tortugas. Captain Slott returned to the fort at nightfall, having found nothing—neither the boat, nor bodies, nor oars. Grenfell and his companions had been swallowed up by the waters without leaving a trace.

Not until four days later did Lieutenant MacConnell report Grenfell's escape to General Hill at Key West.[3] Hill received the report on March 14 and at once cabled the United States Con-

---

[1] "A. O'D.," "Dry Tortugas," 287.
[2] McElrath, "Annals of the War."
[3] C. C. MacConnell to B. H. Hill, March 12, 1868, Letter Book, Hq. (JL-39), 1866–1870, p. 94, in National Archives.

sul in Havana to inquire if the fugitives had reached Cuba.[4] At the same time, he informed the headquarters of the Military District of Florida, at Jacksonville, of the escape and recommended that a full investigation be made into the circumstances surrounding it.[5]

The American consul in Havana had no information about the fugitives, but he reported their escape to the Cuban authorities, and the civil governor warned the police to be on the lookout for the five men and to report their arrival promptly if they reached the island.[6] Had Grenfell made good his escape and arrived safely in Cuba, he would undoubtedly have become the center of another international controversy, this time between Spain, Great Britain, and the United States. The diplomatic maneuvers to determine whether he should be allowed to go free or be returned to the United States might well have gone on for years. He was spared this much, at least.

But Grenfell's story was not yet at its end. His utter disappearance predictably provided a field day for speculations and mendacious reports about his fate. No sooner had the newspapers carried their accounts of his escape and almost certain death, than rumors began to circulate in the United States and in Britain that he had ridden out the storm and in some mysterious fashion had made his way to Canada. Many years after his death the story was still current that on the day before his escape a yacht was seen cruising off the Tortugas and that Grenfell, whose escape was made possible by the connivance of "prison officials" bribed by his wealthy English connections, reached the yacht and was taken to England.[7] There is no mention of the mysterious yacht in Lieutenant Roemer's report, presumably because it had no existence ex-

[4] Hill to H. R. DeLarentrie, March 14, 1868, in Grenfell Papers-National Archives.
[5] Hill to C. F. Larrabee, March 14, 1868, in *ibid.*
[6] Count de Valmaseda to H. R. DeLarentrie, March 14, 1868, in *ibid.*
[7] Waterloo, "The Great Chicago Conspiracy," 149. Thomas Keefe, who follows Waterloo in this and in practically everything else, adds to the story of the yacht his belief that in 1900 Grenfell was still living happily in England.

cept in someone's imagination. Another rumor had it that the escape was engineered by a group headed by Mayor Monroe of New Orleans, and that the fugitives had reached sanctuary in the Crescent City.[8] In England, it was believed that Grenfell had made good his escape and was "with the Paraguayans or Brazilians." [9] Still another version saw the light of day sixty years later. One A. W. McMullen wrote *The Confederate Veteran* in 1929 that "in 1866 or maybe the early part of 1867," when he was a boy of twelve, a stranger came to his parents' home near the coast, not far from Tampa. The man said that he had escaped from the Tortugas; McMullen thought he was English and remembered his father and the stranger discussing the Crimean War. The visitor, who was "pretty well worn out," stayed with the McMullens for several days and left to go on to Pensacola. Recalling the incident many years later, McMullen thought the stranger might have been Grenfell.[10]

The most persistent of the contemporary rumors had it that Grenfell and his companions had reached Cuba and were actually seen in Havana. So widespread and durable were these reports that at the request of his cousin, Henry Riversdale Grenfell, the Foreign Office sent an inquiry to the British consul in Havana, who responded with the information that,

> upon inquiry at the Chief of Police's office, the only information there . . . is a letter from the United States Consul General requesting the authorities to arrest Grenfell. . . . Orders were issued to all the Lieutenant Governors and to all police authorities to be on the lookout for these men, but up to this date nothing has been heard of them. As I was personally acquainted with Colonel Grenfell, I do not think he would have passed through Havana without calling upon me, and this circumstance, added to that of his not having

[8] The source of the rumor was Acting Assistant Surgeon William E. Day, U.S.A. George Meade to B. H. Hill, June 27, 1868; return endorsement dated June 28, 1868, in Grenfell Papers-National Archives.
[9] "Col. George Grenfell, of Penzance," *Cornish Monthly Illustrated Journal*, May, 1868, n. p.
[10] A. W. McMullen, "Was It Colonel Grenfell?" *Confederate Veteran*, XXXVII (1929), 25.

been heard of by the Police, induces me to believe that he did not come to this Island.[11]

A copy of this dispatch was forwarded to Henry Grenfell on September 11, 1868, and now the Foreign Office was at last able to close its voluminous files on George St. Leger Grenfell.

The American government still had to clear up some loose ends and deal with a brief aftermath of the Grenfell story before it too could cease to be concerned about his affairs. On April 21, 1868, General in Chief Grant directed that orders be sent to Major General George Meade, commanding the Third Military District, to convene a Court of Inquiry to investigate and report on Grenfell's escape.[12] In reply, Meade sent to Washington a copy of Lieutenant Roemer's report of April 8.[13] This was evidently sufficient to satisfy Grant, who was too deeply involved at that moment in the political infighting over Johnson's impeachment and his own candidacy for the presidency to be overly concerned about Grenfell's escape; for whatever reason, no more was heard about a Court of Inquiry. At the same time, also, Edward Thornton, who had repeatedly asked the State Department for a verification of the reports in the newspapers of Grenfell's escape, finally succeeded in inducing Secretary Seward to address an official inquiry on the subject to the War Department.[14] Not until three weeks after receiving Seward's inquiry did General John M. Schofield, Stanton's successor as secretary of war, confirm to Seward that Grenfell had indeed escaped, which information Seward forwarded to Thornton a short time later.[15]

Then, in February, 1869, F. F. Marbury, Jr., a New York lawyer, wrote to General Schofield for information about Grenfell's

[11] Foreign Office to Acting Consul John Crawford, July 4, 1868; Crawford to Lord Stanley, August 18, 1868; Foreign Office to H. R. Grenfell, September 11, 1868, in FO-U.S.-General Correspondence, FO 5/1155.
[12] E. D. Townsend to George Meade, April 21, 1868, in Grenfell Papers-National Archives.
[13] Meade to Townsend, April 27, 1868, in *ibid*.
[14] William H. Seward to John M. Schofield, May 9, 1868, in *ibid*.
[15] Edward Thornton to Lord Stanley, June 9, 1868, in FO-U.S.-General Correspondence, FO 5/1155.

actual or probable fate. He acted on behalf of Mrs. Grenfell, who, he said, had been conducting "a young Ladies school of high repute in Paris" since her separation from her husband many years before and who needed the information to clear up her own status, that is, to determine whether she was legally a widow or was in the eyes of the law still married to a man presumed to be living. Marbury was not hampered by diplomatic niceties in his quest for information, and badgered the War Department until he got his answer in the remarkably short time, for those days, of six weeks.[16] He forwarded the information to Mrs. Grenfell, who was enabled thereby to remarry a short time later.[17]

In the winter of 1863, while Grenfell was still serving with Jeb Stuart, Colonel Fremantle published in England the diary of his tour of the Confederacy; in the following year, the diary was also published in New York and Mobile. Then, in 1867, two years after the end of the war, a Cincinnati publisher brought out one of the first, and certainly one of the best and most attractive of the legion of books about the Civil War written by participants; this was General—as he had deservedly become—Basil Duke's *A History of Morgan's Cavalry*. Both Fremantle and Duke had much to say about Colonel Grenfell—his reckless bravery, his eccentricities, and above all, his fascinating past. And thus, while still very much alive, Grenfell was started on the way to becoming one of the legendary figures of the war. But neither Fremantle, nor Duke, nor the many who followed their lead and even embroidered on their accounts had any reason to suspect that the legend they helped to foster and to perpetuate about Grenfell's adventures before the Civil War, was largely the product of his dreaming, created out of a need to replace with the products of his own imagination actions and events whose memory he could not face with comfort, or which were too prosaic to conform to the glamorous world of his own fancy. Standards of behavior were far more rigidly enforced a hundred years ago than they are today, and the line between venial

---

[16] F. F. Marbury, Jr., to John M. Schofield, February 16, March 2, 15, 1869, in Grenfell Papers-National Archives.
[17] Information furnished by A. H. Packe.

error and unforgivable sin much more straitly drawn. Would Fremantle and Duke have thought differently of Grenfell had they known the whole truth about his past, instead of the gaudy fictions he chose to tell them? It would be rash to answer for Colonel Fremantle; his judgment on a fellow Englishman of his own caste might not have been tempered with charity. But in the case of General Duke, the answer is as certain as such things can well be; had he known the actual transactions of Grenfell's chequered life, it would not have affected in the slightest his liking and his admiration for a frequently misguided, frequently unfortunate, but always gallant gentleman. And where General Duke might have led, we are content to follow.

Bibliography

MANUSCRIPT SOURCES

Ministère des Affaires Étrangères. Archives Diplomatiques et de la Documentation, Paris.

Algérie, Series F-80. Archives de France, Paris.

Baptismal Register, St. Paul's, Covent Garden. Parish Office, London.

S. L. M. Barlow Papers, Henry E. Huntington Library and Art Gallery, San Marino, California.

Colonial Office-Gibraltar, General Correspondence. Public Record Office, London.

Foreign Office-Argentina, General Correspondence. Public Record Office, London.

Foreign Office-British Legation, Washington, Archives. Public Record Office, London.

Foreign Office-Monte Video, General Correspondence, 1841-43. Public Record Office, London.

Foreign Office-Morocco, General Correspondence. Public Record Office, London.

Foreign Office-U.S., General Correspondence. Public Record Office, London.

Founders Company, Minutes of the Court of Assistants, MS6331, Vol. VIII. Guildhall, London.

Grenfell Family Papers in the possession of A. H. Packe, Tile House, Burnham, Bucks., England.

Grenfell-Granville Family Papers in the possession of Major General R. F. B. Naylor, C.B., C.B.E., D.S.O. (Ret.), Barnet, Herts., England.

Ministère de la Guerre, Archives. Vincennes, France.

Thomas Henry Hines Papers. Margaret I. King Library, University of Kentucky, Lexington.

Office of the Judge Advocate General, General Courts Martial, 1812–1938, MM2185, Boxes 675-7. National Archives, Washington, D.C.

Ministère de la Justice, Series BB-17, 18, and 30. Archives de France, Paris.

John A. McMaster Papers. University of Notre Dame Archives, Notre Dame, Indiana.

John Hunt Morgan Papers, Southern Historical Collection. University of North Carolina Library, Chapel Hill.

Police Générale, Series F-7. Archives de France, Paris.

Register of Appointments, C.S.A., Confederate Archives, Ch. I, File 86. National Archives, Washington, D.C.

Lord John Russell Papers. Public Record Office, London.

Stone Family Papers. Kentucky Historical Society, Frankfort.

British Ministry of Transport, General Register and Record Office of Shipping and Seamen. Llandaff, Cardiff, Wales.

War Department Collection of Confederate Records, RG 109; General and Staff Officers; File of G. St. Leger Grenfell. National Archives, Washington, D.C.

War Office-Crimea, Miscellaneous Letters. Public Record Office, London.

War Office-Memorandum Papers, Commander in Chief. Public Record Office, London.

GOVERNMENT PUBLICATIONS

Congressional Globe for the Second Session Thirty-Ninth Congress, Part I.

Message from the President of the United States, in Answer to a Resolution of the House of Representatives of the 19th of December, Transmitting Papers Relative to the Case of George St. Leger Grenfel [sic]; House Executive Documents, 39th Cong., 2nd Sess., No. 50 (Serial 1290).

U.S. War Department. *The War of the Rebellion: A Compilation of the Official Records of the Union and Confederate Armies.* 73 vols. Washington, 1880–1901.

NEWSPAPERS

Chicago *Tribune*
Cincinnati *Commercial*
Cincinnati *Daily Enquirer*

Cincinnati *Daily Gazette*
London *Gazette*
London *Illustrated London News*
Paris *Gazette du Palais*

BOOKS

The Annual Army List. London, 1855, 1856.
The Annual Register for 1837. London, 1838.
Anonymous. *History of Cincinnati and Hamilton County.* Cincinnati, 1894.
Azan, Paul J. L. *L'Emir Abd-el-Kader.* Paris, 1925.
Benet, Stephen Vincent. *A Treatise on Military Law and the Practice of Courts-Martial.* New York, 1862.
Berry, Thomas F. *Four Years with Morgan and Forrest.* Oklahoma City, 1914.
Brooks, L. A. E. *A Memoir of Sir John Drummond Hay.* London, 1896.
Bross, A. *Biographical Sketch of the Late Gen. B. J. Sweet.* Chicago, 1878.
Brown, Dee Alexander. *The Bold Cavaliers: Morgan's 2nd Kentucky Cavalry Raiders.* Philadelphia, 1959.
Buchan, John. *Francis and Riversdale Grenfell.* London, 1920.
————. *Pilgrim's Way.* Cambridge, Eng., 1940.
Cable, George W., ed. *Famous Adventures and Prison Escapes of the Civil War.* New York, 1939.
Castleman, John B. *Active Service.* Louisville, 1917.
Clift, G. Glenn, ed. *The Private War of Lizzie Hardin.* Frankfort, 1963.
Coffman, E. McK. "The Civil War Career of Thomas Henry Hines." M. A. thesis. University of Kentucky, Lexington.
Cook, Frederick F. *Bygone Days in Chicago.* Chicago, 1910.
Costigan, Giovanni. *Sir Robert Wilson: A Soldier of Fortune in the Napoleonic Wars.* Madison, 1932.
Crawford, Samuel J. *Kansas in the Sixties.* Chicago, 1911.
Cullum, G. W. *Biographical Register of the Officers and Graduates of the U.S. Military Academy.* Boston, 1891.
Daviess, Maria T. *History of Mercer and Boyle Counties.* Harrodsburg, Ky., 1924.
Dictionary of American Biography. New York, 1929.
Dictionary of National Biography. London, 1917.
Duke, Basil W. *A History of Morgan's Cavalry.* Bloomington, 1960.

335

————. *Reminiscences of General Basil W. Duke, C.S.A.* New York, 1911.

Dumas, Alexandre. *Impressions de Voyage—Le Veloce.* Paris, 1871.

Durrieux, Xavier. *The Present State of Morocco: A Chapter of Mussulman Civilization.* London, 1854.

Dyer, J. W. *Reminiscences: or Four Years in the Confederate Army.* Evansville, 1898.

Dyer, John P. *"Fightin' Joe" Wheeler.* Baton Rouge, 1941.

Elwick, George. *The Bankrupt Directory: . . . complete register of all bankrupts . . . from December 1820 to April 1843 . . . .* London, 1843.

Flournoy, Francis R. *British Policy Towards Morocco in the Age of Palmerston, 1830–1865.* London, 1935.

Ford, Sally R. *Raids and Romance of Morgan and His Men.* Mobile, 1864.

Freeman, Douglas Southall. *Lee's Lieutenants.* New York, 1942.

————. *R. E. Lee: A Biography.* 4 vols. New York, 1941.

————and Grady McWhiney, eds. *Lee's Dispatches.* New York, 1957.

Fremantle, Arthur J. L. *The Fremantle Diary.* Boston, 1960.

Grant, Ulysses S. *The Personal Memoirs of U. S. Grant.* 2 vols. New York, 1885–86.

Gray, Wood. *The Hidden Civil War: The Story of the Copperheads.* New York, 1942.

Hamley, Sir Edward. *The War in the Crimea.* London, 1891.

Harris, Walter B. *France, Spain and the Rif.* London, 1927.

Headley, John W. *Confederate Operations in Canada and New York.* New York, 1906.

Holland, Cecil F. *Morgan and His Raiders.* New York, 1942.

Horan, James D. *Confederate Agent: A Discovery in History.* New York, 1945.

Johnson, Robert U. and Clarence C. Buel, eds. *Battles and Leaders of the Civil War.* 4 vols. New York, 1888.

Johnston, Joseph E. *Narrative of Military Operations.* Bloomington, 1959.

D'Orleans, François, Prince de Joinville. Tr. W. H. Hulbert. *The Army of the Potomac, Its Organization, Its Commander, and Its Campaigns.* New York, 1862.

————. *Vieux Souvenirs, 1818–1848.* Paris, 1894.

Keefe, Thomas H. *The Great Chicago Conspiracy.* Chicago, n. d.

Kirkland, Edward Chase. *The Peacemakers of 1864.* New York, 1927.

Klement, Frank L. *The Copperheads of the Middle West.* Chicago, 1960.

Laurie, G. B. *The French Conquest of Algeria.* London, 1909.

Leech, Margaret. *Reveille in Washington.* New York, 1941.

Logan, India W. P., ed. *Kelion Franklin Pedicord of Quirk's Scouts, Morgan's Kentucky Cavalry, C.S.A.* New York, 1908.

Lonn, Ella. *Foreigners in the Confederacy.* Chapel Hill, 1940.

Lucas-Dubreton, J. *The Restoration and the July Monarchy.* New York, 1929.

McClellan, H. B. *I Rode with Jeb Stuart.* Bloomington, 1958.

Milton, George Fort. *Abraham Lincoln and the Fifth Column.* New York, 1942.

Morgan, Julia. *How It Was: Four Years Among the Rebels.* Nashville, 1892.

Mudd, Nettie, ed. *The Life of Samuel A. Mudd.* New York, 1906.

Pitman, Benn, ed. *The Trials for Treason at Indianapolis, Disclosing the Plans for Establishing a North-Western Confederacy.* Cincinnati, 1865.

Price, F. G. Hilton. *A Handbook of London Bankers.* London, 1890–91.

Ross, Fitzgerald. *Cities and Camps of the Confederate States.* Urbana, 1958.

Russell, W. H. *The British Expedition to the Crimea.* London. 1858.

————. *The War: From the Landing at Gallipoli to the Death of Lord Raglan.* London, 1855.

Sandburg, Carl. *Abraham Lincoln: The War Years.* 4 vols. New York, 1939.

Seitz, Don C. *Braxton Bragg: General of the Confederacy.* Columbia, 1924.

Senour, F. *Morgan and His Captors.* Cincinnati, 1865.

Sensing, Thurman. *Champ Ferguson: Confederate Guerilla.* Nashville, 1942.

Sipes, William B. *The Seventh Pennsylvania Volunteer Cavalry.* Pottsville, Pa., n. d.

Slade, Sir Adolphus. *Turkey and the Crimean War: A Narrative of Historical Events.* London, 1867.

Smith, Edward Conrad. *The Borderland in the Civil War.* New York, 1927.

Stone, Henry L. *"Morgan's Men": A Narrative of Personal Experience.* Louisville, 1919.

Swiggett, Howard. *The Rebel Raider: A Life of John Hunt Morgan.* Indianapolis, 1934.

Tarrant, Sergeant E. *The Wild Riders of the First Kentucky Cavalry.* Louisville, 1894.

Tenney, Luman Harris. *War Diary, 1861–1865.* Cleveland, 1914.

Thomas, Benjamin P. and Harold M. Hyman. *Stanton: The Life and Times of Lincoln's Secretary of War.* New York, 1962.

Trevelyan, G. Otto. *The Life and Letters of Lord Macaulay.* New York, 1876.

Tuttle, E. B. *The History of Camp Douglas.* Chicago, 1865.

[Vallandigham, James L.] *Biographical Memoir of Clement L. Vallandigham, by his Brother.* New York, 1864.

Vallandigham, James L. *A Life of Clement Vallandigham.* Baltimore, 1872.

Wheeler, Joseph. *A Revised System of Cavalry Tactics for the Use of the Cavalry and Mounted Infantry, C.S.A.* Mobile, 1863.

Williams, Kenneth P. *Lincoln Finds a General: A Military Study of the Civil War.* 4 vols. New York, 1949–59.

Williams, T. Harry. *P. G. T. Beauregard: Napoleon in Gray.* Baton Rouge, 1954.

Winks, Robin W. *Canada and the United States: The Civil War Years.* Baltimore, 1960.

ARTICLES IN PERIODICALS AND NEWSPAPERS

Abernethy, Thomas Perkins. "Aaron Burr at Blennerhasset Island and in Ohio," *Bulletin of the Historical and Philosophical Society of Ohio,* XII (January, 1954), 3–16.

Anonymous. "Col. George Grenfell, of Penzance," *Cornish Monthly Illustrated Journal* (May, 1868).

Arnold, Samuel. "The Lincoln Plot," New York *Sun,* December 14, 15, 16, 17, 18, 1902.

Bovey, Wilfrid. "Confederate Agents in Canada during the American Civil War," *Canadian Historical Review,* II (1921), 46–57.

Chew, W. L. "Col. St. Leger Grenfell, C.S.A." *Confederate Veteran,* XXXVI (1928), 446.

Cochran, William C. "The Dream of a Northwestern Confederacy," *Publications of the State Historical Society of Wisconsin, 1916,* (Madison, 1917), 213–53.

Crenshaw, Ollinger. "The Knights of the Golden Circle: The Career of George Bickley," *American Historical Review*, XLVII (October, 1941), 23–50.

Curry, Richard O. "The Union As It Was: A Critique of Recent Interpretations of the 'Copperheads,' " *Civil War History*, XIII (1967), 25–39.

England, George A. "Tortugas Tales," *Saturday Evening Post*, CIC-II (1926), 10–11, 174–82.

Fesler, Mayo. "Secret Political Societies in the North during the Civil War," *Indiana Magazine of History*, XIV (1918), 183–286.

Gilmore, James Roberts, under pen name, "Edmund Kirke," "The Chicago Conspiracy," *Atlantic Monthly*, XVI (1865), 108–20.

Henning, James W. "Basil Wilson Duke, 1838–1916," *Filson Club History Quarterly*, XIV (1940), 59–64.

Hines, Thomas Henry. "The Northwestern Conspiracy," *Southern Bivouac*, N.S., II (June, 1886–March, 1887), 437–45, 500–10, 567–74.

Holder, J. B. "The Dry Tortugas," *Harper's Magazine*, XXXVII (July, 1868), 260–67.

Keefe, Thomas H. "How the Northwest Was Saved," *Everybody's Magazine* (January, 1900), 82–91.

Manucy, Albert. "The Gibraltar of the Gulf of Mexico," *Florida Historical Quarterly*, XXI (1943), 303–31.

McElrath, T. P. "Annals of the War . . . Story of a Soldier of Fortune," Philadelphia *Weekly Times*, May 3, 1879.

McMullen, A. W. "Was It Colonel Grenfell?" *Confederate Veteran*, XXXVII (1929), 25.

"A. O'D." "Thirty Months at the Dry Tortugas," *Galaxy*, VII (1869). 282–88.

Overley, Milford. "Old St. Leger," *Confederate Veteran*, XIII (1905), 80–81.

Russell, Thomas L. "Told by Thomas L. Russell," Pittsburgh *Dispatch*, February 25, 1894.

Sharp, Grace Marmaduke. "The Marmaduke and Some Allied Families," *William and Mary College Quarterly Historical Magazine*, XV (1935), 151–72.

Smith, Bethania Meradith. "Civil War Subversives," *Journal of the Illinois State Historical Society*, XLV (1952), 220–40.

Starr, Stephen Z. "Colonel George St. Leger Grenfell: His Pre-Civil War Career," *Journal of Southern History*, XXX (1964), 278–98.

———. "Was There a Northwest Conspiracy?" *Filson Club History Quarterly*, XXXVIII (1964), 323–41.

Vallandigham, Edward N. "Clement L. Vallandigham—Copperhead," *Putnam's Monthly*, II (1907), 590–99.

Waterloo, Stanley. "The Great Chicago Conspiracy," *Nickell Magazine*, VII (1897), 131–49.

Weaks, Mabel Clare, ed. "Colonel George St. Leger Grenfell," *Filson Club History Quarterly*, XXXIV (1960), 8–23.

Index

Bright, John: declines to help Grenfell, 298–99
Bruce, Sir Frederick: 126, 257, 259, 266, 271, 272, 284, 287, 289, 290, 295, 296, 297, 298, 314, 317, 318; appointed minister to Washington, 252; interviews acting Secretary of State William Hunter, 253; on civil liberties in U.S., 254; report to foreign secretary on Grenfell case, 254–55; asks permission to have Robert Hervey discuss Grenfell case with Joseph Holt, 255; on U.S. politics in 1865, p. 256; seeks commutation of Grenfell sentence, 260; discusses Grenfell case with Andrew Johnson, 267–68; forwards Bradley T. Johnson's offer to help Grenfell, 291; letter to T. F. Maguire, 299; interviews James Speed, 300; death, 313
Buchanan, James, 136, 149, 261
Buell, Don Carlos: 60, 67, 73, 75, 79, 80, 81; orders John Hunt Morgan driven from Gallatin, Tenn., 76
Buena Vista, battle of, 45, 163
Buford, Adam, 92
Buford, John, 108
Bull Run, battle of, 59
Bullitt, Joshua: leader, Kentucky Copperheads, 163; arrested, 164
Burnett, Henry L.: 8, 219, 228, 229, 230, 233, 249, 250, 252, 253, 257, 258, 264; closing address to military commission, 6–7, 245–47; objects to naming witnesses, 220; leads off with evidence against Grenfell, 221; examines John T. Shanks, 221–26; intimidates defense witnesses, 226; announces Charles T. Daniel's escape, 234; petitions Andrew Johnson to pardon Grenfell, 297
Burnley, J. Hume: 235, 253; ordered to inquire about Grenfell case, 211; directs I. E. Wilkins to make inquiries, 212; makes no official intervention in Grenfell case, 236–37; interview with William Seward, 237–38
Burr, Aaron, 145
Burton, Sir Richard F., 13
Butler, Benjamin F., 125, 150

Camp Douglas: 159, 160–62, 164–66, 174, 175, 178, 187, 188, 191, 193, 194, 196, 197, 199, 201, 202, 205, 209, 214, 222, 229, 231, 235, 243, 263, 294; established, 152–53; conditions in, 153; obvious choice for attack, 154; plan for November 8, attack, 184
Camp Morton, 162, 184
Cantrill, George E.: 204, 207, 213, 246, 316; granted separate trial, 5; arrested, 202
Carrington, Henry B.: 174, 183, 184, 298; persuades Felix Stidger to join OAK, 163; arrests Kentucky and Indiana Copperheads, 163–64
Castleman, John: 171, 173, 177, 229, 230, 236; career, 95; to lead attack on Confederate prisoner camp at Rock Island, 156, 166; selects Confederates for Camp Douglas attack, 165; on Grenfell's involvement, 167; arrested, 183; asks John Bright to intercede for Grenfell, 298–99
Chase, Salmon P.: opinion in *Ex parte Milligan*, 289
Cheatham, Benjamin F.: at John Hunt Morgan's wedding, 86
Chicago Conspiracy: 179, 239; northern opinion of, 6
Chicago Conspirators: 3, 213, 216, 293; names listed, 4–5; indictment, 5
Churchill, B. P., 250
Churchill, Winston Spencer, 17
Clay, Clement C.: 132; appointed Confederate commissioner, 149
Cleburne, Patrick, 102
Cole, Charles H.: to aid Camp Douglas attack, 156
Conover, Sanford, 262, 263
Cook, John, 201
Cooper, Samuel: 97, 100; 122, 123, 124; interview with Grenfell, 121
Copperheads, 143–44, 146–47, 149, 154–55, 157–59, 163, 165, 170, 173–78, 180–85, 201, 207, 214, 215, 216, 227, 243, 288, 297
Crawford, Samuel J.: story of Grenfell at Democratic Convention, 178–79
Crimean War, 10, 11, 34
Crook, George, 125, 150

344

saddle, and coat, 71; drills and disciplines regiment at Sparta, Tenn., 72; his role in Morgan's success, 73–74; at capture of Gallatin, Tenn., 75; article about Grenfell in Knoxville *Register*, 77–78; in fight at Gallatin, Tenn., 78; with Morgan at Lexington, Ky., 79; orders halt of seizure of horses in Lexington, 79; negotiates independent command for Morgan, 81–82; obtains battery and funds for Morgan, 82; dispatch to Joseph Wheeler, 83; at capture of Hartsville, Tenn., garrison, 84–85; at Morgan's wedding, 85–87; quarrel with Morgan, 87–90; stories of his eccentricities, 91; his stories of his pre-Civil War adventures, 92; horses seized by John T. Shanks, 92; kindness to Henry Stone, 93; appointed aide by Braxton Bragg, 95; appointed Wheeler's inspector of cavalry, 95–96; commissioned lieutenant colonel, 97; inspection report, Roddey's and Patterson's regiments, 98–99; Bragg's and Wheeler's opinion of Grenfell, 99–100; reports French recognition of Confederacy, 101; meets Arthur J. L. Fremantle, 101–103; difficulties with Tennessee authorities, 102–103; arrested in Shelbyville, Tenn., 103; leaves Army of Tennessee, 103–105; Jefferson Davis' opinion of Grenfell, 105; source of Grenfell's funds in America, 105–106; appointed assistant inspector general, Cavalry Corps, Army of Northern Virginia, 107; unwelcome on J. E. B. Stuart's staff, 107–108; fight at Jack's Shop (Liberty Mills), 108–109; relations with Stuart, 108–12; leaves Stuart, 112; rejoins Morgan 114–15; ordered to report to Joseph E. Johnston, 115; resigns commission, 115; and Kentucky delegation in Confederate Congress, 116; opinion of Jefferson Davis, 117; screens volunteers for Morgan's command, 117–18; warns Morgan about Captain Kleber, 118–19; informs Morgan of Thomas Henry Hines's project, 119; flattering letter to Morgan, 119–20; decides to leave Confederacy, 120–25; "rejects" captain's commission, 121; "dispute with Jefferson Davis," 122–23; agrees to join Hines, 124; sails from Wilmington, 125; explanation of trip to New York, 125–26; interviews John A. Dix in New York, 126; interviews Colonels Wiswell and Hardie in Washington, 126; interview with Edwin M. Stanton, 126–31; travels with Fitzgerald Ross in upstate New York, 132; at Niagara Falls, 132; in touch with Hines in Canada, 132; fishing in Canada, 164; devotion to the South, 165; joins Hines in Toronto, 167; story of "black flag" and mistreatment of prisoners, 169; travels from Toronto to Chicago, 172; meets with Copperheads, 173; hunts in Carlyle, Ill., 175–76; supposed presence at Democratic Convention, 178–79; illness in Carlyle, 180–82; returns to Chicago, 182–83; visited by John T. Shanks, 194–98; arrested, 202–203; news reports of his arrest, 204–205; imprisoned at Camp Douglas, 205; asked to turn state's evidence, 206; moved to larger cell, 207; communicates with British consul, 208–209; retains counsel, 209; asks family to request help of Foreign Office, 210; transferred to Cincinnati, 213; opinion of military commission, 215; challenges jurisdiction of military commission, 218; pleads not guilty, 220; ill during trial, 234–35; protests innocence, 235–36; letter to Frederic Bernal, 239; asks to be released on bail, 239–40; offers to write article for *Harper's Magazine*, 249–50; asks for help of British legation, 252; asks John Minor Botts's help, 259; transferred to Ohio Penitentiary, 269–70; transferred to Fort Jefferson, 273–74; begins diary, 278; shares cell with "Lincoln conspirators," 279–80; disciplinary problems, 281; ordered treated as a "State Prisoner," 282; complains of hardships in prison, 283; comment on Bennett Hill, 284; describes his gardening, 285; petitions

President for pardon, 286; asks to be released on basis of Milligan case, 290; appeals to Lord Edward Stanley, 295; asks James A. McMaster for help, 297; second appeal to Lord Stanley, 300; describes James Dunn's punishment, 301; describes own punishment, 303; praises George P. Andrews, 306; becomes "chief nurse," 309–12; survives yellow fever, 312–13; corresponds with S. L. M. Barlow, 316–17; escapes from Fort Jefferson, 324–36

Grenfell, Henry Riversdale: 330; inquires about Grenfell's fate, 329

Grenfell, Hortense Louise Wyatt: 331; marries George St. Leger Grenfell, 20; establishes school in Gibraltar, 32–33; leaves husband, 33

Grenfell, John Pascoe, 16

Grenfell, Julian, 16, 40

Grenfell, Pascoe (George St. Leger Grenfell's grandfather): 179; career, 15–16

Grenfell, Pascoe (George St. Leger Grenfell's uncle), 15, 40, 179

Grenfell, Pascoe, and Company, 179, 209

Grenfell, Riversdale, 16

Grenfell, Robert: killed at Omdurman, 17

Guernsey, Alfred H.: rejects Grenfell's offer of article, 250–51

Hall, Frederick: 130, 131, 229; present at Grenfell-Stanton interview, 128; testifies in Cincinnati trial, 226–27

Halleck, Henry W., 48, 60, 85

Hardee, William J.: 102; at John Hunt Morgan's wedding, 86

Hardie, James A.: 127; interviews Grenfell, 126

Harrodsburg, Ky.: reception of John Hunt Morgan's raiders, 64–66

Hartsville, Tenn.: Federal garrison captured, 84–85

Hay, E. W. A. Drummond: mediates between France and Morocco, 23

Hay, John Drummond: reports Grenfell's visit to Abd-el-Kader, 24–25; reports Grenfell's difficulties with Moroccan government, 28; requested to order Grenfell to leave Morocco, 28; persuades Grenfell to leave Tangier, 29

Heintzelman, Samuel P.: reinforces Camp Douglas, 176

Herbert, Auberon Thomas, 41

Hervey, Robert: 209, 224, 257, 259, 269, 273, 297; addresses military commission for Grenfell, 6, 244; cross-examines John T. Shanks, 223; belief in Grenfell's innocence, 252; offers to visit Washington on Grenfell case, 253; prepares brief on Grenfell case for War Department, 255; suggests tactics for freeing Grenfell, 260; instructs A. J. Peeler to sue out habeas corpus, 296; urges Edward Thornton to help Grenfell, 318

Hill, Bennett H.: 163, 170, 176, 228, 283, 297, 306, 327; learns of Chicago conspiracy, 161–62; commandant of Fort Jefferson, 281–82; describes Grenfell at Fort Jefferson, 284; allows Grenfell to correspond freely, 285; approves Grenfell's petition for pardon, 286; relieved as commandant of Fort Jefferson, 305; protests inadequate garrison at Fort Jefferson, 321

Hines, Thomas Henry: 132, 150, 159, 161, 162, 164, 169, 170, 171, 176, 179, 180, 182, 185-87, 191, 192, 194–96, 199, 201, 204, 206, 225, 229, 230, 236, 243, 248, 270; pre-Civil War career, 93–95; escapes from Ohio Penitentiary, 113, 119; arrives in Richmond, 119; understanding with Grenfell, 124; discusses project with Jefferson Davis, Judah P. Benjamin, and James A. Seddon, 144; description of project, 146–47; priority in proposing plan, 148; given instructions by Seddon, 148–49; expects help of Morgan's men in Camp Douglas, 153–54; selects Camp Douglas for attack, 154; July 4 set as attack date, 154; meets with Clement L. Vallandigham in Canada, 155; to lead attack, 156; reports plans to Seddon, 156; agrees to postponement to August 29, 157–58; chooses Confederates for attack, 165; plans tactics for attack, 165–66; meeting with Copperheads, 173–75; agrees to postponement to November 8, 177; November 8 attack plans, 183–84; pays conspirators' legal expenses, 210; pays B. P. Churchill to free Grenfell, 250; writes pro-Grenfell editorial, 297–98

Holcomb, James P.: Confederate commissioner to Canada, 149

Holroyd, Joseph: 325; joins escape party, 320

Holt, Joseph: 205, 225, 255, 256, 267, 271–290, 318, 322; career, 261–62; comments on Shank's credibility, 262–66; suggest commutation of Grenfell death sentence, 266; declines to recommend pardon for Grenfell, 286–87; hostility to Grenfell, 292

Hood, John B.: 107; sends Vincent Marmaduke to Richmond, 147–48

Hooker, Joseph: 217, 218, 229, 232–34, 251, 283; constitutes military commission, 214–15; sentences Mrs. Buckner S. Morris, 230; forwards trial record to War Department, 248

Hull, George W.: story of seizure of Grenfell's horses, 92; testifies in Cincinnati trial, 231

Indian Mutiny (Sepoy Mutiny), 11
Island No. 10, p. 60

Jack's Shop (Liberty Mills): fight at, 108–109

Jackson, Obadiah, 206

Jackson, Thomas J. (Stonewall), 106, 111, 296

Johnson, Adam R.: offered command of John Hunt Morgan's Second Brigade, 87; collects funds for Morgan, 114

Johnson, Andrew: 257, 259, 267, 268, 270, 272, 290–92, 296–97, 300, 315, 322; attitude toward treason, 260; commutes Grenfell's death sentence, 271; declines to pardon Grenfell, 287; remarks to S. L. M. Barlow about Grenfell case, 317

Johnson, Bradley T.: 296, 301, 313; offers to act for Grenfell, 291; sends Grenfell letter about James Dunn to N. Y. *World,* 302

Johnson, Richard W.: ordered to drive John Hunt Morgan from Gallatin, Tenn., 76; in fight at Gallatin, 76–77

Johnson, Wesley: testifies about Shank's criminal record, 265

Johnston, Albert Sidney, 93

Johnston, Joseph E.: 59, 115, 117, 150; approves lieutenant colonel's commission for Grenfell, 97; complains of tactics of John Hunt Morgan's recruiting agents, 118

Keefe, Thomas H.: 184, 189–92, 193–94, 198; sent to Toronto by Benjamin H. Sweet, 161; comments on Grenfell, 168–69; arrests Grenfell, 203

Kendall, John: 241; testifies about Grenfell's stay in Carlyle, Ill., 181

Key, Thomas M.: 297; visits Grenfell in prison, 268–69

Kilpatrick, Judson, 108

King, "Captain": George Ellsworth attempts to capture, 71

Kingsley, Charles, 16

Kirke, Edmund (pen name of James Roberts Gilmore): 186, 188, 189, 194, 199; story of John T. Shank's "escape" from Camp Douglas, 190–91

Knapp, J. D.: 241; testifies about Grenfell's stay in Carlyle, Ill., 181

Knights of the Golden Circle (KGC): 178; founded by G. W. L. Bickley, 134–35; organization, objectives, 135–39; membership in the North, 137, 147

Knoxville *Register:* laudatory article on Grenfell, 77–78

Landram, John J.: at battle of Cynthiana, Ky., 69–70

Langhore, Maurice: 192, 230–31, 246, 250, 262, 282; on Grenfell's trip to Chicago, 172; history, 185–86; betrays November 8 attack plans, 185–87; offers Grenfell freedom, 206; testifies in Cincinnati trial, 227–29; high opinion of Grenfell, 228

Layard, Austin Henry, 211

Leathers, "Colonel" Frank, 53

Lebanon, Ky.: and John Hunt Morgan's first Kentucky raid, 64

347

Lebanon, Tenn.: John Hunt Morgan's defeat at, 48–49

Lee, Robert E.: 106, 111, 129, 150, 226, 244; surrenders, 3; interviews Grenfell, 42–43; gives Grenfell letter of recommendation to P. G. T. Beauregard, 43; appoints Grenfell assistant inspector general of Cavalry Corps, 107; on "Stuart's intrigues" to get rid of Grenfell, 110; complains of John Hunt Morgan's recruiting agents, 118

Leek, Richard: testifies about John T. Shank's criminal record, 265

Lexington, Ky.: John Hunt Morgan ordered to join Kirby Smith at, 78; entry of Morgan, 78–79

Lincoln, Abraham: 85, 129, 141, 159, 177, 178, 179, 240, 253, 260, 261, 268, 271, 275, 279, 294; assassinated, 6, 7; and John Hunt Morgan's first Kentucky raid, 67; calls for draft of 500,-000, p. 150; doubts reelection, 151; and trials for sedition, 208

Louisville & Nashville Railroad, 60, 63, 68, 73, 75, 90

Lyons, Richard P. B. (Earl Lyons), 210, 211, 252

MacConnell, C. C.: becomes post commandant at Fort Jefferson, 320–21; attitude toward Grenfell, 321; believes Grenfell bribed William Noreil, 323; reports Grenfell's escape, 327

Macrae, W. C.: 259; urges Andrew Johnson to pardon Grenfell, 257

McClellan, George B., 59, 268

McClellan, Henry B.: on Grenfell at Jack's Shop (Liberty Mills), 108–109, 111

McElrath, T. P.: 304; description of Grenfell's gardening, 284–85; on James Dunn's punishment, 301; on Grenfell's punishment, 302–303

McLaws, Lafayette, 111

McLean Military Prison (McLean Barracks), 213, 217, 229, 235, 240, 249, 250, 269, 270

McMaster, James A.: Grenfell solicits help of, 297

McMullen, A. W.: story of Grenfell's "escape," 329

Maguire, T. F.: 299, 300; asks Bruce to help Grenfell, 298

Mahon, William: 251–52; escorts Grenfell to Ohio Penitentiary, 269–70

Manifest Destiny, 134–35, 137

Marbury, F. F., Jr.: inquires about Grenfell's fate, 330–31

Marmaduke, Vincent: 187, 201, 207, 214, 219, 227, 229, 316; acquitted by military commission, 5, 33; credited with idea of freeing Confederate prisoners to aid Copperheads, 147; arrested, 204

Marshall, Humphrey, 80

Marshall, John, 51

Maynard, William, 179, 180, 209, 210, 235

Meade, George G., 106, 125, 330

Meigs, Montgomery C.: draws plans for Fort Jefferson, 275

Melford, Major: 123; interviews Grenfell at Confederate War Department, 121

Memphis *Appeal*: publishes Hines's pro-Grenfell editorial, 298

Merritt, James E., 262, 263

Milligan, Lambdin P.: 215, 288, 289, 290, 291; decision of the Supreme Court in *Ex parte Milligan*, 288–89

Mobile *Register*: reports Grenfell's seizure of "deserter's" horses and equipment, 102–103

Montgomery, Richard, 262, 263

Moore, Absalom B.: 233, 296; captured by John Hunt Morgan at Hartsville, Tenn., 84–85; testifies in Cincinnati trial, 231–32; denounces Grenfell, 293–94

Morgan, Charlton, 297

Morgan, George W., 80

Morgan, John Hunt: 5, 8, 51, 53, 56, 66, 68, 91, 93, 94, 98, 100, 102, 104, 105, 107, 109, 110, 116, 122, 124, 147, 148, 153, 154, 165, 166, 173, 178, 185, 188, 189, 201, 232, 270, 272, 293, 297, 305; meets Grenfell, 44; prewar career, 45–46; personal and military character, 46–47; raids Henry W. Halleck's line of communications, 48;

defeated at Lebanon, Tenn., 48–49; praises Grenfell, 59; first Kentucky raid, 60–70; with George Ellsworth at Horse Cave, Ky., 63; at Lebanon, Ky., 64; battle of Cynthiana, Ky., 70; reports on raid to Kirby Smith, 72; urges invasion of Kentucky, 73; ordered to break up Louisville & Nashville Railroad, 73; at capture of Gallatin, Tenn., 74; fight with Richard W. Johnson at Gallatin, 76–77; ordered to join Kirby Smith at Lexington, Ky., 78; triumphal march into Lexington, 78–79; ordered to intercept retreat of George W. Morgan, 80; ordered to act as rear guard on retreat from Kentucky, 80; permitted by Kirby Smith to choose own route to Tennessee, 80; disregards orders to guard Saltville, Va., 80–81; sends Grenfell to negotiate independent command, 81–82; subordinated to Joseph Wheeler, 83; captures garrison of Hartsville, Tenn., 84–85; marries Martha Ready, 85–87; organizes command into brigades, 87–88; quarrel with Grenfell, 87–90; under Wheeler, 96; reports Grenfell dismissed by Braxton Bragg, 103; arrives in Richmond, 113; asks War Department help to reconstitute command, 113–14; moves headquarters to Abingdon, Va., 117; complaints of his recruiting activities, 117–18; warned by Grenfell about Captain Kleber, 118–19; lacks equipment for new command, 120; requests captain's commission for Grenfell, 123; last raid into Kentucky, 125

Morgan, Martha Ready: marries John Hunt Morgan, 85–87; visits Richmond, 113

Morocco: 25, 27, 28; source of Abd-el-Kader's supplies, 21; controversy with France, 22

Morris, Buckner S.: 6, 194, 195, 207, 209, 210, 213, 217, 223, 231, 246, 316; prewar career, 4; acquitted, 8, 247; visited by John T. Shanks, 191; ar-

rested, 204; his character witnesses, 241

Morris, Mrs. Buckner S.: visited by John T. Shanks, 191; letter to Joseph Hooker, 229–30

Morton, Oliver P.: requests assignment of Henry L. Burnett to prosecute Indiana Copperheads, 216

Mudd, Samuel: 262, 278, 282, 283, 286, 290, 302, 309, at Fort Jefferson, 279; describes Grenfell, 280; yellow fever epidemic, 308, 310–12; attends Grenfell, 312; as a musician, 313

Mullen, James: testifies in Cincinnati trial, 241

Murray, Charles D.: 215; reads verdict of military commission, 8

Murray, Henry John: 22; sends Grenfell to Gibraltar, 23; on leave, 24; instructed by Lord Palmerston on Grenfell case, 30; reports to Palmerston on Grenfell's return to Tangier, 31–32; consul at Portland, Me., 238–39

Napoleon III, 42, 101

New York *World*: prints Grenfell's letter on punishment of James Dunn, 302

Niles, Gordon E.: publishes *The Vidette*, 77

Ninth Kentucky Cavalry, 94, 95, 305

Ninth Pennsylvania Cavalry: fight with Second Kentucky Cavalry at Tompkinsville, Ky., 62–63

Noreil, William: joins escape attempts, 322–23; escapes, 324–26; absence noticed, 327

Northwest Conspiracy, 133

Northwestern Confederacy: 150, 155, 177, 183; Thomas Henry Hines reports plan to form, 144; ideas of a, 145–46

Norton, A. Banning: testifies about John T. Shank's criminal record, 266

O'Laughlin, Michael: 280; at Fort Jefferson, 279; dies of yellow fever, 312

104th Illinois Infantry: captured by

John Hunt Morgan at Hartsville, Tenn., 84–85; 232, 293

Ord, E. O. C.: orders Grenfell's transfer to Fort Jefferson, 274

Order of American Knights (OAK) (Sons of Liberty): 161, 163, 165, 178, 182, 191, 206, 226, 231, 240, 243, 246; founded, 139; hierarchy of command, 140; Clement L. Vallandigham elected supreme grand commander, 140–41; renamed Sons of Liberty, 141; opposition to the war, 142–43; Thomas Henry Hines proposes to aid OAK uprising, 146–47; claim large membership in Illinois and Chicago, 154; Hines enlists OAK cooperation, 155–56; agree to July 4 attack on Camp Douglas, 156; agree on postponement to August 29, 157–58; boast of forthcoming uprising, 159

D'Orleans, Philippe, 58; Prince de Joinville: commands French warships at Tangier, 22

Orr, James: 325; joins escape party, 320

Osmanli Irregular Cavalry (Beatson's Horse): attached to Turkish Contingent, 35

Paine, Lewis, 253

Palmerston, Lord (Henry Temple): 26, 27; instructions to Henry John Murray on Grenfell case, 30

Pearce-Serocold, Marie Emilie Jeanne Grenfell: 100, 180, 271, 283, 285, 321; born 1838, p. 20; marries Charles Pearce-Serocold, 41; sends money to father, 314

Peeler, A. J.: instructed by Robert Hervey to sue for writ of habeas corpus for Grenfell, 296

Phelps, John: 265; testifies about John T. Shanks's criminal record, 264

Pickett, George, 129, 244

Polk, Leonidas: 102, 103; officiates at John Hunt Morgan wedding, 86

Price, Sterling, 150

Purcell, Archbishop John: 259, 297; asks William Dennison to help Grenfell, 257

Quantrill, William, 61

Ramsey, George D.: comments on Grenfell at Fort Jefferson, 284; tries to influence War Department in Grenfell's favor, 287

Ray, T. M.: addresses military commission on Buckner S. Morris' behalf, 6

Ready, Charles: daughter marries John Hunt Morgan, 86-87

Regiment of Mounted Rifles, 98

Riff pirates: 10, 12; attack Grenfell, 33

Robinson, Lieut. ——: 304, 305; punishes Grenfell, 303

Roddey, P. D., 99

Roemer, Paul: 328, 330; believes Grenfell bribed William Noreil, 323

Rosecrans, William S., 100–101

Ross, Fitzgerald: 12, 107, 109; meets Grenfell, 11; prewar career, 11; fishes and hunts with Grenfell, 132

Russell, Lord John: 254, 257, 268, 272; instructs J. H. Burnley to inquire about Grenfell case, 211; urges leniency for Grenfell, 255–56

St. Leger, Georgina: marries Pascoe Grenfell, 16; godmother of George St. Leger Grenfell, 17

Ste. Marie, Count: engaged in smuggling with Grenfell, 27

Savarin, Jean Brillat, 315

Schofield, John M.: confirms report of Grenfell's escape, 330

Second Kentucky Cavalry: 92, 231; joined by Grenfell, 8; defeated at Lebanon, Tenn., 48–49; reorganized after Lebanon defeat, 49; description, 52–55; resent Grenfell's efforts to establish discipline, 56; admire Grenfell as officer and "character," 57; first Kentucky Raid, 60–70; fight at Tompkinsville, Ky., 62–63; appearance at Lebanon, Ky., 64; Union spy "enlists" in regiment, 68; the "Spartan Life" at Sparta, Tenn., 72; fight at Gallatin, Tenn., 76–77; triumphal entry into Lexington, Ky., 78–79

Second Ohio Cavalry, 215

Seddon, James A.: 156; interviews Thomas Henry Hines, 144; formal instructions to Hines, 148–49

Semmes, R. T.: 207, 213; convicted by military commission, 5, 233; sentence remitted, 248

Seward, William: 253, 255, 256, 260, 268, 300, 315, 330; interviewed by J. H. Burnley, 237–38; asked to help to obtain Grenfell's release, 238; informs Sir Frederick Bruce of commutation of Grenfell's death sentence, 271–72

Seymour, Horatio, 178

Shanks, John T.: 199, 200, 201, 228, 229, 230, 235, 246, 250, 262, 263, 264, 265; seizes Grenfell's horses, 92; prewar career, 187–88; selected to spy on conspirators, 188–90; visits Buckner S. Morris home, 192; registers at Richmond House, 193; visit to Grenfell's room, 194–98; "arrested," 204; testifies in Cincinnati trial, 221–27; denies conviction for forgery, 222–25; identified by Maurice Davis, 241–42

Sheridan, Philip H.: 125, 183, 244

Sherman, William T., 50, 107, 125, 129, 157, 183, 244, 247, 269

Shiloh, battle of, 48, 60

Sidi Bou Selham: asks John Drummond Hay to order Grenfell to leave Morocco, 28; gives Grenfell permit to return to Tangier to wind up affairs, 29

Sigel, Franz, 125

Sixth Wisconsin Infantry, 160

Skinner, Lewis C.: 190, 191, 201; raids Charles Walsh home, 202

Slidell, John: gives Grenfell letter of introduction to Robert E. Lee, 42

Slott, Captain ——: searches for Grenfell after escape, 327

Smith, Edmund Kirby: 72, 80; recommends invasion of Kentucky, 73; invades Kentucky, 78; wins battle of Richmond, Ky., 79

Smith, J. Sim: 310; dies in yellow fever epidemic, 309

Sons of Liberty: see Order of American Knights

Spangler, Edward: 280, 290; at Fort Jefferson, 279

Speed, James: interviewed by Sir Frederick Bruce, 300

Stanley, Lord Edward: 300, letter to Grenfell, 295–96

Stanton, Edwin M.: 3, 68, 122, 226, 261, 262, 270, 273, 290, 291, 292, 307, 317, 318, 322, 330; orders Henry L. Burnett to Washington, 7; interview with Grenfell, 126–31; and disloyalty trials before military commissions, 207–208; asked to allow Robert Hervey to discuss Grenfell case with Joseph Holt, 255, 256; hostility toward Grenfell, 260–61, 272

Steuben, Baron von, 59

Stidger, Felix: becomes undercover agent, 163

Stone, Henry Lane: 312, 313; Grenfell's kindness to, 93; asks brother to be considerate of Grenfell, 305–306

Stone, Valentine: acting commandant at Fort Jefferson, 305; dies of yellow fever, 311

Stuart, J. E. B. ("Jeb"): 5, 11, 107–108, 115, 226, 258, 331; relations with Grenfell, 109–12; mortally wounded at Yellow Tavern, 125

Sweet, Benjamin, J.: 123, 162, 163, 166, 168, 169, 184, 191, 192, 193, 204, 206, 207, 208, 237, 240, 245, 250, 260, 281; history, 159–60; learns of plan to attack Camp Douglas, 160–61; prepares for August 29 attack, 175–77; learns of plan for November 8 attack, 185–87; selects John T. Shanks to spy on conspirators, 188–90; decides to arrest conspirators November 6–7, pp. 200–201; testifies in Cincinnati trial, 231; recommends executive clemency for Grenfell, 259; petitions Andrew Johnson to pardon Grenfell, 297

Tangier: 9, 10, 21, 25, 27, 28; description, 22; French warships arrive, 23; bombardment, 23–24

Tenth Kentucky Cavalry, 87

Thibaudeau, Adolphe, 42

Thibaudeau, Blanche Wyatt, 42

Thomas, George H., 90

Thompson, Jacob: 157, 158, 164, 168, 171, 179, 199, 210, 243, 250, 316; appointed Confederate commissioner to Canada, 149; receives his instructions from Jefferson Davis, 149–50; meets with Thomas Henry Hines and Clement L. Vallandigham, 155–56; gullibility, 155

Thornton, Edward: 317, 322, 330; appointed British minister to Washington, 313; promises to do utmost for Grenfell, 318

Tompkinsville, Ky.: fight at, 62

Turkish Contingent (Anglo-Turkish Contingent): 11; organized, 34–35; reported ready for action, 35; infantry and artillery occupy Kerch, 35; cavalry unable to land, 35–36; disbanded, 37

Twain, Mark, 53

Vallandigham, Clement L.: 102, 171; elected head of OAK, 140–41; runs for governor of Ohio, 143; advocates Northwestern Confederacy, 145; interview with Thomas Henry Hines and Jacob Thompson, 155–56; returns to U.S. in disguise, 158–59; testifies in Cincinnati trial, 242–43

Victoria, Queen, 24

The Vidette: published August [27], 1862, p. 77; reprints Grenfell article from Knoxville *Register*, 77–78

Vivian, Robert J. H.: reports Turkish Contingent ready for action, 36; occupies Kerch, 36

Vyvyan, Mrs. ——, 284, 285, 286

Walker, William S., 134

Walsh, Charles: 6, 165, 166, 173, 175, 182, 187, 206, 207, 209, 226, 227, 231, 243, 244, 245, 246, 267, 316; career, 4–5; convicted, 8, 247; promises Copperhead aid for Camp Douglas attack, 156; suggests postponement of attack to November 8, p. 177; arrested, 201–202; his character witnesses, 241; his daughters testify, 241; his pardon recommended, 248

Washington, George, 59

Wellington, Duke of, 9

Wentworth, John: 296, 297, 299; resolution for papers on Grenfell case, 293; denounces Grenfell in Congress, 294–95

Wharton, John A., 96

Wheeler, Joseph: 83, 87, 99, 102, 105, 109, 115; Grenfell appointed his inspector of cavalry, 95–96; description of his command, 96; requests lieutenant colonel's commission for Grenfell, 97; tactical and strategic ideas, 97–98; opinion of Grenfell, 100; raids Federal supply lines, 100–101; invites Grenfell to rejoin him, 104

Whitehurst, D. W.: ordered to Fort Jefferson, 309; works with Samuel Mudd, 310; praises Grenfell's conduct in yellow fever epidemic, 317–18

Wigman, E.: escorts Grenfell to Fort Jefferson, 274

Wilberforce, William, 16

Wilkins, I. Edward: 236; inquires about Grenfell's arrest, 208–209; his instructions from J. H. Burnley, 212; visits Chicago on Grenfell case, 237; on severity of Grenfell's sentence, 252–53

Wilson, Sir Robert: reports Grenfell's return to Tangier, 32; reports Grenfell's attempted visit to Abd-el-Kader, 32

Wilson, Robert S.: 257, 259, 269; addresses military commission on behalf of Charles Walsh, 3, 6, 244; retained by Grenfell, 209; cross-examines John T. Shanks, 223; cross-examines Maurice Langhorne, 228; suggests tactics to Sir Frederick Bruce, 260; advises habeas corpus proceedings for Grenfell, 289–90

Wiswel, M. N.: 127, 259, 260; interviews Grenfell in Washington, 126; urges Andrew Johnson to pardon Grenfell, 257

Wolford, Frank: defeats John Hunt Morgan at Lebanon, Tenn., 48–49

Wright, Horatio G.: builds Fort Jefferson, 275

Wright, Phineas C.: founds Order of American Knights, 139